MADE IN CHINA YEARBOOK 2018
DOG DAYS

Edited by
Ivan Franceschini and **Nicholas Loubere**

with the Made in China Editorial Board
Kevin Lin, **Elisa Nesossi**, **Andrea E. Pia**, and **Christian Sorace**

MADE IN CHINA JOURNAL

中華全球研究中心
AUSTRALIAN CENTRE ON CHINA IN THE WORLD

Australian National University
PRESS

LUND UNIVERSITY

ANU PRESS

First published April 2019 by ANU Press
The Australian National University
Acton ACT 2601, Australia
Email: anupress@anu.edu.au
Available to download for free at press.anu.edu.au

ISBN (print): 9781760462925
ISBN (online): 9781760462932

WorldCat (print): 1091373612
WorldCat (online): 1091373755

DOI: 10.22459/MIC.04.2019

Design Concept & Typesetting by Tommaso Facchin; Illustrations by Marc Verdugo. Proofreading by Sharon Strange.

The Australian Centre on China in the World is an initiative of the Commonwealth Government of Australia and The Australian National University.

This project has been produced with the financial assistance of the Australian Centre on China in the World (CIW), Australian National University, and the European Union Horizon 2020 research and innovation programme under the Marie Skłodowska-Curie grant agreement No 654852. The views expressed are those of the individual authors and do not represent the views of the European Union, CIW, or the institutions to which the authors are affiliated.

Sirius rises late in the dark, liquid sky
On summer nights, star of stars,
Orion's Dog they call it, brightest
Of all, but an evil portent, bringing heat
And fevers to suffering humanity

Homer, *The Iliad*
(Translated by Stanley Lombardo)

TABLE OF CONTENTS

DOG DAYS

Dog Days

Sirius rises late in the dark, liquid sky
On summer nights, star of stars,
Orion's Dog they call it, brightest
Of all, but an evil portent, bringing heat
And fevers to suffering humanity

Homer, *The Iliad*

According to the Chinese zodiac, 2018 was the year of the 'earthly dog'. Legends about dogs abound in Chinese mythology, but the most famous one undoubtedly is that of the 'heavenly dog' (*tiangou*). As the story goes, after divine archer Hou Yi shot down the nine suns that had simultaneously risen up in the sky, the Queen Mother of the West decided to reward him with the elixir of immortality. Unfortunately for him, his wife Chang'e—who, depending on whom you listen to, was either a selfish woman willing to sacrifice her marriage to preserve her youth or simply very disgruntled with her husband—beat him to the holy beverage and, with her body growing lighter and lighter as an effect of the magic potion, flew away towards the moon. Here enters the dog, a big black hound that Hou Yi was rearing. Seeing the wife of his master floating away, the dog lapped what was left of the elixir and started giving chase, his body growing in size all the while. Hiding on the moon did not save Chang'e, as the giant mutt swallowed the celestial object whole, with her on it. It took the intervention of the Queen Mother of the West to tame the dog and force him to spit out both the moon and the Chang'e. Instead of being punished, the gigantic animal was pressed into service as the guard dog at the gates of the heavens.

Some identify the heavenly dog with a particular star—Sirius, which in Chinese is *tianlangxing*, or 'star of the heavenly wolf'. As Homer's words at the beginning of this introduction make abundantly clear, Sirius has an ominous reputation. Since ancient times, Roman and Greeks linked the star with the hottest days of the year. They even coined an expression—'dog days'—to indicate that span of time in the summer of the northern hemisphere when Sirius rose in conjunction with the sun. Those were inauspicious days, characterised by heat, spells of dryness, thunderstorms, and a sudden loss of energy and industriousness, if not outright madness. Curiously, it was in the middle of the long, hot, and feverish dog days of the summer of 2018 that some workers at Shenzhen Jasic Technology took their chances and attempted to form an independent union to challenge their employer. This brave action did not take long to provoke a coordinated response from the company and the local government, with the workers quickly being terminated, beaten, and detained. The fever did not break there, however, as the governmental immune response continued, triggered by solidarity groups springing up both inside and outside the country in support of the arrested workers and their struggle. Of particular embarrassment for the Chinese authorities was the participation of Maoist and Marxist student groups in the protests, with many travelling to Shenzhen from around China to join the workers. In late August over 50 activists were arrested in both Shenzhen and Beijing. This incident is emblematic of China's contemporary situation, with any challenge to the status quo being immediately and severely suppressed.

China's year of the dog was also imbued with the spirit of another canine, Cerberus—the three-headed hound of Hades—with the ravenous advance of the surveillance state and the increasing securitisation of Chinese society. Over the past several months the Chinese government has rapidly ramped up its acquisition and development of surveillance technology, deploying facial recognition cameras across the country and moving to integrate the huge amounts of data being collected through online activity into new modes of predictive algorithmic governance.

Nowhere is this large-scale experiment in social control more evident than Xinjiang, where the authorities have detained perhaps more than one million Uyghur and other ethnic minority citizens in vast 'reeducation camps', resulting in family separations, forced labour, and the destruction of lives on a mass scale. While the Chinese government was able to quickly build their mass detention apparatus with little attention from the international community, there have since been herculean efforts to bring to light the logistics of what is going on and the devastating toll it is taking on people's lives. While the government now admits to the existence of the camps, there is a stubborn refusal to acknowledge them for what they really are. At the same time, there have been incidents around the globe of Chinese citizens threatening and attempting to silence those speaking out about what is happening in public forums.

Anybody Out There?

In this *Yearbook*, we follow the events of 2018 through the essays that appeared throughout the year in the *Made in China Journal*. We have regrouped the essays into seven thematic sections. The first—entitled 'Anybody Out There?'—examines the current predicament of the Chinese labour movement. Labour activism has undergone significant transformation in China over the last decade. Between the mid-2000s and mid-2010s, an increase in labour protests seemed to herald a growing and more self-confident labour movement. A series of high-profile collective actions that took place in 2010—in particular a strike at a Honda auto parts factory in Foshan in 2010—sparked a renewed optimism, during which the public debate on Chinese labour came to be dominated by the idea of China's workers 'awakening' and taking their fate into their own hands. This new narrative was largely focussed on the so-called 'new generation of migrant workers', presented in much of the academic literature and public debate as the engine of the new wave of worker struggle. Far from the optimism of those years, today the effects of economic slowdown and the tightening of controls on civil society have thrown China's workers into a state of uncertainty and disorientation, and the Chinese labour movement has once again found itself at an impasse.

This section offers a series of essays that aim at assessing and understanding the current conjuncture. In 'Changes and Continuity', Chris King-Chi Chan offers a retrospective of the development of industrial relations in China over the past four decades. In 'China's Labour Movement in Transition', Geoffrey Crothall draws from China Labour Bulletin's impressive trove of data to analyse the latest trends in Chinese labour unrest. In '*Gongyou*, the New Dangerous Class in China?', Yu Chunsen looks into the discourses that Chinese migrant workers use to define their shared identity, probing the possibility of them becoming the foundation of a new class consciousness. In 'Reconfiguring Supply Chains', Nellie Chu shows how infrastructure projects that link China's interior and coastal manufacturing regions have intensified key aspects of the country's informal economy. In 'The Struggles of Temporary Agency Workers in Xi's China', Zhang Lu tracks the activism of dispatch workers in Chinese auto factories, examining the potential for this group to successfully bargain for their rights. In 'Robot Threat or Robot Dividend?', Huang Yu considers the possible consequences of automation and robotisation on employment and labour activism in China. In 'A Pessoptimistic View of Chinese Labour NGOs', Ivan Franceschini and Kevin Lin revisit the debate on labour NGOs in China, offering their own reading of the current situation. Finally, in 'The Jasic Strike and the Future of the Chinese Labour Movement' and 'The Jasic Mobilisation: A High Tide for the Chinese Labour Movement?', Zhang Yueran and Au Loong Yu provide insights into the struggle of the Jasic workers mentioned at the beginning of this introduction.

To the Soil

In December 2018, the Chinese authorities commemorated the 40th anniversary of China's reform and opening up, an event generally hailed as the beginning of the country's rise as a global economic and political power. The unprecedented economic growth and transformation of these four decades has been rooted in a fundamental restructuring of local society. Contemporary China has changed from a largely agrarian society predominantly inhabited by peasants, to a rapidly urbanising one, characterised by a floating populace moving back and forth between rural and urban spaces, which are in a continuous state of flux. Going hand in hand with China's ascent into modernity is the subordination of rural areas and people. While rural China has historically been a site of extraction and exploitation, in the post-reform period this has intensified, and rurality itself has become a problem, best typified through the ubiquitous propaganda about the need to revitalise the countryside, and ongoing attempts to reconstruct rural areas in a new image.

Against this background, the second section—'To the Soil'—focuses on the labour that these attempts to restructure and reformulate rural China have entailed, and the ways in which they have transformed rural lives and communities. In 'China's Land Reform and the Logic of Capital Accumulation', Jane Hayward examines how rural land reforms in China are being driven by the imperative of capital accumulation. In 'Manufactured Modernity', Sarah Rogers reflects on poverty resettlement projects to try to make sense of the intent and impact of such large-scale interventions on both the lives of individuals and the transformation of the Chinese countryside as a whole. In 'Managing the Anthropocene', John Aloysius Zinda highlights how scholars and journalists alike tend to place environment and labour in separate boxes and seldom consider the labour of environmental protection or the people who perform it. In 'Beyond Proletarianisation', Thomas Sætre Jakobsen bemoans the fact that China labour studies' bias towards urban contexts is neglecting the reality of hundreds of millions of workers who live between the farmlands in the countryside and the workplaces of the city. In 'Inside Work', Tamara Jacka shows how the development trajectory of modern China has been underpinned and enabled by the exploitation of the 'inside work' of rural women. In 'Rural Transformations and Urbanisation', Marina Svensson describes her experience at the Third Ningbo International Photography Week, which this year focussed on documenting rural transformations and processes of urbanisation. Finally, in 'Domestic Archaeology', Daniele Dainelli presents a photographic project on the Chinese countryside that took him seven years to complete.

On a Chinese Screen

The third section—'On a Chinese Screen'—looks into the role of the media in relation to labour issues and beyond. The previous decade saw widespread discussions about the role of the Internet in reshaping power relations in Chinese society. New media—it was widely believed—would give voice to the poor and downtrodden, allow citizens to better supervise government activity, and foster lively cultural exchanges. Workers would also benefit from this, as the Internet provided them with the tools needed to bring their grievances into the spotlight and enhance their ability to connect with their peers to establish new forms of solidarity. A decade later, what is left of that cyber-utopian discourse? As the Chinese Party-state steps up the censorship and manipulation of online information, and as new media is increasingly used as a means of reinforcing control and surveillance over the population, a more sombre assessment of the role of the Internet seems to have gained traction in the court of public opinion. The scandals that in recent years have engulfed those social media companies that in the late 2000s and early 2010s gave rise to many of those thwarted expectations—Facebook in primis—have nothing but contributed to the disillusion.

The essays included in this section assess the relevance of the cyber-utopian discourse against the background of the latest developments in Chinese politics and society. In 'Changing Representations of China's Workers', Sun Wanning considers how the struggles of Chinese migrant workers have been constructed in public discourse and how media has come to play a role in their struggles. In 'Platform Economies', Julie Chen analyses the plight of Chinese platform workers. In 'Rethinking Online privacy in the Chinese Workplace', Mimi Zou shows how social media provides considerable scope for employers to monitor employees. In 'Visualising Labour and Labourscapes in China', Marina Svensson examines how Chinese workers have been portrayed through the lens of photography. In 'Documenting China's Influence', David Bandurski investigates an 'independent' Chinese documentary, revealing how foreign media can inadvertently become co-producers of state propaganda. Finally, in 'The Global Age of the Algorithm', Nicholas Loubere and Stefan Brehm look into the development of the social credit system in China.

Human Rights Made in China

The fourth section—Human Rights Made in China—offers a variety of perspectives on issues related to human rights and state violence in China. In 'Beijing Evictions: A Winter Tale', Li Qiaochu, Song Jiani, and Zhang Shuchi discuss the reaction of local civil society to the evictions of migrants from the suburbs of Beijing that took place at the end of 2017. In 'Evictions and the Right to the City', Kevin Lin ponders whether migrants in today's China have a right to the city. In 'Outsourcing Coercion and Social Control', Lynette Ong examines how the Chinese state outsources violence and social control to private actors, including thugs-for-hire, profit-seeking brokers, and even commercial enterprises. In 'Justice Restored Under Xi Jinping', Elisa Nesossi considers two decades of miscarriages of justice in China and recent efforts to remedy the situation. In 'Confessions Made in China', Magnus Fiskesjö discusses how mass media outside of the control of Chinese state authorities should deal with the coerced televised confessions of political prisoners in China. In 'Will the Future of Human Rights Be "Made in China"?', Sarah Brooks looks at how the Chinese government has stepped into the role of international player, focussing on China's activities at the United Nations. In 'Remembering Liu Xiaobo One Year On', Jean-Philippe Béja offers some glimpses into Liu's life, highlighting the significance of his legacy for new generations of activists. Finally, in 'Xinjiang Today', Tom Cliff recounts how in the past couple of years Xinjiang has witnessed the rise of a composite version of twentieth century authoritarian fantasies and popular dystopias made possible by twenty-first century technology.

States of Emergency

On 12 May 2008, a 7.9 magnitude earthquake hit Wenchuan county, Sichuan province. Felt as far as Beijing, the tremors caused horrific damage: 69,229 people died and 17,923 went missing. Yet, the aftermath of the earthquake was also a time of hope. Chinese citizens from all over the country outdid each other to show solidarity with the victims, not only donating money and goods, but also rushing to the disaster zones to provide assistance. Young volunteers from all walks of life poured into Sichuan to help, with many of them going on to establish their own social organisations. As local governments began to recognise the importance of NGOs in providing disaster relief and social services, 2008 was widely seen as a 'Year Zero' for Chinese civil society. At that time, hardly anybody could have foreseen the wave of repression against civil society that was to come and that is today the norm. Indeed, there were worrying signals even then—the threats against the parents of children who had died in the disaster and the trial of Tan Zuoren, for instance—but the general atmosphere remained forward-looking and optimistic.

The essays included in the fifth section—'States of Emergency'—revisit the optimism of those early days and examines what is left. In 'Be Grateful to the Party!', Christian Sorace probes how the Chinese Communist Party has used propaganda and other means to boost its 'affective sovereignty' in the wake of the disaster. In 'The World Is Yours!', Bin Xu describes the moral dilemmas that afflicted him as a scholar and volunteer in the earthquake areas. In 'Sichuan, Year Zero?'; Yi Kang offers a retrospective on NGO development in Sichuan since 2008, challenging the idea that it was a 'dawn' for Chinese civil society. In 'Civic Transformation in the Wake of the Wenchuan Earthquake', Sun Taiyi examines the evolution of state-society relations by looking at the interactions between state, society, and individuals. In 'The Power of the Square', Gao Huan explores the specific case study of an emergency shelter in Mianyang. Finally, in 'Documenting the Sichuan Earthquake', Marina Svensson analyses the most significant Chinese documentaries portraying the catastrophe to audiences around the world.

Window on Asia and Work of Arts

The sixth section—'Window on Asia'—offers a series of perspectives on the latest developments in the field of labour and civil society across Asia. In '"Hun Sen Won't Die, Workers Will Die"', Sabina Lawreniuk examines the ways in which both labour politics and China have played a role in determining the latest assault on freedoms of expression, association, and assembly in Cambodia. In 'My Rights Have Been Left behind in Papua New Guinea', Zhang Shuchi describes the plight of Chinese workers abroad. In 'Online Activism and South Korea's Candlelight Movement', Hyejin Kim looks at the role of the Internet and new media in fostering a new generation of activists in South Korea. In 'China and Development Aid', Sverre Molland assesses the impact of China's increasing influence in mainland Southeast Asia on the attempts to introduce humanitarian and human rights standards in labour migration. In 'Illicit Economies of the Internet', Johan Lindquist looks into the 'like economy' of click farms in Indonesia, taking click farmers not as an aberration, but rather as a starting point for approaching this kind of phenomenon. In 'Chinese Digital Ecosystems Go Abroad', Elisa Oreglia ponders the implications of the spread of WeChat among Internet users in the Shan State, Myanmar. Finally, in 'Ulaanbaatar, City of the Future', Christian Sorace explores the political implications of chronic pollution in the Mongolian capital.

We wrap up the volume with a cultural section entitled 'Work of Arts'. In 'Communist Hibernation, Christian Sorace offers his take on the oeuvre of movie director Geng Jun against the background of China's Rustbelt. In 'Crime and Punishment on a Chinese Border', Suzanne Scoggins reviews Zhao Liang's documentary *Crime and Punishment* about the harsh reality of police enforcement in a small Chinese town on the border with North Korea. In 'Figuring Post-worker Shenzhen', Mary Ann O'Donnell introduces several works of art that depict the post-worker demographics of Shenzhen, and its emergence as a 'creative' city. In 'Rural Migrant Workers in Independent Films', Eric Florence examines how the representation of migrant workers in China has evolved over the years through the lens of independent Chinese movies. In 'Plastic China', Yvan Schulz reviews Wang Jiuliang's recent documentary about waste management in China. Finally, in 'The Last Days of Shi Yang',

Ivan Franceschini presents a fictionalised account of a revolutionary martyr of the 1920s—a lawyer that played an important role in the labour struggles of those years.

Keeping the Candles Burning

This volume recaps the third year of our *Made in China Journal*. Since the journal's launch in 2016, the publication has grown beyond our wildest expectations, and we are grateful to both our contributors our readers for the continued support. The aim of *Made in China* is to create a bridge between academia and a wider audience, making the research and work of our authors accessible to everybody, especially to those who might make use of their findings and ideas. For this reason, we strongly believe in open access. As the Chinese authorities step up their attempts to censor academic publications and to influence global public discourse on China—and as commercial academic publishers all over the world capitulate to the demands coming from Beijing—we are convinced that open access publishing remains key to academic freedom and integrity. It is this belief that motivates us to keep *Made in China* going, and it is with this conviction that we continue into our fourth year. We believe that the conformity and sycophancy that are increasingly underlining the debate in and on China can only be fought through critical engagement and inclusion. To return to the heavenly dog, legends say that *tiangou* had an enemy in the figure of the Daoist immortal Zhang Xian, who protects children from the animal with his bow and arrows. More often, Chinese people would simply take matters in their own hands and, whenever an eclipse of the sun or the moon occurred, they would beat on drums or light firecrackers in an attempt to scare away the giant invisible hound that had devoured the celestial bodies. It always worked. However, in today's world, with the light going out around the globe, it will take more than some noise to set things right. This book is our small attempt to keep the candles burning while we hope that the year of the pig will bring better tidings. ■

BRIEFS
Jan–Dec 2018

JAN/MAR 2018

Members of Student Reading Group Detained and Harassed

In November 2017, the police detained two recent graduates and four students who were attending a reading group at the Guangdong University of Technology in Guangzhou. The self-described Maoist reading group organised critical discussions of social and political issues. While most of the members were soon released, the organisers Zhang Yunfan—a recent graduate of Peking University—and Ye Jianke were detained for 'gathering a crowd to disturb social order'. In December, more individuals affiliated with the reading groups were either interrogated or detained, but news of their detention was only made public in early January 2018. Starting with Zhang Yunfan, several members issued public statements explaining the personal and political reasons that led them to become involved with the group, disclosing their experience of harassment and torture under detention in order to mobilise public support. A statement signed by hundreds of academics, students, and public intellectuals—many affiliated with Peking University—called on the local authorities to review the case, release Zhang Yunfan from police custody, and protect his rights under residential surveillance. By the end of March, all detained members of the reading group had negotiated an end to their detention and regained their freedom. *KL*

(Sources: **Chuang**; **Hong Kong Free Press**; **Radio Free Asia**)

Constitutional Amendment Approved by the National People's Congress

On 11 March, during the annual Two Sessions (*lianghui*), the National People's Congress passed a number of historical constitutional amendments with 1,958 votes in favour, two against, and three abstentions. Among the 21 changes to the Constitution, the most controversial revision was the removal of term limits for the posts of President and Vice-President, which had been announced by Xinhua as early as 25 February. This amendment potentially paves the way for Xi Jinping to rule indefinitely. The legislature also amended the Preamble of the Constitution to include 'Xi Jinping Thought' and the sentence 'the leadership of the Communist Party of China is the defining feature of socialism with Chinese characteristics'—key tenets of what has officially become known as 'Xi Jinping Thought on Socialism with Chinese Characteristics for a New Era'—to promote the supremacy of the Chinese Communist Party over the state. The amendments also pave the way for a major overhaul of the government, a move which will affect more than two dozens ministries and agencies with the aim of reinforcing Party control. Most importantly, the revision enshrines in the Constitution a powerful new watchdog, the National Supervision Commission. This new organ is equal in power to the State Council; it outranks all ministries as it reports directly to the Party centre. It will take charge of a national network of supervision commissions, linked with local anti-corruption offices. This will widen the scope of the Party's authority over all civil servants, whether they are Party members or not, excluding the protections envisaged by Chinese civil law. *EN*

(Sources: **Financial Times**; **South China Morning Post 1**; **South China Morning Post 2**; **South China Morning Post 3**; **Xinhua**; **The New York Times 1**; **The New York Times 2**; **Xinhua 1**; **Xinhua 2**)

Unrelenting Repression of both Lawyers and Activists

The first quarter of 2018 saw continuous and unrelenting repression of both lawyers and activists in China. Four days into the new year, 32-year-old Tibetan activist Tashi Wangchuk went on trial for 'inciting separatism', a crime that carries a punishment of up to 15 years in jail. He was detained in January 2016, after appearing in a *New York Times* video that documented his efforts to preserve Tibetan culture and language. According to Wangchuk's lawyer, the video—in which the activist criticises the education policies of the Chinese authorities—constituted the prosecution's main piece of evidence. Also in January, prominent *weiquan* lawyer Yu Wensheng had his legal licence revoked, and was subsequently detained while walking his son to school. This was in retaliation for an open letter in which he criticised President Xi and called for political reform. In 2014, Yu had already been detained for 99 days, enduring interrogations lasting 17 hours, as well as physical abuse that resulted in a hernia. In February, it was reported that jailed *weiquan* lawyer Jiang Tianyong's health had severely deteriorated. According to his sister, Jiang was suffering from memory loss, raising concerns that he was being force-fed psychoactive medication—a method commonly employed by Chinese authorities against political prisoners. Likewise, in March, former state prosecutor Shen Liangqing was briefly detained after speaking out against President Xi's constitutional changes. In the same month, Fu Zhenghua, previously a deputy head of China's Ministry of Public Security, who had led several high-profile investigations and crackdowns, was appointed Minister of Justice. *EN & TS*

(Sources: **Amnesty International 1**; **Amnesty International 2**; **BBC**; **Business Insider**; **China Digital Times 1**; **China Digital Times 2**; **The Guardian**; **The New York Times 1**; **The New York Times 2**; **Radio Free Asia**; **Reuters 1**; **Reuters 2**)

Gui Minhai Seized in the Presence of Swedish Diplomats

On 20 January, Swedish bookseller Gui Minhai, who was abducted from Thailand in 2015 and was just granted limited freedom in October 2017, was again detained by the Chinese authorities while in the presence of Swedish diplomats. Gui was traveling from Shanghai to Beijing with two Swedish consular officials to seek medical attention. However, at Jinan station, Shandong province, plainclothes security agents forcibly took him away. He reappeared three weeks later in a forced confession filmed in front of a group of reporters from pro-Beijing news media, including the *South China Morning Post* (see Fiskesjö's essay in this volume). In the forced statement, Gui was coerced into saying that his trip to Beijing was part of a Swedish plot to get him out of China. Chinese authorities subsequently stated that he was then being held in captivity for leaking state secrets. Gui, a Hong Kong resident and Swedish citizen, was originally abducted from his holiday home in Thailand in October 2015, and brought to China under the pretence of facing charges related to a traffic accident that had occurred more than a decade before. In October 2017 he was released under partial house arrest and allowed to communicate with his family using video chat. The Swedish foreign ministry and the European Union demanded that Beijing release Gui, with Sweden calling the most recent abduction a 'brutal intervention'. The Chinese government responded by denouncing Sweden's 'irresponsible remarks' and suggesting that continued protest could threaten bilateral relations. Gui's case exemplifies the Chinese government's intensifying crackdown on dissident voices, both in China and globally. China has repatriated thousands of suspected criminals and dissidents from 90 countries, including the US, despite the fact that extradition treaties only exist with 36 nations. The tactics range from abduction to threats aimed at inducing 'voluntary' repatriation. *NL*

(Sources: **China Digital Times 1**; **China Digital Times 2**; **Foreign Policy**; **Human Rights Watch**; **Radio Free Asia**; **The Washington Post**)

Surveillance and Repression of Uyghurs Intensifies in Xinjiang and Globally

In the first quarter of 2018, the human rights situation in the restive northwestern Xinjiang Uyghur Autonomous Region deteriorated rapidly. Hundreds of thousands of Uyghurs, the Muslim ethnic minority that constitutes the majority of the local population, were sent to reeducation camps. Stories from the camps painted a stark picture, with detainees being held indefinitely as part of a newly normalised predictive policing regime. This followed a continuing crackdown targeting Uyghurs since 2014, which banned religious practices and dress, and was ostensibly aimed at stamping out religious extremism. With this anti-terror rationale, since then Xinjiang has become a testing ground for a state-of-the-art high-tech surveillance state. Authorities have been collecting biometric data at state-organised medical check ups, and Uyghurs are now required to install surveillance apps on their mobile phones. These actions have been accompanied by the rapid increase in the use of facial recognition software, iris scans at police checkpoints, and a range of other types of data collection that feed into an 'Integrated Joint Operations Platform' (*tihua lianhe zuozhan pingtai*) providing real-time analysis of 'security threats'. Xinjiang residents are also being assigned 'safety scores', with those deemed 'unsafe' being sent to the reeducation camps (see Loubere and Brehm's essay in this volume). The Chinese government has also increased pressure on Uyghurs outside of the country. Family members of Uyghur reporters for Radio Free Asia have gone missing in an apparent attempt at intimidation. Uyghurs in other countries, even those with foreign nationalities, have also been pressured to provide personal information—such as addresses, photos, and scans of foreign identity documents—to Chinese security forces. Those who refuse are compelled through threats to their families. *NL*

(Sources: **China Digital Times 1**; **China Digital Times 2**; **Foreign Policy**; **Human Rights Watch**; **Radio Free Asia**; **The Washington Post**)

Foreign Companies Bow to Pressure from Beijing

In January, the Chinese authorities blocked the website and app of the Marriott hotel group for one week after the company listed Tibet, Hong Kong, Macau, and Taiwan as separate countries in an online customer survey. To make things worse, a Marriott employee used a corporate Twitter account to 'like' a tweet in which a pro-Tibet group expressed approval for the survey's identification of Tibet as a country. In the midst of a public relations nightmare, Marriott profusely apologised and fired Roy Jones, 49, the hourly worker at a customer engagement centre in Omaha, Nebraska, who had liked the tweet. A similar incident involved Daimler, when its subsidiary Mercedes-Benz posted on Instagram a photo of a car along with an inspirational quote from the Dalai Lama. Delta Airlines, Qantas Airlines, clothing designer Zara, and medical instruments maker Medtronic were also involved in similar spats in late 2017 and early 2018. Far more consequential is the capitulation of Apple. On 28 February, the Cupertino-based company formally transferred its Chinese iCloud operations to Guizhou-Cloud Big Data, a local firm with close ties to the Chinese authorities. Apple also began hosting its iCloud encryption keys in China. Although Apple publicly declared that it would not transfer accounts over to the new data centre unless users first agree to the updated terms of service, the move caused widespread concerns regarding the privacy and data protection of users. Companies are not the only targets of pressure from Beijing. On 30 March, the organisers of the Man Booker International Prize admitted that, after receiving a complaint from the Chinese embassy in London, they had changed the nationality of Professor Wu Ming-yi, one of the writers included on the 2018 longlist, from 'Taiwan' to 'Taiwan, China'. The organisers only backed down after a public uproar, announcing that in the future they would list the 'country/territory' of authors, rather than their nationalities. *IF*

(Sources: **ChinaFile**; **Quartz**; **Reuters**; **SupChina**; **The Guardian**; **The Telegraph**; **The Verge**)

APR/JUN 2018

Gender Issues in the Spotlight

The second quarter of 2018 brought renewed scrutiny of gender issues in China. Chinese women still face perilous conditions in society and the workplace, often falling victim to sexual harassment and discrimination of various kinds. The #MeToo campaign that swept Peking University (PKU) in April this year well exemplifies female vulnerability to sexual harassment on campus and in the workplace. This movement culminated in activists' demand for the university to disclose information on a rape-suicide case that occurred two decades ago, when Gao Yan, a student at PKU, committed suicide after being sexually assaulted by Shen Yang, at that time a professor at that institution (he would keep the position until 2011). Having failed to intimidate the activists, PKU pledged to reinvestigate the case and introduce regulations against sexual misconduct. Sexual harassment aside, Chinese and international media highlighted how women in China are discriminated against in job applications. Research conducted by Human Rights Watch found that almost 20 percent of civil service positions released in early 2018 either required job applicants to be male or expressed a preference for male candidates, whereas only one job post indicated a preference for females. It was also found that private companies—including tech giants Alibaba and Tencent—had opened up special positions to hire 'beautiful girls', so-called 'goddesses', to lure more male applicants. *NLiu*

(Sources: **Business Insider**; **Caixin**; **Human Rights Watch**; **The New York Times**; **Xinhua**)

Liu Xia Is Released, but Repression Continues Unabated

In the second quarter of 2018, repression of human rights practitioners continued unabated in China. In those months, foreign media widely reported on the situation of Liu Xia, the widow of late Chinese dissident and Nobel laureate Liu Xiaobo. Without having been formally accused of any offence, Liu was placed under house arrest in October 2010. While earlier reports claiming that Chinese officials were preparing to allow Liu to leave the country proved unfounded, diplomatic pressure from German Chancellor Angela Merkel led to the release of Liu Xia on 10 July, just days before the first anniversary of her husband's death. On that day, Liu left China on a flight that brought her to Berlin via Helsinki. During her visit to China on 24 May, Merkel also met the wives of two detained lawyers—Li Wenzu, wife of Wang Quanzhang, and Xu Yan, wife of Yu Wensheng. Earlier in April, Li attempted to walk over 100 kilometres from Beijing to Tianjin in search of answers regarding her husband's whereabouts, as he had been held incommunicado since July 2015. However, her planned 12-day protest march was cut short by Chinese authorities, who placed her under house arrest and later charged her with subversion. In the meantime, Yu fired his defence team, an action that contradicted a pre-recorded video in which he asserted he would never dismiss his lawyers under his own volition. This raised suspicions that he was acting under duress. There were also bad news for Tashi Wangchuk, a Tibetan activist who campaigned for Tibetan language education and who had been detained since 2016, after appearing in a *New York Times* video in which he discussed his campaign. At the end of May he was sentenced to five years in jail for 'inciting separatism'. *TS*

(Sources: **Amnesty International**; **China Change**; **The Guardian 1**; **The Guardian 2**; **Radio Free Asia 1**; **Radio Free Asia 2**; **Radio Free Asia 3**; **South China Morning Post 1**; **South China Morning Post 2**; **South China Morning Post 3**)

Labour NGOs Stigmatised on National Security Day

Since the passing of the National Security Law back in 2015, the Chinese government has declared 15 April as 'National Security Education Day', i.e. a day for raising public awareness of national security issues. In 2017, the authorities promised informants who reported on spies rewards ranging from 10,000 to 500,000 yuan. According to local media, in the following year the public had provided about 5,000 tipoffs, some of which were useful in catching alleged foreign spies. In 2018, the government disseminated among workers in defence-related industries a comic strip targetting labour NGOs. In it, we see a blonde, bespectacled foreign NGO staff member introducing himself to a plump, bald Chinese labour NGO leader. In the next panel, an NGO trainer is talking to an audience of workers about three key points—how to organise workers to protect their rights, how to establish a free trade union, and how to take to the street to raise demands—while the same foreigner is seen stuffing banknotes in the pocket of the Chinese activist. From this, the story progresses with the foreigner reporting on the success of his activities to his bosses abroad; the Chinese NGO leader holding another training session on 'Western ideas of labour' and 'Western ideas of trade unions' for workers; and the workers launching a demonstration to demand higher wages, shorter work hours, and 'decent work'. However, the exchanges of money between Chinese and foreign NGO staff members catch the eye of one of the workers, who reports them. The story ends with the local NGO leader being interrogated by state security officials and admitting to his wrongdoings while the foreign NGO employee flees China in terror. This was just the latest and most explicit instance of state propaganda portraying labour NGOs as agents of 'hostile foreign forces'. *IF*

(Sources: **China File**; **Global Times**; **People's Public Security University of China**; **The New York Times**)

Strikes in Non-manufacturing Sectors Gain Traction

Between late March and June 2018, a number of strikes and protests in China's non-manufacturing sectors gained international attention. In late March more than 2,000 sanitation workers in Shanghai went on a six-day strike to protest against waste management companies' cuts to their income. After the local government had increased the minimum wage, these sanitation workers—who were barely paid the legal minimum—had their meal subsidies and morning and evening shift allowances cut. Later that month, up to 500 coal miners suffering from pneumoconiosis in Hunan province petitioned the local health authorities to protest the delay in providing them with medical examination records crucial to securing compensation. Then, for days leading up to International Workers' Day on 1 May, crane operators on construction sites across a dozen provinces staged protests to demand a pay raise, citing relatively low pay for their high-risk work, the lack of paid overtime, and little annual leave. In April, teachers from kindergartens, and public and private schools organised at least 19 protests over pay, performance bonuses, and pensions. The following month, around 200 retired teachers in Anhui province protested to the local government twice within a single week to demand unpaid bonuses. Finally, in early June thousands of truck drivers in at least three cities used their trucks to block roads in protest against rising fuel costs and falling haulage rates that cut into their incomes. Strikes in non-manufacturing sectors such as education, retail, sanitation, and logistics have gained prominence in recent years. In particular, the nationally coordinated strikes by crane operators and truck drivers were significant, hinting at the potential for non-manufacturing workers to organise more networked and less atomised industrial actions. *KL*

(Sources: **China Change 1**; **China Change 2**; **China Digital Times**; **China Labour Bulletin 1**; **China Labour Bulletin 2**; **Radio Free Asia 1**; **Radio Free Asia 2**; **Wall Street Journal**)

New Statistical Report on Migrant Workers Released

In April, the National Bureau of Statistics released its latest annual report on Chinese migrant workers. According to this document, in 2017 China had a total of 286.52 million migrant workers, an increase of 4.81 million or 1.7 percent from the previous year. At the same time the migrant population was clearly aging: for the first time those born after 1980—the so-called 'new generation of migrant workers' (*xinshengdai nongmingong*)—made up more than half of all migrants. The Report also hinted at significant changes in the employment structure, with a gradual decline of occupation in the manufacturing (–0.6 percent) and construction sectors (–0.8 percent), and an increase (+1.3 percent) in the service sector. Average monthly wages grew by 6.4 percent to 3,485 yuan, but growth was 0.2 percent slower than the previous year, likely due to the minimum wage freeze in places like Guangdong since 2016. The 2018 Report added a new satisfaction indicator, with 56.1 percent of migrant workers declaring that they were very satisfied with their current living situation. The Report suggested that the Chinese government improve housing and education opportunities for migrants and their children in order to promote migrants' social integration in the cities. The Report also revealed that migrants had become more likely to report labour to government bureaus and use legal mechanisms, and that they were slightly less likely to negotiate directly with their employers—a finding which might reflect either improved government responsiveness or a weakening of migrant workers' bargaining power. Notably absent compared to previous reports was a section on rights protection, including statistics on overtime, labour contract coverage, and wage arrears. Labour contract coverage has been in decline for several years in a row—in 2016 it was down to only 35.1 percent from 43.9 percent in 2012. Also absent in this new report were data on unionisation and migrant workers' awareness of unions. *KL*

(Sources: **National Bureau of Statistics**)

Revolutionary Martyrs 'Slandered'

In May 2018, Rage Comic, a popular online cartoon and video platform, fell prey to China's recently passed Law on the Protection of Heroes and Martyrs. Taking effect on 1 May 2018, the Law requires all of Chinese society to respect heroes and martyrs of the Communist Party, and subjects anyone who fails to do so to civil or even criminal charges. The turbulence surrounding Rage Comic resulted from a 58-second video it posted on 8 May 2018 on Toutiao, a Beijing-based news content platform. In this video, Rage Comic made fun of Dong Cunrui, a People's Liberation Army soldier who is both famous and revered in China for his brave self-sacrifice in order to destroy a Kuomintang bunker during China's War of Liberation. Playing on the rhyme between 'bunker' and 'burger' in Chinese, Rage Comic substituted the former with the latter and, thus, turned Hero Dong into a starving diner. This joke backfired, however. The Ministry of Culture and Tourism ordered the Cultural Department in Shaanxi province, where the company is based, to impose executive punishment on Rage Comic. CEO Ren Jia first apologised on Weibo on 17 May, stating that the company would reflect on its grave mistake and educate all its staff on pertinent laws and regulations. On 23 May, he brought his employees to the Cemetery of Martyr Dong Cunrui in Hebei Province, laying a wreath there and reading out an apology letter. Toutiao was also under official investigation for having failed to oversee its platform. Rage Comic and Toutiao aside, Sougou and Douyin, a popular Chinese search engine and video platform respectively, also received official punishments for publishing content that insulted 'heroic deeds and spirits' on their platforms. *NLiu*

(Sources: **China Daily**; **China Digital Times**; **Global Times**; **QQ News**; **Sohu**; **Wall Street Journal**)

JUL/SEPT 2018

Vaccine Scandal Rocks China

Consumer scandals continued to engulf China in the third quarter of 2018. News broke out in late July that Changsheng Bio-technology Co. and Wuhan Institute of Biological Products Co. had respectively manufactured more than 250,000 and 400,000 substandard infant vaccines, an unknown number of which may have been administered to Chinese toddlers. This revelation sparked outrage across Chinese society. Social media platforms were inundated with criticism of unscrupulous corporate conduct and lax government supervision. On 30 and 31 July, furious parents even staged a protest in Beijing outside the offices of the National Health Commission and National State Drug Administration. Such massive public backlash was not only due to the fact that defective vaccines would fail to protect infants from common diseases—such as diphtheria, pertussis, and tetanus—but also due to the revelation that government officials had covered up for Changsheng Bio-technology Co. when it was discovered that the company had been falsifying its production data in October 2017. In response to the public outcry, President Xi Jinping and Prime Minister Li Keqiang vowed to conduct a thorough investigation. Fines were enforced on the two corporations involved, their executives detained, and more than 40 government officials punished. These efforts, however, did little to restore Chinese consumer confidence in domestic products, as this was just the latest in a series of repeated scandals since the milk powder incident in 2008. *NLiu*

(Sources: **Bloomberg; Caixin; CNN; Ershiyi Shiji Jingji Baodao; SCMP; Wall Street Journal**)

Xinjiang Garners Global Attention

Since October 2017, the Xinjiang Uyghur Autonomous Region has been marked by intensified surveillance of Uyghurs, a Muslim ethnic minority. According to scholar Rian Thum, an 'entire culture is being criminalised', as reports have emerged that up to one million Uyghurs have been detained in political re-education camps. Prominent Uyghur figures, such as Professor Rahile Dawut, football star Erfan Hezim, and musician Abdurehim Heyit are all believed to be currently held in such camps. For several months, this was met with silence from the international community. However, in August 2018 the United Nations Committee on the Elimination of Racial Discrimination released a report expressing concern, and called for the immediate release of all wrongfully and unlawfully detained individuals, as well as for the end of ethno-religious profiling. Likewise, in September, Human Rights Watch—an NGO based in the United States—released an extensive report detailing and providing evidence about the Chinese government's mass internment camps; abuse and mistreatment of ethnic Uyghurs, Kazakhs, and other minorities; as well as the increasingly intrusive controls on everyday life in Xinjiang. Government leaders in Muslim countries—in particular Malaysia and Pakistan—also expressed concern. Meanwhile, the Chinese government continued to deny all allegations, and the Chinese Ministry of Foreign Affairs attempted to discredit the reports as 'one-sided information', claiming instead that the Autonomous Region was 'enjoying overall social stability, sound economic development, and harmonious coexistence of different ethnic groups'. The Ministry further stated that the 'policies and measures in Xinjiang are aimed at preserving stability, promoting development and unity, and improving livelihood.' *TS*

(Sources: **CNN; Human Rights Watch; Radio Free Asia 1; Radio Free Asia 2; Reuters; SupChina; The Economist; The Independent; The New York Times 1; The New York Times 2**)

#MeToo Lands in China

In the third quarter of 2018, in spite of almost immediate censorship from the Chinese government, China's nascent #MeToo movement refused to be stifled. During the summer of 2018, the movement—predominantly led by student activists—resonated across university campuses in China. Online, the #MeToo hashtag collected over 4.5 million hits on Weibo, with activists sidestepping online censors through the use of homophones, including #MiTu, which roughly translates to #RiceBunny. #MeToo in China led to accusations against multiple high-profile men in the realms of academia, media, and civil society, including activist Lei Chuang, environmentalist Feng Yongfeng, and journalists Zhang Wen and Xiong Peiyun. In August, accusations against two other well-known men emerged—Buddhist Master Xuecheng and billionaire Richard Qiangdong Liu, founder and CEO of JD.com. On 15 August, Xuecheng resigned from his tenure as head of China's government-run Buddhist Association after being accused of sexual assault and harassment. A 95-page dossier, compiled by two supervisory chancellors at Beijing's Longquan Temple, contained several reports of Xuecheng sending sexually aggressive texts to nuns and disciples, with one woman accusing him of rape. Liu was arrested on 31 August following allegations of rape from a Chinese student at the University of Minnesota. If found guilty, Liu faces up to 30 years in prison. Although the movement stopped short of attacking any powerful figure in the Party-state apparatus, the downfall of such high-profile and influential individuals was well-received as a victory for China's #MeToo movement. *TS*

(Sources: **Chublic Opinion; Reuters 1; Reuters 2; SBS; South China Morning Post 1; South China Morning Post 2; The Atlantic; The Wall Street Journal; The Washington Post 1; The Washington Post 2**)

One Step Forward, Ten Steps Back for Human Rights

The third quarter of 2018 saw continued repression of human rights in China. However, there was some welcome news on 9 July, when Liu Xia—widow of late Chinese Nobel Peace Prize laureate Liu Xiaobo—was released from effective house arrest and moved to Germany. Sadly, 9 July also marked the third anniversary of the '709' crackdown, which saw the arrest of over 300 human rights lawyers and activists. On the anniversary, the European Union urged the Chinese government to release almost 30 detained activists, including publisher Gui Minhai (a Swedish citizen) and lawyer Wang Quanzhang. At the same time, in Hong Kong a group of lawyers and activists held a silent protest outside the Hong Kong Court of Final Appeal. In response, the Party-state stepped up repression. On 11 July, Qin Yongmin, a veteran pro-democracy campaigner, was sentenced to 13 years in prison on charges of 'subversion of a state power'. On the same day, Mongolian historian and author Lhamjab A. Borjigin was detained following charges of ethnic separatist activities. These charges are reportedly related to his book, documenting the life of ethnic Mongolians during the Cultural Revolution, wherein Borjigin claims that at least 27,900 Mongolians died, and 346,000 were imprisoned and tortured. A few days later independent liberal think tank Unirule Institute of Economics—which has often taken a critical stance toward government policies—was evicted from their Beijing office following an apparent tenancy dispute. Likewise, Jianjiao Bulao (roughly translated 'Pepper Tribe'), an online platform where female factory workers 'screamed' about workplace issues, was also shut down in July. *TS*

(Sources: **Hong Kong Free Press; Quartz; Radio Free Asia 1; Radio Free Asia 2; Reuters 1; Reuters 2; South China Morning Post 1; South China Morning Post 2; Voice of America News)**

OCT/DEC 2018

The Chinese Trade Union Holds Its National Congress

Between 22 and 26 October 2018, the All-China Federation of Trade Unions (ACFTU) convened its Seventeenth National Congress. In delivering his Report on the Economic Situation in front of the convened unionists, Premier Li Keqiang reemphasised the role of the ACFTU as a 'transmission belt' between the Chinese Communist Party and the Chinese workers. Politburo member Wang Huning reiterated the obligation of the ACFTU to motivate, unite, and guide Chinese workers under the Party's leadership. The Congress passed some amendments to the Constitution of the ACFTU. One remarkable change lies in the addition of 'sincerely serving the mass of workers' to the Union's earlier mission of 'protecting the legal rights of the workers'. Union officials said this change was largely in response to the evolving contradictions in Chinese society. Another noteworthy amendment pertained to the incorporation of Xi Jinping Thought as an essential part of the ACFTU's guiding ideology. In endorsing this amendment, the Congress reaffirmed the core status of President Xi Jinping in the Chinese Communist Party. Similar rhetoric also prevailed during the Twelfth National Congress of the All-China Women's Federation, convened in late October. In his speech at the Congress, President Xi asserted that upholding the leadership of the Party was fundamental to advancing the cause of women in China and realising the great rejuvenation of the Chinese nation. *NLiu*

(Sources: **ACFTU**; **China Labour Bulletin 1**; **China Labour Bulletin 2**; **Sohu**; **The State Council**; **Workercn**; **Xinhua 1**; **Xinhua 2**)

Fare Thee Well Private Economy?

As China prepared to celebrate the 40th anniversary of the launch of economic reforms in December 2018, concerns grew about the Chinese government's commitment to further liberalise the economy. Despite their economic contributions over the last four decades, private firms in China were finding themselves embroiled in an ever-challenging situation, plagued by slower economic growth, tighter credit lines, tougher regulations, and stronger Party interference. These hardships resulted in at least ten private firms being nationalised by state-owned enterprises in the first nine months of 2018. Some Chinese intellectuals went as far as to publicly assert that private companies should be eliminated from China's economy, considering that they had completed their job of helping China prosper. Amid these arguments, President Xi Jinping reiterated the government's support for private firms in October. His assurance was, however, quickly called into question. In early November, authorities in Beijing first banned the executive director of Unirule, a liberal think tank, from travelling to the United States to attend a symposium on China's economic reforms, and then revoked the business licence of the organisation, forcing it to suspend all its activities. Such occurrences show how the Chinese leadership has become increasingly intolerant of dissenting views, not only in the political realm, but also on economic matters. This can be seen in the repeated attempts at rewriting Chinese history, as evidenced by an exhibition titled 'The Great Revolution' that opened at the National Museum in Beijing on 13 November to celebrate the anniversary of economic reforms. While Xi Jinping enjoyed numerous displays about his achievements, Deng Xiaoping, the architect of China's economic reforms, was much less visible, and other key actors of the past decades, such as Zhu Rongji, China's former reformist premier, were nowhere to be seen. *NLiu*

(Sources: **Economic Information Daily**; **Financial Times**; **The New York Times**; **Radio Free Asia**; **South China Morning Post**; **Wall Street Journal**; **Xinhua**)

China's Human Rights Record in Xinjiang under International Scrutiny

In November 2018, China's human rights record was scrutinised by the United Nations Human Rights Council. In a process known as a 'universal periodic review' (UPR), the nation in question must demonstrate its ability to follow previous United Nations (UN) recommendations and answer questions posed by other states, NGOs, and other institutions. On 6 November, China was called to address human rights issues including its treatment of ethnic minorities, specifically Uyghurs in Xinjiang; its crackdown on lawyers and activists; as well as issues regarding civil, religious, and press freedoms. Unsurprisingly, China responded by defending its human rights record, deeming the UN assessment to be 'politically driven' and 'fraught with biases'. At the end of 2018, China's worsening human rights record was increasingly drawing international scrutiny. The UN's high commissioner for human rights, Michelle Bachelet, requested direct access to Xinjiang amid growing concerns over China's treatment of the Uyghur minority. In addition, spearheaded by Canada, 15 Western ambassadors issued a letter requesting Xinjiang's Communist Party leader to meet with them and provide an explanation of the alleged human rights abuses. Such actions were rebuffed by Beijing, with the Chinese foreign ministry spokeswoman Hua Chunying claiming that the ambassadors had exceeded their diplomatic capacities. While this heated exchange was still in the making, internationally renowned photographer Lu Guang went missing while visiting Xinjiang. He has not been heard from since. Moreover, in early December reports from international media began detailing the emergence of a forced labour regime in factories attached to reeducation camps in Xinjiang, prompting new criticisms. *TS*

(Sources: **BBC**; **The Guardian 1**; **The Guardian 2**; **The Independent 1**; **The Independent 2**; **Radio Free Asia 1**; **SBS News**; **South China Morning Post**; **The New York Times**; **United Nations Human Rights Office of the High Commissioner**)

As One High-level Official Disappears, Nobody is Safe from Repression

In the last quarter of 2018, China's human rights record continued to deteriorate. October began with the disappearance of a high-level official—Meng Hongwei, then President of Interpol and Deputy Minister of Public Security in China—who was reported missing after travelling from France to China. The Central Commission for Discipline Inspection subsequently stated that Meng is being investigated on allegations of taking bribes. On 5 November, rights groups released a statement urging the Chinese government to release 'cyber-dissident' Huang Qi who was arrested in 2016 on charges of 'leaking state secrets'. His condition had drastically declined during his time in custody. It was reported that Huang suffered from chronic kidney disease, hydrocephalus, and heart disease. In the same month, Fengrui, the Chinese law firm raided at the start of the '709' campaign in July 2015, was officially shut down. On 29 November, Li Wenzu, a 709 campaigner and the wife of detained human rights lawyer Wang Quanzhang, was barred from leaving China. She was on her way to Sweden, where she was to receive the Edelstam Prize for outstanding contributions to advancing human rights. At the end of the month, authorities in Guangdong formally arrested two individuals who witnessed the beating and stripping of human rights lawyer Sun Shihua. Since September, Sun had been pursuing a complaint after being beaten, illegally detained, strip-searched, and drug-tested for seven hours in Guangzhou. Lawyers were not the only victims of state repression: in mid-November, a Chinese author known by the pen name Tianyi, was sentenced to over 10 years in jail for writing and selling a 'pornographic' erotic novel that featured gay sex scenes; and in early December, Xu Lin, a musician who sang about the late Nobel peace laureate and political prisoner Liu Xiaobo, was given a three-year jail term. *TS*

(Sources: **ABC News**; **Radio Free Asia 1; Radio Free Asia 2; Radio Free Asia 3; Reuters**; **South China Morning Post 1**; **South China Morning Post 2**)

Hong Kong under Siege

In the final quarter of 2018, the political situation in Hong Kong was increasingly tense, as the former British colony's special status under the 'one country, two systems' arrangement appeared to be faltering. The inauguration of a high-speed railway connecting Hong Kong to Guangzhou on 23 September and a new bridge that links Hong Kong to Zhuhai and Macau on 23 October raised fears among Hong Kongers that closer linkages to the mainland would allow the Chinese government to exert more control over their society. These fears were mainly rooted in the decision to enforce mainland Chinese laws at the West Kowloon Terminus in Hong Kong, which critics argued would eventually undermine the independent judicial system of Hong Kong. The deterioration of Hong Kong's political situation was also apparent in a string of other incidents. In early October, Victor Mallet, Asia News Editor at the *Financial Times*, was first denied renewal of his work visa in Hong Kong and then, one month later, refused entry to the city, a de facto expulsion ostensibly related to his chairing a public meeting with a leader of an independentist party in the city. On 3 November, an exhibition by Badiucao, a Chinese-Australian political artist, was cancelled in Hong Kong over 'threats' from Chinese authorities. One week later, Ma Jian, a renowned Chinese writer residing in England, had two scheduled speeches at a literary festival in Hong Kong cancelled due to his criticisms of the Chinese government—the events were later rearranged as the hosts changed their mind at the last minute. Adding to these worrisome situations was the trial on 19 November of Chan Kin-man, co-founder of the Occupy Central Movement in 2014, and of his fellow campaigners. The controversies surrounding the proceedings, along with the other aforementioned contentious events, stained Hong Kong's image as a beacon of freedom in Asia. *NLiu*

(Sources: **ABC**; **CCTV.com**; **Financial Times**; **Hong Kong Free Press**; **Reuters**; **South China Morning Post**; **The Guardian**; **Washington Post**; **Xinhua**)

Jasic Crackdown Widens

In early November 2018, more than a dozen students and recent college graduates who had expressed their support for the Jasic mobilisation were detained. Staff of a social work organisation in Shenzhen and two employees of a district-level ACFTU branch in the same city were also caught up in the crackdown. Those who were detained earlier—including one NGO staff member and three workers—continued to be held incommunicado. This development followed weeks of harassment against those students and activists who had mobilised to demand the release of those detained during the summer. A number of prominent Chinese universities attempted to block Marxism clubs on campus—with which the Jasic student supporters were affiliated—from renewing their registration. In response to the university's punitive actions against a dozen of its students, Cornell University's School of Industrial and Labor Relations took the unprecedented step of suspending an academic labour exchange programme with People's University in Beijing. This action drew a rebuke from the *Global Times*, which accused Cornell of echoing Trump's strategy against China. Following the arrests in November, a number of renowned Marxist and left-wing international scholars, including Noam Chomsky, issued personal statements in support of those detained, and announced their intention to boycott China's officially sponsored Marxism conferences. At the end of the year, in spite of mounting international solidarity, the situation for labour activism in China remained dire. In another instance of state repression, on 7 November, riot police in Shenzhen assaulted and pepper-sprayed former blast workers with silicosis who were protesting to demand compensation for their occupational disease. *KL*

(Sources: **China Daily**; **Financial Times**; **Global Times**; **Guardian**; **Reuters**; **Radio Free Asia**; **The New York Times**)

ANYBODY OUT THERE?

The Chinese Labour Movement under Xi

June 2010, workers at Foshan Fengfu Auto Parts Co. a supply factory to Honda Motor's joint-ventures in China, strike to demand higher wages. PC: People's World/AP.

Changes and Continuity

Four Decades of Industrial Relations in China

Chris King-Chi CHAN

China's economic reforms started exactly 40 years ago. Labour scholars today are debating the extent to which labour relations and the labour movement in China have changed, and where they may be heading. Positions are polarised between pessimists who emphasise the structural power of the market and the authoritarian state, and optimists who envision the rise of a strong and independent labour movement in China. In this essay, Chris King-Chi Chan advocates for a different approach.

The year 2018 marks the fortieth anniversary of the beginning of China's economic reform programme. The rise of migrant workers' strikes since early 2000s and the efforts of the Chinese government to rebalance and reregulate workplace relations have created fertile ground for labour studies and labour activism in China. One of the key debates in this scholarly/activist community concerns the extent to which labour relations and the 'labour movement' in China have changed, and where they may be heading. Pessimists highlight the structural power of the market and the ability of the authoritarian state to undermine worker solidarity and collective action, while optimists envision the ongoing emergence of a strong and independent labour movement in China, supported by labour NGOs and international civil society.

In the midst of this debate, on 3 December 2015 there was a major crackdown on labour NGOs in Guangzhou and Foshan. Between 2012 and 2015, most of the affected NGOs had been active in assisting the collective struggles of workers by promoting collective bargaining. Some labour lawyers and academics referred to this new type of NGO as 'labour movement-oriented NGOs' (*gongyunxing NGOs*) to distinguish them from 'social service-oriented NGOs' (*fuwuxing* NGOs) and 'legal rights-oriented NGOs' (*weiquanxing NGOs*) (Duan 2015; see also Franceschini and Lin's essay in this volume). This crackdown was a major setback for Chinese activists who had worked to build a labour movement from the ground up. For scholars, by the time their studies on labour movement-oriented NGOs were published, these organisations had essentially ceased to exist.

Does this portend a gloomy future for Chinese workers? To respond to this question, I advocate a Marxian approach built on two observations. First, class struggle between capital and labour around the issues of production, which is constrained by global political economy, defines the history of China's integration into global capitalism. Second, the state remains a contested terrain of class struggle in China (Chan 2010 and 2012; Chan and Hui 2017). It is only through a worker-centred historical approach that we can understand the rapidly shifting landscape in contemporary China, and what the future may hold.

Harmonious Labour Relations

Since the early 1990s, China has established itself as a 'world factory', with the cities in the Pearl River Delta (PRD) as its powerhouse. Major ethnographic research conducted in the PRD has found that the politics of place and gender were often exploited by management to maintain class domination and despotism throughout the 1990s (Lee 1998; Pun 2005). But labour relations have undergone change in the new millennium. Politically, after President Hu Jintao and Premier Wen Jiabao took office in 2002, a series of socioeconomic reforms reforms were introduced in the name of building a 'harmonious society' (*hexie shehui*). Social challenges related to farmers, rural areas, and agriculture—the so-called 'three rural problems' (*sannong wenti*)—have since become a greater concern for the Party-state. Economically, since 2003, China has surpassed the United States as the country with the largest foreign direct investment inflow in the world. China's GDP also shocked the world, with an average annual growth rate of 10.5 percent from 2001 to 2011 (National Bureau of Statistics of China 2012).

The dramatic changes in China's urban and rural economies since 2003 have given rise to a shortage of labour (*mingonghuang*)—a situation in stark contrast with the labour surplus (*mingongchao*) of the early 1990s. Within this context, rising waves of strikes and protests have taken place in the PRD since 2004. This unrest has forced the government to increase the minimum wage and introduce new labour laws, culminating in the 2008 Labour Contract Law. This law was intended to stabilise and regulate labour relations by making written contracts a legal obligation for employers. Workers were entitled to double pay if their employers did not sign a contract with them and, after they completed two consecutive contracts or were employed for ten continuous years, the employer was required to give them a permanent contract. Employers had to pay severance of one month's wages for each year of service if they wanted to dismiss a worker. This was an important step to the formalisation of employment relations for the migrant workers, who had previously existed in a precarious state (Lee 1998; Pun 2005).

Class Struggle Intensified

The global economic crisis of 2008 had a major effect on the Chinese economy. In 2009, China's total exports decreased by 16 percent (National Bureau of Statistics of China 2010). Many factories in South China faced closure or bankruptcy, but the Chinese economy recovered quickly due to the government's huge stimulus investment in infrastructure and social spending. In 2010, the GDP growth rate returned to double digits (10.3 percent). Concomitant with this economic revival was the reemergence of labour shortages. Against this backdrop, a more significant wave of strikes led by Honda workers in June 2010 attracted global attention. These industrial actions gave impetus to the process of trade union reform (Chan and Hui 2014), and the All-China Federation of Trade Unions (ACFTU) began to promote a policy of wage bargaining and trade union direct election.

The next turning point for labour relations in China came in 2012, as President Xi Jinping took power. Unlike the Hu–Wen administration which emphasised harmonious society and pursued reformist social and labour policies, Xi's government has adopted a hard-line policy to pacify labour activism. The foundation of this political change has been the economic slowdown since 2012, with many factory closures and relocations. The GDP growth rate decreased from 10.1 percent in 2011 to 8.1 percent in 2012 and 6.7 percent in 2016—a situation that Xi has called the 'new normal' for the Chinese economy (National Bureau of Statistics of China 2016).

Since 2012, many factories announced their relocation plans with minimal or no compensation to workers. In response, workers increasingly took collective action. During this period, pension insurance became one of the main demands of migrant workers on strike. This demand was encouraged by the Social Insurance Law, in effect since 2011, and was also pressing because many migrant workers had reached or were nearing retirement age. The strike at the Yue Yuen shoe factory in Dongguan in April 2014 was the most influential collective action concerning pension issues (Chen 2015). More than 40,000 workers went on strike for more than ten days, gaining global attention. The strike ended with the company agreeing to pay the social insurance owed to the workers (Chan and Hui 2017). Another successful case took place at the Lide shoe factory in Guangzhou in August 2014. Lide workers were able to receive compensation and social insurance before the factory's relocation with the help of the Panyu Migrant Workers Service Center, one of the major 'labour movement oriented NGOs' (Froissart 2018).

Since then, in the face of the economic slowdown, the Party-state has lowered the standard of labour rights protection. For instance, in February 2017, Guangdong province announced that the minimum wage now would be adjusted every three years, rather than every two years, in order to lower operation costs of enterprises. Thus, the minimum wage in 2018 would remain at the 2015 level (Caixin 2017). At the same time, police intervention in labour protests has escalated, strikes that affected public order can be directly shut down, and worker leaders risk arrest. Wu Guijun, one of the leaders of a strike in Shenzhen in 2013, was detained for 371 days (Mitchell 2015). Labour NGOs have also been targeted by the government. This has had dramatic negative repercussions for the development of labour NGOs in China, with many organisations becoming severely constrained in the ways they are able to support workers' collective actions.

The Future

The latest developments show that some labour NGOs seem to have reduced capacity to support workers in their struggle due to the shrinking political space for civil society—particularly civil society working in the labour sphere. But challenges to labour activism do not put an end to class struggle. Therefore, in order to understand the trajectory of China's labour situation there are two key points that must be considered.

First, workplace conflict is embedded within the capitalist production regime. Strikes and other forms of labour protests will not be eliminated without structural change in industrial relations. In an attempt to smooth over the contradictions and strengthen the existing system, in recent years the Chinese Party-state has made great effort to reform local trade unions, and to strengthen their capability to intervene in workplace conflict and promote collective bargaining. One example is the pilot project of the Shenzhen Federation of Trade Unions to establish community-based worker service centres and worker training programmes (Dou 2017). If these projects are successful, an authoritarian hegemonic labour regime will emerge in some sectors and regions, but at least workers will enjoy slightly better protections. If, on the contrary, the state-led reformist policies are not well implemented and detrimental working conditions remain, the workers' struggle will carry on.

In fact, the dramatic growth of the service sector in China has resulted in surging labour unrest in relevant industries. Workers' collective actions in the service industries have accounted for 21 percent of all collective action cases, surpassing the manufacturing industries for the first time in the third quarter of 2016 (China Labour Bulletin 2016). Information about labour strikes and protests are generally difficult to access. Still on May Day of 2018, the *Global Times*, an official Chinese newspaper, reported that crane operators in the construction sector had launched protests across China demanding better pay and an eight-hour working day. In the city of Chengdu alone, at least 10,000 workers joined the protest (Yin 2018).

Second, regarding the role of NGOs, it should be noted that they are a tool, rather than the goal, of civil society in supporting workers. Historically, labour NGOs in the PRD were initiated by Hong Kong labour organisations, activists, and academics (Chan 2018). In the late 1990s and early 2000s, with the more relaxed policies of the Party-state, labour activists and intellectuals in mainland China began to establish their own organisations. In this way, the existence of labour NGOs can be seen as emerging from a particular historical and political moment. As long as intellectuals and social activists maintain their concerns for labour issues, the measures they take to support the workers struggle can vary across time and space. For instance, eight university students from Beijing were detained or wanted by the government as they organised a reading group with workers in a university campus in Guangzhou (Chuang 2018). This instigated an enormous outpouring of support from Chinese scholars and other intellectuals. It illustrates that the struggle around labour rights between pro-labour civil society actors and the state is far from dead. It is ongoing, developing, and changing. Under a new political context, new strategies have been created to support workers and resist pressure from the state. ■

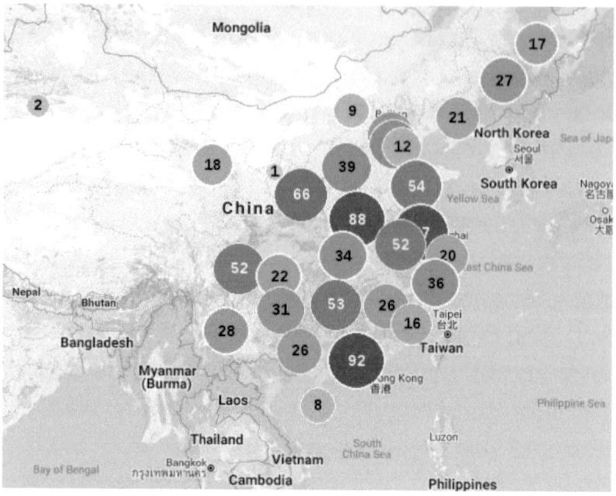

A map of workers' strikes in China in 2018 provided by China Labour Bulletin (maps.clb.org.hk/strikes).

China's Labour Movement in Transition

Geoffrey CROTHALL

In the first five years of Xi Jinping's rule, China was characterised by slowing economic growth, the decline of traditional industries, a rapid growth in service industries, and the increasing use of flexible or precarious labour. This has had a clear impact on Chinese workers. In this essay, Geoffrey Crothall illustrates the latest trends in labour activism in China, examining the workers' main demands, the types of protest, the number of participants, and the responses of the local authorities and police.

For China's workers, the first five years of Xi Jinping's rule (2013–18) were characterised by slower economic growth, the decline of traditional industries such as manufacturing and mining, a rapid growth in service industries, and the increasing use of flexible or precarious labour.

This led to a commensurate change in the nature and scale of worker protests, with the focus shifting away from factories in Guangdong, the traditional heartland of worker activism in China, to a more broad-based response to economic hardship across a wide range of industries around the country. In the vast majority of cases, collective action during this period was triggered not by demands for better pay and working conditions but rather by the failure of employers in both traditional and new industries to comply with even the most basic provisions of labour law.

To better understand the changing face of worker activism in China, this essay will use China Labour Bulletin's (CLB) Strike Map to illustrate the geographical and sectoral distribution of worker protests in China between 2013 and 2017. This allows for an examination of the workers' main demands, the types of protest, the number of participants, and the response, if any, of the local authorities and police.

The CLB Strike Map recorded a total of 8,696 collective worker protests from 1 January 2013 to 31 December 2017. This, of course, is not a definitive record of all the strikes in China; it is merely the incidents posted on Chinese social media and occasionally in the official media that we were able to collect during key word searches. Our sampling rate has varied over the five years but we estimate—based on the occasional and partial statistics issued by the national and local governments in China—that the CLB Strike Map accounts for about 5 to 10 percent of all incidents of worker collective action in China during this period. The sampling rate was likely higher in Guangdong and major cities in 2013, but coverage has since been more universal.

Distribution across Industries

In the early 2010s, the manufacturing sector was by far the most important locus of worker activism in China. Factory workers first started organising to demand higher wages, social insurance payments, and then, as the factories started to close down or relocate, compensation for the termination of their employment contracts. As the decade progressed, however, the proportion of factory-based protests declined as the manufacturing industry consolidated and protests in other sectors, particularly in services, increased. The proportion of protests in the manufacturing sector declined from around 47 percent in 2013 to just 21 percent in 2017, roughly the same proportion as collective protests in the retail and service industries that year. See chart below.

The growing number of protests in the service and retail industries were spread out over a vast array of businesses, including shops, bars, restaurants, hotels, gyms, IT companies, banks and finance companies, medical facilities, kindergartens, as well as other private education facilities like driving schools, golf courses and amusement parks, television stations, and other local media outlets. Public sector teachers also took collective action over a wide range of issues from low pay, pensions, bonus payments, and wages in arrears. Many service sector workers were hired as informal service providers rather than formal employees and when disputes over payment of wages or severance pay broke out they often had no idea who their actual employer was.

One of the most active and effective groups in this period were sanitation workers, who accounted for 8 percent of all service sector protests (CLB 2014b). Sanitation workers across China faced low pay, lack of benefits,

Distribution of Worker Protests across Different Industries, as a Percentage of Total Protests (2013–17)

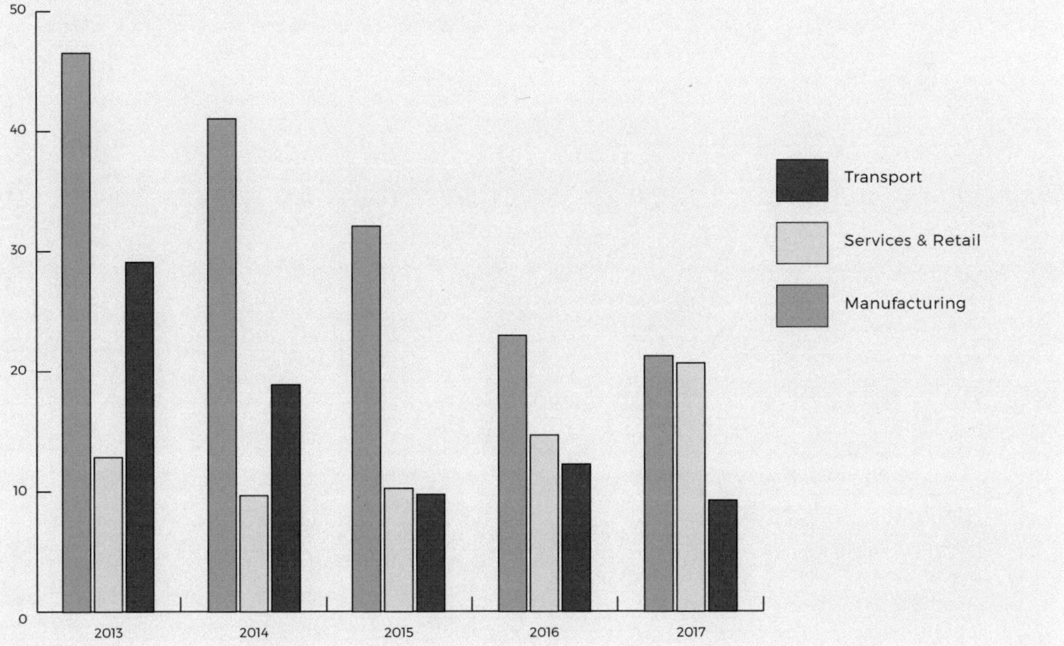

insecure employment, and hazardous working conditions. The only way to improve their situation was through collective action.

During this period, the transport sector also became a more precarious profession as the market for traditional taxis declined with ride-hailing apps gaining a larger market share. At the same time, the job security of bus drivers and conductors was threatened by increased competition from Internet-based services, and couriers and food delivery workers, nearly all of whom had little or no job security, became an integral part of the urban economy. In 2013, the majority of protests in the transport sector (105 out of 188) were staged by traditional taxi drivers complaining primarily about high vehicle rental fees and competition from unlicensed cabs. By 2017, of the 117 incidents recorded in the transport sector, only 43 were by traditional taxi drivers, 10 incidents involved drivers with the main ride-hailing service Didi Chuxing, and 28 incidents involved delivery workers.

Broader Geographic Distribution of Worker Protests

In the first year of this study, more than a third of all worker protests recorded on the CLB Strike Map occurred in the southern province of Guangdong, and most of those incidents were concentrated in the manufacturing districts of the Pearl River Delta (PRD). Five years later, in 2017, the proportion of incidents in Guangdong had fallen steadily to stand at just under 12 percent of the total (see the graph below). This may be partially due to a higher sampling rate for the CLB Strike Map in Guangdong in 2013 but sampling rates alone cannot explain such a dramatic shift.

This dramatic fall was the result of two concurrent and related trends: the closure of low-end manufacturing facilities in the

Proportion of China's Collective Worker Incidents in Guangdong (%)

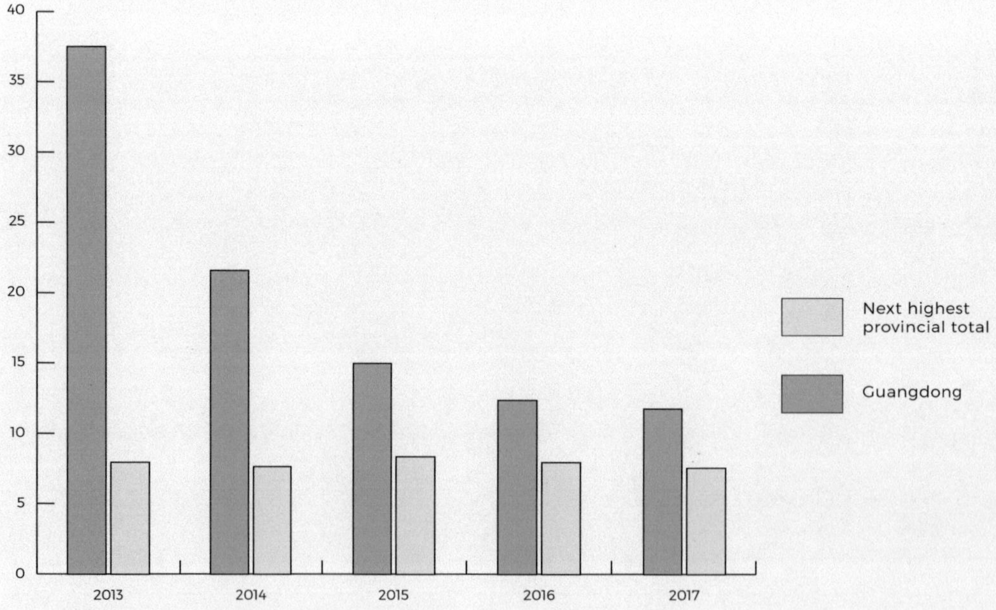

PRD, and the development of construction, manufacturing, and service industries across the whole of China.

The majority of labour disputes in Guangdong, especially from 2013 to 2015, were directly related to the decline of manufacturing in the region. As the economy faltered and more factories closed down, an increasingly elderly workforce realised they would have to take action if their legally mandated social security benefits and housing fund contributions were to be paid in full before their factory closed its doors for good, or the owner simply skipped town owing them months of unpaid wages. In some cases, factory bosses did pay their workers what they were owed before closing down the factory and protests were thus avoided (CLB 2016a). In many other cases however management dragged their feet or refused payment outright, leading to long, drawn out, and bitter disputes such as the Lide shoe factory workers' campaign for relocation compensation, which lasted from August 2014 to April 2015 (CLB 2015).

By 2017, tens of thousands of factories in the PRD had closed, while those that remained tended to be more stable and economically viable (Tu 2015). In September 2017, the municipal authorities in Dongguan—once known as China's factory to the world—boasted of a 69 percent reduction in the number of collective protests by workers over the year and a 71 percent reduction in the incidence of factory bosses skipping town without paying wages (CLB 2017). The local labour officials claimed the credit themselves for reducing the number of disputes, but it seems much more likely that the majority of problematic factories had already closed down or relocated to lower-cost inland or overseas locations by 2017.

In 2017, the coastal manufacturing centres of Zhejiang, Jiangsu, and Shandong—as well as inland provinces like Henan, Hebei, Shaanxi, Anhui, and even Sichuan—all had substantial numbers of worker protests. In the first three months of 2018, Henan had the highest number of protests in China—44 incidents compared to 29 in Guangdong.

Many inland provinces experienced rapid urbanisation and a boom in infrastructure and property development during this period. This, in turn, led to the creation of manufacturing facilities and services in these newly urbanised areas. Local governments were keen to attract new investment with the promise of a plentiful labour supply and a business-friendly environment, which usually meant the lax enforcement of labour law. In addition, there was over-investment in unsustainable sectors of the economy, leading to numerous business failures, lay-offs, and wage arrears. Typically, disputes in inland areas tended to be relatively small-scale and short-lived, but occasionally larger protests did break out, such as when 2,000 workers at a toy factory in Luoning, Henan, went on strike in June 2015 over non-payment of wages.

It should be noted that the rapid spread of smartphones and social media platforms across much of China during this period probably contributed to the greater visibility of worker disputes in smaller cities that might have previously slipped under the radar.

Workers' Demands

In the early 2010s, China's factory workers, exemplified by the Nanhai Honda auto workers in Foshan, launched a series of strikes demanding better pay and working conditions. These strikes were a direct response to rapidly rising living costs and a long period of wage stagnation during the global economic crisis. Wages in the manufacturing sector did increase significantly in the first few years of the decade although wages in service industries tended to lag behind. As economic growth slowed in the mid-2010s, however, wage increases started to level off and the problem of wage arrears came more and more to the fore.

As the chart above illustrates, workers' demands for pay increases steadily declined during the five-year period of this study. At the

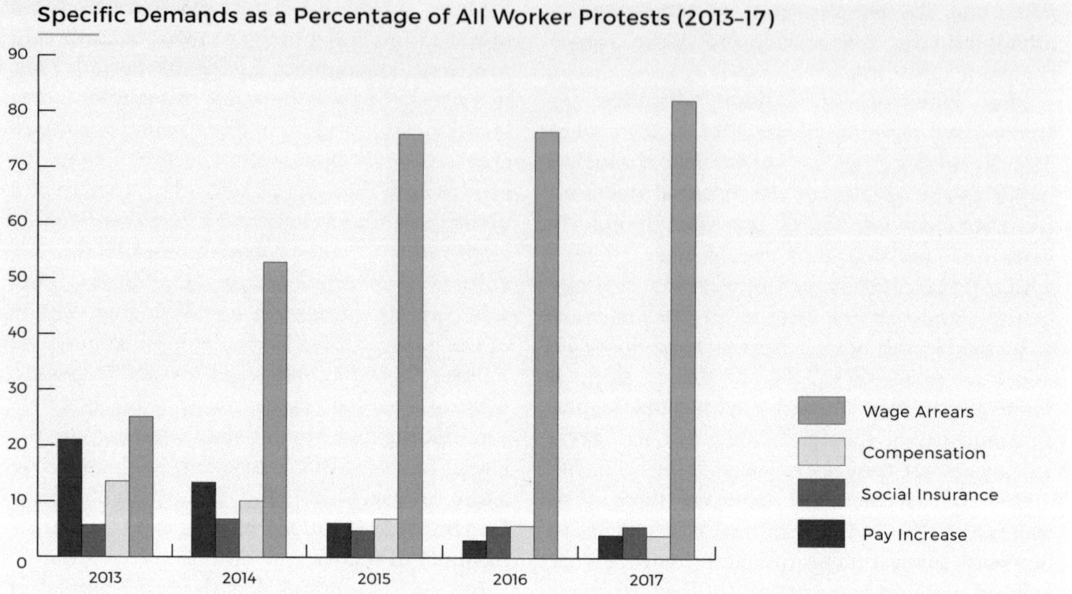

same time, demands for payment of wages in arrears shot up from 25 percent of all protests in 2013 to 82 percent in 2017.

The non-payment of wages has been a perennial problem in China's construction industry for decades. Construction workers are separated from the main project developer and financier by numerous layers of sub-contractors and, in most cases, they are only paid on completion of the job. Every year, in the run-up to the Lunar New Year, millions of migrant workers are forced to stage desperate protests just to get paid in time for the holiday.

As noted above, the issue of wage arrears has persistently dogged the manufacturing sector, with factories suddenly closing and the boss vanishing. However, the deliberate non-payment of wages is increasingly spreading to other industries as well, particularly services and new start-up enterprises. Of the 1,033 wage arrears cases recorded on the CLB Strike Map in 2017, just under half (507) were in the construction industry, while 212 were in manufacturing, and 223 were in services and retail.

The growth of new industries in China has created new problems for workers. Many of the jobs in service industries, such as couriers, food delivery, and telecom sales, are insecure, low-paid with little or no benefits, and place excessive demands on the time of individual workers. The Chinese government, and in particular Premier Li Keqiang, has placed excessive faith in the ability of start-up enterprises to generate decent and stable jobs (China Daily 2015). Many start-ups fail within a year or so of being established, and when they do collapse or get into financial difficulty, their employees simply do not get paid.

Worker Organising and Participation

One of the most obvious trends discernible from the CLB Strike Map over the last five years has been the decline in the number of major protests. In 2013, nearly 10 percent of all protests involved more than 1,000 workers.

The following year, the proportion had dropped to 7.2 percent, even including five massive protests with more than 10,000 workers, such as the Yue Yuen shoe factory strike in Dongguan in April 2014, which saw up to 40,000 workers out on strike for two weeks. In the next three years the proportion of major protests dropped dramatically to the point in 2017 where we recorded just one incident involving more than 1,000 workers (see graph below). At the time of writing (May 2018), we have recorded another 7 incidents with more than 1,000 participants. Please note, however, that CLB takes a quite conservative approach to protest size and we are more likely to under-estimate than over-estimate the number of participants.

This steady fall is partly explained by the fact that the traditional sources of major protests, such as large-scale factories, have been in decline and no longer provide the huge numbers of workers in one place who can rally around a common cause. It perhaps also indicates the authorities' determination to preempt large-scale protests that have the potential to threaten social stability China. Following the high-profile protest over wage arrears by coal miners in Shuangyashan, Heilongjiang province, which occurred during the 2016 National People's Congress, the authorities went to great lengths subsequently to ensure that laid-off workers in the state sector were paid in full and adequately compensated during the closure or contraction of major state-owned enterprises (Financial Times 2017).

While the number of large-scale protests has fallen significantly in the state sector, this does not necessarily mean that workers are no longer organising on a larger scale. In 2016, for example, tens of thousands of Walmart workers joined online groups in response to the company's attempts to impose a flexible working system on its roughly 100,000 employees in China. The online groups created a sense of solidarity among Walmart workers across the country and allowed them to share information and strategies that could be used to resist management attempts to erode their benefits (CLB 2016b). Workers in other service industries also used social media platforms to organise simultaneous small-scale protests in

Percentage of Protests Involving More than 1,000 Workers

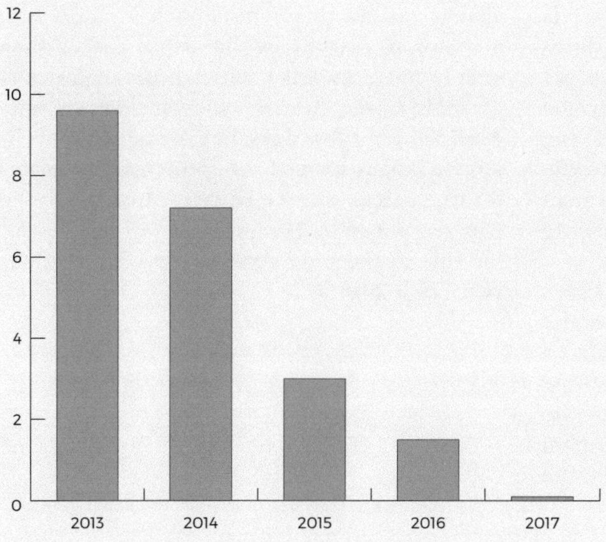

different cities. For example, on 27 June 2016, sales staff at Neutrogena organised coordinated protests outside the company's offices in Beijing, Guangzhou, and Shanghai.

Government and Police Response

Most collective labour disputes in China are short-lived and are resolved or dissipate without the need for government intervention. It is difficult to gauge exactly how often local governments do get involved in labour disputes because such actions are not often detailed in social media posts about collective protests. When local officials do turn up it is clear that their primary concern is to contain and resolve the dispute as quickly as possible. Local government officials will often attempt to mediate or intervene by putting pressure on both labour and management to make some concessions and compromise so that production can return to normal. However, these quick fixes rarely address the fundamental grievances of workers and do little to mitigate the tensions in labour relations that gave rise to the workers' collective action in the first place.

If there is a trade union branch at the enterprise at the centre of a dispute, it is usually a passive bystander or it will sometimes side with management in its attempts to get the employees back to work. Just about the only exception during this period was Huang Xingguo, the head of the Walmart store trade union in the central city of Changde, Hunan province, who led staff in a month-long dispute over severance pay in 2014 (CLB 2014a).

District trade union officials do sometimes get involved in labour disputes but, like the local government officials they are associated with, their primary concern is to get striking employees back to work. That said, the municipal trade union federations in Shanghai and Shenzhen have taken some steps in the last two years to help organise food delivery workers and support Walmart employees in their campaign against the unilateral imposition of flexible working hours.

Police do not normally get involved in labour disputes unless the incident is deemed a threat to public order or the business owner specifically requests police assistance. Police officers intervened in about a quarter of all incidents recorded on the CLB Strike Map during the five-year period from 2013 to 2017. As indicated in the graph in the next page, there was a spike in police interventions in 2015, which coincided with an intense period of worker activism in Guangdong but also elsewhere, and directives from Beijing to take a tougher stand against civil society in general. As might be expected, the police were far more likely to get involved in larger-scale protests. In collective protests involving more than 1,000 workers, for example, police intervened in about 50 percent of cases and made arrests in 20 percent of them.

It is clear from the data that a police presence does not necessarily lead to the arrest or detention of worker activists. In most cases, the main concern of the police is to contain the protest as much as possible and prevent it from causing a disruption to public order or traffic. If arrests are made, they are nearly always related to offences such as 'gathering a crowd to disrupt public order' rather than simply going on strike, which is not technically illegal in China. In most cases workers are only detained for a few days, but occasionally well-known labour activists are sentenced to longer terms, such as veteran activist Meng Han who was sentenced to 21 months in jail in 2016 for his role in the Lide shoe factory the previous year (CLB 2016c).

Police Intervention in Collective Worker Incidents 2013–17 (%)

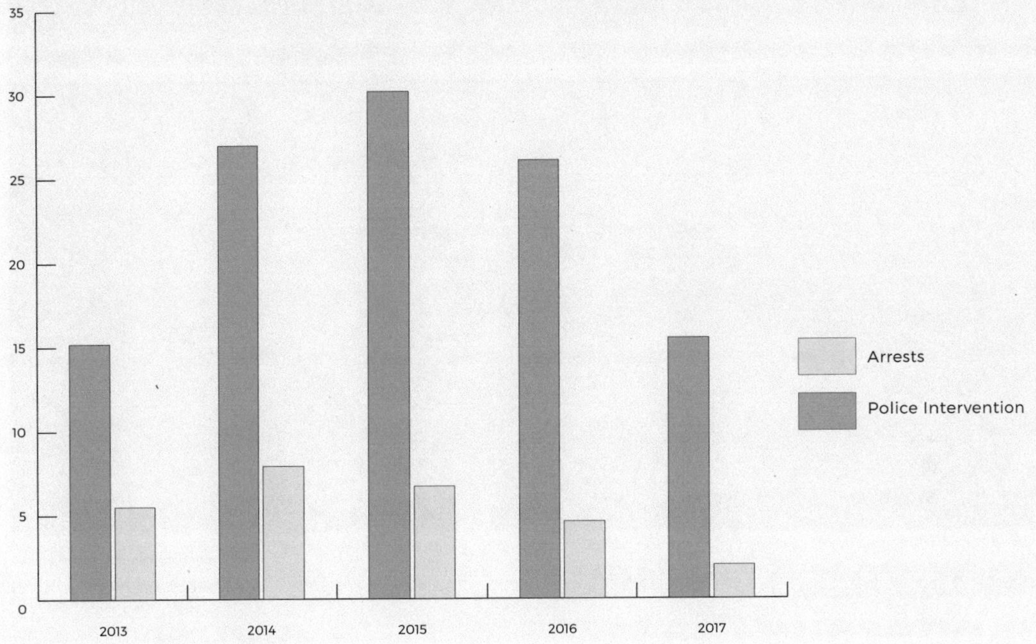

Challenges Ahead

The last five years have been a period of rapid transition for China's workers as they adapted and responded to a new economic and political reality under Xi Jinping. Workers were challenged by the decline in traditional industries and the emergence of new and precarious patterns of employment in the service industry.

The lack of an effective trade union that could represent workers in collective bargaining with management and the absence of institutions or accepted practices that might help resolve collective labour disputes peacefully and constructively meant that workers had little option but to resort to strikes and other forms of collective action to air their grievances.

Although we do not have any definitive data on the number of collective worker protests during this period, we can conclude with some confidence that while large-scale factory protests probably reached a peak around 2015, smaller-scale protests over a much broader range of industries and regions continued to erupt on a very regular basis across the entire country.

These persistent protests have presented the authorities with a serious challenge as they struggle to fulfil Xi Jinping's pledge to improve the lives of ordinary working women and men in China. In particular, the increasingly casual and precarious nature of employment in China today will make it very difficult for local government officials, who are already notoriously lax in enforcing labour law, to guarantee that labour rights are adequately protected. ■

Chinese workers in Shenzhen. PC: jordanpouille.com.

Gongyou, the New Dangerous Class in China?

YU Chunsen

For decades, labour scholars have been debating the transformation of the identity of Chinese migrants from 'peasants' to 'workers' in an attempt to assess the extent of their class consciousness. In this essay, Yu Chunsen examines a new identity—framed as 'gongyou', or 'workmate'—that is developing among the new generation of migrant workers in China.

After four decades of rural-to-urban migration, the class identity of more than 280 million rural migrant workers in China remains ambiguous. Many scholars have attempted to capture the transformation of their identity from 'peasants' to 'workers' by resorting to such labels as 'new industrial workers' (*xin chanye gongren*), 'semi-proletariat', 'full proletariat', 'precarious proletariat' (*buwending wuchanzhe*), and even 'Chinese new workers' (*zhongguo xin gongren*) (Lee 2007; Lü 2012 and 2014; Pun and Chan 2008; Pun and Lu 2010; Smith and Pun 2017; Standing 2016; Swider 2015; Woronov 2016; Xie 2005; Yang 2010).

Drawing on semi-structured interviews with 164 rural migrant workers in six high-tech processing and assembly manufacturing factories in Chongqing and Shenzhen conducted between 2014 and 2016, in this essay I contribute to this debate by discussing how rural migrant workers I have encountered during fieldwork in China describe and identify themselves. In particular, I examine a new identity—framed as *gongyou*, or 'workmate'—that is developing among the new generation of migrant workers in China. I argue that organically forming identities such as this one have the potential to transcend divisions of gender, industry, and geographic area, and could thus provide a means of challenging the state and capital going forward.

A New *Gongyou* Identity

The term *gongyou* is widely used by migrant workers in the manufacturing, construction, and service sectors in both Chongqing and Shenzhen. In Chinese-English dictionaries, *gongyou* is usually translated as 'maintenance worker', 'workmate', 'factory worker', 'workfellow', or 'working partner'. The fact that migrant workers in labour-intensive industries with precarious employment and limited social security refer to themselves as gongyou instead of using the official designation *nongmingong* (literally, 'peasant-worker')—a term that often carries derogatory connotations—indicates a willingness to challenge the official discourse, and suggests the development of a new type of collective identity.

While this self-identification is common in both Chongqing and Shenzhen, the term *gongyou* can also be found among different types of rural migrants with precarious jobs elsewhere in urban China. Interestingly, this *gongyou* identity does not include what is traditionally considered the Chinese proletariat, i.e. those workers who enjoy stable employment and social security in state-owned enterprises. Although Hurst (2017) has pointed out that, since 2008, China's fragmented working class has shown increasing solidarity, those identifying as *gongyou* remain nonetheless detached and differentiated from the traditional working class by the precarity of their employment. The *gongyou* identity, therefore, is distinguished by its rural origins, and should not be seen as forming an integrated class with the traditionally secure urban proletariat, nor with the whole spectrum of the insecure precariat with formal rights to the city—including, for instance, members of the urban middle class and urban laid-off workers. From this point of view, the household registration system (*hukou*) still constitutes a formidable obstacle to the development of a unitary class consciousness among Chinese workers at large.

However, in spite of these barriers, my fieldwork suggests that the *gongyou* discourse seems to be emerging as a unifying factor for those precarious rural migrants, numbering in the hundreds of millions, who constitute one of the main groups within the precariat in China. As Owen et al. (2010, 478) have suggested, 'identities that guide social action can come from role relationships, affiliation within social groups, identification with social categories, or personal narratives.' According to them, class consciousness is also primarily based on individual identity and group membership-based identity, which stem from individuals themselves, and the group as a whole (Owen et al. 2010, 479). In other words, collective identities are an important catalyst to form class consciousness. In this sense, the fact that most precarious rural migrant factory workers that I spoke with in both Chongqing and Shenzhen refer to themselves and their colleagues as *gongyou*, indicates that there is potential for the future development of a unified class identity.

The Diffusion of *Gongyou*

There is no English or Chinese study that focuses specifically on the *gongyou* identity and discourse. The term has been used in Chinese literature since the 1920s. For instance, writer Ye Shengtao in his novel *Among the People*

(*Zai minjian*) referred to factory labourers as *gongyou* (Ye 1925). Lu Xun also used the term in his essay 'On the Clock Tower' (*Zai zhonglou shang*), this time with a more specific meaning of handymen or manual workers, such as janitors and cleaners, in schools and other public institutions (Lu 1927). Another famous Chinese writer, Yang Shuo, also used *gongyou* specifically to refer to railway construction workers in his work of prose *North and South of the Yalu River* (*Yalujiang nanbei*) (Yang 1950). However, in spite of this widespread diffusion in Republican China, *gongyou* lost currency during the Maoist period, dying out in the 1950s.

It was not revived until the 2000s when rural migrant workers seem to have taken up the term *gongyou* due to its neutral connotation, preferring it to the derogatory *nongmingong*. The term *nongmingong* has gradually been replaced by *gongyou* and other terms even in official state discourse. For instance, the Hubei Federation of Trade Unions and the Shandong Federation of Trade Unions respectively launched a *Gongyou Magazine* (*Gongyou zazhi*) and a '*Gongyou* Action to Start a Business' (*Gongyou chuangye xingdong*) (SFTU 2006). These branches of the official trade union have recognised the use of the term *gongyou* to refer to blue-collar workers, especially rural migrants in the mining, construction, manufacturing, and service industries.

Civil society has also played a role in reviving the *gongyou* discourse. Since the early 2000s, several labour NGOs in China have begun calling rural migrants in different industrial sectors *gongyou* while helping them to pursue legal rights and labour protections. According to my interviews, these organisations have taken up the *gongyou* discourse, and even included the term in their names, in order to create a common identity among migrant workers and boost a sense of belonging. Examples include the Beijing Workers' Home (*Beijing gongyou zhijia*) and the Pearl River Gongyou Service Centre (*Zhujiang gongyou fuwu zhongxin*). A member of the research staff from the Beijing Workers' Home has even written two books about the 'Chinese new workers' (*Zhongguo xin gongren*), outlining the working and living conditions of rural migrant workers in different cities, including Chongqing, Shenzhen, Suzhou, and Dongguan (Lü 2012 and 2014). According to her research, rural migrant workers identify and call themselves and their colleagues *gongyou* as a means of asserting a collective identity.

Beyond Boundaries

Both the male and female rural migrant workers whom I interviewed in the high-tech sector in Chongqing and Shenzhen commonly refer to themselves and their colleagues as *gongyou*, explaining the meaning of the word in terms similar to those that can be found in Chinese literature from the 1920s. More specifically, all 82 rural migrants whom I interviewed in Shenzhen called themselves *gongyou*. In Chongqing, over 80 percent of my 82 interviewees used the term. When they transfer between different industries, these migrants maintain the name and identity of *gongyou*, indicating the potential for widespread diffusion due to the high levels of worker mobility.

Wang and Wang's research (2013) on the living and working conditions of the new generation of rural migrants in Shenzhen suggests that rural migrants tend to belong to a similar social stratum, united by their rural *hukou* or by their village backgrounds and customs. Due to these circumstances, they more easily forge a common identity based on closed and fixed social networks (Wang and Wang 2013, 64). Over 90 percent of the rural migrant workers I interviewed feel that the *gongyou* term builds a sense of closeness and solidarity. Most of them believe that, as members of the *gongyou* group, together they can help each other when labour disputes occur, because they share a common identity.

Considering how often these workers change jobs, and even industries, this self-identification as *gongyou* is clearly not linked solely to manufacturing or factory work. In fact, this identity goes well beyond the high-tech sector and appears to be linked to the core features of the 'precariat', such as the precarity of employment and low wages, which binds them together as a potential 'class in the making'. Extending beyond boundaries of gender and industry, the *gongyou* identity spreads beyond one single geographical area. As stated above, my research finds that the use of the term *gongyou* is significant for rural migrants in both Chongqing and Shenzhen. Although rural migrants in Shenzhen use the term more actively and spontaneously, those in Chongqing report having been influenced by interactions with their colleagues who have previously worked in Shenzhen, indicating direct identity transfer and diffusion.

A typical case was that of a 28-year-old migrant woman from rural Chongqing, who worked in a high-tech manufacturing factory called Pegatron in the Liangjiang New Area. She explained that she had worked in Foxconn Shenzhen for four years before returning to Chongqing. She spontaneously called her colleagues *gongyou*, exactly as she had called her previous colleagues in Shenzhen. After working in Chongqing for four months, she reported that many of her colleagues had begun to use the term *gongyou* too. She did not want to identify herself as *nongmingong*, because this term made her feel like a subordinate citizen, a symbol of backwardness.

Forming a Dangerous *Gongyou* Class?

While the household registration system remains one of the main barriers to the formation of the precariat as a 'class for itself', the *gongyou* identity represents a social status specifically embraced by migrant workers engaged in urban industries. The use of this term among this group is also an empirical example of the emergence of a nascent collective class consciousness in an important segment of the Chinese precariat. That many young migrant workers in Shenzhen spontaneously express their collective identity by organising members of the *gongyou* group together to protect their legitimate labour rights can be regarded as a potential signal of a rising collective class consciousness facilitating future class struggles in high-tech manufacturing in China.

The Nanhai Honda strike in Foshan of 2010 is an example of a successful class struggle between rural migrants identifying as *gongyou* and factory owners. It was an important event for rural migrants pursuing their own labour protections in terms of increasing their basic salaries in Guangdong province, and at that time it deeply influenced the struggles of other rural migrants for higher wages and better labour protections across different factories, industries, and regions (Friedman 2012; Lau and Choi 2010). According to Chinese labour NGO and media reports, the striking Honda workers called each other *gongyou*, a fact that highlights the importance of this identity for the ensuing worker mobilisation (China Labour Bulletin 2010; China News Weekly 2010; The Economic Observer 2010).

Since then, strikes have been widespread in various industries (see Crothall's essay in this volume). From an analysis of news reports, it can be seen that the *gongyou* identity has contributed to solidarity in mobilisations. This type of cross-sector, cross-region identity formation has the potential to present a significant challenge to both the state and capitalists in China.

Through their increasing willingness to undertake collective action in order to seek more stable employment and better working conditions, these precarious workers may play an important role in shaping the future direction of Chinese society. As those taking on collective identities with their fellow workers—such as the *gongyou* identity—grow larger in number, their voices will be increasingly hard to ignore. ■

Urban landscape of Guigang, Guangxi province, where the Wongs set up their secondary factory. PC: Nellie Chu.

Reconfiguring Supply Chains

Transregional Infrastructure and Informal Manufacturing in Southern China

Nellie CHU

In recent years, rising labour costs and unstable market conditions in coastal areas have prompted former migrant workers and small-scale entrepreneurs to move their manufacturing activities to interior provinces. While this has been made possible by China's infrastructural upgrade, in this essay Nellie Chu shows how infrastructure projects that link China's interior and coastal manufacturing regions have ended up intensifying key aspects of the country's informal economy.

In recent years, rising labour costs and unstable market conditions characteristic of China's garment manufacturing sector in the Pearl River Delta (PRD) region have prompted former migrant workers and small-scale entrepreneurs to move their wholesaling and informal manufacturing activities to interior provinces. Their entrepreneurial activities restructure global supply chains by using logistical and transport systems that connect interior regions to major industrial and trading hubs historically built along the coastal Special Economic Zones. These transregional linkages, as I will show, have been accompanied by an expansion of informal entrepreneurship and manufacturing practices that are primarily driven by early generations of migrant workers who arrived in Shenzhen, Dongguan, and Guangzhou in the early 1980s, and who have relocated back to their native places in smaller cities or in the countryside. After relocating, they typically establish satellite factories and small-scale warehouses that support the manufacturing capacities of larger factories in the metropolitan regions and traditional manufacturing areas.

This cross-regional movement of labour and capital highlights the reconfiguration of the country's industrial base away from the coastal regions to the interior provinces. At the same time, these infrastructure and economic developments underscore the tenacity and initiative of China's migrant population, whose entrepreneurial activities impact China's informal manufacturing sector. In this essay, I show how infrastructure projects that link China's interior and coastal manufacturing regions have intensified key aspects of the country's informal economy. In particular, I examine the labour conditions of temporary wage workers, as well as the extractive practices of landowners and government officials in the interior regions through their collection of fees and other forms of rent-seeking. These place-based and informal extractive practices remain part and parcel of migrants' experiences of small-scale entrepreneurship as they reconfigure garment supply chains transregionally across China.

In what follows, I draw from my anthropological research in Guangzhou's garment district, where I have conducted extensive ethnographic fieldwork since 2010. First, I trace the historical linkages of this informal industrial hub to transnational export and trade; then, I elaborate on the current socioeconomic conditions that have compelled migrant labourers to establish secondary markets of garment manufacture and trade in their native places. By focussing on the case study of a migrant family who has extended their garment manufacturing operations to their hometown in Guangxi province, I will highlight the challenges that migrant entrepreneurs face in light of the central government's ambitions for industrial upgrading and engagement with world markets.

Migration, Informality, and Cross-border Trade

Transnational connections initially fuelled the emergence of informal manufacturing and the export of low-cost clothes in what would become Guangzhou's garment district in the early to mid-1970s. Before the beginning of Deng Xiaoping's market reforms in 1978, the area's proximity to Hong Kong facilitated the cross-border smuggling of leftover fabrics and second-hand clothing to and from what at that time still was a British colony. Since then, garment manufacturing and export operations have mushroomed in this working-class district, which was formed from several neighbouring urban villages. This growth compelled traders and brokers from the Middle East, Southeast Asia, Africa, and Euro-America to bypass Hong Kong as an intermediary port of exchange, and to source goods directly from manufacturers in Guangzhou.

The cross-border flows of commodities and capital impacted generations of migrants who floated in and out of the garment district. Migrants from the coastal regions of Fujian, Wenzhou, and Chaozhou—among the first to engage in the mass-manufacture and trade of low-cost garments during the 1980s and 1990s—gradually elevated their social standing to that of the rentier class by leasing small-scale industrial spaces and market stalls to the subsequent generation of migrant entrepreneurs. In the late 1990s to early 2000s, new waves of migrants from the interior provinces of Sichuan, Henan, Hunan, and Guangxi settled in this district in order to take up piece rate labour in the informal garment workshops, as well as to experiment in running their own small-scale factories and wholesale business ventures.

Since the onset of the reform era, the financial success of these migrant entrepreneurs has been highly uneven and unpredictable. While some migrants have managed to accumulate modest amounts of wealth in the early years of market reform, the majority of middle-aged migrant men and women today can only find temporary piece rate work by moving in and out of the garment factories in the area. Others float between running their own businesses in the fabric markets during the day, while taking up piece rate work in informal garment workshops in the evening. Elderly migrants struggle to maintain a livelihood by collecting scrap metal and other recyclables from the nearby factories and fabric markets, and by delivering passengers, fabric bolts, and raw materials to the surrounding garment workshops. Here, the average lifespan of a migrant-owned business is only two or three years.

Speculation and Surveillance

Recent speculation surrounding rising labour costs in Guangzhou and across the PRD region, as well as increasing competition from low-cost garment manufacturing in other developing countries, has intensified the sense of financial insecurity and precariousness among migrants. Indeed, since my arrival in the city's garment district in 2010, migrant bosses (*laoban*) in the garment district have blamed the 2008 global financial crisis for curbing foot traffic and slowing market growth in Guangzhou's garment sector. They have also predicted that the fashion industry in southern China will soon be eclipsed by developing economies in Thailand, Cambodia, and Vietnam, where labour costs are lower, clothes are cheaper, and styles are more appealing to transnational clients.

At the same time, since 2010 migrant entrepreneurs in Guangzhou are facing stricter surveillance and disciplinary measures by local enforcement agents who are exerting tighter control over the flows of people, commodities, and cash in the interest of extracting fees. At the same time, they have been curbing cash-based market activities not falling within the regulatory purview of the state. Prior to 2016, migrant women, both young and old, would set up outdoor tables and racks full of clothing, accessories, and other novelties for sale along the narrow alleyways of the urban villages during the evening hours. Over the last two years, however, unlicensed business activities have largely been prohibited along the main pedestrian roads. Some garment factories and wholesale stalls have been ordered to close, attesting to the tighter regulation of production and other economic activities within the district.

Outside of the geographic boundaries of the garment district, uniformed officers are stationed along the major intersections. At certain times of day, officers collect parking fees from truckers and other drivers entering the area, and they prohibit pedicab drivers from riding anywhere within the district. Those caught driving pedicabs at certain times of the day are arrested and fined. Such regulatory controls by municipal government agencies have led to dwindling business activities that rely critically on the foot traffic of their overseas clients, resulting in increasingly precarious livelihoods for migrant labourers there.

In response to such socioeconomic uncertainties, migrant entrepreneurs in the garment district have begun to extend their businesses from Guangzhou to their native places in the countryside and in smaller cities. There, they attempt to establish secondary wholesale shops or small-scale factories in their homes so that they can tap into the local labour markets. While some migrants move their entire factory or wholesale operations to the interior regions, others establish satellite industrial and retail sites in their native places.

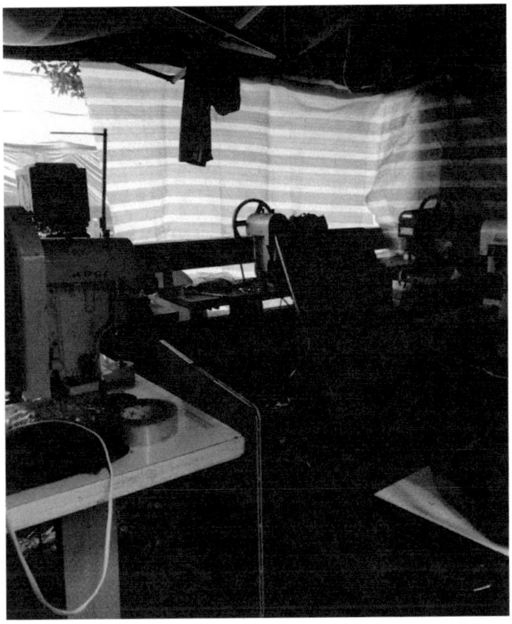

(Left) Typical street scene in an urban village in Guangzhou. (Right) A sewing machine in a makeshift garment assembly space in Guangzhou's garment district. PC: Nellie Chu.

These business developments have been made possible by the proliferation of high-speed railways and other transport systems connecting major metropolises with more marginal areas all over the country. By moving or extending their business endeavours to the interior, 'less-developed' regions in China, migrant entrepreneurs exploit labour markets which offer lower costs, while bringing their manufacturing skills, knowledge of global consumer markets, and transnational client networks to these newly developed frontiers of accumulation and extraction.

Informal Manufacturing across Local Economies

In the course of extending their production links across local economies, however, some migrants face unreasonable demands for various payments and bribes, thus adding administrative burdens and capital costs to their entrepreneurial endeavours. As a case in point, a migrant couple I interviewed in the garment district had recently opened a satellite factory inside their new five-storey house in a smaller city in Guangxi province. Since labour costs were lower in Guangxi than in Guangzhou, the Wongs maintained their small-scale workshop in Guangzhou, where Mr Wong received production orders from domestic and transnational clients who passed through the garment district. Meanwhile, mass manufacture took place in Guangxi, where Mrs Wong managed and oversaw the entire production process. After the garments were manufactured, the finished products were delivered overnight via the newly built high-speed train that connects the interior regions of Guangxi to Guangzhou in a matter of three to four hours. Mr Wong and his employees in Guangzhou then packaged the finished

(Left) Informal street vendor in Guangzhou before these markets were officially prohibited in the city's urban villages. (Right) A row of informal garment factories in Guangzhou. PC: Nellie Chu.

garments before sending them to their clients. These cross-region linkages of labour, capital, and commodities were spatially segmented and temporally coordinated by the Wongs to serve the 'just-in-time' delivery and export of fast fashion.

The scheduled cycles of cross-region production and delivery worked seamlessly when the Wongs began their operations in Guangxi in the summer of 2016. However, in the weeks leading up to my visit with Mrs Wong in the summer of 2017, a number of public utility officials asked the family to pay a certain amount in fees for setting up the electricity line in their house in Guangxi. She informed me that they had visited their home and demanded a few hundred to a few thousand yuan here and there. 'It's so corrupt over there,' Mrs Wong told me. 'In Guangzhou, once they get the electricity line, they just asked for a few hundred yuan, and that would be it. They find reasons to ask for more money [in Guangxi]. That's not how they do it over there [in Guangzhou].'

The Wongs paid officials up to 20,000 yuan over the course of the two years that they were in operation in Guangxi. 'Initially, they asked for only a few hundred yuan to complete jobs. As soon as they figure out that you are building a house, more and more people come by and demand various forms of payment from you. Now I have to deal with the bills.' As Mrs Wong explained her dilemma to me, I realised the particularities of how a commercial land or industrial space was governed and managed. Through Mrs Wong's broad comparisons between doing business in Guangzhou and in her native place in Guangxi, I surmised that networks of patron-client relationships—presumably between landowners, lessors, and other interested people or third parties—were implicated in a division of profits and rents that were collected through the extension of infrastructure, such as electricity lines, in and across particular locations.

She then further explained: 'At first, we thought that the intermediary agent who helped us submit our payment was trustworthy, but then the problems [the demands for payment] kept coming.' While the Wongs assumed that hiring workers in Guangxi would save labour costs, they did not anticipate the extra costs of bribes and other fees. To be sure, the movement of labour and infrastructure involves negotiations and compromises that, at times, might hamper the seemingly smooth and seamless movement of people, commodities, and production facilities. Having operation facilities both in Guangdong and Guangxi might have offered them flexibility, but keeping machines and employees idle imposed unforeseen costs. In light of these financial demands, Mrs Wong explained that she could not provide work and pay for her current seven or eight employees in Guangxi. She simply informed them that she needed to return to Guangzhou without a precise date of return and rehire. At the time of writing (May 2018), her employees in Guangxi remain unemployed.

Infrastructure Projects and the Informal Economy

The central government's plans for industrial upgrading and increased engagement in global markets call for attention to infrastructure projects that restructure global supply chains across China's interior and coastal regions. It should also prompt us to examine the ways in which these domestic projects link up with various aspects of the nation's informal economy. Indeed, the practices of informal and precarious labour, as well as various forms of rent-seeking, within China's rural spaces and smaller cities have intensified as China's global experiments in cross-border scaling and industrial upgrading are increasingly connected. These dual developments have socioeconomic impacts on the mobility and labour of rural migrants. Though the successes (or failures) of China's infrastructure projects remain ambiguous to many observers, China's migrant population is definitively being displaced through the ongoing shifts in the extraction and accumulation of capital, even when they return to their native places. As these policies and investments continue to unfold, attention must be focussed on the migrant labour population within China's informal economies, many of whom remain vulnerable to the societal effects of large-scale displacement and dispossession. ■

Changchun FAW-Volkswagen assembly line. PC: Wang Yuwen.

The Struggles of Temporary Agency Workers in Xi's China

ZHANG Lu

In China, temporary agency workers often receive as little as half the pay and none of the benefits enjoyed by their 'regular' counterparts, which has resulted in high-profile struggles across sectors. In his essay, Zhang Lu examines their recent collective actions in the automotive industry, pointing to the challenges and potentials for future labour activism in contemporary China.

In recent years, China has witnessed rising activism among temporary agency workers—workers who are hired through labour agencies and are now a main component of the Chinese workforce across sectors. Several high-profile struggles by agency workers in the automotive industry have highlighted their grievances and their ability to mobilise. These include collective actions from workers at FAW-Volkswagen (FAW-VW), Guangzhou Ai Paike Auto Parts Co., Ltd (APAC), and Guangzhou NHK Spring Precision Co., Ltd (NHK) for equal pay and unpaid benefits. What is the nature of their grievances and the extent of their bargaining power? What strategies do agency workers use to protest and to make their claims to employers? What are the trends and implications of agency workers' struggles for labour relations and worker activism in Xi's China? This essay seeks to address these questions by taking a close look at the recent struggles by agency workers in the automotive industry.

Labour Dispatch and Contested Regulation

The growth of precarious work has come to characterise a significant global trend over the last few decades. One of the fast-growing forms of precarious work in many countries has been temporary agency work (TAW), better known as labour dispatch (*laowu paiqian*) in the Chinese context. The core feature of TAW is a triangular structure that separates employment from the actual use of labour: a temporary agency worker is employed by a temporary staffing agency, and then dispatched to work at the user company. TAW has attracted much public and scholarly scrutiny, as it challenges the conventional definition of employment relationships and complicates the legal and financial obligations employers have to their employees (Gonos 1997; Vosko 2010).

In China, the dramatic rise of labour dispatch since the late 1990s has had far-reaching consequences for Chinese workers and labour relations. Although China does not provide official statistics on labour dispatch, according to a survey conducted by the All-China Federation of Trade Unions (ACFTU), the country's agency workers reached 37 million in 2011, accounting for 13.1 percent of the total actively employed population. Moreover, instead of being confined to temporary, auxiliary, or substitute positions, agency workers are increasingly being used in permanent positions or on a long-term basis in a wide range of industries. In fact, 39.5 percent of the surveyed agency workers had worked for the same client firms for more than six years. In particular, state-owned enterprises (SOEs) had the highest percentage of agency workers, accounting for 16.2 percent of their total workforce (ACFTU 2012). Agency workers have been subjected to discriminatory treatment at work, including lower pay, fewer benefits, harsher disciplinary action, and lack of job security and advancement opportunities compared to regular employees at the client firms. The ambiguous triangular employment relationship, combined with the lack of regulation, has led to rampant violations of workers' rights.

It was against this backdrop that the 2008 Labour Contract Law devoted 12 articles to the regulation of labour dispatch. However, the lack of specific, enforceable measures, led to an explosive growth of agency workers since the passage of the Law. In 2013, the Law was amended to close the loophole and address the rampant use of labour dispatch. On 1 March 2014, the Interim Provisions on Labour Dispatching took effect, which requires companies in China to reduce the use of agency workers to 10 percent of their total employees by 1 March 2016. Faced with stricter regulations, many employers responded by laying off agency workers or continuing to use labour dispatch under the guise of outsourcing or subcontracting to bypass the 10 percent limit (Peng 2016). To defend their employment and legal rights, temporary agency workers across a range of industries have been protesting, petitioning, and filing lawsuits against layoffs and unequal treatment at work. The year-long struggles by FAW-VW agency workers for 'equal pay for equal work' highlight the plight of agency workers and their determination to defend their legal rights.

The Struggles of AFW-VW Workers

The use of temporary agency workers has proliferated throughout the automotive industry since the mid-2000s, along with the restructuring and rapid expansion of the industry (Zhang 2015). As of 2016, there were around 3,500 agency workers at FAW-VW Changchun plant, and many of them had been working at the company for more than ten years in skilled core production positions. Despite doing the same work as regular workers, the agency workers were only paid half as much and did not enjoy the same benefits. Emboldened by the new regulations, in November 2016 several thousand temporary agency workers in FAW-VW's Changchun plant began their struggle for equal pay for equal work, when the two-year transitional period for compliance with the 2014 Interim Provisions on Labour Dispatching expired and their employer had still not made the legally required adjustments to limit the use of agency labour (China Labour Bulletin 2017a).

The agency workers at FAW-VW demonstrated tremendous determination, persistence, and unity throughout their struggles. They first filed a complaint with the ACFTU, demanding compensation for years of unequal pay and the signing of formal employment contracts with FAW-VW. Then, they elected three representatives who, alongside trade union officials, engaged in collective bargaining with the management of FAW-VW and their labour agencies between December 2016 and January 2017. After several failed bargaining sessions, the workers filed a collective dispute case with the Changchun labour dispute arbitration committee, and later brought FAW-VW to court. After the court rejected their case, between February and May in 2017 the agency workers organised several demonstrations (China Labour Bulletin 2017a). However, their protests were met with police harassment. In May 2017, the three worker representatives, Fu Tianbo, Wang Shuai, and Ai Zhenyu, were arrested for 'gathering crowds to disrupt public order'—an accusation commonly used by local governments to quell labour and social unrest. While Wang and Ai were released, Fu remained in custody and was officially charged in early June 2017 (China Labour Bulletin 2017b). The agency workers continued their struggles for equal pay and for the release of Fu Tianbo from prison. In July and August 2017, they issued public letters to the Volkswagen Group and Volkswagen's work council in Germany, asking for their intervention in the legal violations in the Changchun plants and for the release of Fu. However, VW decided not to intervene (China Labour Bulletin 2017c). On 18 August 2017, the workers wrote a jointly signed letter to the local Public Security Bureau demanding the unconditional release of Fu (Ruckus 2018).

At the same time, management and the local government took various measures to break up the protest: the workers' posts on social media were blocked and management cooperated with the police to criminalise the worker representatives. In addition, in April 2017 FAW-VW made a concession by announcing 2,400 new regular jobs for its agency workers who had worked at the company for more than ten years. However, only 500 positions were to be located in Changchun. Moreover, if the agency workers accepted the new contract, they would have to give up their demand for compensation for years of unequal pay. About 1,500 agency workers took the offer. Although not all of the workers who signed the new contract gave up their demands for back pay, they basically withdrew from the protest. On 21 December 2017, FAW-VW launched a second round of recruitment and offered all the remaining agency workers in the Changchun plant five-year regular contracts, on the condition that they give up their claims on all the remuneration issues. Workers who would not sign the new contracts would be terminated and sent back to the labour agencies. The workers were only given one day to accept the new offer. It was clearly a management strategy to quell the protest. Under this pressure, all but five agency workers eventually signed the contract. The five workers who did not give up were dismissed by FAW-VW at the end of 2017. They included worker representatives Fu Tianbo and Ai Zhenyu, who decried the contract as illegal and were determined to continue their struggle until justice was served (Xia 2018).

As of writing (June 2018), the agency workers have not achieved their demands for open-ended contracts and compensation for the unequal pay since 2008. It is fair to say, however, that the agency workers' tenacious struggle was one of the main reasons for the FAW-VW decision to stop using labour dispatch in the Changchun plant at the end of 2017. It is also important to point out that the agency workers involved in the struggles at FAW-VW tend to have more workplace and marketplace bargaining power than in other sectors. For one, FAW-VW and other automakers have been rapidly expanding production capacity alongside the construction of new manufacturing facilities across China in recent years. These new plants require a large number of workers, especially skilled and well-trained ones like this group of temporary agency workers who already had ten years of experience working at the company (Xia 2018). Meanwhile, shortly after it stopped using agency workers, FAW-VW started using more outsourced workers on production lines to increase staff flexibility. Yet, it did not take long for the outsourced workers to begin their protest against unequal treatment as well. According to the interviews that I conducted at the FAW-VW Changchun plants in June 2018, over 400 outsourced workers have been involved in struggles against unequal pay and the illegal practice of 'fake outsourcing, real dispatching' at FAW-VW since early 2018.

As many employers resort to outsourced/subcontracted workers to evade the 10 percent limit on the use of dispatch labour, a growing number of these workers have joined agency workers to demand equal pay, the signing of regular contracts, and mandatory insurance payments and public housing funds in back pay. This has been demonstrated by the ongoing struggles at auto parts companies such as APAC and NHK in Guangzhou.

Shaping Labour Relations

On the one hand, agency workers have deep grievances after being subjected to years of unequal and substandard treatment, and they have become increasingly restive and emboldened by the stricter regulations on labour dispatch. They have demonstrated great determination, persistence, and unity in their struggles for equal pay, regular contracts, and mandatory insurance payment and public housing funds required by the laws. On the other hand, it has proven extremely difficult for them to defend their legitimate rights through formal legal channels, given the power asymmetry between workers and employers, and the fact that local authorities often side disproportionally with employers in labour disputes.

Furthermore, the Chinese Communist Party under the new leadership of Xi Jinping has moved towards tightened political and ideological control, and an increasingly repressive approach to worker activism. Strikes are often treated as 'social stability maintenance' (*wei wen*) incidents, the police is frequently called in, and criminal charges are filed against striking workers, rights lawyers, and labour activists (Pringle 2016). In addition, central leaders have taken steps to curb increases in the minimum wage and cut social security burdens on companies. A recent government-led consultation on revising the Labour Contract Law to improve 'labour market flexibility' and to roll back some job-security protections for workers is widely seen as a harbinger of more business-friendly policies to keep companies afloat as China's growth continues to slow (Wong 2016).

Thus, it is likely to become even harder for agency and outsourced workers to defend their rights through official legal channels. Still, recent battles partially won by the agency workers at NHK and other auto parts companies in Guangzhou suggest there is potential for this group of workers to successfully bargain for their rights. Considering the sheer scale and far-reaching consequences of labour dispatch for the employment terms and conditions of millions of Chinese workers, further research into the strategies and tactics of agency workers' struggles in different industries and regions is essential to understanding the current and future trends of labour relations and worker activism in the era of Xi. ■

Robotisation shortens the training period of cutting bicycle helmet venting holes from six months to only three days. PC: Huang Yu.

Robot Threat or Robot Dividend?

A Struggle between Two Lines

HUANG Yu

With China being the world's largest market for industrial robots, robotisation has become a hot topic in the Chinese public discourse. While media reactions have been polarised between those who fear large-scale displacement and those who emphasise the rise of newly created jobs, there has been little solid research looking into the impact of robotisation on labour market and shop floor dynamics. In this essay, Huang Yu assesses both the 'robot threat' and the 'robot dividend' discourses, offering some views on how workers should react to the ongoing technological revolution.

Since 2013, China has become the world's largest market for industrial robots, recording record sales of 87,000 units in 2017. With the publication of the 'Made in China 2025' plan in 2015, robotisation has become a hot topic in public discourse. While media reactions have been polarised between those who fear large-scale displacement and those who emphasise the rise of newly created jobs, there has been little solid research looking into the impact of robotisation on both the labour market and shop floor dynamics. Based on fieldwork conducted in the Pearl River Delta (PRD) since late 2015, in this essay I try to assess both the 'robot threat' and the 'robot dividend' discourses, offering some views on how workers should react to the ongoing technological revolution.

From 'Workerless Factory' to 'Robots Create Jobs!'

China's robotic revolution took off against the backdrop of periodic labour shortages much bemoaned by companies. Soon after the publication of the 'Made in China 2025' plan, official media enthusiastically applauded the ability of robots to reduce the labour force. Two news stories were widely circulated at that time. The first regarded the debut of a 'workerless factory' (*wuren gongchang*) in Dongguan in 2015, a mobile phone module manufacturer which claimed that an industrial robot could replace up to eight workers while reducing the product defect rate by over 20 percent (Xinhua 2015). Significantly, the firm was awarded a subsidy by the Dongguan government under the policy of 'replacing humans with machines' (*jiqi huanren*), underlining how a coalition between government and industry planned to overcome the labour shortage problem.

The second focussed on how the Foxconn factory in Kunshan, Jiangsu province, retrenched 60,000 workers, over half of the total work force in 2016 (Zuo 2016). The public could still remember how, a few years earlier, just after the notorious spat of worker suicides (Pun and Chan 2012), Terry Gou—the CEO and founder of the company—had haphazardly announced the plan to use one million robots to replace its human labour force. He unabashedly praised the advantage of robots over humans, stating that 'human beings are also animals, to manage one million animals gives me a headache' (Kwong 2012).

Although most media reporting embraced the discourse of the 'workerless factory', a minority of reporters criticised the motivation behind the robotisation initiative of local governments. For instance, writing for *Beijing Youth Daily*, Lijian Xing stated:

> After robots were introduced to replace humans, local governments did not need to take up the responsibility of offering job retraining to the displaced workers. When tens of thousands, hundreds of thousands, and ever more migrant workers sullenly left, local governments could enjoy a significant cut in their budgets for security, education, healthcare, housing, and other public facility provision (Xing 2016).

As media coverage began to highlight the risks of large-scale unemployment as a potential social threat over the last couple years (Guo 2016; Zhou and Jiang 2016), the public discourse has begun to shift from robots replacing workers to robots creating jobs. Media reports have either been tracing historical cases to downplay the threat of new technologies, or have cited research to demonstrate how Artificial Intelligence (AI) and/or robotics can generate more jobs than they eliminate. For instance, several reports have backed the notion of the 'Luddite fallacy' (*lude miulun*) by arguing that new technology does not lead to higher overall unemployment. One journalist contended that when horse-drawn carriages were phased out by automobiles, film cameras by digital cameras, or pagers by mobile phones, more jobs were created than culled (Wuhua 2017).

More recently, a report issued by the International Federation of Robots has been widely cited, as it determined a job-creation ratio of 3.6 jobs for every robot deployed (Tian and Cai 2018; Zheng 2017). After the State Council rolled out the 'Next Generation AI Development Plan' in July 2017, media further focussed on the positives. One report claimed that in England AI had eliminated 800,000 'low-end jobs', but had simultaneously created 3.5 million new positions (Jin 2017). Another suggested that the trend of job shrinkage caused by robots would end in 2019, as after 2020 AI would become a positive force generating 2 million new jobs (net) by 2025 in the United States alone (Xia 2018).

The Robot Contradiction

In the Chinese media, AI and robotisation are largely portrayed not only as an inevitable trend but also as a boon for society. However, the damaging effects of robots on the labour market should not be overlooked. A recent study reviewing employment in the United States from 1997 to 2007 found that each new robot added to the workforce meant the loss of between 3 and 5.6 jobs in the local commuting area, not to mention a decline of between 0.25 percent to 0.5 percent in local wages (Acemoglu and Restrepo 2017). Since China's robotic industrialisation has just begun its dramatic expansion, there has not been much aggregate research on the potential impacts of robotisation on workers. However, my research has found that, among the four firms that possessed comparative employment data before and after automation, the workforce reduction rate in the production line ranged between an alarming 67 and 85 percent (Huang and Sharif 2017). Moreover, although media and firm representatives have tried to downplay automation's impact on the workforce, with talks of a 'labour shortage' already under way, it is important to note that by early 2017 Dongguan's subsidy plan had already culled 190,000 workers, a figure that far outnumbers the estimated labour shortage of 100,000 reported in 2015 (Huang and Fu 2017).

Still, so far we have not witnessed the kind of widespread use of robots that throws workers onto the streets in great numbers. Although robot demand has continued to soar in the last five years in China, in 2016 a total of 87,000 robots were sold in the country while robot density remained at only 68 units per 10,000 employees (IFR 2017 and 2018), a minor number in comparison with China's 282 million migrant workers in that year. This is largely because technological upgrading itself is not a linear and smooth process, but is subject to gaps and disruptions. For instance, despite the initial hype over robotisation in its Kunshan plant, Foxconn failed to put its 'Foxbots' into widespread application on the assembly line due to frequent problems and breakdowns (Jianxiaojiao 2017). Part of the reason is that since their invention, industrial robots have mostly targeted the automobile industry for heavy-duty tasks such as welding and painting, but robots that excel in light-duty, flexible, and versatile tasks are relatively recent additions. The first collaborative robots that are designed for versatile tasks and can work around humans debuted in 2014, and their demand is expected to increase roughly tenfold by 2020 (Trobe 2016).

Therefore, we will likely see a shrinking labour market in the manufacturing sector in the coming decades, and many migrant workers in China will either have to shift to the service industry or return to the countryside. In fact, employment in the service industry has already exceeded manufacturing since 2011. However, labour conditions in the service sector have been identified as even more precarious and deregulated than in manufacturing, with opaque labour relations, low contractualisation rates, and inconsistent payment of overtime in several sub-sectors (Worker Empowerment 2017). Moreover, robots have also found their way into the service industry and might have a significant impact on labour even there (Youshino 2017). What about going back to farming? The prospect that agriculture can sustain a living is not very promising. The Ministry of Agriculture recently announced that 35.1 percent of the country's farmland has been transferred from small farmers to rural elites or agribusinesses (Ministry of Agriculture 2018). If workers are displaced by robots but have no land to return to, China might soon see the rise of urban ghettos and mounting social problems. However, the national government has not yet conducted a comprehensive study of the impact of automation on workers, nor has it offered any prospective solution to the potential problems (Butollo and Lüthje 2017). Local governments are reluctant to treat migrants as permanent residents and are unwilling to shoulder the negative consequences that industrial upgrading might pose for those workers.

Deskilling or Upskilling?

Unlike the debate on the effect of robots on employment, the media's attention on how automation impacts workers' skills is relatively scant. Although the issue today is largely overlooked, decades ago this used to be a hot topic that captured much scholarly attention. Sociologists who explored the processes of industrial automation in the United States and Japan from the 1960s to the 1980s revealed how the introduction of numerical control machines rendered machinists deskilled by separating concept from execution. As automatic machines forced workers to surrender the control of the labour process to the management, managers quickly replace unionised, skilled machinists with non-union, white-collar employees as a way to curb labour activism (Braverman 1988; Morris-Suzuki 1988; Noble 1979). My research has found that for sectors that used to rely on manual skills, such as woodwork, clothing, and metal processing, the impact of deskilling is very obvious. For example, in a factory that manufactured bicycle helmets, robotisation shortened the training period of cutting venting holes from six months to only three days. Similarly, in a door-making factory, automation rendered carpenters deskilled and replaceable by novice workers. Here, the deskilling effect brought on by automation might have some potential for promoting common interests between veteran and young workers. However, with the government's restriction on collective labour rights, combined with more and more stringent control of worker organisation and activism, the chances of seeing a broader base for labour solidarity seem to be slim.

Still, the lack of a skilled workforce has been identified as a main obstacle to China's drive for 'intelligent manufacturing'. In December 2016, the central government issued the 'Development Planning Guidelines for Manufacturing Talents', in which it projected an alarming gap—3 million in 2020 and 4.5 million in 2025—of skilled personnel for numerical control tools and robotics (Ministry of Industry and Information Technology 2017). The guidelines also suggested that by 2020, apart from the 22 percent college-educated 'talents', the majority (78 percent) should be skilled blue-collar workers able to handle robots and automatic equipment coming from two sources: job retraining or vocational schools.

Given China's past development path that has hinged on labour-intensive and low-skill manual work, a lot of manufacturers were either slow or even reluctant to take up labour retraining. Among the eight manufacturers that I studied in Dongguan, only one invested in training workers, and this was because the company engaged in high precision metalwork that requires substantial levels of skill in the production process. Mr Zhou, the owner who used to work in a state-owned enterprise, had set up an in-house apprenticeship programme to train skilled workers who could handle tasks such as changing fixtures and jigs, adjusting computer numerical control machines to new functions, and who could, eventually, participate in designing the production process (Sharif and Huang 2019). He understood that while technology was important, the true value of the machines could only be harnessed if the technology was combined with the relevant and appropriate human-embedded skills. In his words: 'Machinery is something everybody can buy, but a good production process (*gongyi liucheng*) needs to be designed. One component is hardware and the other is *software*.' As a small and medium enterprise, the case of Mr Zhou's company is quite exceptional. Given the high turnover rate, very few employers in Dongguan are willing to invest in worker training. Recently, a survey has identified that in the Pearl River Delta from 2010 to 2013, the percentage of migrant workers who ascended to management or technician positions dropped from 24.85 percent to only 12.86 percent, while those who remained operators increased from 75.15 percent to 87.14 percent (Xu 2016).

The contradiction between the high demand for robot operators and the manufacturers' low initiative in offering in-house training has prompted the emergence of market-based job retraining programmes operated by labour recruitment agencies. In 2016, I visited one of these programmes in Dongguan to assess the upskilling potential of robotisation. Is it possible that through training, factory operators who were replaced by robots could ascend to be controllers of advanced equipment? This programme offered two kinds of courses: one primary programme charging 6,000 yuan either for full-time instruction lasting two months or for part-time weekend learning lasting five and a half months; and one advanced programme running for four months for 15,800 yuan. However, most of the students were not low-skilled, assembly line operators, but trained workers equipped with electrician and machine maintenance knowledge who sought to improve their skills. One of the students I interviewed had a senior high school diploma, had worked as an electrician in a metal processing company for four years, had taught himself programmable logic controller (PLC) programming when he worked in elevator maintenance in a home appliance company, and eventually found a position as an engineer in a firm that supplied abrasive blasting equipment. In 2016, he decided to quit his 7,000-yuan-a-month salary job and signed up for the robotics-training programme after observing the large-scale robotisation in some of the client firms of his company. The director of the vocational school assured students that their salary could jump to over 10,000 yuan per month one year after completion of the programme. While some media coverage touted the potential of robotisation for upskilling the labour force, they have generally concealed the fact that only those with certain skills in electrical circuits and PLC programming could advance to become robotic engineers. For the vast majority of assembly-line operators, the chances remain very slim.

Vocational schools might serve as the most viable source to supply skilled workers for a roboticised manufacturing sector. In China, the projected demand for vocational labour in 2020 is expected to reach 79 million despite a supply of only 63 million, leaving a gap of 16 million—a staggering 20 percent shortage (Chen et al. 2013). While both the state and enterprises agree on the need to expand technical and vocational education and training (TVET), the question of who should take up the responsibility remains a hotly debated issue. Recently, China released the 'Modern Vocational Education Development Strategy (2014–20)', a document that outlines a roadmap for TVET. Here, the government has called for companies to be a key provider of TVET and has pushed forward the privatisation of the TVET sector, requiring that 80 percent of the large- and medium-sized enterprises become 'providers of TVET services' by 2020. The government will reward this act of 'corporate social responsibility' with tax relief (Kloer and Stepan 2015; Liu 2014). However, pundits question whether support of vocational training by large corporations through privatisation measures will lead to systematic improvement, especially considering that small and medium enterprises suffer from a severe shortage of talent, and that their size and financial constraints render them unable to enter into cooperation agreements with vocational colleges.

At the same time, the TVET privatisation drive has also attracted the investment of firms not specialised in manufacturing. Recently, I visited a vocational school located in a poor province in western China, a newly established institution that has adopted a policy of 'being run privately with public support' (*minban gongzhu*), a model in which the local government sponsors the salary of teachers, while the owner, a real estate developer, covers the other expenses necessary to maintain the school's operation. In fact, the developer decided to invest in vocational education in order to grab land cheaply to build commercial apartments. When we visited the school, we could see that an upscale residential block was under construction adjacent to the campus. To respond to the state's poverty reduction initiative, this province has sought to become a big data hub and has encouraged local vocational schools to set up related programmes to meet the labour market demands. In 2017, this school started to offer programmes on big data, intelligent product development, and industrial robot technology. However, as these new concepts and technologies still look unfamiliar to most parents who live in this mountainous region, each programme recruited less than ten students. Now, the students have almost finished the first year of instruction, but the practical training lab is still under construction. Having little confidence in their ability to become proficient programmers after they graduate, many of them are planning to work in sales of these high-tech products.

Learning from the Past

The discursive transition from 'workerless factory' to 'robots create jobs' seeks to downplay the effect of job displacement that industrial automation brings to the most populous country in the world. These two terms both echo the notion of 'robot dividend' that designates machines, rather than human labour, as the source of value, further marginalising the position of workers in society. In light of this, it is unsurprising that the Guangdong government froze the minimum wage for three years from 2015 to 2017. However, since technological upgrading helps many firms reduce costs and increase profits, workers should fight to get a proper share of the 'robot dividend'. At least that was the main agenda that trade unions in the United States adopted, as a way to acclimate the workers to the new modes of production 'when the capitalist drive for a greater intensity of labour oversteps the bounds of physical and mental capacity' (Braverman 1998, 104). Now, for firms in China that have already established collective bargaining—especially those in the profitable automotive sector—increased wages and shorter working hours should be key agendas. For the vast majority of small and medium enterprises, this demand might be harder to achieve. Still, once, after I presented my preliminary findings to some workers at the end of 2015, they started to question why the Dongguan government only offered subsidies to firms but not to displaced workers. Raising workers' awareness of their entitlements might be the first step towards devising suitable strategies.

Workers need to be aware of the long-term impacts that industrial automation might have on labour. Such awareness can be gained by examining previous cases. Back in the 1970s, Harry Braverman unveiled how increased labour productivity and levels of working-class consumption have the potential to leave a negative legacy for the labour movement, as the unionised working-class 'increasingly lost the will and ambition to wrest control of production from capitalist hands and turned ever more to bargaining over labour's share in the production' (1988, 8). Similarly, under a drive to maximise profit, firms in the Soviet Union pursued a strategy of shrinking the labour force and increasing work intensity, resulting in severe unemployment nationwide (Writing Group for 'Socialist Political Economy' 1976). Learning from Soviet lessons, Maoist policy emphasised that workers, rather than machines, should be the main propagator of the technological revolution. In the Mao era, it was believed that industrial upgrading could only be accomplished through 'mass movements', rather than the reign of technical experts. Overall, workers should understand that technological change is never a neutral process but a site of struggle between two lines. As capital further consolidates its position through investment in roboticisation, workers must seize the moment and struggle for their rights and positions. ■

Sola, Alone.
PC: Alexandra Antonini.

A 'Pessoptimistic' View of Chinese Labour NGOs

Ivan FRANCESCHINI
Kevin LIN

In the wake of the 2015 crackdown on labour NGOs, pessimism about the future of Chinese civil society has been unavoidable even for the most assured optimists. Still, pessimism and optimism in discussions of Chinese labour NGOs have roots that go far deeper than this latest turn of events. In this essay, Ivan Franceschini and Kevin Lin take stock of the existing literature and reconsider the debate in light of the latest developments, proposing a possible synthesis between 'optimistic' and 'pessimistic' views.

'We've entered a grey area: we're not organisations anymore, and maybe in the future we'll be reduced to only a few individuals.'

This was the ominous prediction of one Chinese labour activist in Shenzhen in 2016. If we consider that these words were proffered in the midst of the worst crackdown that labour NGOs had experienced since their appearance in China two decades before, his pessimism was warranted. A few months earlier, with little warning, the police in Guangdong province had arrested a couple dozen labour activists in various organisations, bringing charges against five of them. At the time of the interview, it was still unclear what would happen to the detained activists—only later would they be sentenced to detention for 18 to 36 months, suspended in all cases but one—and tension was running high within the community of Chinese labour NGOs. In addition, there was widespread concern that the enforcement of the Foreign NGO Management Law the following year would restrict or even cut off foreign funding for these organisations and, thus, jeopardise their very survival (Franceschini and Nesossi 2017).

At such a bleak time, pessimism was unavoidable even for the most assured optimists. Still, pessimism and optimism in discussions of Chinese labour NGOs—either among activists or among scholars—have roots that go far deeper than this latest turn of events. Proponents of negative and positive views of labour NGOs have been sparring with each other for at least a decade. In the latest addition to the discussion, Chris Chan (2018) has critiqued both mindsets. In his opinion, 'over-optimism or over-pessimism can be harmful in hard times', with optimists 'preferring not to face the mistakes of their strategies' and pessimists accusing labour NGOs of undermining worker solidarity and arguing that they are no longer needed, when this is, in fact, not the case. However, it is important to acknowledge that these organisations are not static entities, but rather dynamic institutions that change over time, adapting to the shifting political context. For this reason, any analysis of labour NGOs should take into account the changing environment, and evaluations of their 'effectiveness' must necessarily vary markedly over time.

In this essay, we take stock of the existing literature and reconsider it in light of the latest developments. In the next section we begin by outlining the main features of the scholarly debate over labour NGOs. This is followed by a description of how in recent years some organisations have attempted to adopt a new approach. We conclude by offering some remarks on the prospects for the survival of these organisations going forward.

A Polarised Field

The earliest labour NGOs appeared in China in the mid-1990s, benefitting from an inflow of foreign funding in the wake of the Chinese government's more open stance towards civil society (Chan 2013; Howell 2008; Pun and Chan 2004). Since the beginning, these organisations have focussed on four kinds of activities: a) the establishment of worker centres, which usually include a small library and offer special interest classes, educational classes, and recreational activities; b) the provision of legal consultation services and, in some rare cases, legal representation; c) outreach programmes on labour rights; and d) social surveys and policy advocacy (Chan 2013; Xu 2013). It has been this choice of limiting themselves to such non-confrontational activities, adopting a strictly legalistic conception of rights—instead of focussing on promoting the interests of the workers or aggressively pushing for new progressive laws and regulations through collective struggle—that has attracted scrutiny in the existing literature.

Most scholars have maintained a positive assessment of these organisations' focus on community building and legal mobilisation. For instance, Xu Yi has contended that the legal mobilisation strategy of many labour NGOs has important political implications, since 'through legal mobilising, labour NGOs foster consciousness and the skills of organising [among the workers]' (2013, 250). Diana Fu has argued that these organisations are actually resorting to 'disguised collective actions,' which she defines as 'a form of *organised* activism in which civil society groups play a vital but under-the-radar role in coaching citizens to advance rights claims' (2017b, 501). In this way, labour activists 'rather than mounting the scale of disruption... guide citizens toward direct but individual confrontation with the state,' assisting workers in claiming their rights without engaging in potentially perilous protests (2017b, 502). While admitting that from this perspective labour NGOs may be seen as unwitting tools of state domination, Fu believes this strategy still helps '[lower] the cost of coordinating contention in a repressive state that forbids these organisations from operating,' allowing their survival and fostering the collective consciousness of the workers through a pedagogical process.

Other scholars have remained more sceptical. Among the earliest and harshest critics, Ching Kwan Lee and Shen Yuan have accused labour NGOs of being an 'anti-solidarity machine', with their individualistic approach to labour rights allegedly undermining the emergence of a collective consciousness among Chinese workers (2011). On a similar note, back in 2005 Chloé Froissart observed that labour NGOs are 'also working for the benefit of the Party-state, to which they adhere, minimising social conflict and orienting reforms in a direction that can help the Party to maintain its power. While an integral part of the social movement of migrant workers, these organisations also delimit this social movement in their own way. These limitations are why some migrants question these NGOs' legitimacy to represent them' (2005, 11). Chris Chan (2013), meanwhile, has noted that not all workers can benefit from the assistance of these organisations, as most NGOs rely on funding coming from overseas foundations that prefer to support the most vulnerable or exploited social groups, and thus overlook the issues faced by ordinary workers. Finally, Ivan Franceschini has argued that labour NGOs in China are undermined by a significant lack of 'social capital', which can be seen, among other things, in their difficulties to gain the trust of workers who 'believe that anybody who offers voluntarily to help them must have an ulterior motive' (2014, 485).

These criticisms have managed to polarise the field of Chinese labour studies, with 'optimist' and 'pessimist' scholars criticising each other, respectively, for wishful thinking or lacking long-term vision. Yet, in most cases 'pessimist' scholars have also acknowledged the importance of labour NGOs in assisting Chinese workers who otherwise would have been left entirely to their own devices; similarly, 'optimist' scholars do not refrain from acknowledging some shortcomings of these organisations. We believe that the two views are not necessarily in conflict. Labour NGOs are not static entities, they respond to opportunities and constraints. While some criticisms—and expectations—might hold true for a certain kinds of labour NGOs in specific times and places, the situation is varied and continually shifting. For instance, in recent years some organisations have changed their approach in a bid to overcome their limitations, thus transforming their relationship with the workers from one of subordination and dependency to one of partnership (A. Chan 2018).

From Legal Mobilisation to Collective Struggle

In the early 2010s, some labour NGOs started abandoning their traditional legalistic approach, and instead began promoting a new strategy focussed on the interests of the workers, articulated around the concept of 'collective bargaining' (*jiti tanpan*). Writing before the latest crackdown, Duan Yi (2015), a prominent labour lawyer based in Shenzhen, argued that Chinese labour NGOs were in the process of transforming from traditional 'service-oriented' (*fuwuxing*) and 'rights protection-oriented' (*weiquanxing*) organisations to real 'labour movement organisations' (*gongyunxing zuzhi*). Academics provided ample evidence of NGO intervention in collective disputes. In 2014, Chih-Jou Jay Chen followed the (attempted) involvement of Chinese labour NGOs in a protest by more than 40,000 workers in the Dongguan plant of Yue Yuen, a Taiwanese footwear company that had failed to pay social security to its employees (Chen 2015). We ourselves have tracked the involvement of labour NGOs in a case of collective mobilisation over several months between 2014 and 2015 at Lide, a footwear company based in Guangzhou that had decided to relocate production.

Some scholars have built a more comprehensive framework to account for these changes. In a recent study, Chen Feng and Yang Xuehui have argued that the new 'movement-oriented' labour NGOs promote a kind of 'displaced unionism'—where 'unionism' indicates 'certain union-like roles these groups play, in contrast with many of their counterparts operating mainly as service providers, social workers, legal advisors, or advocates', and 'displaced' denotes the 'actual social location of these groups and where they perform their roles' (2017, 159). In another study, Chloé Froissart has provided an impressively detailed account of the role that labour NGOs play in promoting an authentic 'worker-led collective bargaining'—in contrast to state-sponsored 'collective negotiations' (*jiti xieshang*)—helping workers to design strategies to engage with employers, trade unions, and local authorities so that they can '[exercise] their rights before they are granted and by putting pressure on authorities to act as real authorities rather than representatives of a rogue state' (Froissart 2018, 13).

An Interrupted Transition?

Most likely, it was the shift of these few organisations from atomised legal mobilisation to union-like collective struggle that prompted the Chinese authorities to harshly clamp down on them. While repression was never far from the surface, with activists having to deal with harassment and surveillance on a daily basis (Fu 2017a), the latest attack poses a more fundamental challenge to labour NGOs for at least two reasons: first, it was not a local initiative, but in all likelihood part of a nationwide campaign supported by the highest echelons of the Party-state. Second, in coordination with the new Foreign NGO Management Law, this latest crackdown has threatened to cut off access to foreign funding vital for the survival of domestic labour NGOs.

However, we should not underestimate the ability of labour NGOs to adapt. It is true that some have simply stopped operating, prevented by a combination of state repression and declining financial support. Others have scaled down their activities, limiting themselves to realms deemed acceptable to the authorities, such as community building and, in some instances, individual legal mobilisation. In both cases, this has led activists—including the one cited at the beginning of the article—to go underground in the hope of keeping up their work under the radar. However, a few organisations are still continuing to support workers in collective bargaining, even if much less directly. In doing so, they are more careful in screening their cases, warning the workers about possible consequences, and staying away from politically delicate situations (Franceschini and Nesossi 2018). In the meantime, in conversations with labour NGOs, it is clear that this crisis is also forcing some activists to rethink and reinvent their strategies.

Where does this leave us in the debate between pessimistic and optimistic views of labour NGOs? While the current situation does not warrant the optimism of those who see labour NGOs as the spearhead of a broader labour movement in China, we agree with Chris Chan that 'we should not simply describe or understand these organisations and their members as "being mollified" ' (2018). It is undoubtedly true that the space of collective bargaining has narrowed, to the point that some scholars have argued that collective bargaining as a political project is dead (Friedman 2018). Still if the experience of the past two decades teaches us anything, it is that Chinese labour NGOs, in spite of their shortcomings, are resilient entities, apt at navigating the vagaries of the Chinese political landscape and taking advantage of any political opening. In following Lee's (2016) suggestions for the study of labour activism in China, we should now, more than ever, adhere to Gramsci's dictum: 'I'm a pessimist because of intelligence, but an *optimist* because of *will*' (1963, 310). ■

Demonstrators holding posters of Mao Zedong, reminiscent not only of political rallies in the 1960s, but also of worker protests in state-owned enterprises in the late 1990s. PC: Mimi Lau, *South China Morning Post*.

The Jasic Strike and the Future of the Chinese Labour Movement

ZHANG Yueran

In the summer of 2018, the struggles of workers to form a labour union at Shenzhen Jasic Technology triggered an unprecedented crackdown that has attracted widespread attention and sparked solidarity movements both inside and outside China. In this essay, Zhang Yueran takes a deeper look at the dynamics and various twists and turns of the Jasic workers' unionisation campaign, and reveals how this episode has important implications for the broader labour movement in China.

In the summer of 2018, the struggles of workers at Shenzhen Jasic Technology, a publicly listed private firm specialising in the manufacturing of welding machinery (hereafter referred to as Jasic), to form a labour union have attracted widespread attention both inside and outside China. The worker activists decided to push for unionisation in order to address a wide range of workplace grievances, such as an inflexible work schedules, under- and late compensation for overtime work, excessive and unreasonable fines, and

PC: Mimi Lau, *South China Morning Post*.

stringent workplace regulations (for instance, regulations that restricted access to bathroom breaks).

The campaign was initiated in May, in the wake of the arbitrary firing of a worker. In mid-July, the workers' efforts towards unionisation led to heightened repression from the employer, with the leading worker activists fired and physically beaten. After staging a series of collective actions protesting their employer's repression and the highly biased handling of the case on the part of the police, on 27 July a total of 30 worker activists and their supporters were detained by the police in Pingshan district, Shenzhen, on suspicion of 'causing disturbances' (*xunxin zishi*). About a month later, on 24 August, more than 50 workers, students, and activists who had organised or participated in solidarity actions with the detained workers, were themselves detained in several police raids in Shenzhen and Beijing. At the time of writing (September 2018), some of the arrested activists have been sent back home but remain under heavy state surveillance, some are still detained or have been put under house arrest in unspecified locations, and others are facing formal legal prosecution.

Reports from foreign media have tended to focus either on the involvement of the Maoist students in the solidarity actions or on the gigantic scale of state repression, especially with regard to the raids that took place in August. However, within China, the Jasic struggles first became a hot topic in late July, largely thanks to the determination, bravery, and audacity displayed by the Jasic workers themselves in their struggles. Videos of Jasic workers delivering impassioned speeches as they staged protest actions outside the police station went viral. Articulate, touching, and inspiring, their speeches have all left heartfelt impressions on both bystanders and online audiences. It is for this reason that the videos and related articles were widely read and shared even on many online media platforms that usually had nothing to do with politics and activism, such as the sports forum Hupu, where a trending post in late July (since deleted) was titled 'the guy [referring to a leading worker giving a speech] is so handsome!'

A deeper look at the dynamics and various twists and turns of the Jasic workers' unionisation struggles reveals how this episode has important implications for the broader labour movement in China on at least two different levels.

Organisational Effectiveness

First, the aspect of the struggles that I personally find most inspiring is the organisational effectiveness demonstrated by the workers. Worker activists at Jasic first proposed the idea of unionising in May, then in late June and early July started to organise coworkers, collecting their signatures on a unionisation petition. In the end, they were able to garner more than 80 coworkers' signatures within only a couple of weeks. Although at this point the prospect of establishing a democratic, worker-run union at Jasic is bleak—with rumours suggesting that since the leading worker activists were detained in late July, the employer and the district-level branch of the official trade union, the All-China Federation of Trade Unions (ACFTU), have already established a company-run 'yellow' union at Jasic—the very fact that within less than a month more than 80 coworkers came out to publicly support the worker-run campaign is, in itself, a huge achievement.

I have participated in previous unionisation campaigns (albeit in the United States), and have attempted to persuade coworkers to support unionisation efforts. Such personal experiences have taught me that convincing colleagues to support the establishment of a union goes far beyond simply asking them to write down their names; rather, it involves considerable amounts of organisation. Worker activists need to explain to their colleagues what a union does, how it will be managed once established, and why setting up a union could effectively help solve the issues that have been plaguing them. More importantly, they need to nurture trust and solidarity among coworkers, and convince them that workers will indeed become powerful enough to defend their own rights when everyone unites together. Worker activists also need to show coworkers that achieving such large-scale solidarity at the workplace is possible. Lastly, they need to ensure that their coworkers' commitment to this kind of unity outweighs their fear of potential employer retaliation, so they will be courageous enough to sign petition forms. All these steps entail endless communication, persuasion, and encouragement, and require worker activists to forge strong bonds with their coworkers to win their trust.

Despite such arduous organisational work and the challenges associated with it, worker activists from Jasic still managed to garner support from more than 80 coworkers—approximately 10 percent of the workforce—within a very short period. Such an achievement should not be underestimated. Consider, for instance, the fact that in manufacturing factories of the same scale in the United States, where unions enjoy more leeway and independence in running unionisation campaigns, the whole process of organising and mobilising workers—from the starting point of a unionisation campaign to winning majority support—normally takes about three years, if not more. Seen in this light, the Jasic worker activists' ability to win over 10 percent of their coworkers in a couple of weeks in such a restrictive environment is little short of a miracle.

However, whether a unionisation campaign succeeds or fails does not just depend on the organisational ability and dedication of the workers. A unionisation campaign is also essentially a race between workers and the employer, who tries to react as harshly and swiftly as possible before the unionisation spreads like wildfire. In the case of Jasic, the

PC: Mimi Lau, *South China Morning Post*.

employer's reaction was both extremely harsh and extremely swift. All of the leading worker activists were fired at a very early stage of the campaign, before unionisation could seriously pick up steam in the factory. Winning over more than 10 percent of their coworkers' support was undoubtedly very impressive, but a couple of weeks was not enough for these worker activists to cultivate a far-reaching, well-connected support network in the factory and to turn the colleagues who signed the petition from *supporters* to *fellow leaders*. In other words, despite growing rapidly, the campaign was crushed by the employer almost as soon as it started—long before it could become strong enough to survive sustained repression.

Therefore, after the leading worker activists were fired, and especially after they were detained, the worker-led unionisation effectively came to a halt because no other Jasic workers could step up to become new leaders inside the factory. The lack of new leaders was surely compounded by the fact that the whole factory was placed under heavy police surveillance after 27 July. When workers from other factories and students from all over China flocked to Shenzhen to stage solidarity initiatives and advocate the release of the detained workers, almost no Jasic workers publicly participated in these actions—though a few Jasic workers did play the role of informants for the solidarity groups—and no industrial action was staged inside Jasic. In the end, the blossoming worker solidarity, which the leading Jasic worker activists worked so hard to build, was quickly dismantled in the face of heavy-handed repression by the employer and the state alike.

Slogans on the back of a protester's T-shirt. PC: Mimi Lau, *South China Morning Post*.

A Trigger for Union Reform

Second, it is also important to reflect on the role of the ACFTU in this struggle. In May 2018, when receiving workers from Jasic who had come to lodge complaints, leaders of the ACFTU branch of Pingshan district pitched to the workers the idea of unionising as one possible way to address their workplace grievances. This official encouragement was one of the crucial factors that sparked and encouraged the workers' efforts to organise towards unionisation. In early June, the Pingshan union officials further suggested that the first step for the workers seeking to unionise should be to ask coworkers to put their signature on petition forms to express their support for establishing a union. Up until that point, it had seemed that the official trade union was supportive of the unionisation efforts. In July, however, leaders at the Pingshan union drastically changed tack, demanding that Mi Jiuping, one of the leading worker activists, write a statement declaring that the workers' endeavours to establish a union had nothing to do with the ACFTU. From there on out, leaders of the Pingshan union sided with the employer, decrying the worker activists' attempts to unionise autonomously as nonsense and threatening that they 'shall bear legal responsibility' for their actions.

Nevertheless, on 23 July, after the worker activists had already been fired and had staged a series of protest actions, the official WeChat account of the Pingshan union published a post declaring that it would support and guide Jasic 'to set up a union in the company as per laws, regulations and procedures', seemingly registering a note that was sympathetic to the workers' cause. On 29 July, however, when people from all walks of life rushed to Yanziling police station to voice their support for the worker activists detained two days earlier, leaders from the Pingshan union were seen standing alongside representatives of the employer, secretly observing all the actions taken by supporters of the workers.

In this way, the official trade union vacillated throughout this episode—at times acting in a supporting role, and at others repressing the workers on behalf of the employer. Eventually, when workers needed the union's help the most in the face of an impending crackdown, the ACFTU did not hesitate to turn its back on them and side with the employer and the Party-state.

This is where the ACFTU stands after two waves of reform efforts in the Pearl River Delta. After earlier tentative attempts, the first wave of union reforms took place in the wake of the hugely influential 2010 strike at the Honda plant in Nanhai, Foshan (see Chan's essay in this volume). On this occasion workers advanced democratic reform of the union branch in their company as one of several demands. After 2010, a wave of labour protests ensued in the Pearl River Delta, calling for either the reform of existing local unions or the establishment of new ones, the enhancement of internal union democracy, and the implementation of the collective bargaining mechanism. These movements, to some extent, achieved positive outcomes. Local unions were formed, union leaders were elected through open nomination and secret ballot, and collective bargaining was implemented often resulting in significant wage increases. In addition to the struggles of the workers themselves, this wave of reform was also facilitated by a degree of political openness on part of the official leadership of the ACFTU at various levels. Nevertheless, starting from 2013, the space of operation for these reformist leaders has increasingly shrunk, and the attitudes of the ACFTU leadership towards workers has became increasingly ambiguous, ultimately leading to the end of the first wave of reforms.

As the space for labour organising further narrowed in the Pearl River Delta after the crackdown on labour NGOs that took place at the end of 2015 (see Franceschini and Lin's essay in this volume), a second wave of ACFTU reforms ensued. This time the protagonists were not workers but some prominent Chinese labour scholars. They pinned their hopes on the official trade union not because they saw the ACFTU as a particularly fertile ground for organising, but because the other possibilities for labour organising were perceived to be essentially blocked. They set up various programmes in collaboration with the official union to train a new generation of young and dedicated unionists who were seriously committed to advancing labour rights, in the hope that they would be able to breath new life into the ACFTU. In particular, as organising at the workplace became increasingly difficult and collective bargaining became increasingly formalised and hollowed out, they put an emphasis on reorienting the ACFTU towards community- and neighbourhood-based organising. The idea was to turn the ACFTU into a vehicle through which to build a sense of solidarity in workers' everyday life.

In part, the appeal of this second wave of reforms is due to the fact that it is politically more feasible and less risky given the current political situation. It allows the ACFTU to frame what it does as a 'community service' that has nothing to do with politics, and thus to eschew the terrain of contentious struggle between labour and the state-capital alliance. In other words, the Jasic struggle puts the ACFTU back in the position from which it has been trying to escape through its 'retreat' from the workplace to the community. It is on this ground that the promise of the second wave of ACFTU reforms can be assessed. These reforms might make some marginal improvements that deliver various services workers need in their communities and cultivate a community-based sense of solidarity among workers, possibly making their lives better in a meaningful way. However, as long as the ACFTU opts to shy away from workplace struggles, whatever improvements it might deliver in communities and neighbourhoods will remain fleeting. ■

An earlier version of this op-ed was translated from Chinese into English by Nan Liu.

The Jasic Strike
Timeline

MAY 2018

MID-MAY
Jasic workers complain to the local authorities about their dire working conditions and the local branch of the ACFTU suggests that they establish a factory-level trade union.

JUNE 2018

EARLY JUNE
Jasic workers submit their application for establishing a trade union to the local branch of the ACFTU, but are told that first they have to gather the signatures of potential members.

MID-JUNE
Management at Jasic preemptively sets up an Employee General Meeting and appoints trusted aides as leaders.

JULY 2018

EARLY JULY
Worker representatives gather 89 signatures for the unionisation petition but are accused by Jasic management of deceiving workers into signing the form.

MID-JULY
Worker representatives are expelled from the factory and beaten by both security guards and other unidentified people before being detained by the local authorities.

20 JULY
Over 20 workers protest in front of the police station where their representatives are being held, but end up being arrested as well.

21 JULY
All detained workers are released but are prevented from returning to work by managers at Jasic, who barricade the factory.

27 JULY
30 protesters, including dismissed workers, their families, and supporters, stage a protest in front of the Jasic factory to demand to be reinstated, but are all arrested by the police.

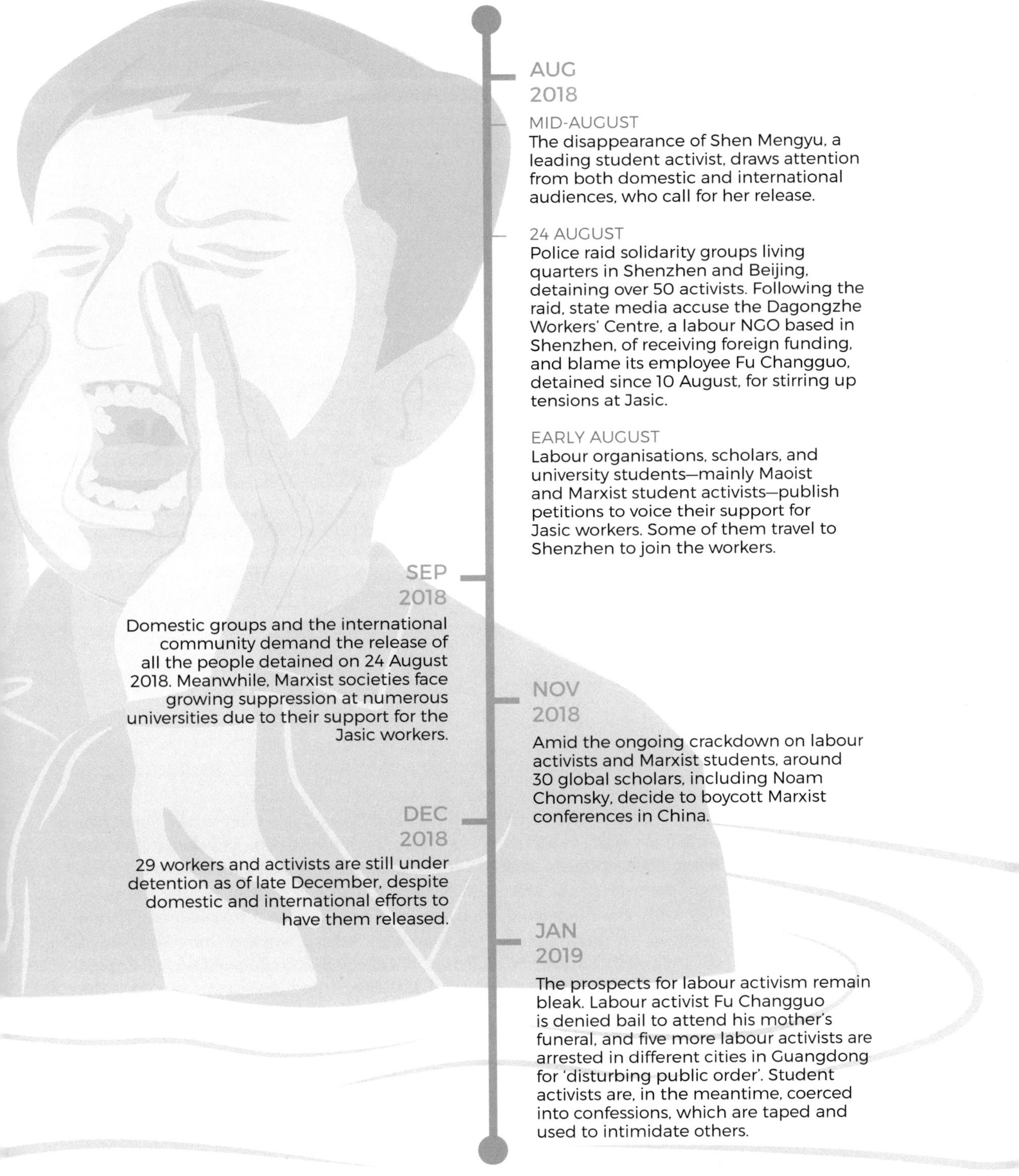

AUG 2018

MID-AUGUST
The disappearance of Shen Mengyu, a leading student activist, draws attention from both domestic and international audiences, who call for her release.

24 AUGUST
Police raid solidarity groups living quarters in Shenzhen and Beijing, detaining over 50 activists. Following the raid, state media accuse the Dagongzhe Workers' Centre, a labour NGO based in Shenzhen, of receiving foreign funding, and blame its employee Fu Changguo, detained since 10 August, for stirring up tensions at Jasic.

EARLY AUGUST
Labour organisations, scholars, and university students—mainly Maoist and Marxist student activists—publish petitions to voice their support for Jasic workers. Some of them travel to Shenzhen to join the workers.

SEP 2018

Domestic groups and the international community demand the release of all the people detained on 24 August 2018. Meanwhile, Marxist societies face growing suppression at numerous universities due to their support for the Jasic workers.

NOV 2018

Amid the ongoing crackdown on labour activists and Marxist students, around 30 global scholars, including Noam Chomsky, decide to boycott Marxist conferences in China.

DEC 2018

29 workers and activists are still under detention as of late December, despite domestic and international efforts to have them released.

JAN 2019

The prospects for labour activism remain bleak. Labour activist Fu Changguo is denied bail to attend his mother's funeral, and five more labour activists are arrested in different cities in Guangdong for 'disturbing public order'. Student activists are, in the meantime, coerced into confessions, which are taped and used to intimidate others.

Jasic workers holding Mao's picture.
PC: Mimi Lau, *South China Morning Post*.

The Jasic Mobilisation

A High Tide for the Chinese Labour Movement?

AU Loong Yu

In the summer of 2018, workers at Shenzhen Jasic Technology demanded the right to set up a workplace union. What differentiates this episode from other labour struggles in the area is the fact that the Jasic case was supported openly by a group of some 50 self-proclaimed Maoist and Marxist university students, along with a small group of older citizens. In this essay, Au Loong Yu assesses this unprecedented incident in which students and workers struggle together across institutions, provinces, generations, and class boundaries.

In July this year, 89 workers at the Shenzhen Jasic Technology Co. Ltd demanded the right to set up a workplace union. In the past decade there has been an explosion of strikes in Shenzhen, and this dispute is one of the many where workers have demanded better working conditions, owed wages, unpaid social insurance, and severance pay. Yet, the Jasic case is unusual in that it was supported

[1] Part of this essay first appeared in Chinese in the Mingpao Daily, 30 August 2018. A more lengthy discussion on the issue by the same author appeared in the January 2019 issue of New Politics (newpol.org). All information reported here comes from the Internet or personal contacts.

openly by a group of some 50 self-proclaimed Maoists and Marxist university students, along with a small group of older citizens. Coming from different parts of China, they organised themselves into a 'Jasic Worker Support Group' and descended on Jasic to stand in solidarity with the workers who were battling the police.

At the height of the Jasic campaign, these old and young Maoist supporters held up photos of Chairman Mao and a banner reading 'To Be Good Students of Chairman Mao Forever'. They created a website—which has now been removed from the Internet—called 'Vanguard of the Era' (*Shidai xianfeng*) calling for more support for their cause, 'for the sake of the working class's awakening, for the sake of Chairman Mao!' (Wu 2018). They uploaded photographs of themselves on social media posing in Maoist-like revolutionary heroic postures, disciplined and determined to fight for their cause. One of them posted an article entitled 'Where Has Jinggangshan Gone? On the Jasic Struggle and the Future of Revolutionary Revival' (Luo 2018). Referring to the mountain where Mao first established his guerrilla base in 1927 and to Mao's revolutionary strategy of 'encircling cities from the rural areas' (*nongcun baowei chengshi*), it proclaimed 'Jinggangshan is here right now at Jasic and in all industrial areas.'

Although Jasic supporters might not really be advocating for an armed uprising, they do believe that the time is ripe for leftists in China to escalate worker struggle from economic to political. The very moment the Maoists got involved, the incident quickly escalated from a workplace trade union organising drive to a political struggle against local officials. The heroic campaign was quickly and violently suppressed. Four workers were arrested, charged with disturbing the peace, and are now awaiting trial. At the time of writing (December 2018), 28 supporters remain either under house arrest or have been forcibly disappeared (HRIC 2018). As for the students, after they went back to their universities, they were interrogated, disciplined, investigated, threatened, and in some cases expelled. In the past three months, more than 20 students have been fiercely manhandled—some were beaten up, some were attacked and kidnapped by thugs right on campus, and some have simply disappeared. How are we to assess this unprecedented incident in which students and workers struggle together across institutions, across provinces, across generations, and across class boundaries?

Making History?

Professor Pun Ngai at the University of Hong Kong has argued that the Jasic mobilisation is a movement of 'unity between workers and students' and is of 'historical significance' (Pun 2018). Indeed, the case is significant because it was the first time in the past few decades that students have emerged in such a high profile and organised manner to support a worker protest. This stands in sharp contrast to what happened in Tiananmen Square in 1989, when intellectuals and students cordoned themselves off from the workers at the very beginning of the protests. After the democratic movement of the late 1980s failed, intellectuals soon split into two main groups: Liberals (*ziyoupai*) and the New Left (*xinzuopai*). Both of these groups subscribed to the false dichotomy of 'state versus market', while remaining indifferent to the plight of the working masses. At best, only a handful of the New Left intellectuals adopted a rhetoric of 'fairness' in their writings by counterposing the liberal slogan of 'prioritising efficiency' for future reform with 'prioritising justice' instead. As for the students, they simply retreated to their study. It was not until the 2009 Guangzhou sanitation workers strike that workers began to receive some support from students, who mostly participated as individuals, rather than as a coordinated group. Thus, the fact that in the Jasic incident, more than 50 students put themselves at risk by acting in solidarity with the workers was indeed a new development.

Nevertheless, Professor Pun goes on to make two other points that I have reservations about. Firstly, she commends the incident as having a second historical significance in that for 'the first time the workers consciously organised a trade union.' The reality is that there have been numerous cases of workers going on strike to demand the reelecting or establishment of workplace unions. For example, as early as 2004–05, workers at the Shenzhen Japanese company Uniden went on strike five times in one year. They finally succeeded in setting up a union but it was quickly suppressed. Other examples were the Ole Wolff case in Yantai in 2006, the Yantian Container strike of 2007, and last but not least, the Nanhai Honda strike of 2010.

Secondly, she remarks that 'the actions of the Jasic workers also show that Chinese workers have already transformed from purely economic subjects into political subjects with class consciousness.' True, the protest was initially quite promising. The factory has just over a thousand workers. So the fact that 89 workers signed on to request that a labour union be established—with 20 remaining in the struggle after the crackdown—is significant, particularly considering the difficulty of labour organising in this type of context (see Zhang Yueran's essay in this volume). However, is it possible to conclude that the average Chinese worker has become a 'political subject with class consciousness' based on the actions of a less than 100 people in a single workplace?

Red Resurgence

Now that the suppression of students has captured the attention of the international media, it is worth looking at the origins of these Maoist student groups in a bit more detail. The reemergence of Maoist ideology among the younger generation can be traced to the turn of the century. At that time, some older Maoists in North China began to resist the privatisation of state-owned enterprises (SOEs) from behind the scenes. They also invited rural migrant activists and students to their classes and trainings. In 2005, they founded the 'China Labour Research Web' (*Zhongguo gongren yanjiu wang*), later renamed 'Red China' (*Hongse Zhongguo*), which was closed down by the authorities in 2010. At that time, these Maoists prioritised state workers over rural migrant workers as they regarded the former as more 'revolutionary' and the latter as lacking class consciousness. They mostly focussed their activities around the state workers in the North, and if there were Maoist NGOs working in the South they maintained a very low profile. The current rise of a new generation of young Maoist students engaging so deeply in the Jasic struggle indicates the Maoists are turning their attention to rural migrant workers in the South. That in the Jasic case they have decided to adopt a tactic of high-profile confrontational resistance, was evidence of their determination and commitment given the highly repressive situation.

Left and Right Maoists

Earlier this decade, 'Red China'—along with 'Utopia' (*wuyouzhixiang*), a Maoist website founded in 2003 by the well known Maoist/Nationalists Fan Jinggang and Han Deqiang—had placed their hopes in Bo Xilai to lead a left turn in the Party. For instance, Minqi Li, an academic based in the United States and a theoretician of 'Red China', placed great expectations in Bo as 'the last significant faction that was in opposition to neoliberal capitalism', and argued that 'by purging Bo Xilai from the Party, the Chinese Communist Party (CCP) leadership may have foregone their last and best opportunity to resolve China's rapidly escalating economic and social contradictions in a relatively peaceful manner' (Li 2016, 183 and 38).

The fall of Bo in 2012 shattered these hopes, and since then the two labels 'Left Maoists' (*maozuo*) and 'Right Maoists' (*maoyou*) have become common currency in online debates. This means that the Maoists have definitely split into at least two camps: Right Maoists continue to advocate for the support of the Party, as summed up in the slogan, 'Defend the Party and Save the State' (*baodangjiuguo*), while Left Maoists, such as 'Red China', have become more radical in criticising the Party, having finally come to recognise that a qualitative transformation to capitalism has taken place in China. Since the rise of Xi Jinping onwards, they have become more explicit in advocating resistance from below while continuing to try to win over leading Party cadres through the invocation of the 'socialist' principles enshrined in the Constitution or in Mao's work.

Although the Maoists have accumulated a lot of experience in the North in supporting the rights of state workers, their experiences cannot be applied to the workers in the private enterprises of the South without being substantially adapted. When the SOEs underwent privatisation in the late 1990s to early 2000s, the workers sometimes directly confronted corrupt local officials who were responsible for the theft of public property. They deployed the revolutionary ethos of the CCP to legitimise their political resistance. This was natural and was even sometimes useful. But in the private companies of the South it is different. The conflict is chiefly one between employees and employers. Moreover, the revolutionary ethos of the CCP is less likely to resonate with migrant workers, and so if actions escalate into political resistance the workers are less likely to be motivated. Therefore, in the Jasic case, as in many other cases, when the local government cracked down on workers the struggle turned political. But when looking at the possibility to escalate this type of struggle one must also ask the question: are workers fully prepared for a political confrontation? Experience already tells us that in this specific case they were not.

A Fundamental Betrayal

The Chinese authorities in reality do not have any interest in 'socialist' principles, nor in Mao or Maoism. While Xi Jinping continues to demand that the people learn from Marxism, Leninism, and Mao's Thought, paradoxically, the Party-state continues to crack down on any independent and collective efforts to seriously study the classic texts of the left, and ramps up its attacks even more when these efforts carry an aspiration to sympathise with the working people. Repressing the resurgence of Maoism among the people is not new. Back in 2004 the Zhengzhou police arrested and charged local Maoists who tried to assemble to pay tribute to Mao. The Party-state's crackdown on the Jasic workers and students today is just another incident reminding us that the CCP has long since betrayed its own founding doctrine and is hostile to anyone who wants to interpret Maoism differently from the officially sanctioned line.

There is much for us to learn from the Jasic case. It should be the catalyst for us to begin a long overdue public debate on the situation and strategy of China's labour movement in the midst of a crisis-ridden society. Whereas previously labour constituted a silent majority which remained basically absent from the debate between Liberals and the New Left, the Jasic case reminds us that the situation is changing, that more workers now want their voices to be heard, and that a debate on all these issues is increasingly urgent. ■

TO THE SOIL

The Labour of Rural Transformation in China

Farmer and buffalo in a rural village in Hubei Province. PC: Tauno Tohk.

China's Land Reforms and the Logic of Capital Accumulation

Jane HAYWARD

In this essay, Jane Hayward briefly examines how rural land reforms in China are being driven by the imperative of capital accumulation. She looks at how policies of agricultural land transfer, new rural community construction, and the urban-rural land linking system, are all too often driven by the urban real estate industry in league with local governments and agribusinesses, rather than by villagers themselves.

China's integration into the world market, and its ever-tightening embrace of the logic of capital, is manifested in the ongoing mass reorganisation of land—both urban and rural—to create spaces for capital accumulation. This short essay will discuss how these processes are taking place in three ways: through agricultural land transfers, new rural community construction, and the urban-rural land linking system. Since the late 1950s, China's urban-rural relations have been organised on the basis of the household registration system, or *hukou*, under which Chinese people are allocated either a rural or an urban registration permit. Mobility between the countryside and cities has been restricted, and urban and rural land is governed under different systems. Urban land is state-owned, and its use rights can be sold on the market. Agricultural land is collective, and cannot be sold. Access to public services, including healthcare and social security, has been determined by the *hukou*. Those living in the cities have enjoyed far better facilities, while those in the countryside have had to rely on their collective land rights as a form of guaranteed livelihood. This system, originally intended to preserve resources in the cities for urban industrialisation, institutionalised an unequal urban-rural relationship under which living conditions were, and continue to be, harsher for China's peasantry.

The *Hukou* Under Market Reforms

Following the start of market reforms in 1978, agricultural land was reorganised from the large communes of the Mao period to what was known as the household responsibility system. Ownership remained collective while the management rights to plots of land were contracted out to village households for production. Special Economic Zones were set up in China's eastern and southern coastal cities which attracted large amounts of foreign investment. The *hukou* system slackened as local governments turned a blind eye to peasants flooding into these areas in their millions, providing cheap labour for the export industry. Rural-urban migration accelerated further after the mid-1990s following fiscal reforms which stemmed the flow of money from the central government to the rural localities, redirecting it instead into urban industrial projects. Rural cadres were compelled to replenish their coffers by squeezing peasant households with extra taxes and fees, and also by expropriating plots of collective farmland to lease to developers in lucrative but often illegal deals. As a result, living conditions for China's peasantry deteriorated sharply. More and more people were forced to seek low-paid work in the cities. Once there, due to the *hukou* system, they were discriminated against as second-class citizens and denied access to many basic facilities.

By 2002, China's countryside was in a state of emergency marked by impoverished households, corrupt local governments, and lack of investment in infrastructure. Large swathes of farmland risked the double jeopardy of abandonment by migrating villagers and illegal requisitions. China's entry into the World Trade Organisation in 2001, which would see agriculture exposed to world market competition, threatened to make matters worse. In order to address this crisis, a new set of policy guidelines was introduced under the slogan 'combined urban-rural planning' (*chengxiang tongchou*). This called for a complete renegotiation of the hierarchy between city and countryside, and the even distribution of the fruits of China's reforms across both urban and rural areas. Broadly speaking, the overhauling and modernisation of the countryside was to be achieved by the inward flow of capital investment, and the outward movement of people into towns and cities. This was intended to equalise the urban-rural wealth gap—the urban areas which had benefitted up until now would 'pay back' the countryside, while former peasants would be able to enjoy the benefits of urbanisation and modern life.

Agricultural Land Transfers

Meanwhile, Chinese policymakers fiercely debated how to reorganise agricultural land. A strong cohort resisted calls to privatise it outright on the basis that individual peasant households with little bargaining power in the face of largescale corporations would too easily be separated from their property rights, leading to widespread landlessness and extreme poverty, as had already occurred in many other parts of the world (Hayward

Construction work in a rural village in Hubei. PC: Tauno Tohk.

2017, 528–31). Instead, at the key meeting of the Third Plenary Session of the Seventeenth Central Committee in October 2008, China's leaders formally recognised the practice of land transfers (*tudi liuzhuan*). This meant that land remaining nominally under collective village ownership, and under contract to peasant households, could be 'transferred' (leased out) to third parties. These measures in effect divided the dual land rights of the household responsibility system into three—ownership, contract, and management rights—a system which has come to be known as the 'separation of three rights' (*san quan fen zhi*).

This shrewd innovation seeks to scale up the scattered household land plots by consolidating them in the hands of a smaller number of highly skilled, professionalised farming entities—usually large farm households or agribusinesses. The result is a quasi-land market, albeit one that functions under restricted conditions. While this brings more capital into the countryside, it amounts to the manipulation of the institution of collective property such that peasant land entitlements can more easily be exploited in the interests of capital accumulation. The rental fee paid to peasant households may be more than they would make by working the land themselves, but it is not high, and studies have reported on the coercive tactics which may be used to get unwilling villagers to transfer their land (Gong and Zhang 2017).

New Rural Community Construction

Meanwhile, rural villages are being reorganised under programmes of 'new rural community construction' (*xinxing nongcun shequ jianshe*). The goal is to 'civilise' villages by subjecting them to modern urban planning practices (Bray 2013, 54). Under this programme, village layouts are landscaped and reorganised on the basis of 'three concentrations': segregated zones of scaled-up agricultural land, consolidated industrial areas, and dense housing settlements (Bray 2013,

55–56). This means that, with a view to organising the village in a more 'rational' way, traditional houses scattered around the village are demolished and villagers are relocated into high-rise tower blocks, freeing up village land for agricultural or industrial use to attract outside investment. These 'community construction' projects are expensive and, since local governments are already short of funds, financing them is not easy. Local officials may demand that peasant households, many already struggling on low incomes, pay for the projects themselves, driving them into debt. Alternatively, funding may come from corporate donors, with the donor then securing the management rights to the freed-up land. Surveys have shown that such deals are often made by corporations in league with local governments, bypassing village participation and against the wishes of householders. Once in the tower blocks, villagers have access to modern facilities such as water, sanitation, gas, electricity, and Internet access. However, with the associated fees and the low income from the land which is now leased out, many villagers find that their net expenditures have risen, rather than fallen (Rosenberg 2013; Cui and Sun 2014).

Urban–Rural Land Linking System

Both of these institutional transformations are closely bound up with a third: the urban-rural land linking system, or 'linking system' (*guagou*) for short. This hinges on China's shortage of agricultural land. Despite the country's vast land area, a relatively small amount of it is suitable for agricultural cultivation. The central government has decreed it should not fall below a minimum level of approximately 1.8 billion *mu* (1 *mu* is about 0.16 acres). Due to China's extraordinary rate of urban expansion, by 2005 China's agricultural land had fallen almost to this level already. This means that no more agricultural land can be used for urban development, unless a corresponding plot elsewhere of equal size is brought *back* under cultivation—for example, land which was previously fallow or had been built over. Any such *new* plots can be 'swapped'—added to a regional system of land quotas and auctioned to urban developers, allowing them to build on a plot of agricultural land elsewhere—generally in a more lucrative location on the borders of a city or township.

This ingenious system is designed to facilitate urban development without reducing the national agricultural land area, while enabling villagers to benefit financially from urban development elsewhere (Cui 2011). Yet, as a number of surveys have indicated, the system incentivises the widespread exploitation of rural assets in the interests of both urban and agrarian capital. While peasants continue to have little bargaining power in the exchanges, many cases have been reported of peasants losing their homes against their will, and for little or sometimes no compensation. Meanwhile, local officials have every incentive to auction land areas exceeding their assigned quota to gain extra funds (Chen and Ma 2012).

Alliances and Accumulation

While many of these changes appear to be geared towards the modernisation of the countryside and the improvement of peasant livelihoods, the overriding logic governing these processes, all too often, is that of capital accumulation. What is crucial is how the land linking system ties transformations in the countryside to processes of urbanisation in and around townships and cities. Thus, these rural transformations are themselves being driven largely by the urban real estate industry, in alliance with agribusiness and local governments in need of land revenue. These work together to shift peasants off their land, out of the villages, and into cities, while they may have little say in the matter (Zhan 2017). ■

New resettlement communities in southern Shaanxi. PC: Sarah Rogers.

Manufactured Modernity

Dwelling, Labour, and Enclosure in China's Poverty Resettlements

Sarah ROGERS

Between 2016 and 2020, the Chinese authorities will have resettled nearly 10 million people throughout China's inland provinces with the aim of eliminating absolute poverty in rural areas. Looking at the case of southern Shaanxi, in this essay Sarah Rogers reflects on specific poverty resettlement projects, and Chinese resettlement practice more broadly, to try to make sense of the intent and impact of such large-scale interventions on both the lives of individuals and the transformation of the Chinese countryside as a whole.

I first encountered resettled farmers in 2005 to the west of Hohhot in Inner Mongolia. The resettlement village in which I conducted research was the new home of Han Chinese herders from several natural villages who had been moved down off the mountains and into a consolidated settlement near a major highway. Herding had been banned and the mountains effectively enclosed for environmental protection. While people still travelled back to their old villages to tend ancestral graves, they were now embedded in the dairy economy, raising small numbers of cows and selling the milk to Yili Group—a massive state-owned dairy producer. It was in Inner Mongolia and later in Shanxi province that I learnt about the Chinese practice of resettlement *as* development: these people were not in the way of a dam or major infrastructure project, they were relocated seemingly for their own benefit and to protect a 'fragile' environment. Hundreds of thousands of Han and ethnic Mongolian herders were resettled in this way. Herding was once a highly visible livelihood activity in places like Inner Mongolia and throughout the Loess Plateau. These days, however, while narrow trails still visibly criss-cross the hillsides, a herder with his or her livestock is a rare sight indeed, largely supplanted by industrial livestock production.

Thirteen years on and I am still conducting research in resettlement villages, nowadays in southern Shaanxi and central Gansu. Much has changed in the way that resettlement projects are managed. Perhaps most notably, the scale has only intensified: 2.4 million people are being resettled this decade in just three prefectures in Shaanxi under the Southern Shaanxi Relocation and Settlement Project (*shan nan yimin banqian anzhi gongcheng*). A total of nearly ten million people are being resettled between 2016 and 2020 throughout China's inland provinces (NDRC 2016). One of the key reasons for this escalation is the central government's stated goal of eliminating absolute poverty in rural areas by 2020, which has been accompanied by massive commitments of funding and intense pressure on local officials to achieve poverty reduction targets. In what follows, I reflect on specific poverty resettlement projects, and Chinese resettlement practice more broadly, to try to make sense of the intent and impact of such large-scale interventions. Why does China turn to resettlement as a solution to so many of the country's ills? And what role is resettlement playing in the ongoing transformation of the Chinese countryside?

New resettlement communities in Southern Shaanxi. PC: Sarah Rogers.

Dwelling

One of the most visible and calculable changes in the lives of resettled farmers is where and how they dwell. Poverty resettlement projects in southern Shaanxi (see images) attempt to manufacture an entirely new way of living. Formerly living in sprawling homesteads with several built structures in which extended families, animals, machinery, and stored crops resided, resettled farmers now occupy high-rise apartments with precise measurements of 60, 80, or 100 square metres. Nothing grows except ornamental trees and flowers, and the odd indoor plant, and no livestock can be found. Unlike most old farmhouses, these apartments feature kitchens connected to gas cooking and with proper ventilation, as well as indoor bathrooms with showers and flushing toilets. Local officials are rightly pleased to show outsiders through soon-to-be-occupied apartments (for which household contributions are now capped at 10,000 yuan) and models of various sized apartments complete with toy furniture. Compared to the 'dangerous' conditions in the village, here people can live in a modern, clean, and safe way.

On one level this all makes perfect sense. The condition of housing in poorer villages is often hazardous, particularly to women cooking inside with firewood. And who, having spent any time in a Chinese village, can decry an indoor toilet? But as critical scholars, it is our role to pose additional questions. Why is it that people *have to move* to enjoy these benefits? Why is it not possible for such 'development' to take place *in* villages? What has changed such that some villages are suddenly considered uninhabitable and some environments fragile? And if people must be moved because of natural disasters or poor infrastructure, why are they not reallocated farmland or given any space to grow vegetables or raise animals?

That the nature of dwelling is so abruptly transformed points to the various motivations and networks of interests that underpin poverty resettlement projects. First, for reasons of food security, land use in China is circumscribed to the point where any loss of farmland to urban or industrial development must be compensated by an equal conversion of land somewhere else into farmland (see Hayward's essay in this volume). This quota system means that sprawling rural residences (*zhai jidi*) are suddenly of great interest to local officials. By relocating farmers to high-rise apartments, demolishing homesteads, and converting this residential land to farmland, a land quota is freed up allowing for urbanisation somewhere more profitable.

Second, under intense pressure to meet the 2020 poverty target, local officials, and the evaluation system within which they are embedded, lean towards visible, quantifiable changes in people's lives. Relocating a poor household from an old farmhouse to a modern apartment fits the bill perfectly: once relocated, with an asset and a new job (see below) you are no longer poor. Third, resettlement drives a construction boom from which local governments, state-owned enterprises, private firms, and local labourers all reap the benefits. It is difficult to make sense of the proliferation of high-rise resettlement communities without reference to these intersecting motives.

Labour

Resettlement can also transform the nature and place of people's labour. While earlier resettlement projects like the ones in Inner Mongolia seemed more about agricultural intensification and embedding smallholders within domestic and international supply chains, the imperative to alleviate poverty is now driving a focus on off-farm wage labour. To paraphrase local officials: resettlement allows people to have a 'stable' life with a salaried job.

Back in the old villages, farmland is often transferred to cooperatives or agribusinesses, where some resettled farmers might return to work seasonally or simply receive an annual dividend as shareholders. The new settlements, however, often lie alongside purpose-built industrial parks, tourism sites, or agricultural processing facilities, where poor people are prioritised for low-skilled jobs that guarantee a wage of at least 1,500 yuan a month. Such 'public welfare' positions also include jobs as gardeners, cleaners, and security guards in the new communities, and are aimed at guaranteeing that at least one person in a poor household has a salaried job and is developing new skills. Given income is so critical to how China measures poverty, these subsidised positions are used as evidence of 'shedding' poverty.

One way of interpreting poverty resettlement, therefore, is that it is designed to bring a low-cost labour force into close proximity with capitalist enterprises, many of which are incentivised to move inland by rising wages in wealthier provinces, but also through the use of sweeteners offered by local governments. Farmland is not necessarily fully appropriated, though, and can only be used in certain ways, which means that poverty resettlement—following Julia Chuang (2015)—might lie somewhere between David Harvey's accumulation *by* dispossession and Giovanni Arrighi's accumulation *without* dispossession. Resettlement certainly dovetails neatly with the central government's stated preference for larger-scale farms run by 'new agricultural operators' (*xinxing nongye jingying zhuti*)—i.e. anyone but smallholders.

To better understand the impact of these structural forces, we might also examine labour in terms of work practices, or what Ingold (2000) calls the 'taskscape'. While rural household livelihoods have long been composed of both agricultural work and off-farm labour, resettlement is an attempt to accelerate a shift from the rhythms, tasks, and places of agricultural production and subsistence to those of wage labour and consumption. I say attempt, because in reality things are of course much messier.

In the new industrial parks, some older men and women spend their days indoors on repetitive low-skilled tasks, while younger men might earn slightly more doing higher-skilled metalwork. Those working in walnut or dried tofu processing factories must undergo training to ensure they behave in the necessary way and abide by sanitary regulations. Wages are used to purchase not just the basics, but also the food that is no longer grown. However, given the low pay on offer locally, most young people continue to work in larger cities or in far-flung provinces. Some young women stay behind in the new apartments to care for children and the elderly (see Jacka's essay in the this volume). Others completely reject these new rhythms and in doing so complicate the clean rural/urban break envisaged by authorities. It is typically the elderly who choose to stay in their village homes and continue the labour of growing vegetables, tending fruit trees, and raising livestock, leaving their allocated apartments to the next generation. Furthermore, resettled people's household registration (*hukou*) is not transferred, meaning their medical insurance, pensions, and voting rights are still tied to the village. For some time to come, therefore, there will be continued movement between these places as people negotiate new or modified patterns of work, care, and citizenship.

Enclosure

If, as one resettled farmer described, almost all families have people who have stayed behind in the original villages, then extensive poverty resettlement in China's mountainous areas might not so dramatically cleave the urban from the rural. However, there is little doubt that the various interests that are tied up in this latest resettlement campaign are seeking to fundamentally remake rural localities.

Poverty resettlement is often linked to poor environmental conditions. Farmers must be resettled because the landscape is 'unsafe', suddenly incapable of supporting livelihoods, or because they now reside in a designated water conservancy or biodiversity zone. Entry into some of these areas is now prohibited. Poverty resettlement is also linked to extensive land transfers to agribusinesses. If land usage rights are transferred and farmers receive rent or dividends, then it kills two birds with one stone: poor households have a new income stream, and the way is smoothed for larger-scale operators. People's reluctance to let go of their old homesteads is the one major sticking point: local officials are now asking people to sign agreements that the old structures will be demolished within three years with the promise of a subsidy. With the farmhouses gone, large-scale operators making decisions about land use, an influx of urbanites enjoying some country respite, and only seasonal farm labour available for former residents, the Chinese countryside will have been remade.

The nostalgia of outsiders would be unhelpful here. After all, China's mountainous villages can be places of deprivation, illness, toxicity, sexism, and gruelling labour. But that does not preclude a diagnosis that through enclosure, resettlement is an attempt to erase what came before. A dwelling perspective posits that a landscape 'is constituted as an enduring record of—and testimony to—the lives and works of past generations who have dwelt within it, and in so doing, have left there something of themselves' (Ingold 2000, 188). From such a perspective, while poverty resettlement projects may seek to (yet again) remake human-environment relations in rural China, the practices, memories, and stories of the landscape cannot be so easily expunged. ■

Ladu view: Fields and community-managed forests in northwestern Yunnan. PC: J. A. Zinda.

Managing the Anthropocene

The Labour of Environmental Regeneration

John Aloysius ZINDA

Since 2010, China has seen new carbon markets, closures of polluting factories, and expanded efforts to regenerate degraded landscapes and protect wildlife in intact ecosystems. All of this entails a great deal of labour. Yet when reporters or researchers discuss China's environmental management efforts, they may chronicle policies, regulatory actions, infrastructures, carbon figures, or impacts on humans and animals, but they seldom say much about the labour of environmental protection or the people who perform it. This is because scholars and journalists alike tend to place environment and labour in separate boxes.

Undoing environmental calamity takes a lot of work. For decades, the Chinese Communist Party (CCP) and its agents in the Chinese state have been grappling with the material consequences of socialist extractivism followed by state capitalist economic expansion. Lurching growth machines disgorged catastrophic floods, smog blankets, depleting aquifers, poisoned soils, dead rivers, cancer villages, eroded slopes, creeping deserts, and silent forests. Even as top leaders stressed that they must 'develop first, clean up later' (Hilton 2013), by the late 1990s Chinese state authorities were investing large sums in planting trees on denuded slopes. The next decade saw effectual restrictions on major pollutants and expanding biodiversity conservation efforts. Since 2010, China has seen new carbon markets, closures of polluting factories, and expanded efforts to regenerate degraded landscapes and protect wildlife in intact ecosystems.

All of these efforts entail a great deal of labour. To implement pollution controls, someone needs to perform inspections and analyse monitoring data. Constructing canals and other infrastructure takes millions of worker-hours. Planting trees means moving seedlings, digging holes, and tending plantations. Wildlife conservation requires watching animals, plants, and people, and associated tourism operations employ guides, drivers, shopkeepers, and custodians. Yet when reporters or researchers discuss China's environmental management efforts, they may chronicle policies, regulatory actions, infrastructures, carbon figures, or impacts on humans and animals, but seldom say much about the labour of environmental protection or the people who perform it.

That environmental labour garners little attention is no surprise. Scholars and journalists alike tend to place environment and labour in separate boxes. Distinctions between nature and humanity may not be as stark in Chinese culture as in the West. Still, in China as elsewhere, in conversations about environmental management, people tend to be absent or appear as either incorrigible destroyers or nature's saviours. Given that many think of environmental regeneration as a matter of getting people out of the way so that nature can recover, it is hard to expect much attention to the people who do the labour of environmental regeneration. This state of affairs makes it all the more important to highlight these people's experiences.

Environmental labour is especially salient in the Chinese state's efforts to manage landscapes. These projects almost invariably summon the residents of rural communities in those landscapes to patrol, manage, or restore ecosystems. Much of this work happens in formally protected spaces. In this essay, I will use the terms 'parks' and 'protected areas' interchangeably to refer to a broad array of units, from national nature reserves to wetland preserves to local forest parks, that have rules intended to constrain human activity in the interest of conserving or preserving objects of environmental, cultural, and historical importance. Still, a great deal of environmental labour also takes place outside of protected areas, in lands and waters that belong to rural collectives. In the following pages, I show how environmental labour plays out in efforts to protect intact ecosystems, to restore environments judged degraded, and to remove people and their labour from restricted lands.

Labour of Protection

We scurried through the brush. The two young women trailed quick, wiry Feng, who scampered between tree trunks and bamboo culms. We had been hiking all day, checking research transects for signs of the giant panda that trudge the ridges. Clad in green camouflage gear, Feng guided us with cheer and courtesy.

'Quick, come over here!' Feng called out. The rest of us clambered up. Feng held back a few bamboo fronds and pointed down to three balls of green fibrous muck. 'Panda scat!' The women scribbled in their notebooks. Nearby, Feng pointed to several truncated stalks likely chomped by the same animal.

Wanglang National Nature Reserve had hired Feng after a stint in the military. He and his cohorts, most of them ex-soldiers, do much of the reserve's day-to-day work. They walk transects, monitoring signs of pandas and other wildlife as well as watching for poachers and people grazing cattle in the park. They keep track of the infrared-triggered cameras that take pictures when animals' body heat sets them off. Much of their time goes to assisting researchers like the two doctoral students from Beijing—leading them through the woods, helping with their observations, and tending to their instruments.

This work is physically demanding, but government pay is steady, and room and board are covered. It also equips men from rural areas without much schooling with technical skills. They work scientific instruments and log data on computers. Back in the nature reserve office, professional analysts process and analyse the data.

In other parks, alongside full-time staff, people living nearby perform conservation labour. Baima Snow Mountain National Nature Reserve in Yunnan hires residents of villages within the reserve to patrol for poaching, illegal timber harvest, and fire control. These residents, usually men, must walk set routes, filling in checklists to return to park management offices. This means days of walking through forest and meadow. For locals, that burden may not be especially onerous. Depending on the season, villagers can work patrolling in with gathering mushrooms or medicinal plants, or start from pastures where they graze yaks and cattle in the summer. Why hire locals? First and foremost, they know the land. Locals need little guidance to find their way along patrol routes. They know where poachers or timber harvesters are likely to go. This familiarity can cut both ways. Working for the reserve can mean regulating their kin and neighbours, in which case patrollers' loyalty may not be with the reserve. Another reason for employing locals is that, with little education and with housing and agricultural livelihoods in the village, they may not demand high wages compared to personnel hired from outside.

Parks with tourism operations employ local residents in many more ways. They run shops and guesthouses, drive buses, sell tickets, and do custodial work. As with patrolling, residents present a convenient and low-cost labour pool. But they also raise challenges. Tourism operations often make use of land residents farm, graze, and harvest. That can mean limiting these uses. Moreover, seeing parks and outside entrepreneurs make large sums using land that had belonged to their village collectives, residents often demand a cut. Protests and drawn-out negotiations are common. Villagers in Pudacuo National Park in Yunnan secured annual payments from the Park, guaranteed employment, and investment in village infrastructure. That guaranteed employment usually means a household member being hired to gather trash and clean out toilets. Residents receive preference for other jobs but usually lack qualifications for higher-paying jobs as tour guides, which go to people from other localities who have vocational training. While not directly related to conservation, tourism labour underpins these parks' management by making possible the activity that managers really care about: revenue-generating tourism. Managers also argue that tourism contributes to conservation by giving residents 'alternative livelihoods'. The idea is that with income from tourism, residents will no longer rely on grazing livestock or harvesting forest products. However, if a household has time and people available for the work, its members often prefer to continue using forests and meadows, treating tourism income as a supplement (Zinda et al. 2014). Where tourism does displace resource use, it is more common that by imposing restrictions on farming and livestock husbandry, park management forces residents into tourism alternatives.

The labour of environmental protection is not limited to formal protected areas. Across China, 60 percent of forestland belongs to rural collectives, usually villager committees. A substantial proportion of these forests are designated 'public benefit forests', managed to maintain ecological functions like erosion control and habitat provision. In much of the country, members of rural communities are charged with this work. Administrative villages employ forest guards (*hulinyuan*) who oversee forest stewards (*senlin guanhuyuan*) recruited from hamlets within each village.

In northwestern Yunnan province, forest stewards and forest guards are assigned to prevent forest fires, control illegal harvest of timber and other forest products, and assemble their neighbours to implement forest conservation projects. Specific duties and arrangements vary across locales.

Forest stewards and forest guards with whom I have spoken report that patrolling forests takes most of their time. Forest stewards have to walk the forests under their charge once or twice a week, more in the dry autumn and winter, when fire risk is greater. Depending on the size of a community's forests, that could take a few hours or a full day. Once a month, an administrative village's forest guard leads all the village's forest stewards upslope to patrol state forests abutting village lands. They often spend several days and nights in the woods.

While patrolling takes up time, enforcement is the harder part of the job. When harvest season arrives, forest guards have to keep watch for people burning chaff, a common practice that breaks down plant matter and releases nutrients into the soil. At every hint of smoke, one has to rush out, put out the fire, and reprimand the person who set it. One forest guard speaks of having to disrupt funeral rituals: 'It's happened three times this year. After someone dies, they take their old clothes up the mountain and burn them. When that happens, if I discover it, I call them up right away—please, can you understand, this could cause a forest fire, at least don't do it by the forest.'

Whether the issue is fire, cutting down protected trees, or digging up the forest floor to gather mushrooms, forest guards and stewards are supposed to confront the perpetrator. Minor infractions bring only a warning, but serious ones must be reported to the township forestry office, which may impose a fine or other penalty. Enforcement actions can stir up tension—especially if stewards impose them preferentially. They can also cause trouble for people who use forests because they depend on them. Often, rules for forest use imposed from above conflict with customary practices and present needs. Strict limits on harvesting live pine trees for firewood can mean long forays into the forest. Forest guards and stewards can find themselves caught between official duties and relationships with kin and neighbours.

Forest stewards are compensated from funds given to communities as 'ecological benefit compensation' (*shengtai xiaoyi buchang*) for maintaining forests for the public good. Because these payments are based on forest area, stewards in villages with large forests, and thus more area to patrol, are paid more. Given the amount of time they spend patrolling, this remuneration is less than a day's pay for wage labour in nearby towns. This and the hassles of meetings and enforcement make many reluctant to serve as forest stewards. There is a lot of turnover. Forest guards are paid more—around 2,000 yuan a month—and tend to keep their positions for a decade or longer.

Labour of Restoration

Environmental labour goes beyond holding off poachers and fires on intact wildlands. Rural dwellers are at the front lines of the CCP's efforts to restore degraded environments. This is nowhere clearer than in the thousands of villages whose residents have been enlisted to plant trees in endeavours like the Returning Farmland to Forest Programme (RFFP, also known as the Sloping Land Conversion Programme and Grain for Green Programme) and the Three-Norths Shelter Forest Programme. In the RFFP, state authorities called on some 30 million households to retire erosion-prone farmland and plant trees there in exchange for annual payments. The programme's primary goal was to reduce the amount of soil washed into riverbeds, where it could build up and worsen floods or deposit behind dams. In the process, state agents aimed to restore forest habitats, sequester carbon, alleviate poverty, and transform agriculture.

Government reports and large-scale studies suggest that the RFFP and related programmes have brought modest net increases in tree cover and income. However, when researchers examine implementation on the ground, they often find situations contrary to official reports: failed plantations, forests that are actually fruit orchards, and uneven delivery of payments (Zinda et al. 2017). The RFFP has increased tree cover and assisted poor farmers in many places, but more is going on than official accounts disclose.

Firsthand observers also reveal the considerable labour that tree-planting has required. In Yunnan, people would have to pick up seedlings at a delivery point, then haul them up to the village on horseback. There followed several days of digging holes, placing seedlings, and shovelling on dirt and fertiliser. In the years that followed, smallholders were responsible for making sure these seedlings flourished by fertilising, pruning, and managing pests.

It was an uphill battle. Tree varieties poorly suited to the area languished. As one farmer recounted: 'At first where the walnuts were doing poorly, the government distributed seedlings for replanting. But there weren't enough, so we had to go into the forest and find them. It would take two days to gather up seedlings in the forest, then another two to plant them. We had to do this every year for three or four years.' Year after year, people tracked into the woods to gather new seedlings and plant again. Beyond the RFFP, people who dwell in landscapes targeted for rehabilitation do much of the work of implementing efforts to control desertification, restore wetlands, revive wildlife populations, and reverse rangeland degradation.

Labour Removal

It takes a lot of labour to restore landscapes, but many restoration projects also remove labour. State authorities urge or order people, along with their crops and livestock, to be removed from a landscape. This can take place through bans on resource use in particular areas while people remain in place or through wholesale resettlement. While grazers, gatherers, and smallholders do not always use resources in benign ways, in many cases they manage landscapes to ensure that plants and animals they use stay abundant, enriching biological communities. The removal of this labour transforms these landscapes, and not always beneficially. In the name of grassland restoration, tens of thousands of nomadic herders have been resettled. This has been done in spite of evidence that mobile grazing often does not degrade rangelands, and can enhance them (Cao et al. 2013)—in part because settlement makes these groups of people more easily subject to surveillance (Yeh 2005).

Protected areas, set up to limit human activity, are commonly sites of labour removal. Officially, most nature reserves have core and buffer zones where productive activities are not allowed—but across China, thousands of villages are located within these zones. Protected area managers facing hundreds or thousands of residents in their jurisdictions take varied approaches. In the Jiuzhaigou National Scenic Area in Sichuan, authorities banned grazing and farming. Not only did this make residents dependent on tourism, but it changed ecosystems. Absent yaks and herders, meadows once rich in grasses, forbs, and shrubs turned into uniform stretches of pine (Urgenson et al. 2014). Managers at Pudacuo National Park let residents continue farming and grazing, incorporating their agricultural labour into the tourism attraction. Tour buses pause to let visitors view herders on the high pasture, and a hotel near Lawzong village releases tourists to observe smallholders at work in their fields. Still, residents are not always allowed to stay. State authorities recently announced that between 70,000 and 80,000 people would be resettled from a reserve for tigers and snow leopards in northeastern China (Standaert 2017). In a broader wave of 'ecological migration', government agencies are uprooting entire villages in poor and remote areas to resettle residents in urbanised settings. In addition to their impacts on the people concerned, these removals of labour—as well as the knowledge people have acquired through dwelling in these places—have profound and varied impacts on biological communities.

Working for Ecological Civilisation

Environmental regeneration is labour-intensive. People do it through work in offices, fields, and forests. Analysts following expenditures, policy impacts, and vegetation measures often overlook these activities that accomplish environmental intervention on the ground.

Given the importance of this work, we need to ask, what are the conditions of environmental labour? In some cases, like tourism in protected areas, environmental workers are wage labourers working for corporations. Their working conditions and concerns present analogies with wage work elsewhere. Yet, far from the factory floors that dominate most labour scholarship, the kinds of domination and contestation that take place in tourism attractions are little known.

But much of the labour of protection and restoration is not wage work. People who patrol protected areas and village forests receive payments that are often effectively lower than wage employment. Compensation for reforestation and landscape management targets environmental impacts more than the work itself. Working conditions are difficult to gauge, too, as environmental labour intertwines with other livelihood activities in landscapes. As people are increasingly compelled to manage environments for the state's environmental mandates, and to do so in a transactional way, alienation from the landscapes within which they dwell is likely to follow.

Recognising environmental labour is all the more important as the CCP unrolls its proposal to create an 'ecological civilisation' (*shengtai wenming*). With this policy rubric, Party leaders recognise that managing China's economy and society for growth only cannot continue. From forest cover to air pollution to energy to hydrology, state authorities are implementing projects that use regulations alongside market instruments to promote durable ways of using resources. They also propose inculcating citizens with an 'ecological culture' (*shengtai wenhua*) centred on thrift and care for nature (Geall 2015).

Discussions of ecological civilisation move beyond a picture of the world that pits humans against nature to a recognition that the social and the biophysical are always intertwined—a sensibility that may resonate with people who speak of 'socionatures' or the 'anthropocene' epoch. Rather than embrace humility, as some participants in these discussions have urged, Chinese authorities have seized the anthropocene, declaring that nature must and will be managed by technocrats. In visions of ecological civilisation, from now on China's natures will be defined, built, and maintained by humans, in the vision of the CCP. This is no longer a matter of conquering nature, but of establishing flexible mechanisms of monitoring and response around complex and unpredictable social and environmental processes. Technocratic monitoring, maintenance, and intervention will require more environmental labour. Who does this labour and how will have lasting repercussions for the people and the landscapes involved. ■

'Different Dusk,'
PC: Mingjia Zhou.

Beyond Proletarianisation

The Everyday Politics of Chinese Migrant Labour

Thomas Sætre JAKOBSEN

In China as elsewhere, labour studies typically focus on visibility, organisation, and collective endeavours taken on by workers and their organisations to improve the collective situation of the labouring class as a whole. The privileged site remains focussed on urban areas in general, and on manufacturing work in particular. In this essay, Thomas Jakobsen argues that this view is reductive, in that it only takes migrant labourers seriously as political actors once they enter the urban workplace. This risks neglecting the reality of hundreds of millions of workers who live between the farmlands and the city.

In the aftermath of the Global Financial Crisis of 2008, labour scholars focussing on China have started questioning the modernist narrative of the movement of peasants from farm to factory. The migrant condition in contemporary China has been reconceptualised as a form of politics of disillusionment, replacing 'the old promise of formal or continuous employment' (Smith and Pun 2018, 44), and with precarious employment being characterised as the 'new normal' for Chinese workers (Lee 2016). This urges us to reflect upon the opportunities for alternative political visions for Chinese rural migrant workers. Familiar narratives concerning labour politics typically focus on visibility, organisation, and collective endeavours taken on by workers and their 'political arms', such as labour unions or political parties, to improve the collective situation of the labouring class as a whole. The privileged site for these overt manifestations of labour movement politics remains focussed on urban areas in general, and on manufacturing work in particular. This is probably the reason why rural migrant workers toiling in the workshops of foreign subsidiaries in the industrial Sunbelt of southeast China have taken such a prominent position in academic and popular discourse on China's working class (Chang 2009; Pun 2005).

Yet, little evidence of a self-assertive labour movement at a higher level than the single workplace exists in contemporary China (Lee 2016). If the political imaginaries attached to the path of proletarianisation give rise to the political aim of mobilising around the imagery of the 'proper job', then scholars and activists need to raise the question of what emergent political imaginaries arise from the 'new normal' of precarious work. In this essay, I first argue for the need to look beyond proletarianisation as a prism for understanding the politics of labour migrants from the countryside to urban China. Building from this, I then suggest that everyday practices of mobile precarious labour provide a fruitful point of departure for sketching emergent political imaginaries. Finally, based on fieldwork in Yunnan province, I focus on a young generation of smallholders to highlight how autonomy *from* wage work becomes central to the formation of their aspirations.

Beyond the Inherited Class Maps

'Old' ideas (Ferguson 1999; Rigg 2012) about the transition towards capitalism linger as an often-unspoken background element in the debates among labour scholars over the scope for labour mobilisation and the development of a working-class consciousness among Chinese migrant workers (e.g. Frenkel and Yu 2015; Pun and Lu 2010; Solinger 2012). That is, both in the literature on Chinese migrant workers and in the international literature on smallholders who move from farm to city, there is a tendency to perceive short-term work arrangements and precarious labour as a temporary phenomenon. Informal work used to be perceived as probationary, something to be overcome on the inevitable path towards proletarianisation, industrialisation, and urbanisation (Breman 2013; Huang 2011). Peasants typically enter the mainstream of labour studies only as they become 'true' workers, proletarians, motivated to improve their lot through collective action in the workplace (McMichael 2008). What is problematic about this way of perceiving labour mobilisation and working-class consciousness is that it only takes migrant labourers seriously as political actors once they enter the urban workplace. This risks neglecting the reality of hundreds of millions of workers who live between the farmlands in the countryside and the workplaces of the city (Day and Schneider 2017). Significantly, China's household registration system (*hukou*) contributes to these arrangements, as most of the workers who enter Chinese cities from the vast rural hinterlands are unable to get a permanent residency in the city.

However, the 'new normal' regime of precarious work suggests that simply removing the barriers to permanent urban citizenship will not spontaneously produce an urban working class. While there is no conclusive research on how the Global Financial Crisis affected the labour mobility of smallholders, data suggests that the 'new normal' regime of precarious work also affects workers' aspirations. This is seen as rural migrants now travel shorter distances for work than they did a decade ago (Loyalka 2012). Significantly, many—if not most—rural migrant workers who became unemployed in the aftermath of the Global Financial Crisis returned to their smallholdings (Chan 2010). While this was a temporary arrangement, it threw into stark relief the continued importance of the smallholding for the reproduction of labour in

China (Jakobsen 2018). This highlights the fact that, for the foreseeable future, the Chinese peasant working class will continue to be produced *between* farms and urban workplaces.

Everyday Politics

Where does this leave us in terms of conceptualising the politics of labour? The intervention of Partha Chatterjee (2006, 40) provides a particularly important contribution here, as he advances the idea of a 'political society' that he distinguishes from 'civil society' or the politics of right-bearing. Considering that political society involves claims to habitation and livelihood by 'groups of population whose very livelihood or habitation involve violation of the law', Chatterjee argues that the politics of a migratory peasant labour force are 'political in a way different from that of the elite' (2006, 39). This is suggestive, as it opens up space for conceiving politics as a broader category of action than overt forms of mobilisation. Rather, the 'covert, informal and often individual acts ... attempted to maintain or better their position' (Walker 2009, 295) are brought into purview. These practices are political, in the sense that they are engaged in by workers similarly situated as a precarious mobile workforce who deliberately struggle to bring about a different kind of everyday life (Das and Randeria 2015).

This notion of everyday politics is instructive for two reasons. First, it expands the scope of class struggle beyond the industrial proletariat and thus does not see the urban workplace as the only site of class formation. Second, it breaks with the tendency to only recognise the struggles of workers as a form of politics during overt forms of collective action, such as strikes or demonstrations. Moving beyond proletarianisation means broadening our repertoires of interpretation in order to articulate the not-yet-articulated political imaginaries found in the street and in the fields.

Thus, the practices, aspirations, and livelihood arrangements of migrants become important, as they provide the seeds for alternative political imaginaries under the 'new normal' of precarious work. And while wage work might have become the most important source of livelihood for many—if not most—Chinese peasants, from a household and individual perspective, land, labour, and social benefits still make up a patchwork of livelihood resources allowing for the everyday and intergenerational social reproduction of the household to take place. From this point of view, a multiplicity of unfinished or unarticulated labour politics is highlighted, where minor acts of defiance, avoidance, friendship, as well as a multiplicity of livelihoods, emerge as political projects where autonomy *from* wage work is but one possible trajectory.

Mobile Lives and Multiple Livelihoods

In the countryside adjacent to Kunming where I undertook fieldwork for this essay, families rely on a mixture of subsistence production and cash crop cultivation. In the villages of Kaoyan and Baicai—which I named after the localities' main cash crops, tobacco and Chinese cabbage respectively—emigrating for work was very uncommon before the mid-1980s, and even in the early 1990s only a few unmarried men left the villages to work. These pioneers typically graduated from primary school, worked a few years on their parents' plots, and when the time for marriage was approaching or other siblings started working the land, they left for Kunming to look for employment. Kunming is conveniently positioned about two hours away by car making it possible for migrants to work seasonally. When these men later married, they typically settled down on the farm and lived the whole year in the village, waiting until their offspring grew up to resume their seasonal migrations to the city. In the early 1990s, some unmarried women also started leaving for work.

Looking at today's younger generation—roughly those between 16 and 30 years old—a very different life trajectory emerges. These youths usually spend three more years in school than their parents, before either completing or abandoning middle school to start working outside the village. Once they start middle school, few of them return to work on their parents' farm, as they live at the school during weekdays and only return home during the weekends. When they start working, few of them adopt the seasonal mobility patterns of the previous generation. Rather, they remain in Kunming or other cities the whole year, unless there is some special occasion to go back home. However, in spite of their prolonged absence from the countryside, they still remain very much dependent upon their villages for long-term material support. When they became sick, exhausted, or unemployed, they return to Baicai or Kaoyan to recuperate and reduce their dependence on commodity markets, as they can survive through home-grown food and rearing livestock. Moreover, when they get married they typically return to their village to raise children for a few years, before once more leaving to work in the city.

Against the background of these shifting mobility patterns, there is the gradual emergence of capitalist relations in the villages. First, in the 1980s villagers saw increasing costs for farm inputs, as these were 'liberated' by allowing them to operate based on the price mechanisms of supply and demand. Second, in the 1990s, heavy taxation pushed smallholder farming to its limits, a situation that lasted until 2006, when the Chinese Communist Party (CCP) phased out these taxes in the aftermath of widespread protests. More recently, since 2008 the CCP has been promoting policies for a 'new-style agriculture' (*xinxing nongye jingying tixi*). This signalled a shift away from food security being achieved through initiatives aimed at making peasants stay on the land to produce grains, towards a modernisation of agriculture through scaled-up and input-intensive farming. These policies are part of a larger focus on urban-rural integration (*chengxiang yitihua*), which emphasises investment into the human capital of the countryside in order to transform the rural populace into 'proper' urban subjects and provide increased opportunities to compete in urban marketplaces.

Urban-rural integration is manifested through initiatives aimed at bolstering education, initiating a rural medical insurance system, and direct cash transfers to end users, such as pensioners, disabled people, or poverty-stricken families. As a result of these agricultural and human capital policies, guided by the imperative of letting the market set the 'correct' prices in rural areas, labour and land are becoming increasingly commodified. However, land is not abandoned, and family members who have emigrated still regularly return to their homes during transition periods or times of crisis. More recently, government cash transfers for poverty alleviation have fed into the mixed strategies employed by rural households to support themselves and their next generations. This multiplicity of livelihood strategies, combining wage work with smallholder farming and government transfers, provides families with some autonomy from the ups and downs of the labour market, especially if compared to communities where farmland has been expropriated (Chuang 2015).

Aspirations

The youth born and raised in the countryside that I spoke to during my fieldwork, voiced their feelings of indeterminacy regarding their future in terms of work and citizenship. Although they were not optimistic about the prospects of returning to their farms as a means of earning a livelihood, they nevertheless chose to retreat to their hometowns whenever they got sick, exhausted, or went through life-course transitions such as marriage or parenthood. These youths generally hesitated when confronted with questions over how they perceived their future homes and workplaces, thus revealing their ambiguous positions. As unofficial workers, non-urban subjects, and with diminishing opportunities of returning to the farm in order to live a satisfying life, their aspirations were short-circuited towards focussing on improving the present.

Part of their hesitation also stemmed from their difficulty in perceiving a future either as an urban working subject or a returned farmer. Unlike the army of *nongmingong*—a category applied to rural migrant workers in post-Mao China's industrial heartland—the peasant workers whom I interviewed in Yunnan lacked any official category to facilitate their self-identification. This ambiguity in terms of self-perceived identity was evident in the story of Mrs Li, aged 22, whom I met in one urban village in Kunming. The village was inhabited mainly by rural migrant workers, and had some public buildings, including schools, a police station, and a post office. Mrs Li explained how, after five years of shifting between petty-capitalist workplaces characterised by low wages and intrusive management, she had doubts as to whether wage work would provide her with a satisfying life. She nonetheless felt that returning to the farm without other sources of income was not an option. She foresaw a future where she would return to the farm at some point, but in order to do that she felt the need to work hard in order to save up for the tough times to come. The pragmatic realism conveyed by this kind of testimony reflects an awareness among rural youth that there is no way to get ahead in the urban workplace, accompanied by an acknowledgment that smallholder farming has gradually been emptied of its symbolic and material value.

In terms of domination and resistance, their bosses usually controlled the workplace with a strict hand, illegally forcing the workers to pay a deposit that would only be reimbursed if the employee does not leave their job for an entire year. Moreover, many had experiences of being scolded for minor mistakes in workplaces where workers seldom received proper training, were commanded to work outside of ordinary hours, and were frequently not paid on time. This situation fuelled resentment and sparked a yearning among these young workers for a livelihood not tied to a 'proper' job. The younger generation of interviewees typically constructed a sharp distinction in terms of levels of freedom between working for the boss (*da gong*) and working on the farm. They often explained how in their hometown 'there are fewer restrictions and more freedom' and that 'people control you when you work outside, but when you are at home, you are at your own command.' Nonetheless, they distanced themselves from popular ideas about the 'rural idyll' through elaborate stories of the drudgery and physical toil of tilling their parents' plots.

This younger generation furthered its interests through individual acts of defiance, such as rejecting the commands of their bosses when these felt like a violation of their sense of fairness. There were also some tactics of avoidance, such as returning to the farm when their bosses make unreasonable demands on them. However, the most important tactic the interviewees employed was to 'vote with their feet' (*yi jiao toupiao*), by changing workplace frequently. While from a managerial point of view this is considered to be a problem of high turnover, I would argue that this kind of mobility needs to be understood as part of the repertoire of political acts of resistance for the younger generation of workers. This generation entered the urban labour market under difficult circumstances: on the one hand, with declining prospects for staying on the farm; on the other, against the backdrop of the 'new normal' of precarious work that individualises and pit workers against each other in a highly competitive environment.

In sum, the interviewees did not become subdued by the requirements of their work or ephemeral consumption desires. Nor did they retain a sense of nostalgia for smallholder farming. Rather, they demonstrated a desire for more freedom from the relations of work by claiming forms of subsistence autonomy within a space of limited possibilities. This points to how the formation of expectations, while being informed by the experiences of yesterday and the constraints of the present, might involve limited openings for envisioning other possible futures.

Broadening the Horizon

In conclusion, the notion of working-class politics in contemporary China often tends to focus exclusively on its most visible manifestations, such as the appearance of strikes or riots in urban contexts. This rather constrained view of labour politics often leads to the assumption that we are witnessing a transition of Chinese peasant workers towards proletarianisation and increasing working-class consciousness. However, relying only on these narratives to interpret the current geography and history of class-making in China potentially distorts our understanding of its present trajectory. That is, by laying claim to what is possible in the future based on historical experiences—typically modelled on Western history—we risk losing sight of the emergent projects, aspirations, and common experiences that constitute the potential building blocks for different types of solidarity and resistance among rural migrant workers in China. ■

Picking Tea at Gingko Village, 2016. Photo by the author.

Inside Work

The Hidden Exploitation of Rural Women in Modern China

Tamara JACKA

Conventional wisdom holds that China's modern development has been powered by urban industry and commerce. The agrarian family economy, combining home handcraft production and domestic work with small-scale agriculture, is commonly seen as a remnant of the past. In this essay, Tamara Jacka proposes a different understanding of the development trajectory of modern China as being underpinned and enabled by exploitation in the agrarian family economy, especially of rural women.

Men rule outside, women rule inside
(nan zhu wai, nü zhu nei)
Ancient Chinese saying

In conventional wisdom, China's modern development has been powered by urban industry and commerce. The agrarian family economy, combining home handicraft production and domestic work with small-scale agriculture, is commonly seen as a remnant of the past; a separate sphere that lags behind and is dependent on the modern economy, dragging it down rather than contributing to it.

In this essay, I propose a different understanding of modern development in China as being underpinned and enabled by exploitation in the agrarian family economy. My focus is the exploitation of rural women, working in what is understood in China as the 'inside' sphere. I use the word 'exploitation' here in the Marxist sense, to refer to the unpaid appropriation of labour power, achieved by not compensating workers for the full value of the goods they produce (Zwolinski 2017). I focus on the exploitation of rural women through 'inside work' because I believe it to be unjust, and because it provides the necessary foundations for other forms of unjust exploitation. Yet it has received little attention from scholars and activists.

One might think that inside work is the same as what, in the industrialised West, is understood as a private sphere of unpaid domestic or reproductive work, in contrast to a public sphere of paid production. And indeed, when the Chinese Communist Party (CCP) assumed power in 1949, it introduced to rural China an ideological gender division of labour very similar to that of the modern West. But before that, the Chinese outside/inside division meant something quite different from the Western public/private division. A growing convergence between the two has been one of the main mechanisms through which the state and capitalists in China have exploited rural women undertaking inside work. A mapping of modern Western conceptions of activities in the private sphere as unproductive and insignificant onto Chinese conceptions of inside work has been particularly important in this regard.

In the rest of this essay, I sketch out the transformations between the late nineteenth and early twenty-first centuries through which this ideological convergence has occurred, and discuss how it has enabled the state and capitalist exploitation of women in inland, rural China. To illustrate key trends, I draw on ethnographic fieldwork in Gingko village, an agrarian community of 1,750 people, located in the foothills of the Dabie mountain range in southeastern Henan province. Work patterns in Gingko village are typical of relatively poor, Han villages in central China (for details, see Jacka 2017).

Late Nineteenth Century to Late Twentieth Century

In Europe, modernisation involved a shift from an agrarian family economy to an urban industrial economy, within which emerged an ideological split between families' place of residence—the 'private sphere' of unpaid reproduction and consumption—and industrial workers' place of work—the 'public sphere' of paid production. But early Chinese modernisation was different. It involved considerable commercialisation within the framework of the agrarian peasant family economy and much less industrialisation.

In imperial China, the state-promoted gender division of labour between outside and inside coincided closely with another ideological gender division between farming and textile production, as expressed in the saying 'men plough, women weave' (*nan geng, nü zhi*). Officials equated feminine inside work primarily with textile production, especially spinning and weaving. Women's inside textile production and men's outside agricultural work were equally valued as fundamental to an economic and political order centred on family self-sufficiency. Both cloth and grain supported subsistence and tax payments, as well as being sold (Bray 2013, 93–120). Equal valuation of women's and men's work did not, however, translate into gender equality in the family. In fact, commercialisation in the late imperial period coincided with an increasingly hierarchical neo-Confucian gender ideology, increased stress on women's seclusion in the inside sphere, and the maintenance of male family heads' control over the products of women's labour (Gates 1989; Bray 1997, 252–72).

In the late nineteenth and early twentieth centuries, a perception grew among the political elite that women's home-based textile production was dying out. They believed, as did foreign observers, that such production was collapsing in the face of competition from imported cloth and China's newly emerging cotton mills. As recent studies have shown, though, machine-made yarn did not entirely replace home spinning. Furthermore, while the demand for homespun relative to factory-produced cloth declined, the absolute demand increased as a result of population growth and rising urban living standards (Eyferth 2012, 374). In 1934–36, 24 percent of rural Chinese households were engaged in spinning and weaving. In the central provinces where cotton was grown, home-based weaving was even more common: across Henan, roughly 60 percent of all rural households wove cotton cloth (Peng Zeyi 1957, cited in Eyferth 2012, 374).

That elite perceptions were at odds with this picture may have been due to regional variations, as well as the invisibility of village women working inside their homes. The vision of reformers may also have been clouded by a desire for modernity and a belief, derived from European modernising processes and ideology, that modernisation entailed industrialisation and the demise of village handcrafts.

Reformers appear also to have taken on the Western perception of the private sphere as being one solely of consumption and reproduction. Liang Qichao, for example, complained: 'Out of two hundred million women, every one is a consumer, not one is a producer. Because they cannot support themselves but depend on others for their support, men keep them like dogs and horses' (Liang Qichao 1898, cited in Eyferth 2017, 371). As Jacob Eyferth has pointed out, this statement is extraordinary in the context of late imperial China, as it was underpinned by ideas about gender and work that were very new. It is understandable only if we assume that Liang was imposing a Western ideological model of a modern economy, split between 'producers' in industry and 'consumers' (and 'reproducers') in the home. Yet at the time, China's industrial sector was tiny, the vast majority of the population belonging to an agrarian family economy in which women as well as men were both consumers *and* producers (Eyferth 2012, 371–72). It was not until the mid-twentieth century that significant industrialisation occurred, and a Western-style public/private split emerged.

With collectivisation in rural China in the 1950s, a division between public production and private reproduction was institutionalised through a divide between paid production for the collective, and a private sphere of unpaid work. A key element of collectivisation was the mobilisation of women into public, collective labour. In Gingko village, as elsewhere in the 1960s and 1970s, able-bodied women all worked full-time in collective production. But they were not recognised as full workers; they most commonly received 60 to 80 percent of a man's payment. This exploitation of women in 'public', 'outside' collective labour—crucial to the state's appropriation of rural resources for the ultimate goal of rapid industrialisation—was compounded by a yet greater exploitation of women in private, inside labour.

Through the Maoist period (1949–78), some attempt was made to alleviate women's burden of domestic duties by running collective dining halls, but these generally only lasted for a few years during the Great Leap Forward (1958–62). The state also discouraged home-based spinning and weaving by providing coupons for the purchase of factory-made cloth, the aim being to maximise state appropriation of both raw cotton and women's labour in collective production, and prevent their diversion to village families. But the coupons were insufficient for families' needs, so women continued to spin and weave their own cloth (Eyferth 2012, 387–89).

Aside from this, the state paid almost no attention to women's work in the inside sphere: it was as if it did not exist. And yet, rural families could not have survived, and the labour power necessary for collective production could not have been reproduced, were it not for the work of women caring for children and others, cleaning, producing food, and making clothes, bedding, and shoes. During this period, women toiled for almost as many, and in some cases more, hours in such inside family duties as in collective production.

I stress that women's supposedly 'unproductive' inside duties continued to involve textile production, including spinning and weaving, and the sewing of clothes, shoes, and bedding, as well as domestic work. Almost all women in Gingko village born before the 1960s spun and wove right through the collective period and, indeed, well into the post-Mao period. Even in the mid-2010s, elderly Gingko village women showed me cloth and cloth shoes they had made, and the dismantled parts of wooden spinning wheels and looms, stashed away with other junk less than a decade previously.

Most Gingko village women born after the mid-1960s did not spin or weave. Nor did they sew clothes. Some of their mothers sewed clothes by hand, but this generation mostly had clothes made by one of just a handful of local women who owned a sewing machine. However, through the Maoist period and into the post-Mao years, women of all ages sat with needle and thread each night, long after other family members had gone to bed, patching clothes and sewing cloth shoes and bedding (see also Hershatter 2011, 193–95).

It could be argued that the Maoist state's failure to more fully liberate women from their inside work limited its ability to exploit women in collective production. Perhaps if women had not lost so much sleep caring for and clothing their families, they might have had longer lives and more strength for collective work. But the state did not see women's inside work as either a contribution or a cost—it did not see it as 'work' or 'labour' at all (Hershatter 2011, 186). 'Unpaid and invisible as it was, women's textile [and domestic] work underpinned socialist accumulation, as much as it underpinned the reproduction of village life' (Eyferth 2012, 391).

1980s to 2010s

With decollectivisation and marketisation in the 1980s, rural women gradually stopped making their families' clothes, shoes, and bedding, and bought them instead. But married women still devoted much time to domestic work, including care-work, as well as agriculture. They were supported in this by a post-Mao regime, which repudiated key features of Maoist development strategy and ideology, including its efforts to recruit women into the public sphere. Henceforth, a 'natural' gender order, restoring women to the inside sphere, was promoted (Jacka 1997, 88–89).

As before, the characterisation of inside work as 'unproductive'—as domestic duties, rather than real work—enabled the gross exploitation of the women responsible for such work. But the ideological emphasis shifted: whereas previously it was pretended that inside work did not exist, in the post-Mao period married women were enjoined to be good mothers. With the one-child policy, being a good mother meant having fewer children, but there was also an emphasis on the need for mothers to nurture 'quality' children, with 'scientific' child-rearing and education (Greenhalgh and Winckler 2005, 237–44).

In the countryside between the 1980s and 2000s, responsibility for inside 'mothering' work was increasingly taken by grandmothers. Farming, too, was taken over by middle-aged and elderly women and men. Interestingly, agriculture increasingly came to be perceived not as outside production, but as inside reproduction. These trends were associated with the emergence of large-scale outmigration of villagers seeking waged work in domestic and transnational capitalist enterprises in urban and coastal China's construction, industrial, and service sectors.

In its initial phase, rural outmigration was undertaken primarily by young men. But across inland China by the late 1990s, most adults of both sexes under the age of 50 worked as wage labourers away from home for most of the year. The majority went out alone, leaving behind wives, mothers, and grandparents. The latter group could generally earn less money in the city than younger workers, so for many it seemed more rational to stay in the village to tend the fields and care for family dependants (Jacka 2017).

In Gingko village in the 1990s and 2000s, women generally migrated in their late teens and then returned to the village to get married and have a child (or two). When the child was just a few months old, he or she was handed to a grandmother, so the mother could continue to earn a wage as a migrant worker. Consequently, women in their sixties and seventies, who had previously raised three to six children but expected an easier life in their old age, now found themselves instead responsible for multiple grandchildren. There was also a sizable number of Gingko village women aged between 30 and 60 who effectively subsidised younger family members' migration by staying in the village to care for children, the frail elderly, the ill, and the disabled.

These village carers also did a great deal of farming work to provide food for their families and earn some cash. However, rice production for the market was unmanageably labour-intensive for middle-aged and elderly women burdened with care-work. Some villagers stopped planting rice and grew less labour-intensive crops; some contracted their paddy fields to others; and some simply abandoned them. But even those women who abandoned most of their land still raised chickens, grew vegetables, peanuts, and canola, and picked tea.

They also worked as underpaid farm labourers. Agricultural businesses often preferred to hire female labourers because, as in the collective period, the assumption was that their work deserved less pay than men's. In Gingko village, female farm labourers were paid 20 percent less than men. These women's work was vital to their families, for it not only supported the women themselves, but also covered (grand)children's costs. Most migrant workers remitted some money to their rural families, but few could cover the full costs of their children's upkeep.

However, the economic contribution of women's agricultural work was not recognised. From the point of view of Gingko villagers, migrants working outside (the village) were the breadwinners, while agriculture increasingly became associated with women's inside domestic work, and perceived as 'mere' subsistence and reproduction. And while the state viewed migrants' work in outside production as vital to the economy, if it saw women's work in agriculture at all, it was as a 'problem' for food security. Initially, the supposed problem was that women and the elderly were poor farmers: policymakers were not much concerned with the wellbeing of overworked villagers, but they did worry about declines in agricultural production. From the late 2000s, that concern morphed into one about land: elderly villagers had to get off the land, so it could be contracted to capitalist farmers, who would merge villagers' small plots into large tracts, suitable for 'efficient' mechanised crop farming (Ye 2015).

From the mid-2000s, the state also worried about the 'problem' of grandmothers raising children left behind by migrant parents. No appreciation was expressed for the contribution grandmothers made through their care-work. Instead, scholarship, policy documents, and the media were full of concern about left-behind children's supposed problems in school, poor health, accidental drownings in village ponds, and other misfortunes (e.g., Wang 2015). All these problems were blamed on the failure of 'backward' grandmothers to properly care for their charges. Bent as it was on raising the quality of the next generation, the state was particularly concerned that older rural women had little or no schooling. Motivated in part by this concern, the state pulled resources out of village schools and closed down many, forcing rural parents to send their children to urban boarding schools (Murphy 2014, 35).

By the 2010s, rural parents too had become alarmed by media horror stories about left-behind children. They also worried about the poor quality of their children's education in urban boarding schools as well as village schools. For many, the solution was to have young mothers remove caring and schooling duties from grandmothers and boarding schools, become carers themselves, and send their children to urban day-schools. Through the 2010s, it became increasingly common for women, who had resumed migrant waged labour when their babies were small, to return home when their children reached school-age and become *peidu mama* or 'mums accompanying [children] to school'. Together with their children, they moved to a rented apartment in a nearby town or city, so the children could attend a superior urban day-school (Tang, Liang, and Mu 2017). Other former migrant women in better-off families bought an urban apartment and remained there after marriage and childbirth.

In Gingko village, as a consequence of these trends, enrolments in the village primary school declined from one hundred in 2013 to four in 2017. Most village women with school-aged children lived during the week in the nearby town or county city. None of these women had full-time paid jobs, but some picked up part-time, casual work or ran small businesses. Some returned to the village on weekends to tend land and care for the elderly. Others stayed in town, their parents or parents-in-law joining them there for varying lengths of time, to help care for small children or receive care themselves.

Were these women appreciated for the quality care they provided children, the elderly, and others, and the sacrifices they made in giving up their migrant work? No. On the contrary, some media articles reported that *peidu mama* were envied for being able to afford to withdraw from migrant work (Tang, Liang, and Mu 2017), while others stigmatised them as idle, 'loose' women, engaging in gambling and prostitution because they had 'nothing else to do' (Wu 2016).

A Hidden Engine of Economic Growth

In sum, in the post-Mao period as before, rural Chinese women undertaking inside work have been unrecognised and severely exploited. Between the 1980s and 2000s, middle-aged and older women's unpaid or underpaid inside labour in care-work and agriculture was crucial to the wellbeing of rural families, for it freed younger women and men to migrate in search of waged work. And for the state and capitalists it enabled a double saving: not only could they save on education, the provision of care, and other aspects of social reproduction; in so doing, they could grossly exploit rural migrant workers, paying them wages so low as to have been otherwise unsustainable.

In the 2010s, the state's exploitation and denigration of older rural carers came home to roost: young women increasingly felt compelled to give up their migrant jobs to take over care of their children, so the pool of cheap rural labour available to domestic and transnational capitalist enterprises shrunk. But by then, transnational capitalist enterprises seeing new, even cheaper sources of labour in other countries had already begun moving elsewhere. Faced with this and other concerns, the Chinese state embarked on a new development strategy, oriented more toward domestic consumption. The shift of rural women out of paid production into reproduction was a bonus, not a problem. It both reduced unemployment pressures and created a new group, who boosted consumption and reduced demand on state revenues by providing free care services and subsidising quality education. Yet again, the hidden exploitation of rural women in inside work, marginalised as not real work, was key to state power and capitalist, economic growth. ■

Tao Lina, 'Traditional rural life in Taizhou, Zhejiang.'

Rural Transformations and Urbanisation

Impressions from the Ningbo International Photography Week

Marina SVENSSON

From late October to early December 2018 the Third Ningbo International Photography Week was held at Dongqian Lake in Zhejiang Province. Under the theme Village Images, the exhibition documented rural transformations and processes of urbanisation from a variety of perspectives.

On 27 October 2018, the Third Ningbo International Photography Week opened at the Dongqian Lake Art Centre. Despite the suggestion in its name, the Festival ran significantly longer than a week—until 5 December. The event was curated by photographer Fu Yongjun, currently a lecturer at the Zhejiang University of Media and Communications, but for many years a photojournalist and editor at the Hangzhou newspaper *City Express* (*Dushi kuaibao*) and an accomplished photographer. This year's overarching theme was *Village*

Images (*xiangcun yingxiang*), divided into 12 sub-themes. It displayed works by some 300 Chinese photographers, and also included images taken by foreign photographers in China over the last century. The call for contributions was posted on several websites and platforms—such as *Jinri toutiao*, one of the largest mobile content platforms in China today—and thus received a lot of interest from amateurs, established photographers, artists, and students. Fu Yongjun also invited celebrated photographers such as Zhang Xinmin—whose photographs from Liukeng village, Jiangxi province, were originally published in book form in 2000—and Wang Yong, who has documented photo studios and photographic practices in the countryside. Zhang Xinmin's black-and-white images have become iconic representations of the dramatic changes of village life during the reform period. In imperial times, Liukeng was a rich village with successful merchants and a large number of literati (*jinshi*), but is today poor and marginalised with a large segment of the population engaging in migrant work in urban areas. The Photography Week's opening weekend included conversations with, and talks by, Zhang Xinmin and Taiwanese photographer Ruan Yizhong, who is well known for his work documenting rural transformations and urbanisation in Taiwan.

Participants in the 'Photographic investigation of Hengkantou village, Ningbo, Zhejiang province' at the photo festival.

Through their images, the exhibition's photographers revealed both continuities and rapid changes. They depicted traditions, social and economic life, and rapid developments in villages in different parts of China—including Guizhou, Yunnan, Guangzhou, Zhejiang, Hubei, Shanxi, Sichuan, Shandong, and Xinjiang—with a particularly large number of contributions coming from Zhejiang. Sub-themed exhibitions included *Inheritance*, addressing different types of handicraft and traditions, and *Country Fair*, focussing on the thriving and diverse local markets, and their cultural and religious contexts in the midst of recent changes. Another of the sub-themes focussed on villages in Songyang, Zhejiang, where local photographers have documented the rich local cultural and social life over a number of years. In preparation for the festival, Fu Yongjun brought a group of interested photographers, scholars, and young people to Hengkantou, a 'red' village in Ningbo with a strong revolutionary heritage that has become known for its successful economic modernisation. They spent an intensive week documenting different aspects of the village, such as rural leadership, economic changes, and also cultural and religious beliefs and practices.

Several of the sub-themes addressed different aspects of rural transformation, with a particular focus on how villages have been impacted by patterns of urbanisation that have given rise to the phenomenon of 'villages embracing the cities' (*xiangcun baowei chengshi*) and 'villages in the city' (*cheng zhong cun*). One exhibition called *Scenes* (*changjing*) included works by 14 photographers who documented physical and visual changes with respect to architecture, the emergence of new kinds of landmarks and monuments, and advertisements, signs, and slogans. One exhibition entitled *Urban and Rural* (*cheng xiang*) included works by 15 photographers who documented social and physical encounters between villages and cities. In many parts of China, it is not always so easy to distinguish between urban and rural places—in the

(1) Dong Pin, 'Demolitions in Leqing, Zhejiang.'
(2) Zhang Xinmin, 'Family portrait in front of an ancestral portrait,' Linkeng village, Jiangxi. province.'

(3) Poster for the sub-theme Urban and Rural (*cheng xiang*) with photo by Luo Jinqing.

outskirts of cities one often finds semi-rural spaces and life coexisting with, or rapidly being engulfed by, city life and high rise buildings. In a series called *Temporary Vegetable Farmer* (*linshi cainong*) photographer Luo Jinqing documents farmers who use small plots of land left between new urban buildings to grow vegetables. This series was motivated by his own experience of living in such in-between spaces and buying vegetables from elderly farmers who maintain their attachment to the land and persist in cultivating small plots.

Several photographers trained their cameras on a recent trend of demolitions of entire villages in Zhejiang province. Dong Pin documented the demolition of a village outside of Leqing that only took two months to accomplish. Her photographs of people sitting on the ruins of their homes or looking out from their soon to be demolished houses are imbued with emotional distress and displacement brought about by rapid urbanisation and its non-transparent practices. Another photographer, Liu Yanfeng, documented life in a village outside of Lin'an before its demolition. The speed of demolitions in the city has given rise to the special term 'Lin'an speed' (*lin'an sudu*). Tao Lina's photographs document the changes of a village in Taizhou as a result of the establishment of a so-called economic development zone and the construction of a new village.

In another sub-theme, *Spring Breeze* (*chunfeng*), young photographers born in the 1990s provide new artistic interpretations of village life and urbanisation. Zheng Haoying, a photographer from Hangzhou, exhibited a series called *Empty Chairs* depicting forgotten villages in the city. Whereas in the sub-theme *Long Scrolls* (*chang juan*), photographers were given a one-metre-long paper roll to fill with images of one village. Chen Jianxin, one of those participating, documented urbanisation around Leqing and people's attachment to the land. This is clearly shown in one of his photos, where an ancestral hall is surrounded by high rises and factories. This is a common sight in the Wenzhou area, where lineages remain strong and ancestral halls are preserved and remain central to community life.

The Festival showed that the countryside remains a source of deep attachment and inspiration for Chinese photographers who are very concerned about rural developments. It is also obvious that cultural and religious life holds a fascination, although many photographers also addressed social and economic changes and challenges to traditional life, including urbanisation itself. ■

Chen Jianxin, 'Ancestral hall and rural life in the outskirts of Wenzhou, Zhejiang.'

Domestic Archaeology

Daniele DAINELLI

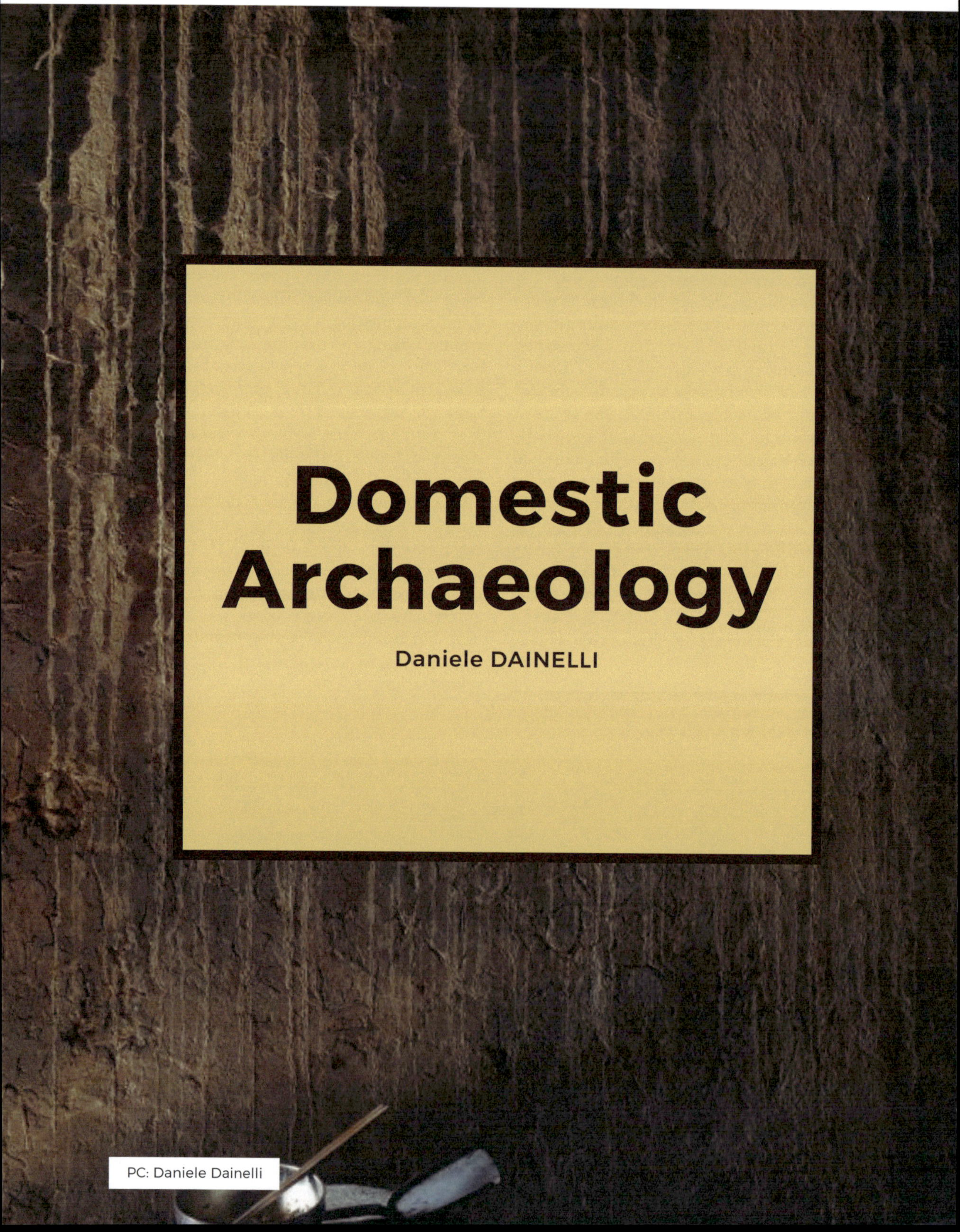

PC: Daniele Dainelli

All Photos by Daniele Dainelli.

The Domestic Archaeology Project is the outcome of seven years of work, from 2009 to 2016. During this period, I undertook dozens of trips to the countryside—exploring the lives of those living in the rural hinterlands of the coast, inland areas, and the western provinces.

In our contemporary era, characterised as it is by change and transformation, rural areas in China are being progressively abandoned. This change is radical, relentless, and epic. It somehow parallels the path of humanity in modern history—a path that has seen the gradual abandonment of the rural way of life in favour of an urbanisation often imposed from above.

Through the juxtaposition of imposing natural landscapes and intimate representations of objects taken from the daily life of rural dwellers, I attempt to show the contrast between these images of indoor solitude and the immensity, enormity, and variety of the land.

In the pictures that I took indoors, I try to give the spectator a tangible sensation, as if it was possible to touch the objects, to feel the textures, the essence, and the soul of these things. At the same time, in the landscape pictures, I attempt to portray the magnificence of the scenery, exasperating and aggravating every little detail through a digital process that allows me to obtain an enlargement of up to three or four metres. Every landscape is composed of 30 to 50 images of medium digital format joined together with the help of the photo stitch technique. Through this method, I can give a precise idea of spaces and distances, providing a more precise representation of reality.

Since the very beginning, I was intensely drawn to the objects I found inside the dwellings of these inhabitants living at the end of rural history: clothes, shoes, bottles, cooking utensils, items grouped together or isolated from the others, hanging on walls as if they have been there for centuries.

I was so fascinated by the 'archaeological' aspect of these objects and by what they tell us about the passing of time that I eventually started collecting them. To this day, I still preserve them exactly the way they were when I first acquired them. In this gallery, I share some of these material possessions—a fleeting glimpse of a life that is already gone before it has disappeared. ■

ON A CHINESE SCREEN
Media, Power, and Voice in China

'Sojourn into Fantasy,' PC: Mimo Khair @flickr.com.

Changing Representations of China's Workers

Wanning SUN

Representations of workers in public discourse in China have changed dramatically over recent decades. Taking a long historical view, in this essay Wanning Sun retraces the shifting narratives of the Chinese working class since the Maoist era. She does so by describing the role played by the media, not only in determining and framing working-class identity politics, but also in influencing the outcomes of worker struggles.

How workers and peasants are constructed in public discourses depends on the specific class relationship between the labour and the political/social elites of the time. If we take a long historical view, we can see a dramatic transformation in the ways in which Chinese workers and peasants are imagined, talked about, and represented in media and also in the broader popular discourse. For instance, as early as the 1920s, the Chinese Communist Party (CCP) introduced Marxist-Leninist notions of class struggle and actively promoted awareness of exploitation among workers. Its political agenda at that time was to mobilise China's peasants and workers to overthrow the old regime (Perry 2012). To raise consciousness, the CCP organised workers to give regular public speeches condemning the evils of private property and the class system, and extolling the virtue of overthrowing exploiters and oppressors.

As the CCP's power base grew, cultural workers in journalism, arts, literature, theatre, and all other domains of cultural production continued to promote the discourse of class struggle. Mao Zedong made it clear that in a class-based society, class differences must trump all other considerations. Combining Leninist ideas of mobilisation with Chinese notions of collectivist cooperation, the Party also actively experimented with new ways of mobilising the rural population for purposes of transforming social structures in its wartime headquarters in Yan'an in the 1930s and 1940s (Clark 2008).

When the CCP founded the People's Republic of China in 1949, it faced the enormous task of building not only a new national economy, but also a new working-class identity politics. China's workers and peasants, previously imagined as being exploited and oppressed by landlords and capitalists, had to be reimagined so that they could identify with, and actively participate in, the socialist modernisation process (Sun 2015).

From Master to Subaltern

Throughout the revolutionary period of the 1950s, 1960s, and 1970s, workers and peasants—the proletariat—were positioned as members of the most advanced forces of production. However, four decades of economic reforms and the embrace of a neoliberal economic order from the late 1970s to the present have seen a gradual loss of such elevated political status. As Guo Yingjie observes, 'there is no denying that large sections of the working class have lost their privilege and joined the new poor since losing their "iron rice bowl" and becoming detached from the CCP's historical mission' (Guo 2008, 40). Lü Xinyu, a Marxist scholar in China, also notes that while Chinese workers and peasants used to be the political and moral backbone of socialist China, in recent decades they have well and truly become a 'subaltern' class (quoted in Zhao 2010).

In contemporary China, the subaltern working class referred to by Lü consists mainly of rural migrant workers (*nongmingong*). In addition to a wide range of employment sectors—such as domestic work, service and hospitality, small businesses, and rubbish collection—the manufacturing sector and seasonal construction work make up the majority of the migrant labour force (Sun 2014).

Class relations between rural migrant labourers and the urban middle class—a socioeconomic elite group—have been profoundly reconfigured in the four decades of economic reforms. Consequently, the CCP has had to make necessary adjustments to its rhetoric on class discourse, necessitating—yet again—another cultural transformation. First, it had to eliminate the class struggle discourse. This meant acknowledging the reality of socioeconomic stratification in China in the reform era, but proposing the doctrine of social harmony as a strategy for managing class inequality and conflict. Second, class consciousness had to be suppressed rather than cultivated. Instead of representing workers and peasants as the politically privileged class, now the middle classes are touted as being exemplary of preferred values, lifestyles, and behaviours in contemporary China.

The social identity of the worker has also changed, along with the political, social, and economic meaning of work. Once upon a time, the term 'worker' (*gongren*) denoted dignity and ownership of the means of production, but workers are now widely described as *dagong* individuals, denoting casual labourers for hire in the capitalist labour market. Workers in the socialist era engaged in labour (*laodong*), which gave them pride and moral legitimacy. In contrast, workers today are referred to as *nongmingong*, meaning 'peasant workers'. *Nongmingong* exist as cheap labour, which is either in excess or short supply, and are in constant need of self-improvement in order to make themselves qualified for capitalist production (Yan 2008). Whereas in the socialist era workers were described as the 'masters of the nation' (*guojia de zhuren*), they have now become, on the one hand, the occasional recipients of urban and middle-class sympathy and compassion, and on the other hand, the objects of their discrimination and contempt (Sun 2009).

Changing Media Responses to Enduring Injustices

Rural migrant workers in the construction sector face a widespread and entrenched problem of wage arrears, whereby workers routinely experience non-payment, wage reduction, and denial of proper compensation for work-related injuries. A closer look at how urban mainstream media cover such issues provides some clues as to how the cultural politics of class changes over time.

How should news media handle the grievances and disputes surrounding wages and other labour issues facing rural migrant workers? To some extent, this depends on whom is asked this question. From the point of view of the Party-state, media should function as a stabiliser, defusing social pressure. According to this view, media should devise a voice-sharing strategy designed to ameliorate social conflict and maintain stability. Others argue that for the sake of self-interest, powerful social groups may want to give some of their discursive space to weaker social groups, so that the latter can have channels to vent their discontent. Others again believe that media should exercise its power to give voice to disadvantaged people, since media has the power and responsibility to expose wrongdoings, mobilise public opinion, and put pressure on the powers that be. Of course, this takes courage, but—according to the proponents of this view—journalists must remember that they represent the conscience of society.

One story is worth telling in this regard. On 7 December 2002, Huang, the wife of a rural migrant worker in Shenzhen, one of China's earliest Special Economic Zones, climbed onto the top of a 30-metre-tall pole near her husband's construction site. Her husband, Luo, had been injured while at work, but was too poor to afford the medical expenses and the company had refused to pay. In desperation, Luo's wife wanted to kill herself. Passersby saw her and alerted the police; journalists rushed to the scene of the incident and extensively covered it. Rescue efforts were successful, and through the mediation of the local police, the company agreed to pay medical expenses upfront. This case was among the first of many incidents to come in following years, whereby aggrieved rural migrants have risked their lives to stage public spectacles in the hope of forcing the local authorities to take immediate action. From the point of view of rural migrant labourers, even though they have been told there is a legal channel to seek redress, very often, they know all too well that they neither have the money nor time to pursue justice this way. The role of media in this specific incident was crucial but fraught. Following the incident, divergent opinions were published online, with some criticising the media for encouraging such 'publicity stunts', and others praising journalists for their social conscience (*People's Daily* 2003).

Sympathetic coverage of the plight of workers was frequent under the leadership of Hu Jintao and Wen Jiabao (2003–13). When incidents such as the one cited above occurred, journalists would often turn up at the scene and, in many cases, mediate between individual migrants, the employers, police, and the local government. Furthermore, reporting of such incidents in the media had the effect of publicly shaming the offending company, as well as putting local authorities on notice.

From the early 2000s onwards, attempts to resolve labour disputes through drastic measures—be it threatening to jump off buildings, blocking the government headquarters, or causing public spectacles in public spaces—have played out in many Chinese towns and cities. However, a closer look at how media has responded to such incidents over the past two decades suggests that such sympathetic coverage was short-lived. Following the end of the Hu–Wen administration, the political mandate for stability maintenance (*weiwen*) has seen the juxtaposition of a number of different narrative frames. These include: the 'social justice' (*shehui gongzheng*) frame, i.e. giving voice to the plight of workers; the 'social harmony' (*shehui hexie*) frame, i.e. emphasising the importance of strategic appeasement in order to defuse social discontent; the 'education and guidance' (*jiaoyu he yingdao*) frame, i.e. chastising migrant labourers for their unlawful actions and urging them to seek 'proper channels' (*zhengdang qudao*); and finally, the 'law and order' (*yifa banshi*) frame, whereby the conduct of migrant workers or labour activists is quickly criminalised and their access to public representation through media—including social media—often denied. Despite its rhetoric of a 'people-centred approach' (*yi ren wei ben*), the current regime has leaned towards a more intolerant, oppressive position on dissenting voices, and has proven to be more than willing to resort to legal force for the purposes of containing, if not eradicating, labour activism.

Middle-class media also oscillate between media-as-spokesperson for rural migrants and media-as-a-pressure valve, while all the time remaining susceptible to the vagaries of the Party-state's mandate of legitimacy production and stability maintenance. Migrant workers seeking justice over wage arrears can be portrayed as deserving of compassion and sympathy on some occasions, while on other occasions they can be criticised for their 'crazy', 'irrational', and 'ignorant' tendencies to resort to extreme measures (Sun 2012).

Digital Technologies and Self-Empowerment?

In the past decade or so, the arrival of digital media technologies, the ubiquitous use of mobile devices, and the spread of social media have afforded rural migrants a hitherto unavailable means and platform to express their political voice. As I have documented elsewhere (Sun 2014), the increasingly widespread affordability of the mini digital video camera has made it increasingly possible for rural migrants to document egregious labour practices on the part of employers. Technological developments from the late 1990s have enabled some rural migrants to become media activists. Nowadays, having access to QQ and WeChat—China's main social media platforms—labour activists and workers can circulate poetry, fiction, blogs, photography, and other forms of creative work produced by themselves and about themselves.

A small but growing number of migrant cultural activists are exploring effective ways to make creative use of digital media to participate in struggles for self-representation and debates on social inequality and citizenship. My own sustained interactions with more than a dozen NGO workers and labour activists in Beijing, Suzhou, and Shenzhen between 2004 and 2013 have convinced me that effective labour activism is becoming virtually synonymous with the effective harnessing of new media technologies.

However, we must caution against technological determinism, which assumes that technology has brought a perfect solution for rural migrants' struggle for economic justice and political voice. While there is plenty of evidence pointing to the subaltern's self-empowerment through social media and digital technologies, there is also plenty of contrary evidence suggesting that rural migrants' embracing of the online and digital world does not necessarily lead to political empowerment (e.g. Wallis 2012). Similarly, for each instance where labour NGOs and grassroots advocates have been successful in mobilising subaltern consciousness through WeChat, microblogging, mobile phones, and other digital platforms, there also seems to be more instances pointing to the limitations of such online activism.

The intention and motivation of rural migrants and labour activists to engage media in struggles for voice, recognition, and economic compensation will continue as long as social and economic injustices exist, but the level of their success is, and will continue to be, determined by the political logic of the situation, and dictated by the imperative of stability maintenance. In view of the authorities' current penchant to enforce censorship, undertake crackdowns, and in some cases even resort to imprisonment in response to various forms of media activism, the space for labour activists to strive for more empowerment via the media has been considerably diminished despite the widespread use of social media. ■

'Selling Online,'
PC: maxpixel.net.

Platform Economies

The Boss's Old and New Clothes

Julie Yujie CHEN

The recent growth of China's platform economy is jaw-dropping. What Chinese platform workers have experienced is the epitome of the intertwining transformations that digital technologies have engendered, not only in the Chinese economy and society, but also in global capitalism more generally. In this essay, Julie Chen argues that a better understanding of the situation of these workers will inform us about China's economic conditions and provide a glimpse into the future of Chinese labour struggles.

In the eyes of both China scholars and the public, the recent growth of China's Internet economy is jaw-dropping. Not only did Baidu, Alibaba, and Tencent enter the top ten most valuable tech companies in the world, but new players have also emerged on the global stage. For instance, ride-hailing platform Didi Chuxing, mobile payment methods Alipay and WeChat Pay, and bicycle-sharing platforms Mobike and ofo have become household names all over the world because of their rapid success and global presence.

The 'platform economy'—a term loosely used to describe the economic activities that are performed by Internet platforms—is estimated to have facilitated transactions worth more than 49 billion yuan (7.7 billion USD) in 2017, involving 700 million users and 70 million workers (China's National Information Center and Internet Society of China Sharing Economy Committee 2018). According to my calculations based on data included in the *China Statistical Yearbook (2017)*, in 2016 the platform economy absorbed 18 percent of the labour force in the tertiary industry. Moreover, an annual increase of ten million workers since 2015 makes the platform economy the fastest growing sector in China (China's National Information Center and Internet Society of China Sharing Economy Committee 2016, 2017, 2018). In the meantime, widespread labour disputes and unrest also make it a site for more labour struggles (CLB 2017, 2018).

Because of the pressure on economic restructuring in the aftermath of the 2018 financial slowdown, and thanks to support from the central government, China's platform economy shows no sign of slowing down. What Chinese platform workers have experienced is the epitome of the intertwining transformations that digital technologies have engendered not only in the Chinese economy and society, but also in global capitalism more generally. Consequently, a better understanding of the situation of these workers will inform us about China's labour and economic conditions, as well as about more general challenges in terms of inclusive and sustainable development with implications that have relevance far beyond China. This essay aims to shed light on these dramatic and overlapping transformations by highlighting two related tensions.

Old Wine in New Bottles?

The first tension exists between a persisting struggle of workers against 'the same old problems' and an emerging new set of challenges related to new modalities of value extraction in the platform economy. It is evident that Chinese workers in the so-called 'new economy' are still fighting against traditional forms of exploitation, like wage theft and unilateral termination of contracts without compensation (CLB 2016). Drivers working on the ride-hailing platforms, for instance, still protest against illegal vehicles and high monthly fees paid to the car companies (Chen 2018; CLB 2018). Nonetheless, the 'old wine in new bottles' of labour struggles should not distract attention from a fundamental shift happening to the value accumulation mechanism in the platform economy—i.e. the fact that the platform economy is, by nature, a form of data capitalism (Srnicek 2016). Data is the foundation upon which a digital platform functions and continues to exist—without data, algorithms cannot work; without a continuous influx of data into the platform system, algorithms cannot improve; without properly functional algorithms, the platform would fail.

A number of scholars have started to grapple with the implications of massive data collection for democracy and the ways in which it is transforming political economy at national and global levels (Foster and McChesney 2014; Zuboff 2015). Big data collection affects all participants in the platform economy, but workers always face more intensive data capture, and harsher control and discipline enacted through algorithms. For instance, the 531,000 delivery riders at Meituan—the largest online takeaway platform, which performed 2.9 million deliveries per hour during the daily peak time in 2017 (Meituan-Dianping 2018)—are all subject to the platform's commands for dispatching and route planning. The 2.9 million hourly deliveries could have never been accomplished without constant influx of real-time data about riders' mobility and performance.

At the core of value extraction and accumulation in the platform economy is a continued trend of shifting surplus away from workers and the general population, and towards capitalists by means of financialisation and automation (Dyer-Witheford 2015). Platform workers' livelihoods, welfare, and reproduction are entangled in data production and manipulation for the growth of the digital platforms, just as factory workers are caught up in the processes of industrialisation. This does not mean to suggest that industrialisation and legacy labour struggles have stopped being relevant nowadays, but that capitalism's turn to datafication has not yet captured substantial interest among labour scholars. It should. Its profound implications for Chinese workers are all the more significant and urgent against the backdrop of China embracing digital technologies for development and governance. The state's centralised data infrastructure is under construction with projects like the social credit system that incorporates both public and private sectors and will be used for political, economic, and social governance (Liang et al. 2018; see also Loubere and Brehm's essay in this volume). Establishing meaningful connections between day-to-day worker struggles and the structural shift to data capture is a daunting task on the horizon for scholars, workers, and activists alike.

Outside the Law?

The second tension emerges between the momentum of what Ching Kwan Lee refers to as 'decentralised legal authoritarianism'—i.e. the central government's institutionalised regime to contain workers' collective actions at the local level—and the elusive position of platform companies that are at once implicated in the local informal labour market, yet are also able to get around local regulations (Lee 2007). The dominance of informal labour in China sets in motion a distinctive trajectory of platform economic behaviour. From the e-commerce boom to the ride-hailing market, platform economies rely heavily on the large pool of cheap and informal labour. Take ride-hailing platforms as an example. Instead of disrupting the traditional taxi industry, most of them—including Didi Chuxing which controls more than 90 percent of the market—also retain traditional taxi services on the platform along with other transport services like ride-sharing. In this way, Chinese ride-hailing platform companies build on the vast pre-existing grey market of illegal and informal taxi services (Chen 2018). This grey market exists in the first place because of the labour segmentations produced by state-owned taxi enterprises and the vastly different regulations at the local levels (Chen 2018). Traditional taxi drivers in one city may find their challenges different from those faced by their counterparts in the neighbouring city or province. They fight local battles, face decentralised regulations, and find it difficult to mobilise for a nationwide cause, which is analogous to other worker struggles as observed by Lee (2007). This pattern carries on to the ride-hailing market as regulations go local.

Ride-hailing apps were legalised in 2016 with the intention to standardise and regulate the market. By the end of 2017, more than 210 municipal governments have passed localised bylaws to regulate the ride-hailing market (China's National Information Center and Internet Society of China Sharing Economy Committee 2018). Local regulations stipulate licence criteria and application procedures for vehicles, drivers, and ride-hailing platform companies. For example, Beijing mandates a 'double-local' rule—that is, only drivers with Beijing *hukou* operating vehicles with Beijing licence plates are eligible to work legally on the platforms (Beijing Transportation Committee 2016). Shenzhen, a migrant city, requires one-year proof of residence in the city from an applicant driver, but in the spring of 2018 it ruled that only electric cars can be used to apply for the operational licence for ride-hailing services (Shenzhen Transportation Committee 2016, 2018). Local policies that set various requirements for vehicles and drivers indeed embody the needs of local authorities, whether for managing population mobility, stimulating new industries, or a variety of other reasons. But the relationship between drivers and platforms is left mostly undefined across the nation and, as a result, platforms have little legally mandated responsibility for drivers' work conditions, social security, and long-term welfare.

Policy orientation of this kind is more likely to make drivers' lives more precarious than to pressure platform companies into compliance. As of June 2018, Didi Chuxing had legal operational licences in only 51 cities out of the more than 400 cities where it operates (Yue 2018). In 2017, it was also reported to have participated in recruiting unqualified drivers to work on the platform (Yangtze Evening

Paper 2017). This quasi-legal position not only fails to prevent the company from collecting massive amounts of data and accumulating value through its information network, but also puts a majority of drivers in a collectively vulnerable position because of illegitimacy *de jure*. They suffer the brunt of market volatility, as well as the penalties inflicted by suddenly-tightened local regulations. For instance, drivers in Beijing, if caught in violations of rules, face up to 30,000 yuan of fines and the temporary seizure of their driver's licence (innoinsights 2018).

Beyond Cyber-control

The relationship between drivers, ride-hailing platforms, and regulatory bodies at different levels is symptomatic of the economic and regulatory environment for the platform economy. Platform companies thrive because of the network effect of digital technologies (Srnicek 2016), as well as their brazen violation of regulations. They also thrive by taking advantage of the existing informal labour market and reinforcing labour segmentation. Subcontracting prevails in sectors like online food-delivery and logistics. Platform companies control the labour process via algorithms across geographies (Rosenblat and Stark 2016), which renders them increasingly significant actors in labour management and segmentation.

It is important to point out that labour control of Chinese on-demand platform workers also goes far beyond the level of algorithms. It takes the shape of both a network and a hierarchy when 'decentralised' regulations compound the effects of cybernetic systems imposed by platforms. In the same way that social media platforms curate users' online content and by extension shape public discourses (Gillespie 2018), digital work platforms broker economic rewards, risks, and opportunities among workers. A clearer definition of platform companies' intermediary and governing roles, and the correspondent liability in the legal framework, is in order.

Indeed, there are many other noteworthy aspects of platform economies in China that this essay does not elaborate on, such as the discourse of flexible work as a new type of employment and robust workers' self-organisations. The two tensions outlined above do not exist in isolation. They intersect. They both contain something old and something new. It is the elusive combination of 'boss's old and new clothes' in the platform economy that underlines the high stakes for regulators and Chinese platform workers—not to mention the working class in general. ■

The Truman Show (1998).

Rethinking Online Privacy in the Chinese Workplace

Employee Dismissals over Social Media Posts

Mimi ZOU

The increasing popularity of social media usage in the workplace, as well as rapid advancements in workplace surveillance technology, have made it easier for employers in China—as elsewhere—to access a vast quantity of information on employees' social media networks. Considering that Chinese privacy and personal data protection laws have been relatively weak, there have been a growing number of cases brought before courts in China involving employer access to, and use of, employee social media content. In this essay, Mimi Zou examines a number of these cases.

Social media has ushered in an age of unprecedented information sharing in the Chinese workplace. According to the 2017 edition of the WeChat's User Report, 83 percent of respondents are utilising the app for work-related purposes. Furthermore, 57.22 percent of respondents indicated that their new contacts on WeChat were work-related (Penguin Intelligence 2017). The increasing popularity of social media usage in the workplace context, as well as rapid advancements in workplace surveillance technology, have made it easier for employers to access, acquire, and utilise a vast quantity of information on employees' social media networks. Social media has become a valuable resource for employers to screen job applicants, monitor employee performance, and investigate employee wrongdoings.

Employers, both in China and elsewhere, often justify such actions on the basis of business concerns about reputational risks, leakage of intellectual property and trade secrets, and other legal liabilities that could arise from employees' social media activities. At the same time, employees' privacy interests are clearly at stake. To tackle these risks, in recent years some state legislatures in the United States have introduced specific laws prohibiting employers from requiring job applicants or employees to disclose usernames and passwords for their personal social networking accounts (Park 2014).

In the Chinese context, however, to date, privacy and personal data protection laws have been relatively weak. At the same time, there have been a growing number of cases brought before Chinese courts involving employer access to, and use of, employee social media content, most commonly in employee dismissal cases. This essay examines a number of these cases, which highlight the extant regulatory gaps in China that provide considerable scope for employers to monitor and inquire into their employees' social media activities, to the detriment of their privacy interests.

Legislating Privacy in China

Until recently, in China there has not been a comprehensive law at the national level that regulates privacy and personal data protection. A patchwork of rules and principles in this domain has developed in a piecemeal and fragmented manner. To start with, the Chinese Constitution does not refer to a general right to privacy (*yinsiquan*). Article 34 provides that a citizen's personal dignity is protected as a fundamental right and Article 40 protects the privacy of citizens' correspondence.

Article 101 of the 1986 General Principles of Civil Law sets out the protection of personal name, portrait, reputation, or honour as 'personal rights' (*renshenquan*) of a natural person, but does not explicitly mention any right to privacy (NPC 1986). In cases involving the written or oral dissemination of a person's private correspondence, which has the practical effect of damaging that person's reputation, the Supreme People's Court has treated such cases as infringement on the rights of reputation (SPC 1988, par. 140).

It was not until the Tort Liability Law, introduced in 2009, that the right to privacy was recognised as one of the civil rights and interests enjoyed by an individual, the infringement of which constitutes an actionable civil tort (NPC 2009, arts. 2 and 62). The new General Provisions of Civil Law of 2017 (hereafter 'General Provisions') further expands the protection of the right to privacy by listing it alongside other personal rights. Article 110 states: 'A natural person enjoys the rights of life, inviolability and integrity of person, health, name, likeness, reputation, honour, privacy, and marital autonomy, among others' (NPC 2017).

It is significant that the General Provisions expressly articulates a broad protection of personal information as an actionable civil claim that is independent of the right to privacy. Article 111 states that: 'The personal information of a natural person are protected by the law. Any organisation or individual who need to obtain the personal information of other persons shall legally obtain and ensure the security of such information, unlawful collection, use, transmission, trade, or disclosure of others' personal data is prohibited.' However, the definition or scope of 'personal information' (*geren xinxi*) is not found in the General Provisions. There is no further elaboration of what activities would constitute 'unlawful' collection, use, transmission, trade, or disclosure.

A recent legislation, the Cybersecurity Law (CSL), is a major step taken by Chinese lawmakers toward establishing a comprehensive framework for regulating online privacy and security issues (NPC 2016). The CSL defines the protected scope of personal information collected, stored, or transmitted electronically. 'Personal information' refers to 'all types of information recorded by electronic or other means that can identify an individual either in itself or in combination with other information, including but not limited to a citizen's name, date of birth, ID card number, personal biometric information, address, and telephone number' (NPC 2016, art. 76). The CSL imposes obligations on 'network operators' (*wangluo yunyingzhe*), including obtaining individual consent for handling personal information, and maintaining the security and preventing unauthorised disclosures of personal information (arts. 40–43).

In December 2017, the Standardisation Administration of China issued the Personal Information Security Specification (hereafter 'Specification'; see SAC 2017), which contains a set of recommended standards regarding the protection of personal information in China (although there are no penalties imposed for breach of such standards). The Specification sets out eight basic principles and standards that cover the collection, storage, use, processing, transfer, disclosure, and any other processing activities involving personal information that are undertaken by 'personal data controllers' (*geren xinxi kongzhizhe*).

PC: maxpixel.net.

Overall, the legal protection of an employee's (online or offline) privacy rights has been relatively weak. Recent developments such as the General Provisions could offer employees a channel for seeking civil damages if their employer has unlawfully collected and disclosed their personal information on social media. If one takes a broad interpretation of the CSL and applies the personal information protection standards under the Specification, employees may indeed enjoy enhanced legal protections where employers fail to obtain their employees' consent in collecting and using their personal information from social media. However, there remains significant ambiguity in how these new regulatory norms will actually apply in practice.

Dismissal Cases Involving Employee Social Media Posts

We now turn to examine a number of cases involving the dismissal of employees based on their social media posts. The cases discussed below represent a 'snapshot' of the common types of such cases that have been brought before local people's courts in China. Under the Labour Contract Law (art. 39), the employee's misconduct must be *serious* in order for the employer to justify the dismissal for the purpose of *not* paying the required economic compensation to the dismissed employee. These circumstances include where the employee has seriously violated the rules and procedures set up by the employer, caused severe damage to the employer due to serious neglect of duties or pursuit of private benefits, has simultaneously entered into an employment relationship with another employer that seriously affects the current position, or is under investigation for criminal liabilities.

The first type of cases involve information posted by the employee on his/her social media networks that entail actual misconduct or wrongdoing that led to his or her dismissal. In one exemplifying case—*Chen v. Di Nuo Wei Ya International Freight Forwarders (Shanghai) Co., Ltd.* (Case 1, 2013)—the employer dismissed the employee on the grounds of unauthorised absence from work for over eight days. Where the employee challenged the dismissal and sought economic compensation, the employer submitted as evidence notarised copies of the employee's Weibo posts during the period of absence. The posts, which included a photo of the employee sunbathing, showed that she was undertaking personal travel without approved leave at the time. The court recognised the Weibo posts submitted by the employer as admissible evidence and ultimately dismissed the employee's claim for wrongful termination.

Another category of such cases relate to statements expressed by employees on social media out of frustration and dissatisfaction with the employer, managers, and/or colleagues. The courts have been more cautious in scrutinising the legal basis for employers to dismiss employees in such cases. In *Beijing Bonatongcheng Technology Co., Ltd. v. Li Chennan* (Case 2, 2014 and 2015), the employee (Li) signed an agreement with his employer that upon the dissolution of his labour contract, he would be paid economic compensation if he refrained from making any comments that would damage the employer's reputation. Shortly before he left his job, Li posted a comment on his Weibo account that the employer frequently withheld wages. The employer claimed that Li's comment seriously harmed its reputation, which was the basis for not paying Li economic compensation upon termination. Li argued that he was merely disclosing a fact, which did not cause malicious damage to the employer. The court at the first instance concluded that while Li's post was detrimental to the employer's reputation, there was no lawful basis for the employer's refusal to pay Li the agreed compensation. The court at the second instance reached the same conclusion and held that it was not entirely up to the parties to decide on the required compensation for termination of employment since the law protected the employee's right to such compensation.

In the third type of cases, an employer has used defamation laws against the employee where the latter's social media communications caused damage to the former's reputation. For example, in *Xi'an Mou Gong Ye Xuexiao v. Tang* (Case 3, 2016), the employer successfully sued a former employee for infringing its right to reputation under Article 101 of the General Principles of Civil Law. The plaintiff was a vocational school and employed the defendant as a teacher. Following his termination based on incompetence, the defendant posted disparaging comments about the school in his WeChat groups, with some of these (closed) groups including his students. His comments consisted of accusations that the plaintiff did not offer proper qualifications, issued fake diplomas, and took a large 'cut' of students' internship wages. In court, the plaintiff argued that the defendant's claims were false and resulted in several students withdrawing their enrolment at the school and many more students were contemplating similar actions. The court ruled for the plaintiff and ordered the defendant to publish a written public apology and pay damages of 2,000 yuan for the plaintiff's loss resulting from reputational damage (which was much less than what the plaintiff sought).

Collective Disputes and Social Media Posts

In some cases, employee dismissals have been based on social media speech relating to the organisation of collective industrial activities. In *Pei Shihai v. Shunfeng Express Group (Shanghai) Express Co., Ltd* (Case 4, 2016), the plaintiff worked as a driver for the defendant, a large courier and logistics company. The defendant dismissed the plaintiff for serious violations of company rules because the plaintiff had sent messages to a WeChat group of coworkers regarding potential workplace disturbances (including strike actions). The plaintiff brought a claim seeking economic compensation for his dismissal. He contended that he did not instigate any strike activity and was merely discussing with his coworkers about defending their rights. His messages to the WeChat group were aimed at resolving the conflict via lawful means. The plaintiff also argued that the WeChat discussions were private speech that occurred outside working hours and it was unreasonable for the defendant to regulate such speech. Moreover, the plaintiff argued that no strike did actually occur and the defendant's evidence before the court was insufficient to prove that the strike would have happened.

In this case, the defendant argued that the plaintiff's WeChat messages showed that he had intended to instigate a strike and rallied his coworkers to participate, including the communication of specific action plans that would have severely threatened the defendant's operations. The strike did not happen because the defendant took action accordingly. The court of first instance ruled that based on the WeChat records furnished by the defendant, the plaintiff's speech was provocative and he should have known the potential consequences. The court was of the view that employees should comply with workplace rules and professional ethics, which the plaintiff did not. The plaintiff appealed to the Shanghai Intermediate People's Court, arguing that he was merely discussing with coworkers how to protect their rights. He asserted that the defendant's records only showed some parts of the WeChat discussions and did not show the messages he had sent to the group seeking to dissuade a potential strike. Upholding the first instance court's ruling, the court decided that the plaintiff's speech was made within a WeChat group consisting of coworkers and, as such, it exceeded the scope of personal freedom of speech. Even though such speech was made outside working hours, it was still inappropriate and unreasonable since the content was likely to cause dire consequences for the defendant.

In a related case involving the same labour dispute—*Sun Liang v. Shunfeng Express Group (Shanghai) Express Co., Ltd.*—the plaintiff sought economic compensation for his dismissal by the defendant. The plaintiff was dismissed on the basis of violating company rules by posting comments in a WeChat group consisting of 117 coworkers that sought to incite participation in industrial action over wage issues (Case 5, 2016). His claim for compensation failed before the labour arbitration committee and court of first instance. He appealed to the Shanghai Intermediate People's Court. Similar to his coworker in the above case (Pei Shihai), the plaintiff claimed that the WeChat record provided to the court by the defendant was incomplete and that he was merely complaining about their wages with his coworkers. The defendant's evidence showed WeChat logs with some of the plaintiff's messages, which proposed plans for work stoppages and road blockages at certain times and places. The plaintiff also claimed that he was inebriated when he posted the comments during non-working time and the comments were of a private nature.

The Shanghai Intermediate Court ruled that the employer was justified in dismissing the plaintiff without compensation. The plaintiff had made provocative speech on WeChat that attempted to instigate collective disruptions in the workplace. The court was of the opinion that the employer had an implied legitimate expectation based on the employment relationship that employees should carry out their duties in good faith, voluntarily maintain the order of the company, and comply with the company's regulations. Even if such duties were not explicitly written in the labour contract and/or employee handbook, they were 'self-evident'. If there is a dispute regarding work arrangements, employees may exercise their 'right to dissent' (*yiyiquan*) but still had the responsibility to observe proper procedures, that is, not disturb the daily operation and the lawful rights and interests of the company. Adopting the same reasoning as the abovementioned case, the court decided that the plaintiff's comments were outside the scope of his personal freedom of speech since they were posted to a WeChat group consisting of coworkers. Even though there were no actual damages caused to the company, his speech was still 'inappropriate and unreasonable'. The plaintiff's actions violated the employer's legitimate expectations arising from the employment relationship and infringed basic professional ethics.

Some comparative insights may be useful here. In the United States, a notable area of protection for collective employee speech has been carved out from Section 7 of the National Labour Relations Act. Section 7 specifically protects workers' rights to self-organise, bargain collectively, and 'engage in other concerted activity … for mutual aid or protection'. In recent years, there have been numerous cases before the National Labour Relations Board (NLRB) that involved challenging employers' policies and disciplinary actions relating to employee social media postings. The NLRB has increased its scrutiny of employer policies that impose overly broad restrictions that prohibit employees from posting negative comments about the employer.

Legal Uncertainties

Recent regulatory developments such as the General Provisions and CSL, as well as the recommended standards under the new Specification, offer some potential for strengthening the protection of employee privacy interests by requiring employers to obtain employee consent for collecting, using, and handling personal information. At the time of writing (August 2018), it remains to be seen how both laws and the Specification will be implemented in practice, especially in cases brought before the courts. This legal uncertainty will continue to leave employers with substantial room for manoeuvre when it comes to monitoring, accessing, and using their employees' social media communications.

The cases brought before Chinese local courts to date highlight the extensive reach of employers' actions in this realm. Power asymmetries in the employment relationship also mean that employees do not readily challenge their employers' social media policies and other interferences with social media activities, including cases where employees are using social media to organise collective industrial activities. Furthermore, employers can use defamation laws against employees for reputational damage from the latter's social media activities, which can result in the chilling of various forms of employee speech. In future cases, the courts are likely to grapple with difficult questions related to if and how the new privacy and personal information protection laws would apply, and how conflicting interests of employers and employees (and, potentially, the state) arising from the use of social media technologies in the workplace ought to be balanced. ■

Portrait of miner Yang Guanlan in Shandong, by Song Chao.

Visualising Labour and Labourscapes in China

From Propaganda to Socially Engaged Photography

Marina SVENSSON

Photography has always been a powerful tool to depict the lives of workers in China. Whereas during the Mao period political control over image production created a visual hegemony that glorified socialism and class struggle, more recent digital developments have enabled ordinary Chinese citizens and workers to document their lives and circulate these images online.

What can photography bring to our understanding of labour in China? This question needs to be addressed taking into account the role and possibilities of photography more generally, its development over time, and the history and special conditions of China. After 1949, political control over image production in China created a visual hegemony that glorified socialism and class struggle, while rendering social problems, inequalities, and injustices invisible. However, like in so many other fields, the reform period has enabled a growing and diverse group of people to challenge earlier prescribed visual aesthetics and ideological control. Photographers today experiment with new ways of documenting Chinese society, and also address hitherto invisible issues as well as new problems. Economic and social reforms have created new types of workers, for instance migrant workers, more precarious labour conditions, for example in factories in the South and in private mines, and new forms of marginalisation and exploitation, such as illegal work within the sex industry.

These socioeconomic developments have drawn the attention of domestic and foreign photographers alike, such as Edward Burtynsky, working on Chinese topics like the steel and coal industries, manufacturing, shipyards, recycling, and the Three Gorges Dam, and Sim Chi Yin, working on issues such as gold miners and migrant workers (Estrin 2015). Digital photography, the Internet, social media platforms, and the expansion of smartphones, not only have provided professional photographers with new possibilities, but they also have enabled ordinary Chinese citizens and workers to document their lives and circulate these images online. Today a wide range of photography tackling social problems and labour conditions can be seen on the Internet, in art spaces, as well as on social media platforms. If, as the filmmaker Wim Wenders (quoted in Levi Strauss 2003, 1) argues, 'the most political decision you make is where you direct people's eyes,' China indeed has gone through a visual revolution challenging the political gaze and visual hegemony. This being said, however, the Chinese Communist Party (CCP) still maintains a strong interest in—and the means to—control and censor both the written word and images.

In such a context, this essay discusses how photography can serve a twofold purpose, as both a valuable historical record that helps us understand how ideology and politics have shaped images of labour and the working class in China, and as an important affective and intellectual tool to analyse current labour issues.

Photography, Social Engagement, and Calls for Change

In the West, photography has long been regarded as a tool to create awareness of social problems, injustices, inequalities, and the life and struggles of marginalised groups of people (Bogre 2012; Franklin 2016; Levi Strauss 2003). Since the late-nineteenth century, documentary photography and photojournalism have addressed topics such as slum housing, landlessness, child labour, poor working conditions, poverty, and migration. Socially engaged photographers and photojournalists have on their own accord or in collaboration with scholars and civil society actors—including news media, photo agencies, and NGOs—documented and uncovered social and political problems with the aim to create awareness and support for social and political change.

In the field of documentary photography on labour issues, one of the earliest and most well-known photographers is Lewis W. Hine, who in 1908 was commissioned by the United States National Child Labor Committee to document child labour in the country. Another example is Dorothea Lange, who during the American depression in the 1930s, together with the economist Paul Taylor, worked for the Farm Security Administration to document the causes and consequences of agricultural intensification and exploitative factory farming. A more recent example is Sebastiâo Salgado, who started out as an economist but in the late 1970s decided to devote himself to photography in the belief that it could be more powerful than pure academic work. While Salgado has been criticised for aestheticising suffering, he has also been widely defended and praised, and in 2010 he was awarded the American Sociological Association Award for Excellence in the Reporting of Social Issues. Salgado maintains a strong belief in the power of photography to give rise to debate and action: 'What I want is the world to remember the problems and the people I photograph. What I want is to create a discussion about what is happening around the world and to provoke some debate with these pictures (Salgado 1994).'

However, the increasing accessibility of photographs has created its own set of challenges. Already in 1974, W. Eugene Smith—who, among other things, is famous for his photographs of the victims of the Minamata mercury scandal in Japan—expressed awareness of how the sheer number of photographs can numb people, although he ultimately held the view that photography can be an important tool for critical thinking. In his words: 'Photography is a small voice at best. Daily, we are deluged with photography at its worst, until its drone of superficiality threatens to numb our sensitivity to all images. Then why photograph? Because sometimes—just sometimes—photographs can lure our senses into greater awareness. Much depends on the viewer; but to some, photographs can demand enough of emotions to be a catalyst to thinking' (quoted in Franklin 2016, 201). This emotional or affective quality of photography is also the reason why so many NGOs and activists today make use of photography in their work.

As a result of the digital revolution, we are today surrounded by ever more images that compete for our attention, and thus visibility remains a question of politics and power

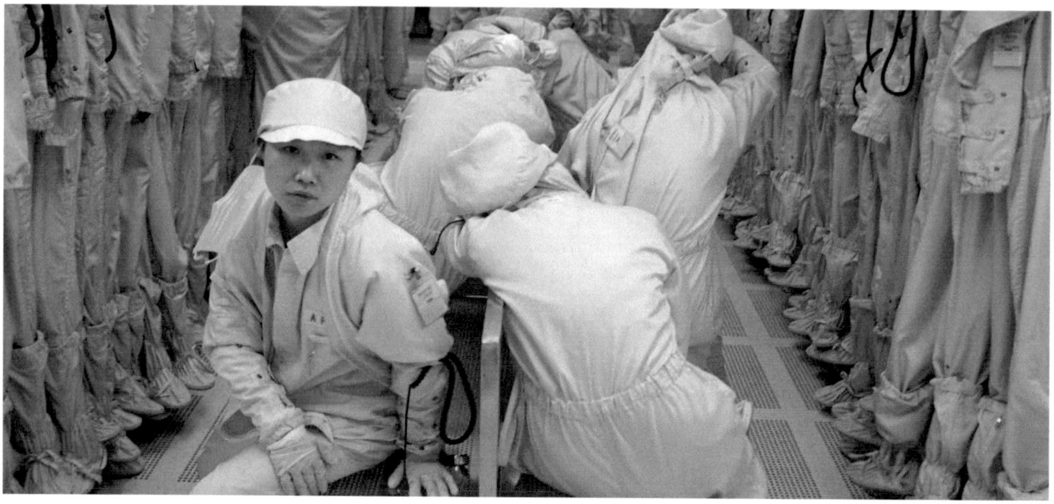

Migrant workers taking a rest in a factory in Dongguan, by Zhan Youbing.

relations. Susan Sontag (2003) has argued that the proliferation of images of violence and pain can result in 'compassion fatigue' that undermines our abilities to feel, connect, and act. Images may thus hinder, rather than foster, action and solidarity, creating a distance that prevents connectivity and civic engagement. Other scholars and photographers have challenged her conclusion, however, and believe that photography can still play an important role in awareness raising, civic engagement, and humanitarian and political activism (Bogre 2012; Franklin 2016; Levi Strauss 2003). One needs to distinguish between images that play on people's sense of guilt and give rise to pity, charity, and good-will, and images that provoke outrage and call for more radical social and political changes. Moreover, one also needs to distinguish between images that portray people as victims and images that portray them with dignity and agency.

From Visual Hegemony to New Visualities

The CCP understood early on that photography can be useful in ideological work and serve as a propaganda tool (see, for instance, Roberts 2013 and Wu 2017). The proper role of photography from the perspective of the CCP was laid down in different speeches and directives, which came to inform Chinese photojournalism in the three decades that preceded the reforms. Photographers were called upon to show the progress and success of communism by documenting technical advances, new factories, and large infrastructural projects. It was not possible to take and publish photographs that hinted at social problems, hardships, or resentments, as this would have been seen as a critique of the political system. For this reason, photographs of the Great Famine of the early 1960s do not exist, but there are ample photographs celebrating the Great Leap Forward and its advances in steel production. In the photographs of the 1950s and 1960s, workers are depicted as heroic and strong, toiling to build the New Socialist China with commitment and revolutionary fervour. They are physically sturdy, well-dressed and clean-faced, and engage in difficult work without flinching. The photographs portray the strength and collective spirit of the working class without hinting at any difficulties or poor working conditions.

Private mine in Henan province in the 1990s, by Niu Guozheng.

With the end of the Cultural Revolution and the death of Mao Zedong in 1976, the role and content of photography began to change. Photojournalists were inspired by the shifting ideological and cultural landscape, and began to experiment with new aesthetics, resulting in the appearance of a new humanitarian realism in photojournalism. At the same time, new artistic uses of photography—inspired in part by the influx of the works of Western photographers—appeared, while family photography became less political and more individualistic in character. Furthermore, the increasing affordability of cameras led to the emergence of a new generation of photographers, artists, and enthusiastic amateurs.

Since the late 1990s, we have seen a growing number of socially engaged photographers who address societal changes and problems, as well as photographers who embark on more personal and artistic explorations. Special photo journals, art spaces, and photo festivals, have given photographers new platforms to showcase their work (Chen 2018). Socially engaged photographers, such as Lü Nan (known for his work on mental patients), Zhang Xinmin (who was among the first to document migrant workers in Guangdong in the early 1990s), Nie Guozheng (who has documented the life of miners), and Lu Guang (famous for his work on the Henan HIV crisis and environmental pollution) have addressed topics and groups of people that previously received scant attention. Many NGOs—Project Hope working on rural education was one of the first—also began to make use of photography to draw attention to their work. The digital revolution, including the Internet, social media platforms, and smartphones, has enabled more people to document their lives and personal memories. On social media, especially Sina Weibo, Chinese citizens have been exposed to images of groups of people and issues that the traditional media are often still silent about, such as the struggle and plight of petitioners, trafficked children, and villagers who have lost their land (Svensson 2016).

Although initially reluctant to take to Weibo, workers, activists, and labour NGOs now use the platform to share photographs about their activities, including protests and strikes. Labour NGOs have also encouraged and trained workers to document their life and work, and have organised a variety of exhibitions (Sun 2014). The Love Save Pneumoconiosis Foundation, an organisation that opened its Weibo account in 2011, has actively used photos and videos of migrant workers suffering from the deadly work-related lung disease. Some migrant workers afflicted by this illness have also begun to use social media to circulate information and images of themselves and their lives. These photos and videos show the workers' weak and emaciated bodies and reveal the seriousness of their condition, arousing empathy and support. Nonetheless, it is beyond doubt that most workers use their smartphones more for fun than as a tool to raise awareness about labour issues (Wallis 2013; Wang 2016).

At the same time, a more activist type of photography—which could be described as inverse surveillance or 'sousveillance'—has developed thanks to new digital technologies and platforms. Although the digital revolution has brought about new forms of visualities and enabled more people to make and circulate their own photographs, the Chinese state can still control and prevent the circulation of unwanted content. This is happening at the same time as the sheer quantity of information available is making it difficult for these images to be seen and actually have an impact.

Reading Labour Issues in and through Photography

How can we read photography in the context of Chinese labour? In 2008, Susan Meiselas and Orville Schell brought together the work of 18 Chinese photographers in the exhibition *Mined in China* which was first shown in the United States and later also in China. In 2011, a new expanded exhibition called *Coal+Ice* was first shown in the Three Shadows Art Centre in Beijing before travelling to other places in China and the United States. Both exhibitions were sponsored by the Asia Institute in New York. These exhibitions included historical photographs from *China Pictorial* (*Renmin huabao*) as well as contemporary photography from the 1990s and 2000s. Historical photographs from *China Pictorial* and other news sources provide rich information about the view and role of the working class during the Mao era but often less information about actual working conditions. The range of photographs illustrate both the changes in visual representation of miners as well as their changing working conditions.

One representative photograph from 1969 shows a group of miners, including a few women, standing and sitting on the underground track leading into a mine. They are not working, however, but busy reading Mao's *Little Red Book* and holding a large portrait of him. The photograph is clearly staged to showcase how studying Mao is helping and inspiring the miners in their work. The miners are well-dressed and clean-faced, and the photograph provides no indication of hardship. Instead, it provides a reminder of how in the Maoist era ideology permeated all workplaces, and how miners were both celebrated and disciplined at a time when work was considered 'glorious'.

This and other historical photographs provide an interesting contrast to the more contemporary photographs in the exhibition. The weakening of the grip of ideology over photography has led to new aesthetics and ways of documenting the life and work of miners. At the same time, the reform period has also led to the emergence of private mines and, in many cases, worsening working conditions. The workforce today includes migrant workers with less skills and lower social status than their predecessors or their counterparts in state mines. Socially engaged photographers capture these changes in the nature and status of the work. For instance, Niu Guozheng's photographs in Henan and Geng Yunsheng's photographs in Yunnan since the 1990s both reveal the precarious situation of those miners who struggle to make a living in a dangerous line of work. Their photographs show bare-chested miners covered in soot engaging in taxing manual labour, carrying buckets of coal in small, private mines that one may assume are not very safe.

One early striking photograph by Niu Guozheng—included in the celebrated 2003 exhibition *Humanism in China*—shows a teenage boy covered in soot on a heap of coal and rocks. He stands with a cheeky and self-confident smile, basket on his arm, dressed only in a pair of shorts and sandals. Slightly ajar on his head, adding to the sense of casualty and humour, sits a helmet that is more for show than for safety. The image works on a number of levels. On the one hand, it raises questions of working conditions, safety, and underage miners; but at the same time it reveals the boy's pride and resourcefulness, and acknowledges his agency.

Showing the more negative and dangerous aspects of mining, Zhang Jie has taken photos of families holding photos of family members who have died in the mines. Wang Mianli's photographs, in contrast, portray technically-advanced mines—seemingly mostly state-owned—where luckier miners work. These photographs privilege the physical settings and the machinery rather than the people working there, and through their composition and colouring give a somewhat techno-optimistic image of the mining industry. Another photographer, Song Chao, worked as a miner himself before taking up photography. His portraits of miners in black and white turn our attention from the mining industry to the individual miners themselves. Although the men are dark and dirty from the soot, their individual character, pride, and strength stand out, and the photos end up highlighting their agency.

These photographs remind us that the mining industry is highly diverse, with quite different working conditions and classes of workers. More importantly, the different styles of the photographers included in the exhibition show how Chinese photography today has diversified and become more individualistic in character. The exhibition obviously can be read and probed in many respects, and it indeed gives rise to a number of questions, some of which can only be answered by turning to academic works and media reports on the mining industry. Nonetheless, the photographs work more affectively than mere text and facilitate both awareness and engagement.

Building Empathy through Photography

Academic work and statistics often fail to capture the lived and embodied experiences of labour in different times, conditions, and places. In the best of circumstances, photography can provide a deeper, more empathic understanding that fosters respect and solidarity. It can also serve as a catalyst for critical thinking and theoretical reflection. Through photography researchers and students of labour can get closer to subjects, sites, and topics that might otherwise be closed and out of reach to them.

Photography, however, may also hide or fail to explain larger institutional and structural contexts and issues. For this reason, one needs to have the necessary background information in order to critically read and analyse visual representations of labour. When looking at photographic records, we need to ask ourselves some critical questions: what are the limitations of photography? What is invisible or has been left out? What photographs are missing? Are workers depicted as victims or as agents of change? Who is taking these photographs and why, and does it matter? Only if we reflect on these questions, will we be able to critically understand the power of photography for engagement and solidarity. ■

The *Mined in China* exhibition can be seen at: www.minedinchina.com/.

Screenshot from the trailer of *China: Time of Xi*.

Documenting China's Influence

David BANDURSKI

Back in 2017, the Discovery Channel aired China: Time of Xi, *a slick documentary series presenting China as a dynamic nation on the cutting edge under the stewardship of its 'people-centred' President, Xi Jinping. While by most accounts the series was simply good programming featuring renowned international personalities, in this essay David Bandurski takes a more critical look at the circumstances surrounding the production, arguing that there was more to it than it meets the eye.*

In 2017, on the eve of the Chinese Communist Party's (CCP) Nineteenth National Congress, the Discovery Channel, one of the world's most recognisable cable television brands, aired a slick documentary series presenting China as a dynamic nation on the cutting edge, under the stewardship of its 'people-centred' President, Xi Jinping. The programme, *China: Time of Xi*, was hosted by international personalities, including American architect Danny Forster and Australian biomedical engineer Jordan Nguyen (Discovery 2017). Produced for Discovery by Meridian Line Films, which identifies itself as a 'UK-based independent production company', it aired in 37 countries and regions across Asia, reaching tens of millions of viewers (2017).

By most accounts, the series was simply good programming—a timely and relevant response to China's political event of the year. A report in the *Straits Times*, Singapore's English-language daily, quoted creative director and executive producer Liz McLeod, the founder of Meridian Line Films, as saying that 'this is obviously a moment when Discovery's audiences will be wanting to know more about President Xi and about Chinese policy, and so it was a very good opportunity to make this series now' (China Daily 2017).

Chinese scholar Hu Angang is one of the famous personalities who make an appearance in *China: Time of Xi*.

Nesting China Dolls

Take a more critical look at the circumstances surrounding *China: Time of Xi*, however, and the plot quickly thickens. The series was in fact the product of a three-year content deal inked in March 2015 between Discovery Networks Asia-Pacific and China Intercontinental Communication Centre (CICC), a company operated by the State Council Information Office (SCIO)—the Chinese government organ, sharing an address with the Central Propaganda Department's Office of Foreign Propaganda (OFP), responsible for spearheading its official messages overseas (Gitter 2017). The news chatter surrounding the series came almost exclusively from official state media, which nevertheless took pains to persuade readers of its independence (People's Daily 2017). Even the *Straits Times* article offering the quote from McLeod was sourced from the *China Daily*, the official English-language newspaper of the SCIO (China Daily 2017).

The UK-based Meridian Line Films was yet another case of nesting dolls ending with the CICC and the SCIO. In its annual report filed in July 2015, Meridian Line lists as company directors both Jing Shuiqing, CICC's deputy director, and Wang Yuanyuan, its creative director (Companies House 2015). According to the same report, 85 percent of Meridian Line shares were held by a company identified as 'China International Communication Center Ltd', a name CICC frequently uses interchangeably with China Intercontinental Communication Center (China Daily 2007). Chinese company records show that the CICC directed by Jing Shuiqing, its legal representative, is fully owned by China Intercontinental Press (SAIC 2000), a company held by the Central Propaganda Department (SCIO) (SAIC 1994). That company's legal representative is Chen Lujun, currently deputy director of the News Bureau of the Central Propaganda Department—and therefore one of the country's top censorship officials for film and the news media (though he regularly appears in the media wearing another hat, as a film industry executive) (DocuChina 2017).

The point of this rapid rewind through what was billed last year as an independent television production is to demonstrate one of the more subtle means the Chinese government has at its disposal to influence the narrative globally about its domestic politics and its foreign policy: international film coproduction.

From Soft to Sharp Power

In a paper released the month after *China: Time of Xi* was broadcast across Asia, authors Christopher Walker and Jessica Ludwig (2017) introduced the term 'sharp power' to describe the efforts of countries like China and Russia to 'distract and manipulate', as opposed to the hard power of economic inducement or outright coercion, or to the appeal and attraction of soft power. Walker and Ludwig cited such 'borrowed boat' tactics as the insertion of *China Daily* supplements like 'China Watch' in foreign newspapers, or the airing of documentaries produced by China Global Television Network (CGTN) on channels outside China. These cases involve utilisation of domestic media channels for what is more or less transparently Chinese state content.

By contrast, the coproduction model is far subtler, and far more recent. As scholar and documentary filmmaker Ming Yu noted in 2017 (Yu 2017), the 2011 release by the State Administration of Radio, Film, and Television (SARFT) of a policy document titled Opinions on Accelerating Development of the Documentary Industry was a key turning point for international coproductions (SARFT 2012). According to the policy, the 'energetic advancement' of the documentary industry would 'have great significance for boosting international cultural dialogue and cooperation, advancing the going out of Chinese culture, and raising Chinese cultural soft power.' Outside official CCP discourse, talk of 'culture' may seem warm and inviting. But for China's leaders culture is twinned with the language of ideological dominance, a link we can spot clearly in President Xi Jinping's August 2013 speech to his first conference on propaganda and ideological work, where he described 'Chinese culture' as a tool of international discourse power (China Copyright and Media 2013). As Li Congjun, the director of the official Xinhua News Agency, wrote at the time: 'In the world today, whose communication methods are most advanced, whose communication capacity is strongest, determines whose ideology, culture, and value system can be spread most widely, and have the greatest influence on the world' (Li 2013).

An Illusion of Independence

Since 2011, CICC has racked up a long list of successes in rolling out its cultural programming, aided by international coproduction partnerships. To offer one more recent example, there is *The Story of Time*, a documentary coproduced by CICC, Guangxi TV, and Vietnam Television (VTV)—Vietnam's national television broadcaster. The film builds on the recollections of teachers and students from Vietnam who spent time in Guangxi to convey what a description by CICC calls 'the deep friendship between China and Vietnam' (VideoChinaTV 2017). The programme was timed to air both in China and in Vietnam during the Asia-Pacific Economic Cooperation Summit held in Da Nang, where Xi Jinping's speech followed that of US President Donald Trump (Tan 2017).

Unlike the 'borrowed boat' approach, or the outright launch of Chinese-produced programmes and channels overseas—such as CGTN America—the coproduction model allows China's state propaganda apparatus to piggyback on the trust and credibility that domestic or regional broadcasters such as Discovery Asia or Vietnam Television have already established with their audiences. Further, it helps project the illusion of distance between the Chinese state and the production process, such that the 'independence' of documentaries like *China: Time of Xi* can be taken seriously, despite obvious alignment with state propaganda messages. That is, until we take the often simple step of lifting the veil—looking, as I did above, at the short trail of breadcrumbs leading back to the centre of China's propaganda regime.

When it comes to international film coproduction, the veil is almost never lifted. Which leads us to the final, and perhaps most important, advantage of China's continued engagement with production cultures overseas through enterprises like CICC: the normalisation of the Chinese state as a creative partner and financier.

Normalising Propaganda

In September 2015, when the executive vice-president of National Geographic Channel (Asia), Simeon Dawes, unveiled the broadcast slot for *China From Above*, a two-part documentary produced jointly with CICC, no one noted the oddity of the fact that Cui Yuying, a deputy director of China's SCIO, was there to address the audience, saying the documentary would 'provide a better understanding of China for foreign audiences' (China.org.cn 2015). Similarly there was no media coverage of the fact that the coproduction partner was fully owned by the Central Propaganda Department, of which Ms Cui was also a deputy director.

Likewise, *Realscreen*, an international magazine covering the television and non-fiction film industries, could write ingenuously in June this year that China was 'making a big comeback as a coproduction partner' at France's Sunny Side of The Doc, one of the world's leading markets for documentary and factual content—despite the fact that all of the partners named, including CICC, were run by the Chinese state (Bruneau 2018). The article even quoted CICC's president, Chen Lujun, speaking excitedly about a new coproduction with Radio and Television of Portugal (RTP) about porcelain and its impact on globalisation. The collaboration may sound innocent enough; but official Chinese coverage makes it crystal clear that the project with RTP is linked to Xi Jinping's signature foreign policy initiative—the Belt and Road—and that the Portuguese broadcaster has joined China's 'Belt and Road Media Cooperation Union', an alliance of media companies around the world committed to working with China on stories linked to the Belt and Road Initiative (BIFF 2018).

Imagine how different this news might look were I to write Chen's remarks in *Realscreen* as a kicker quote with just a bit more context:

> We want to act as a bridge between China and Europe,' said CICC President Chen Lujun, who is also deputy director of the News Bureau of China's Central Propaganda Department. 'Porcelain is a symbol of oriental wisdom and we are happy to introduce that to the world.

As China becomes an ever-present player on the global cultural and intellectual stage, we should be mindful of the deeper political context surrounding what Xi Jinping has enticingly called 'China's story' (An 2018). Always dancing around this story is another chronicle, wilfully or neglectfully untold, about how that story has been directed, manufactured, and influenced by a single dominant protagonist, the Chinese Communist Party. ■

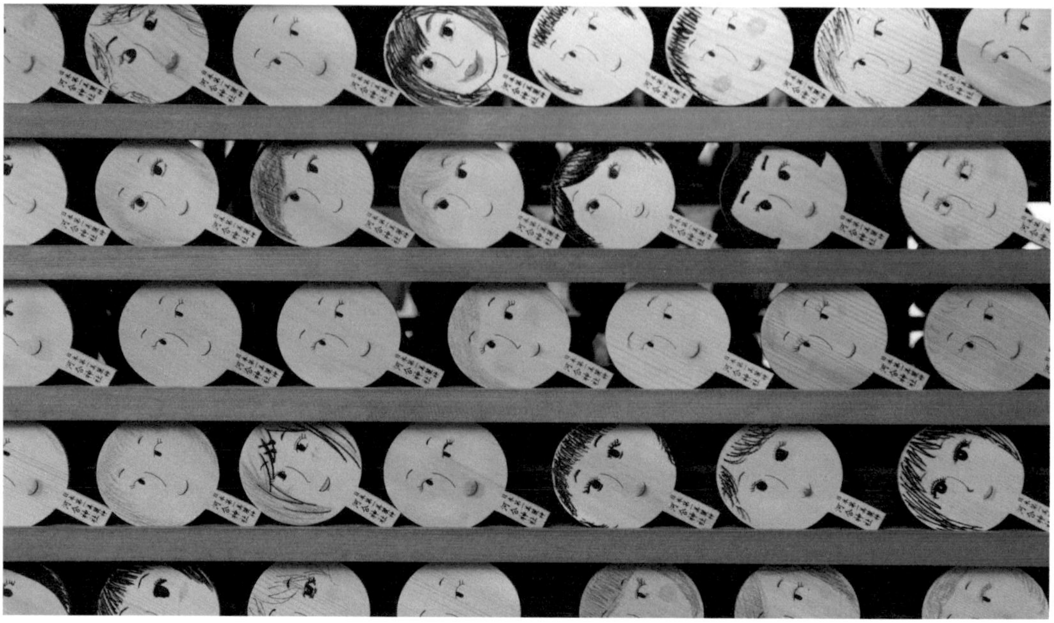

'Face, Face, Face.' PC: Terhide Tomori, Flickr.com.

The Global Age of Algorithm

Social Credit and the Financialisation of Governance in China

Nicholas LOUBERE
Stefan BREHM

Much has been made of the Orwellian social control aspects of the emerging 'social credit system' in China. However, social credit is more than simply a Chinese version of big brother: it is an unprecedented climax of the global financialisation project and a signal of a potential dark digital future dominated by algorithmic rule.

Beautiful credit! The foundation of modern society. Who shall say that this is not the golden age of mutual trust, of unlimited reliance upon human promises?

Mark Twain and Charles Dudley Warner, *The Gilded Age: A Tale of Today* (1873)

In recent years, few news items out of China have resulted in as much anxiety and fear in western media and public discourse than the Chinese government's ongoing attempts to create a 'social credit system' (*shehui xinyong tixi*) aimed at rating the trustworthiness of individuals and companies. Most major Western media outlets have spent significant energy warning about China's efforts to create an Orwellian dystopia. The most hyperbolic of these—*The Economist*—has even run with menacing headlines like 'China Invents the Digital Totalitarian State' and 'China's Digital Dictatorship' (*The Economist* 2016b; *The Economist* 2016c). These articles both implicitly and explicitly depict social credit as something unique to China—a nefarious and perverse digital innovation that could only be conceived of and carried out by a regime like the Chinese Communist Party (Daum 2017).

Social credit is thus seen as signalling the onset of a dystopian future that could only exist in the Chinese context. But how unique to China is this attempt to 'build an environment of trust'—to quote the State Council (2016)—using new digital forms of data collection and analysis? Is this Orwellian social credit system indicative of an inherently Chinese form of digital life, or is it a dark manifestation of our collective impulses to increase transparency and accountability (at the expense of privacy), and to integrate everyone into a single 'inclusive' system to more easily categorise, monitor, and standardise social activity? In this essay, we propose that Chinese social credit should not be exoticised or viewed in isolation. Rather, it must be understood as merely one manifestation of the global age of the algorithm.

Engineering a Trustworthy Society

While there have long been discussions about creating an economic and social rating system in China, they took a much more concrete form in 2014, with the publication of a high-level policy document outlining plans to create a nationwide social credit system by 2020 (State Council 2014). The proposed system will assign ratings to individuals, organisations, and businesses that draw on big data generated from economic, social, and commercial behaviour. The stated aim is to 'provide the trustworthy with benefits and discipline the untrustworthy … [so that] integrity becomes a widespread social value' (State Council 2016). While official policy documents are light on detail with regard to how the social credit system will ultimately operate, they have suggested various ways to punish untrustworthy members of society (i.e. those with low ratings), such as through restrictions on employment, consumption, travel, and access to credit. In recent months, there have already been reports of blacklisting resulting in restrictions for individuals, but as of yet this only applies to those who have broken specific laws or 'failed to perform certain legal obligations' (Daum 2018a).

The Chinese social credit system is emerging rapidly, and the aforementioned blacklists are connecting data from dozens of governmental departments. However, it is still far from being a unified or centralised system. Like most new policies in China, social credit is being subjected to the country's distinctive policy modelling process (Heilmann 2008), where local governments produce their own interpretations of policies, which then vie to become national models. Over 30 local governments have already started piloting social credit systems, which utilise different approaches to arrive at their social credit scores, and which use the scores to achieve different outcomes. In contrast to other policies, however, large Internet companies have also been given licenses to run their own pilots (Loubere 2017a). The most widely used private social credit system is Alibaba's Sesame Credit, which utilises opaque algorithms to arrive at social credit scores for their customers. Those with high scores have been able to access a range of benefits from other Alibaba businesses and their partners (Bislev 2017). Sesame Credit is significant due to the huge amounts of economic data held by Alibaba through Alipay and Ant Financial, but it should not be conflated with governmental social credit system pilots. It is not clear how or if the government and private systems will be integrated in the future, which seems to be causing a degree of tension between regulators and the Internet giants (Hornby, Ju, and Lucas 2018).

Financial(ised) Inclusion

While social credit can be seen as an outgrowth of our collective impulse to achieve a more trustworthy society, a unified fully-functioning social credit system will ultimately turn the quest for trust through transparency and accountability upside down, because it would hold citizens responsible vis-à-vis their rulers. At the core of the emerging system, the state and financial actors define, quantify, and calculate trustworthiness and honesty—it is a technocratic fix based on the logic that, with the correct set of algorithms, the good citizen can be engineered into society. Social credit therefore seeks to transform individuals into a new 'civilised' (and 'credit-conscious') population through the imposition of an incentive and disincentive system that can mould logical profit-maximising citizens into civilised subjects.

In the case of China's proposed social credit system—as with any credit rating system—these rewards and punishments are meted out through engagement with, and incorporation into, the market. The calculation of credit scores requires market activity, which in turn requires a credit score. Moreover, if social credit is to live up to its technocratic promise of systematically eliminating untrustworthiness, everyone must be assessed equally—i.e. everyone must be included in the system. In the absence of a social credit score, the worst must be assumed, meaning that the burden of proving ones trustworthiness falls to the individual. Thus, in a society dominated by social credit, integration into the socioeconomic system is a necessity rather than a choice. In this way, China's social credit resonates with the global financial inclusion project, which seeks to integrate marginal and impoverished populations into the global capitalist system—primarily through expanded access to credit—as a means of promoting economic development and social empowerment.

In the same way that Chinese social credit appears poised to extract huge amounts of personal data from individuals in its quest to create a trustworthy society, proponents of financial inclusion justify intrusive methods of assessing creditworthiness in order to reduce lender risk from untrustworthy borrowers. Indeed, just months before their hyperbolic headlines about China's digital authoritarianism, *The Economist* praised the use of psychometrics and other personal digital data by lenders in developing contexts as being a beneficial financial innovation (*The Economist* 2016a). In this way, the financial inclusion project depicts the application of financialised logics as the means of producing a more fair and accountable inclusive system, where the trustworthy reap rewards that were denied them in the past. However, underpinning this neoliberal fantasy is a glaring contradiction that shatters the illusion of inclusion as being unbiased and fair—those with capital are able to set the terms of their engagement with the capitalist system much more easily than those without.

This points to the fact that the rich will largely be able to extract more of the rewards from their participation in financialised rating systems—such as the social credit system—while avoiding the sanctions. Moreover, punishments are much more dramatic for those without accumulated capital, as their very existence depends on their continued participation in the capitalist system for daily survival. From this perspective, the spectre of China's financialised social credit system portents a society comprising individual micro-entrepreneurs operating in a shared economy mode where livelihoods are determined by credit scores. Indeed, Sesame Credit already works with sharing economy apps, such as Daowei, which provides a platform for a literal gig economy comprised of individuals (with their credit scores listed) advertising the sale of their services or products (Loubere 2017b). Those looking for a plumber in the area can select one with the highest score, just as people in the west decide hotels and restaurants based on Yelp or TripAdvisor reviews.

Financialisation Gone Wild

In this sense, the emergence of social credit represents an unprecedented climax of the global financialisation project. Financialisation can be broadly defined as 'the increasing role of financial motives, financial markets, financial actors, and financial institutions in the operation of domestic and international economy' (Epstein 2005, 3). Social credit opens the door for financialising social behaviour. To elaborate this claim, consider the relation between social and financial capital. The OECD, for example, defines social capital as 'networks together with shared norms, values and understandings that facilitate cooperation within or among groups' (Keeley 2007, 103). In the digital age, these networks become the linchpins between the social and economic spheres. On the one hand, networks are more concrete and easier to observe than the norms and values shaping the perceptions and behaviour of network members. On the other hand, social networks represent a crucial means for both gaining access to material resources and shaping the rules for resource distribution. Thus, analysing and contextualising social networks in a big-data driven world allow for inferences to be made about both the social and economic attributes of an individual.

The invention of social credit establishes an explicit and tangible link between social behaviour and economic benefits. In this context, the State is able to assume a new role not dissimilar to that of a corporate shareholder. Social credit creates a market for social capital and transplants the rationale of profit maximisation into the realm of interpersonal relationships. Through managing networks, digital activity, and private action, an individual or organisation can impact social value and, by extension, financial capital. Thus, social credit creates new incentives that can be used to align the interests of citizens and organisations with those of the government. The state, as a shareholder in 'the people', enjoys the dividends of good behaviour and loyalty, which are rewarded through economic privileges. In this all-encompassing financialised system, social action becomes increasingly entrenched within the economic realm, and individual behaviour is more and more shaped by financial motives. In a nutshell, social credit represents the ultimate marketisation of political control because it provides incentives for maximising citizen value through politically and commercially aligned social behaviour.

Using algorithms to render citizens and organisations compliant with the visions and rationales of the ruling regime reduces the state's information and monitoring costs dramatically. In the context of China, this has the potential to reshape the 'fragmented authoritarian' model, which is characterised by decentralised decision-making and policy implementation (Mertha 2009). One could envision a future in which the many local officials and bureaucrats that enjoy privileges due to the central leadership's reliance on their support to govern the masses will be subject to the rule of algorithms themselves. Only a small elite would be needed to manage algorithmic rule, entailing a dramatic reconcentration of power. If Chinese experiments are successful, they will certainly serve as a model for many other countries: authoritarian regimes, democratic systems with authoritarian tendencies, and eventually democracies that struggle to maintain legitimacy in an increasingly polarised and fragmented political landscape.

The Repressive Logics of Financialised Governance

As noted above, despite the discourse of inclusion resulting in transparency and fairer distribution or resources, social credit and the financialisation of social behaviour are inherently biased and paradoxically result in socioeconomic exclusion within an all-encompassing inclusive system. In addition to being partial to those with capital, social credit will likely also widen other socioeconomic cleavages. Tests and experiments again and again confirm that data and algorithms are just as biased as society is and inevitably reproduce real life segmentation and inequality (Bodkin 2017). Cathy O'Neil, the author of *Weapons of Math Destruction*, for instance, warns that we need algorithmic audits (O'Neil 2016). After all, algorithms are not some naturally occurring phenomena, but are the reflections of the people (and societies) that create them. For this reason, the rule of algorithms must not be mistaken as an upgraded, more rational, and hyper-scientific rule of law 2.0. This is particularly true in China, where the concept of the rule of law has been increasingly developed and theorised by the Party-state to justify its attempts to consolidate control over society (Rosenzweig, Smith, and Treveskes 2017).

In recent years, China has already been providing glimpses of the repressive possibilities of algorithmic rule. In particular, recent reports about the construction of a sophisticated high-tech surveillance state in the Xinjiang Autonomous Region anticipate a near future where a digital social credit system sits at the core of a coercive security apparatus that is inherently biased against certain segments of society—producing dramatically inequitable and ultimately violent results (Human Rights Watch 2018). In an op-ed for the *New York Times*, James A. Millward describes the extent of the surveillance infrastructure primarily targeting the Uyghur ethnic minority. This includes police checkpoints, iris scans, mandatory spyware installed on mobile devises, and pervasive CCTV with facial recognition software. These surveillance technologies feed into, and draw on, a database that includes information about personal identity, family and friends, movement and shopping behaviour, and even DNA that is collected at medical check-ups organised by the government. Ultimately, these data are run through algorithms that assign residents with public safety scores deeming them 'safe', 'unsafe', or somewhere in between (Millward 2018). Those who are deemed to be a threat are often detained and sent to reeducation centres (Foreign Policy 2018). While this is not the government's proposed social credit system per se—as these types of data are not legally allowed to be collected for public or market information (Daum 2018b)—the logics underpinning this type of coercive surveillance infrastructure and the dreams a nationwide citizen rating system are the same.

These developments represent a new reality that, while shocking initially, has become a banal part of everyday existence in a few short years. It is becoming increasingly clear that Xinjiang is a testing ground for technologies and techniques that will be rolled out nationwide—and even beyond—in the near future. For instance, over the spring festival period railway police in Henan used glasses augmented with facial recognition software connected to a centralised database to identify suspected criminals (Wade 2018). China's massive surveillance market is also a global affair, with companies from around the world lining up to develop products for both the Chinese state and private businesses operating in the country (Strumpf and Fan 2017). This points to the fact that China is not developing its surveillance capabilities in isolation but is at the forefront of a global push towards increasingly centralised and interconnected surveillance apparatuses. Rating systems like the proposed social credit system will inevitably sit at the centre of surveillance regimes, providing the basis for how individuals and organisations are monitored and assessed, and what they are able to do (and not do) within society.

Our Dark Digital Futures

China's proposed social credit system and the ongoing construction of a surveillance state in Xinjiang represent the vanguard of more efficient means of socioeconomic control that are being taken up around the globe. They are dark outgrowths of the digital revolution's supposed 'liberation technologies'—underpinned by our very human compulsions for transparency, security, and fairness. Credit systems are, of course, not new, nor are they Chinese in origin. Most industrialised nations have been relying on credit ratings for a long time in order to quantify the financial risk of countries, firms, and individuals (Yu et al. 2015). Indeed, some of the most disturbing aspects of Chinese social credit, such as its integration into social media, are not uniquely or originally Chinese. In the United States, Affirm, a San Francisco-based lender headed by PayPal cofounder Max Levchin, has been experimenting with social media data to evaluate the credit risk of car buyers since 2013. And Lenddo, a Hong Kong-based company, took an even bolder approach and informed debtors' friends on Facebook when they did not pay instalments in time. Even the Orwellian nightmare unfolding in Xinjiang has its parallels elsewhere, such as with the recent revelations that in the United States, the New Orleans Police Department and Immigration and Customs Enforcement have been working with Peter Thiel's company Palantir Technologies (which also has connections with the CIA and the Pentagon) to experiment with 'predictive policing' based on data collected from police databases, social media, and elsewhere (Fang 2018; Winston 2018). Taken together, these developments reveal a vision of a digital future where we are all locked in a continuous and banal system of monitoring, accounting, categorising, and tracking—which has potential far reaching consequences for those who challenge the hegemony in any way, or even just for those who do not have the resources or capacity to participate in the socioeconomic system on the terms mandated.

Big-data driven social benchmarking sparks entrepreneurs' and politicians' imaginations about the opportunities lying ahead. And even though not all visions will be economically or politically viable at any place in the world, the general trend appears to be global and irreversible. Social credit and the dreams of financialised governance are not Chinese or authoritarian particularities, but are, perhaps, our 'shared destiny' (*gongtong mingyun*)—to use a term employed by Xi Jinping when talking about the Chinese vision for the future of humanity (Barmé, Jaivin, and Goldkorn 2015). This, however, does not make it less, but rather more worrisome. The logical conclusion of society-wide financialisation is the blurring of the border between political and commercial realms, and the sharpening of the repressive tools wielded by the rich and powerful. In China this scenario appears to be inevitable. To quote Lucy Peng, the chief executive of Ant financial, '[Sesame Credit] will ensure that the bad people in society don't have a place to go, while good people can move freely and without obstruction' (Hvistendahl 2017). ■

HUMAN
RIGHTS
MADE IN
CHINA

The border of Houchang urban village in Beijing. Photo by the authors.

Beijing Evictions: A Winter's Tale

LI Qiaochu, SONG Jiani, and ZHANG Shuchi

In response to a deadly fire in a Beijing neighbourhood inhabited mostly by migrant workers, the authorities of the Chinese capital launched an unprecedented wave of evictions. Without any notice, migrants who often had spent years in the capital were told to leave their habitations and relocate elsewhere in the midst of the freezing north-China winter. While foreign media widely reported on the unfolding of the crisis, they often overlooked the outpouring of outrage in Chinese public discourse. This essay seeks to fill this gap.

On 18 November 2017, a fire broke out in a building in Beijing's southern Daxing suburb, killing 19 people including 8 children. Most of the victims were migrants who had come to Beijing from other parts of the country. According to the local authorities, around 400 people lived in cramped conditions in the two-story structure, which also served as a workshop and refrigerated warehouse for local vendors (Tu and Kong 2017). In the days that followed the tragedy, nearly 20 people were detained over the fire, including managers and electricians of the building.

In response to the tragedy, on 20 November the Beijing government kicked off 40 days of citywide safety inspections, with a particular focus on warehouses, rental compounds, wholesale markets, and other constructions on the rural-urban fringes across Beijing (Zhu and Gao 2017). This led to a wave of evictions from the suburbs of the city. Without any notice, migrants who often had spent years in the capital were told to leave their dwellings and relocate elsewhere in the midst of the freezing north-China winter. While foreign media widely reported on the unfolding of the crisis, what was often overlooked is the outrage that was expressed in Chinese public opinion over the evictions. This essay seeks to fill this gap in three ways. First, it outlines how Chinese civil society attempted to resist the crackdown. Second, it puts forward a novel comparison between the official response to the fire by government of Beijing and that of London in the wake of the Grenfell tragedy. Finally, it considers the implications that the tragedy has had for local labour NGOs.

Voices from Chinese Civil Society

Chinese academia was the first to stand up against the evictions. In the wake of the crackdown at the end of November, more than 100 Chinese intellectuals signed a petition urging the Beijing government to stop using safety checks as an excuse to evict migrant workers from the city. According to this letter, 'Beijing has an obligation to be grateful towards all Chinese citizens, instead of being forgetful and repaying the country people with arrogance, discrimination and humiliation—especially the low-end population' (Lo 2017). A couple of weeks later, in mid-December, eight top Chinese intellectuals, including legal scholars Jiang Ping and He Weifang, demanded a constitutional review of the Beijing municipal government's actions during the mass eviction (Weiquanwang 2017). They published their petition letter to the Standing Committee of the National People's Congress online. In this document, they argued that the government had infringed upon five constitutional rights of the Chinese citizens, including land rights, the right to participate in the private or individual economy, private property rights, the inviolability of human dignity, and housing rights. Unsurprisingly, the letter was quickly deleted from Chinese social media (Gao 2017). Chinese civil society, in particular those labour NGOs that provide assistance to migrant workers, also did not remain silent. According to Wang Jiangsong, a professor at the China Industrial Relations Institute in Beijing, nearly 50 activists from different labour groups signed another petition letter condemning the government campaign (Wang 2017). Far more consequential was a 'Suggestion Letter', entitled 'Beijing Solidarity', that was released on 25 November by a young graduate using the pseudonym Que Yue. Que suggested the establishment of a network of partners to conduct a field survey in the communities nearby in order to connect those in need of help with professional aid agencies. As more and more volunteers joined the cause, Que also set up a WeChat group aimed at drawing a participatory 'Beijing Eviction Map' that showed both the locations and number of people affected by the evictions (Qi 2018).

In the days that followed, information poured in from different community actors, and a continuously updated document with information related to available assistance became a focal point of action. In charge of the editing was Hao Nan, director of the Zhuoming Disaster Information Centre, a volunteer organisation set up in the wake of the 2008 Sichuan earthquake that specialises in processing disaster-related information and coordinating resources. His job consisted of connecting NGOs, citizen groups, and individual volunteers to work together to collect, check, and spread information. NGOs and the citizen groups conducted investigations in several areas where evictions were taking place and disseminated information about available assistance among migrants. At the same time, volunteers were responsible for collecting useful information online and for checking that the information coming from those who offered assistance was accurate. In an interview with the authors, Hao Nan described the difficulties in assisting the migrants, saying: 'Some of the migrants actually did not need our help, and some of them thought our information was useless. For example, they needed to find places to live nearby, but we could only find cheap places far away from their neighbourhoods.' Furthermore, most migrants could not access this kind of information due to the existence of different, and seldom overlapping, social circles on WeChat.

Meanwhile, some NGOs in Beijing began to mobilise autonomously. On 23 November, the Swan Rescue Team (*Tian'e jiuyuan*), an organisation set up in 2016 to provide emergency relief, began to offer migrants free assistance with their relocation. However, after a few days its leader suddenly announced that they would quit the rescue efforts, asking the public to 'understand that we are nothing more than a particle of dust, what we can do is tremendously limited' (Qi 2018). The New Sunshine Charity Foundation (*Xin yangguang*) provided funding, medical treatment, temporary resettlement, and luggage storage to evicted migrants. The Beijing Facilitators Social Work Development Centre (*Beijing xiezuozhe*) provided mental health support. Staff from the famous labour NGO Home of Workers (*Gongyou zhi jia*), which was located in the area of the evictions, regularly visited migrants nearby and released updates for volunteers and journalists, but quickly received a warning from the government to cease these activities. Finally, the Tongzhou Home (*Tongzhou jiayuan*), a worker cultural centre first opened in 2009, offered evicted migrants the chance to store their luggage or spend the night there. This went on until 28 November, when its director, Mr Yang, was visited by police officers who told him to shut down the organisation. 'I have worked in a factory, been a street vendor, and run a few small businesses—I know how hard it is to be a migrant worker,' Yang said. 'I don't regret helping them. It was the right thing to do and there is nothing to regret' (Qi 2018).

Migrants themselves were not silent. According to witnesses and social media posts, on 10 December many of them took to the streets in Feijia village, Chaoyang district, to protest against evictions. Protesters shouted slogans like 'forced evictions violate human rights', while others held up home-made banners with the same message (Zhou and Zhuang 2017). The voices of the workers were recorded by Beijing-based artist Hua Yong, who in those weeks uploaded dozens of videos documenting the situation and his conversations with migrant workers on YouTube and WeChat. On the night of 15 December, he posted several videos on his Twitter account entitled 'they are here', referring to the police who was at his door to detain him. He was released on bail three days later (AFP 2017).

A Tale of Two Blazes

Though not often linked, the events in Beijing recall the Grenfell Tower fire in London five months earlier. While occurring thousands of miles apart, the two accidents do have something in common. First, they both largely affected migrants. Although no official demographic statistics can be found publicly online, Grenfell appeared to be a very mixed community, with the 71 victims composed of a high proportion of migrants, including people from the Philippines, Iran, Syria, and Italy (Rawlinson 2017). Like in Beijing, there were also concerns about a possible underreported death toll, as some undocumented migrants were among the dead but were not accounted for. This is similar to the case of Daxing, where the community primarily consisted of non-Beijing citizens and 17 out of the 19 victims were migrants who had come from others part of China (Haas 2017). The only difference is that migrants in Daxing were interprovincial, whereas in the Grenfell Tower they were international.

Secondly, migrants in both cases were mostly 'low-skilled', and from relatively poor and deprived segments of society. Being a social housing block in London, the Grenfell Tower accommodated a primarily low-income community. Xinjian village, where the fire broke out in Beijing, served the same functionality. It lies in the so-called 'rural-urban fringe' (*chengxiang jiehebu*), where property is generally cheaper and infrastructure is of poorer quality. While white-collar migrants and college graduates can afford to rent in well-established communities, low-skilled (primarily rural) migrants tend to gather in places like Xinjian.

In light of all these similarities, it is even more interesting to compare how the two governments reacted to the fires. Both had set goals to limit the total population of their cities, and both performed fire safety assessments all over the urban area. Nonetheless, as mentioned earlier, in spite of public outrage, Beijing authorities took this opportunity to evict rural migrant workers. Forced evacuation also occurred in other London high-rise apartment blocks that failed the fire safety checks after the Grenfell Tower incident, but the buildings were not torn down and revamped for weeks, during which time the government promised to 'make sure people had somewhere to stay' (Holton and Knowles 2017). In addition, the British Home Office also published the Grenfell immigration policy, which grants 12 months initial leave to remain and possible future permanent residency to the migrants involved in the fire.

From this comparison, we can draw two lessons. The first is that previously ridged and clear borders have become subtle and invisible. This applies most clearly to Beijing, where, thanks to the economic reforms, the Chinese household registration system (*hukou*) is no longer serving as a de facto internal passport system that stops people from migrating. This means that Chinese citizens do not face explicit barriers in terms of moving within their country. But there are invisible walls in terms of welfare entitlements, as the *hukou* system still links provision of social services to the place of registration. And just as immigration policy in developed countries is more selective towards highly skilled migrants, the conditions for granting a local *hukou* to internal migrants in big cities like Beijing are also geared towards attracting the wealthy or the highly educated. As a result, those low-skilled internal migrants are highly unlikely to obtain a Beijing *hukou*, and the Beijing government is not obliged to provide better housing for them. They are treated as second-class citizens in their own country.

The invisible border is also seen in the living space of those low-skilled migrants. In China, most rural migrant workers have to reside in island-like slums whose connections to other parts of the city are cut off. For instance, the photo that accompanies this essay was taken in December 2017, when one of the authors visited Houchang village, a slum known for being home to many migrant drivers and chauffeurs. On the left side of the picture is the village where migrants live. The rooms are so small that some furniture has to be put outside. Just to the right of the road lies an advanced residential complex with private basketball and badminton courts. Behind this newly built accommodation is the Zhongguancun Software Park, where several high-tech IT companies are based. Right at the crossing, we saw a rubbish truck collecting waste from the software park, but just one street apart, in the village, there was not even one trash bin. We could not get an aerial view of the village, but one can easily imagine a segmented landscape, with the village area stripped of access to public services and composed of basic infrastructure, but surrounded by fancy modern buildings within just ten meters of its perimeter. Every morning, migrants flock out to the city as drivers, delivery workers, etc., providing low-cost labour. In the evening, when they are supposed to relax, they squeeze back into the village. This scenario recalls the science fiction novelette Folding Beijing (Hao 2015), in which the city is physically shared by three classes, who take turns living in the same area in 48-hour cycles.

Another lesson that we can draw from the comparison between London and Beijing is that under all migration management systems, it is low-skilled migrants who bear the brunt of the catastrophe whenever a disaster happens. High-skilled workers are rarely affected and can easily work around the situation, even when they themselves become targets. While the dichotomy between high-skilled and low-skilled seems to be neutral and focuses on learning rather than inherited qualities, we should always bear in mind that when people are low-skilled it is largely due to institutionalised factors, not simply a matter of bad luck or bad choices. Taking education as an example, big cities are rich in experienced teachers, museums, opportunities for international exchange, etc.—a situation that allows urban citizens to receive a much better education than that available to people in underdeveloped areas. Awareness of this is a first step to prevent disasters like the Beijing fire from becoming the justification to victimise already vulnerable segments of society.

New Workers, New Priorities

With a view to labour NGOs, the evictions have at least three layers of meaning: first, they highlight structural and demographic changes in the Chinese workforce; second, they show that there is an urgent need for labour NGO activists to find new strategies to conduct their activities; and third, they demonstrate that the political context is swiftly changing. According to our personal observations, migrant workers who dwell in Beijing's urban villages work in a variety of industries that go far beyond traditional occupations in small retail, decoration, domestic work, vehicle repairing, etc. Today's migrants work in industries that are characterised by the logics of modern large-scale capital investment, including logistics, delivery, and real estate. Although the specific distribution of employment by industry still needs to be investigated thoroughly, the abundant supply of information, as well as the increasing ease of transportation and communication, have already made it possible for the urbanised workers to respond promptly to challenges coming from changes in government policies.

However, while the migrants themselves are increasingly able to respond quickly in the face of new threats, the response of labour NGOs—the traditional champions of migrant workers—to the evictions reveals the serious limitations of their current organisational approaches (see also Franceschini and Lin's essay in this volume). It is well documented that labour NGOs first appeared in China in the late 1990s, and went through a phase of expansion in the Hu and Wen era, especially in the years that preceded the financial crisis. These NGO practitioners are first and foremost professionals in the fields of the law, social services, or occupational safety and health. To this day, these organisations mostly focus on providing individual legal aid, carrying out legal training and legal dissemination among worker communities, investigating violations of labour rights in factories, and organising recreational activities aimed at the working class. Through these activities, they are able to create short-term networks among their clientele, fostering fledgling feelings of solidarity.

The mass evictions clearly exposed the deficiencies of such approach. On the one hand, these labour NGOs have already been hit by a harsh wave of repression in 2015 and 2016 that has severely undermined their ability to operate (Franceschini and Nesossi 2018). While those organisations and individuals that campaigned for a more militant activism based on collective bargaining today are no longer active or are unable to campaign, the remaining NGOs have no choice but to resort to self-censorship and limit their activities in order to survive. In addition, the core members of these organisations tend to consider themselves professionals rather than activists, and find themselves under considerable pressure from their families, peers, and state officials to avoid overly sensitive work. There are also clear class differences between NGO staff and the workers they assist, with the former largely belonging to the urban middle class and having a white-collar background. This gap was evident during the evictions, when the information and assistance services provided by these NGOs scarcely broke through social barriers to reach the workers.

While labour NGOs are marred by these constraints, individual agents appear to be far more active. Not only labour activists, but also ordinary middle-class people decided to step up when confronted by the situation that migrant workers faced in Beijing during the evictions. They felt compelled to appeal for the rights of the urban underclass. For the first time, information and articles concerning labour and the 'low-end population' (*diduan renkou*) grabbed the spotlight on various social media platforms normally used primarily by middle-class users. This resulted in an unprecedented prominence for the 'underclass discourse' in the public discussion, bringing together activists from intellectual backgrounds as diverse as Marxism, Maoism, and liberalism

While labour NGOs are becoming increasingly powerless, the actions of these individual citizens provides some hope in the otherwise stark reality in which migrant workers remain trapped in a dire situation under increasing pressure from the world's most powerful and undisguised police state. In light of this, it is our urgent duty to adapt to the rapidly changing sociopolitical climate, and make new alliance aimed at forging solidarity across different sectors of society. Only in this way, we will be able to develop more effective strategies and organisational models to support marginalised migrant workers and others who are falling victim to state repression in contemporary China. ■

A man pulls his belongings in a cart in Daxing district (Beijing). Photo: *Global Times*.

Evictions and the Right to the City

Kevin LIN

The eviction of tens of thousands of migrants from their dwellings in the suburbs of Beijing in November 2017 poses a question: do migrants in today's China have a right to the city?

Beijing's eviction of migrants from their dwellings in November 2017 following a deadly fire left tens of thousands homeless within days. It was rightly seen not as a legitimate response to a fire hazard but a convenient opportunity to push forward new political goals with regard to the city's migrant population. The evictions were undoubtedly not just an unintended consequence of a disaster. They were preceded by the forced closing of shops, restaurants, and housings in similar areas, and by the announcement of a plan to relocate Beijing's city government and public institutions to a nearby province. This is part of a wider strategy to supposedly slow down the urban growth of the capital—a move that has produced heightened anxiety and uncertainty among the Chinese floating population. This poses the question: do migrants in today's China have a right to the city?

Significantly, those evicted comprised all kinds of migrants: e-commerce couriers, shop owners, street vendors, as well as IT professionals. This heterogeneity reflects the fact that Beijing is not an industrial city: much of its heavy industry has long been shut down or relocated to neighbouring provinces. In contrast to places like Shenzhen or Dongguan, where migrants are the bedrock of the local economy, migrants in Beijing are less central to economic activity, which may be one reason for the harsh measures undertaken by the authorities. However, migrants, if broadly defined as people from outside of Beijing, make up more than a third of the city's long-term residents, or over eight million people.

What the Beijing authorities might not have fully anticipated is that many who have obtained a Beijing *hukou* may continue to identify themselves as migrants, sharing not only the frustration of urban lives with other migrants, but also the feelings of being excluded and disposable. In one sense, migrant as a cultural identity cuts across the *hukou* line, which may explain why the phrase 'low-end' (*diduan*) touched a nerve for wide swaths of the population. So while the eviction speaks of a 'low-end population' (*diduan renkou*), the anxiety (and shared identity) extends beyond just rural migrant workers in the so-called 'low-end economy' (*diduan jingji*).

Such shared sentiments may explain the outpouring of sympathy that followed the eviction (see Li, Song, and Zhang's essay in this volume). But the form such sympathy takes may risk being paternalistic, and the paternalism of caring for the unfortunate can deepen the entrenchment of the social position of the migrant. A common argument against eviction says that if those migrant workers who serve in the restaurants were forced to leave, there would be no one serving Beijing residents. The recognition of the role of migrant workers as servants and builders in a city like Beijing is simultaneously a factual statement and a reaffirmation of their 'low-end' socioeconomic position. It can lead to the thought—comforting for the status quo—that so long as they are not evicted or treated too harshly, their lives on the margins need not be questioned.

Another notable and somewhat unexpected response came from civil society, offering a glimpse of a possible resurgence of the public voice. A public statement in late November signed by academics, independent intellectuals, lawyers, and other civil society activists evokes the language of legality, human rights, and constitutionalism, contending that the eviction of migrants 'is a serious case of violating the law and the constitution and impinging on human rights' (Wang 2017). A second statement released in December by eight legal scholars and lawyers called on the National People's Congress to review the constitutionality of the eviction, citing violations of five constitutional rights centred on land, housing, and private property rights (Weiquanwang 2017).

The framing of the rights of migrants as a liberal-constitutional issue related to property rights—a reminder of the once vocal constitutionalism movement of the 2000s—sheds light on a largely unstated ideological contestation. The rights of migrant workers have been alternatively framed in relation to China's new working class's capacity to organise resistance by labour scholars and activists, or in terms of vulnerability of a social group in need of legal and constitutional protection by rights-oriented intellectuals. In practice, there is an overlap in labour and legal and citizenship rights, as can be seen from the fact that many labour scholars and activists also signed the first statement, where, for pragmatic reasons, a legalistic rights discourse is dominant. Still, such critique based on the protection of individual property rights leaves open the question of why evicted migrants are stuck in their place, socially and geographically, and of their collective rights.

There were acts of defiance in the form of sporadic collective protests and individual assistance to displaced migrants. One activist was detained and an organisation shut down; Hua Yong, a migrant artist who shot videos of the eviction, fled Beijing fearing for his safety, and was later detained and released. However isolated, these acts testify to the existence of alternative visions of what the city may look like, including the right for voluntary assistance to those in need, and documentation of abuses of power. Both are forbidden today.

The threat of urban protests was likely on the minds of the authorities. By some measure, China has one of the highest rates of urban riots. Many of them are expressions and assertions of the kind of city that the citizens want to see. Environmental protests to prevent polluting factories have resulted in some of the most successful mobilisations in recent years. Similarly, riots over the brutality of urban management officers (*chengguan*) have drawn wide support across the country. In light of this, the authorities have been pouring resources into preempting and containing urban riots.

Will China's ambitious urban transformation further deepen tensions among the urban population and migrants? It is hard to escape the conclusion that, as such a policy requires extensive state intervention, the eviction of migrants or other harsh measures will continue to recur. Still, there is hope that faced with this, more and more people will likely start to ask what kind of city they want and demand their right to the city. ■

'Thugs' Shanghai (2012). PC: Rob-Shanghai@flickr.com.

Outsourcing Coercion and Social Control

Lynette H. ONG

To carry out coercion and social control, the Chinese government often resorts to non-state actors, including thugs-for-hire, profit-seeking brokers, and even commercial enterprises. In this essay, Lynette Ong examines the circumstances under which the authorities use these means and the reasons behind their choices, arguing that this is mostly related to the need of reducing the cost of repression and evading responsibility.

During the Occupy Movement in Hong Kong in 2014, protestors were reportedly beaten up by unidentified thugs from neighbouring Guangdong province in China (Lim 2014). In 2012, local authorities hired scores of thugs to lock up the blind activist Chen Guangcheng in order to keep him out of the public eye (Branigan 2012). Local governments also work with professional intermediaries to convince aggrieved citizens to give up their resistance against the state, and engage private security personnel to intercept petitioners heading to Beijing (Wen 2017).

Why does the Chinese government—which is known for its strong-arm tactics—*need or desire* to use non-state actors to carry out coercion and social control? In this essay, I argue the government seeks to deploy non-state actors to perform coercive acts or exercise social control for a wide range of reasons, such as reducing the cost of repression and evading responsibility. These non-state actors range from thugs-for-hire, to profit-seeking brokers and even commercial enterprises (Ong 2018 and 2019).

Thugs-for-Hire

The government is most likely to use thugs-for-hire when it is carrying out *illegal* actions or *unpopular* policies, such as collecting unlawful exactions, evicting farmers and homeowners from their properties, or intimidating petitioners and dissidents. The third-party nature of these actors makes them expedient for carrying out illegal and unpopular policy implementation when formal uniformed agents, such as the police, could not be sent without harming state legitimacy.

The government is also likely to hire thugs when it seeks to evade accountability for its own actions. More often than not, this is related to the use of illegitimate violence to crack down on citizens. To the extent that the government does not want to be seen as using illegitimate force, it is likely to outsource violence to third parties. The thugs' elusive identity allows the government to maintain an arms-length relationship with them and the violent acts they commit.

In China, thugs are most likely to be hired to evict farmers and homeowners from their properties, and to intimidate protestors and dissidents into giving up their actions against the state. Because these state actions are unpopular, if not outright illegal, local governments are very reluctant to deploy formal coercive agents to carry out the work. Thugs, who are hired on a project basis, also help local governments that are weak in fiscal and coercive capacity to carry out central-mandated policies, such as land expropriation, housing demolition, and maintaining social stability by minimising dissent. Thugs-for-hire could be seen as contractual workers, who can be hired and terminated easily, unlike formal agents on government payroll (*bianzhi*) who enjoy a range of work benefits.

Agency Problems

Yet, outsourcing violence is often subject to agency problems. The government cannot exert tight control over these agents' actions. When thugs are sent to intimidate residents and demolish houses, excessive violence is often used, which can result in casualties. When local governments hire private security personnel to intercept petitioners, it is common for these private agents to abuse their power against vulnerable citizens seeking help. When municipal authorities employ ill-trained *chengguan*, some of whom are local ruffians, violence against marginal unlicensed street vendors becomes rampant. Effective and efficient as these coercive measures may be, agent-centred excessive violence often serves to attract sympathisers, which in turn mobilises support for resistance, rather than deterring it.

Violent agents may start off as thugs-for-hire on government projects for local authorities. However, over time they can evolve into mafia groups running vices such as gambling and prostitution rings. Some local authorities in China have grown so reliant on local mafia groups that their own power has been usurped. While it is challenging to estimate the scale or degree of this problem, we know for certain that the nexus between local governments and local mafia groups has become grave enough to warrant the Xi Jinping administration's launch of a massive campaign to fight against local organised crime (Shi 2018).

China is by no means the only country that hires violent agents to do dirty job. The United States government contracted out abuse of prisoners in Abu Ghraib to the security company Blackwater. During the Arab Spring protests, the Mubarak and Assad regimes also mobilised thugs—the 'Baltagiya' in Egypt and 'Shahiba' in Syria—to violently attack pro-democracy protestors (Batal al-Shishani and Elsheikh 2012).

Huangniu

In my research on housing demolition (*fangwu zhengshou*), I write about how the Chinese state also works with profit-seeking middlemen who can help establish trust between officials and citizens to resolve conflicts (Ong 2019). These brokers bring together the state and aggrieved citizens to facilitate state-society bargaining that would not have taken place otherwise. This bargaining may result in payouts or under-the-table deals, which help to resolve protracted stand-offs that might have otherwise spilled over into street protests.

In housing demolition projects in Chinese cities, municipal and local governments not only face tight deadlines, but are also under intense pressure to contain social contention. These two priorities can often be conflicting in nature. When a date for demolition is set, all households in the designated area must vacate by the agreed-upon deadline. Lack of compliance from one or two households can potentially put the entire project in jeopardy, necessitating severe tactics on the part of local governments and property developers. At the same time, however, preventing and repressing popular protests by aggrieved residents being quickly pushed out of their family homes is also a priority of municipal and local governments.

Local governments have limited options in dealing with this dilemma. Even though violence, such as hiring thugs, is often the most efficient means to evict residents, local officials are increasingly constrained in deploying coercive force against recalcitrant urban households. Increased media scrutiny and greater educational attainment of urban dwellers have given rise to a growing rights awareness, especially in major cities across the country. When the state is restrained in using violence but faces strong pressures to complete projects on time, it becomes more receptive to bargaining with citizens. The demand for brokers capable of facilitating a deal has therefore increased.

'Almost Gone,'
Shanghai (2012)
PC: Rob-Shanghai
@flickr.com.

These brokers are called *huangniu* in Chinese—a generally pejorative term that literally means 'cattle', but is used to describe middlemen who provide highly sought-after goods or services at prices above market value. In the context of housing demolition, these brokers are usually hired by disgruntled citizens to bargain with the state for better deals. In general, state officials willingly work with *huangniu* in order to forge agreements with society. The intermediary role of these professionals is enabled by the trust they have established with both the citizens and local officials. The extra payouts that are attributable to intermediary efforts, in terms of extra financial payout or apartment units, are then split between the citizen-client and the *huangniu*.

A Commodification of State–Society Bargaining

These profit-seeking brokers represent a commodification of state-society bargaining by matching demands from discontented citizens with the supply of special favours by state officials. In so doing, a commercial—and technically illegal—deal is secured that involves a compensation over and above that mandated by official policy, or what other citizens in a similar position who do not engage an intermediary are entitled to.

Brokers who collude with insider-government agents help clients to secure favourable treatment. In contexts outside of housing demolition, under-the-table payments are made to corrupt intermediaries who issue drivers' licenses that may otherwise take them a few rounds of tests to obtain. Routine traffic offenders pay a *huangniu* with connections in the transport authority to wipe their records of traffic offences. Similarly, *huangniu* are utilised by truck drivers seeking exemptions from inspections, companies that need registration but do not meet the requirements, and taxpayers who want to pay lower taxes. These examples, and many more, underline the wider implication of intermediated illegal transactions—the widespread abuse of state power bestowed upon government agents.

Corrupt brokers are in a unique position to bring together the state and citizens who are unable to reach demolition agreements. On the one hand, they have intimate connections with government agents that make them privy to insider information about government policies or the decisions of local officials unbeknown to citizens. On the other hand, they are able to gain the trust of clients, either because they are part of their networks or because they publicise their close connections with government agents. The *huangniu* promise their clients compensation higher than that mandated by official policy and, more often than not, they are able to deliver. In addition, *huangniu* provide related services essential for securing higher compensation. These include producing fake marriage and divorce certificates, bogus proof of pregnancy, and other similar documents to inflate the number of household members to be resettled. These services accentuate the illegality of the transactions and the role of corrupt intermediaries in housing demolition. But, they also increase their clients' entitlements to higher compensation.

The case of *huangniu* in housing demolition highlights the state's *willingness* and *ability* to engage with *market agents* who can help to fulfil state's objectives in exchange for profit. Together with thugs-for-hire, the existence of these kinds of intermediaries underscores the Chinese state's adroit use of non-state or market agents to preempt, absorb, and repress social contention and protests, when state actors cannot do it efficiently or effectively. ■

Chinese Justice, PC: Shutterstock.com.

Justice Restored under Xi Jinping
A Political Project

Elisa NESOSSI

Since Xi Jinping's ascendance to power, several cases of miscarriage of justice have been remedied, and significant reforms have been implemented to prevent abuses by the police and the courts. While on the surface these reforms could be considered groundbreaking, they have not found much international admiration or praise, as they are being carried out at the same time as a ferocious crackdown on civil society. It is now clear that in Xi's reforms there is more than meets the eye.

On 5 August 1994, a woman named Kang was found raped and murdered in a cornfield in a western suburb of Shijiazhuang, the capital of Hebei province. A few days later, the Shijiazhuang police established a special taskforce to investigate the case and, based on clues offered by local residents, identified one key suspect: a man named Nie Shubin. In early 1995, Nie was sentenced to death and executed. Back then nobody paid particular attention to the fate of this young alleged criminal. It was only ten years later when another man, Wang Shujin, confessed to that same crime that this case came to light. Following Wang's confession and suspecting that Nie Shubin had been wrongly executed, Ma Yunlong, then a journalist for the *Henan Shangbao*, published a short article on the case. Convinced by Wang's confession and insistent on Nie's innocence, he sent his report to more than 200 newspapers around China. Ma was particularly sympathetic to the relentless suffering of Nie's mother, and he recommended that she employ two lawyers who could help her work on the case. With the aim of seeing justice done, he himself started his own personal investigation into the case—an investigation destined to last for several years and that contributed to his forced early retirement. While the Hebei Court had relied on the alleged confession of Nie Shubin to sentence him to death, it could not equally use Wang Shujin's confession about his guilt to incriminate him. That would have been too politically costly: it would have meant admitting that the police, procuratorate, judges, and the political-legal committee (*zhengfawei*) in Shijiazhuang and Hebei province had got it wrong in the first place. Too many people had been involved in Nie's execution in 1995, and too many interests would have been negatively affected by reversing the verdict and declaring his innocence. Notwithstanding the continued petitioning of Nie's mother, and the work of numerous lawyers and journalists, the Hebei justice authorities maintained an unnerving silence on the case for almost six years.

In 2013, Wang's case was adjudicated for the second and third time but, once again, notwithstanding his insistence on his own guilt, the court did not sentence him for Ms Kang's rape and murder. In 2014, the Supreme People's Court (SPC) ordered the Shandong High Court to review Nie's case and a public hearing was held in April 2015. The term for the review was extended four times until June 2016 when the SPC finally decided to retry the case. Only then was the time politically ripe for justice to be done. Just a few months before, Zhang Yue—the then secretary of the political-legal committee of Hebei province—had been caught up in Xi Jinping's purge against corruption and put under investigation. At last, in December 2016, after a retrial, the SPC declared Nie Shubin's innocent and awarded his family a substantial compensation (Forsythe 2016).

Spanning over two decades, this case fully exposes the influence of politics—both high-politics and institutional politics—on the administration of justice in China. It clearly shows the change in approaches toward criminal justice that have played out during the Jiang Zemin, Hu Jintao, and Xi Jinping eras. Back in the mid-1990s, when Nie Shubin was tried and sentenced, the imperative was to get criminal cases solved swiftly and criminals punished harshly. During this period, leaders perceived this approach as ensuring the maintenance of social order at a time when economic liberalisation had brought a steady increase in criminal activities and the emergence of new forms of crime unheard of just a decade earlier. In 2013, when the case was reopened, Xi's priorities were utterly different. He wanted the justice system to be accountable and transparent, working under the rubric of 'ruling the country in accordance with the law' (*yifa zhiguo*). Having Xi himself engaged in a personal battle against miscarriages of justice, cases of wrongful convictions could no longer be tolerated (Wang 2014).

The Need for Change

Nie Shubin's wrongful conviction was just one of many miscarriages of justice that have been remedied since Xi's ascendance to power. The year 2013 was particularly distressing in this respect. There was first the case of the 'Two Zhangs'—Zhang Hui and his uncle Zhang Gaoping—who were declared innocent after having been sentenced to the death penalty and imprisonment, respectively, on charges of rape and murder in 2004 (Zhou 2013). Then, there was the case of Li Hualiang, a Henan man who was wrongly kept in prison for more than 12 years for the rape and murder of a teenage girl (Lu 2013). This was followed by the case of five men who had unjustly spent 18 years in jail, accused of the robbery and homicide of a taxi driver (Zhu 2017). Later in the year, another man in Anhui—Yu Yingsheng—was declared innocent after serving many years of a life sentence for killing his wife (Jia 2014). The same month, Nian Bin, convicted of fatally poisoning two children in Fujian province, was declared not guilty and freed from death row (Ma 2014).

From 2014 to 2017, courts around China have cleared another nine cases of wrongful conviction and the majority of them have made big news in the Chinese media. Xi has addressed the issue on several occasions, and the political-legal committee, the SPC, along with the other justice institutions, have become heavily involved in identifying the causes behind such unfortunate events. In this general atmosphere of relative openness and political goodwill, Chinese netizens have been allowed to express their anger, journalists to report sad stories of scarred individuals, and legal scholars to discuss in open forums issues of torture and abuses of powers.

These cases of miscarriages of justice—some cleared because the real culprit had confessed to the crime, others on the basis of the legal principle of reasonable doubt and the lack of sufficient evidence—highlight the fact that in the recent past there has been something seriously wrong with China's justice system. They prove unequivocally that the system of collecting evidence has still been based on archaic methods of torture aimed at obtaining confessions from criminal suspects through any means necessary; that the police have played an inordinately large role securing convictions in comparison to the other judicial organs; that lawyers have had only a minimal, if any, voice in the process of defending the accused; and that cases were too often decided behind closed doors by the intervention of the all-too-powerful political-legal committees. A case like that of Nie Shubin's proved that the interests of the police, the procuratorate, and the political-legal committee, were aligned and needed to be protected at all costs, and that courts were powerless in the event of inconvenient truths emerging. Thus, these cases have also indicated that all too often trials have been a mere formality, intended to corroborate what the police and the procuratorate had already established beforehand—leaving judges relatively powerless to play their rightful roles in the justice system.

Xi's Remedial Justice

With Xi's coming to power, it seemed that the time for change had come. The Xi era opened with a new emphasis on procedural justice and building accountability. Reflecting on the weaknesses of China's justice system that cases of wrongful convictions had brought to light, the Chinese leadership under Xi has sought to foster stronger oversight of political and judicial authorities at the local level in order to enhance transparency. Political rhetoric on the promotion of the rule of law accompanied important announcements of reforms during the Third and Fourth Party Plenums in 2013 and 2014, and the issuance of a number of legislative documents aimed at preventing the occurrence of miscarriages of justice (Trevaskes and Nesossi 2015).

One of the key reforms put forward under Xi has placed the trial at the centre of criminal proceedings (*yi shenpan wei zhongxin*) (Biddulph et al. 2017). One of the objectives of this new trial-centred doctrine is to counter the traditional tendency of the Chinese police to rely solely or primarily on confession, rather than other kinds of evidence that are more difficult and time-consuming to obtain. The new approach aims at shifting the focus from police testimony and evidence to the revelations of facts at the trial, with the objective of improving the quality of evidence gathering and reinforcing the supervisory role of the prosecution in ensuring that the police do not abuse their power. Differently from the past, court hearings should become decisive in determining the facts of a case, and evidence provided by the police and the procuratorate should be thoroughly tested in court.

The Political Logic

While on the surface these reforms could be considered groundbreaking, they have not found much international admiration and praise. This is perhaps because they are, paradoxically, being carried out at the same time as the expansion of legally dubious tactics employed to suppress any form of dissent, and to ferociously crack down on human rights lawyers and other civil society representatives. At the very beginning of the Xi era, many China observers anticipated that a renewed emphasis on *yifa zhiguo* and an official commitment to the prevention of miscarriages of justice might cause an overhaul of past abusive practices in the justice system. Since that time, though, the logic behind Xi's governance platforms has unfolded gradually to reveal its political utility.

It is now clear that the intent behind Xi's *yifa zhiguo* is to strengthen Party leadership through the use of the law, in order to further merge Party and state. Reforms of the justice system spurred by cases of injustice have been designed to persuade an increasingly sceptical Chinese population and international audience about the government's good will. Miscarriages of justice have been used strategically to help Xi's leadership distance itself from Hu Jintao's agenda of 'stability maintenance' (*weiwen*) and 'harmonious society' (*hexie shehui*). They have aided him to escape the fallout of the scandal that engulfed Zhou Yongkang, who, as Minister of Public Security and Secretary of the Central Political and Legal Committee under Hu Jintao, had approved and supported some of the abusive practices that had led to egregious errors of justice. In this spirit, miscarriages have been useful to tell a credible story about how the current leadership is doing things differently—perpetuating the myth that the Party can be held accountable by the Chinese citizens and, as such, can be trusted.

Legal reforms prompted by wrongful convictions are also intended to increase the efficiency of the criminal justice system, to curb corrupt practices, and restore the lost legitimacy of the Party-state. By claiming to solve the problem of miscarriages of justice, Xi can legitimise his political authority—indeed, in his view justice can be achieved only if coordinated by the centre of political power. However, contradictory agendas promoted under the broad umbrella of *yifa zhiguo* have made it clear that Xi's aim has not been that of increasing accountability at the expense of coercion, but of intensifying both for the sake of political utility. Rather than shifting its objectives towards fair trial guarantees to help ensure the accountability of the justice system, the Party remains fixated on its coercive power. Thus, when the current administration claims to be willing to deal with past judicial errors in order to prevent them from occurring in the future, they are not doing so merely to increase the accountability of the political-legal system. Their paramount concern is to ensure the preservation of the political status quo and Party's legitimacy. Overall, this means that miscarriages of justice will continue to be remedied selectively to serve a certain political agenda. Only those who are useful for the larger project of legal and political reforms aimed at creating a more 'just' system, so defined by those in power, will have their innocence publicly recognised. ■

Franz Kafka's The Trial.
Photo: Are.na.

Confessions Made in China

Magnus FISKESJÖ

Over the last few years, the Chinese authorities have repeatedly coerced political prisoners to go on television and debase themselves in forced confessions of their 'crimes'. These gruesome spectacles have featured lawyers, journalists, publishers, bloggers, music stars, and many others with an independent voice. In this essay, Magnus Fiskesjö addresses how mass media outside of the control of Chinese state authorities should deal with these grim performances.

Globally, mass media face a difficult dilemma: how to report on the Chinese spectacles of prisoners forced to perform fake, scripted confessions? The Chinese authorities produce these confessions in order to create a new 'truth', one that is to be disseminated through Chinese state media and, if possible, through foreign mass media, and social media as well. Chinese media must, of course, simply obey orders to present, and even assist in the arrangement of these new Orwellian 'truths'. But what should mass media outside of the control of Chinese state authorities do with these grim performances? Some have handled this problem with integrity, others disgracefully.

Over the last few years, there has been a long string of these coerced confessions, in which the Chinese authorities force political prisoners to go on television and debase themselves. These gruesome spectacles have featured lawyers, journalists, publishers, bloggers, music stars, and many others with an independent voice. To the dismay of their friends, colleagues, and relatives, after disappearing into the hands of the authorities, these victims will appear on the screen to denounce themselves and everything they used to stand for. Inside China many, if not most, people know that it is all fake and meant to intimidate and browbeat people into silence. Chinese citizens know that they cannot denounce this game openly, or they could end up on the stand themselves. In this regard, the tactic is largely effective.

Between Stalin and Kafka

These fake confessions represent a modernised version of Stalin's show-trials. They violate both international and Chinese law, and several prominent Chinese judges and legal officials have protested bravely, arguing that legal matters are supposed to be decided in the courts, not on television (Fiskesjö 2017). The spectacles fly in the face of the painstaking effort to build up the 'rule of law' in China over the decades since Mao's death. But today, we no longer hear the admonitions, previously issued by Chinese judicial authorities, to stop police torture and forced confessions (Xinhua 2012). In the increasingly harsh environment inside China, it has become too dangerous to openly criticise these spectacles.

In one of the latest cases, in February 2018 Swedish publisher Gui Minhai—who is an old friend, and who has been detained in China since he was kidnapped from Thailand by Chinese agents in late 2015—was put up for his third mock 'interview' attended by select, pliant Chinese media (Phillips 2018). The previous two occasions involved his self-smearing (along the lines of Josef K. in Kafka's *The Trial*), first with regard to an old criminal offence dug up for the purpose, and secondly with regard to the main issue, his publishing and book-selling in Hong Kong.

This third time, the spectacle's producers included not just the usual propaganda arms of the regime (e.g. the Xinhua News Agency, etc.), but also the formerly independent *South China Morning Post* (SCMP) of Hong Kong. In agreeing to 'interview' a torture victim in between the torture sessions, the paper gave in to pressure from China, exerted by its new Chinese owners (Alibaba). Recently, the paper has given many signs of taking directions from its new masters, and this scandalous decision came on the heels of another similarly planted interview made under duress, with the imprisoned legal assistant Zhao Wei (Phillips 2016). It certainly shows the SCMP can no longer be trusted as an independent news organisation.

Behind the Headlines

But the question for free media organisations remains: how to report the ghastly spectacles? Some have tried to stick to the old journalistic principle of reporting 'both sides', however misplaced this may be with the flagrant gross inequality in the situation of prisoners who are speaking under duress. These media, instead of pointing out the deceit themselves, often cite human rights organisations stating that these are fake events. Readers are then expected to be their own judge. But many people outside of the Chinese context are not used to imagining that an 'interview' could be faked and orchestrated through torture. The news media owe it to their readers to make clear, that this is what is now happening.

Gui Minhai.
Photo: People.cn.

Peter Dahlin pictured during his forced confession on CCTV.
Photo: CCTV13.

Headlines become very important here, since they frame the issue for most readers. It is a perennial issue for newspapers that headline-writing page editors fail to grasp what their journalists reported. Thus, perhaps out of ignorance, we sometimes see headlines on otherwise acceptable articles, which misleadingly say that the victims 'speak' as if they were in a position to freely express themselves. This is bound to mislead readers—many of whom only read the headlines.

One example was the report from NHK World on the day after the 'interview', headlined 'Hong Kong bookseller criticises Sweden' (NHK World 2018). This headline is gravely misleading, as it omits the fact that the bookseller in question, Swedish citizen Gui Minhai, was not voluntarily 'criticising', but *forced to* criticise his adopted country according to a script. In his situation, he is well aware of the fact that following the script is the only way to hope to avoid more torture, harm coming to his relatives, or even death. For news media like the NHK to omit this is truly atrocious. They offer no more than a buried hint, that the victim 'met with reporters … while under supervision at a detention facility.'

Another striking and shameful example came in Norway's leading daily paper, the *Aftenposten*, also on 10 February 2018 (Rønneberg 2018). The headline proclaims, as a matter of fact, that 'Gui thinks' Sweden is using him as a 'chess piece'. This is, of course, the *Aftenposten* itself becoming the chess piece of the Chinese torturers. News reports like this one will mislead many readers into thinking the victim spoke his own mind, and these media all become complicit in the Chinese authorities' scheme. These are successfully planted propaganda victories.

Early on in the saga, while the Chinese authorities were focussed on destroying his bookstore in Hong Kong, Gui Minhai was quite successfully discredited by means of digging up and twisting of an old traffic incident that in fact appears to have been resolved long ago and in accordance with the laws of that time (Bandurski 2016; Huang 2017). Yet many media organisations and even the government in my country, Sweden, fell for this scheme by continually referring to it as a reason for Gui's detainment.

One low point was when, in a television segment that featured Gui's abduction and illegal imprisonment, a national public television journalist spent a great deal of his allotted time on stage pressing the non-question, 'What about the traffic incident?'—probably under the false impression that he was pursuing 'both sides' in the name of 'fairness'. It was a scary display of how authoritarian China managed to stage direct Swedish journalists, without even setting foot in the newsroom. Such victories have allowed the Chinese authorities to focus on their main goals: to close and dismantle Gui's bookstore, while intimidating the entire Hong Kong publishing industry, thus sending a message to the rest of Hong Kong and the world.

Upholding the Truth

Most Swedish media have by now largely woken up to what China is doing, although occasionally there are still ignorant editors who are naïvely continuing to make similar mistakes, unwittingly serving as the conduits of this most insidious form of state propaganda that uses live people as props. The coerced character of these spectacles should be obvious to any independent observer, including how they commonly make use of personal flaws in the prisoners' past, so as to smear and discredit those targeted. This allows the Chinese authorities to achieve their main goal: to silence these voices. Free media owe it to their readers to explain that these performances offer insights *only* into the torturers' scheme, and not into the victim's real views; they should not leave out the fact that no alternative views or protests are tolerated in China.

We actually already know a lot about the concrete procedures behind these fake confessions, and in substantial detail. Multiple victims, when regaining a chance to speak freely, have given us accounts of how it works. Recent major examples include Gui Minhai's heroic colleague Lam Wing-kee and the brave female lawyer Wang Yu—both of whom spoke out despite the immense risk of repercussions (France 24 2018; HKFP 2016). Several foreigners detained and treated according to the same program have also given us similar accounts, including another Swedish citizen, Peter Dahlin (China Change 2017). The victim is intimidated through a series of measures that can be called modern 'clean' or 'stealth' torture (Rejali 2009): sleep deprivation, extended isolation, being forced to stand for long periods, excessive heat or cold, threats against family members and colleagues on the outside, etc. These measures will break down almost anyone. In the end, very few of us, if any, would refuse to read the script for the cameras.

But if we want to avoid being intimidated or becoming complicit, we must refuse to be duped. We must expose and protest against the charade and demand the release of those who, like Gui Minhai, have been violated in this way. And we must ask our media to take it as their duty to spell out the horrible truth: the forced confessions are scripted performances directed by the jailers, from behind a fake stage. We should also clearly distinguish these horrors from the kind of police misconduct, corruption, and torture seen in many, if not all, countries around the world. This is different, because we are not talking about rogue policemen, or even horrifying conspiratorial police torture rings, like the one exposed by the *Chicago Tribune* (Berlatsky 2014).

We are talking about a political crime wave, orchestrated by a government-run propaganda machine that uses living human beings as props and tools for political influence. To be sure, there are other comparable examples, such as the Islamic State in its infamous victim videos shot just before their execution. But China's campaign is especially dangerous because of the country's increasing weight in the world, which it is now throwing around in order to redefine the 'truth' by force. We should not let them. ■

United Nations Geneva
PC: Henry Mühlpfordt.

Will the Future of Human Rights Be 'Made in China'?

Sarah M. BROOKS

In June 2018, the Trump administration announced the withdrawal of the United States from the UN's peak human rights body, the Human Rights Council, this move was widely seen as a 'gift' for China's stated aspirations to 'responsible global leadership'. Against this background, Sarah Brooks looks at how the Chinese government has stepped into the role of international player.

For at least three years, my organisation has been tracking—and helping others to track—the way in which China is expanding its influence in multilateral institutions, in particular the United Nations (UN). However, when on 19 June 2018 the Trump administration announced the withdrawal of the United States from the UN's peak human rights body, the Human Rights Council, the interest in understanding China's methods became an imperative.

Major media outlets published a number of articles focussing on the impact of the US decision (Wade 2018). Several commentators viewed this decision as a 'crushing blow' for efforts by NGOs and victims of abuses to use the Council to hold China accountable. This article examines the idea that the withdrawal is a 'gift' for President Xi Jinping and China's stated aspirations to 'responsible global leadership' (Eve 2018).

To understand just how true this statement is, we must first look at how the Chinese government has stepped into the role of international player. We should then review how China has used its influence and access to change the UN across three broad areas: the politics of intergovernmental bodies, the processes and procedures of the UN bodies and agencies, and the participation of civil society in the UN. Finally, we have to consider why this matters for human rights defenders on the ground, in China and elsewhere.

China's Growing Global Role

On the surface, China's commitment to being an international player in the UN and other multilateral spaces has not actually looked that bad.

In 2015, China committed one billion USD over ten years to support the UN's work in development and security. Human rights are clearly left out. In the last 12 years, China has stood for and won election to the UN's Human Rights Council every term it has been eligible. It also has established nearly single-handedly a new multilateral investment bank, the Asian Infrastructure Investment Bank, and committed to it being 'lean, green, and clean'.

... But Xi Jinping's committed funds privilege two of the UN's 'pillars'—security and development—while not benefitting at all the third: human rights.

... But China's vote in the Council has gone against efforts to see a Commission of Inquiry in Burundi, or an end to the ethnic cleansing in Myanmar, or protections against being targeted for one's sexual orientation or gender identity.

... But few, if any, of China's efforts in overseas investment or assistance, including its much touted Belt and Road Initiative, have benefitted from meaningful civil society participation or been contingent on minimum standards of human rights due diligence.

This is by no means an exhaustive list of steps China has taken to advance its ambitions of global leadership, but it is a demonstration of the ways in which China sees the UN as a key arena for pushing forward and institutionalising its goals and priorities.

The Politics of Intergovernmental Bodies

One clear policy approach of China in UN spaces, in particular at the Human Rights Council, is to leverage political alliances. The Likeminded Group—an amorphous 'regional grouping' of many global South governments—has in many ways taken the place of its twentieth century corollary, the Non-aligned Movement, as the bulky padding for political initiatives by China, Russia, and others.

What begin as anodyne statements by China on behalf of this Likeminded Group, and other governments, increasingly evolve into resolutions of the Council. Human rights experts from governments and civil society alike worry that in such documents, principles of universality and interdependence are being played down, while concepts like sovereignty and territorial integrity are getting more airtime.

UN documents that parrot CCP language emphasising development as a prerequisite for achieving human rights gains provide cover for governments that seek an escape from much-needed scrutiny and international accountability.

Moreover, China increasingly pairs an approach of surrounding itself with its friends, with one of investing time and resources in picking off—one by one—its opposition. To cite just one example, in 2017 year massive Chinese investment in the Greek port of Piraeus and a high-level visit from Li Keqiang had such a significant political impact that Greek representatives in Brussels blocked EU consensus to raise human rights concerns about China. As a result, for the first time in 35 sessions of the Council, the EU failed to make a statement under the Council's debate on serious human rights violations, sometimes referred to as an 'Item 4' statement (Emmott and Koutantou 2017).

The Universal Periodic Review, the Council's process for reviewing the human rights records of all countries. PC: UN Human Rights Council.

Processes and Procedures

The second area where China seeks to develop its influence, and where opportunities exist to amend or adjust the multilateral human rights system, is at the level of process.

The Universal Periodic Review, the Council's process for reviewing the human rights records of all countries, big and small, suffers from serious mutual back-scratching syndrome. In 2015 and 2016, the last years for which full data in the form of official written statements is available through the Human Rights Council extranet, China took the opportunity to comment on the human rights record of every single government under review, often highlighting benefits of the technical cooperation that they themselves had already funded.

The system of treaty bodies, committees of legal and policy experts who assess country compliance and recommend steps for improvement under their respective human rights treaties, has been a particular bugbear for the Chinese government. China's Ministry of Foreign Affairs has filed scathing reports as input into the process of 'strengthening' that system, largely aimed at constraining innovation and restricting dialogue with 'non-credible sources', otherwise known as independent human rights NGOs.

At the same time, the Chinese government seeks to ensure that Chinese nationals stand for—and are duly elected to—positions of responsibility on those very committees. The only problem is that most of those elected come directly from years, if not decades, of government service, which calls into question their independence.

The most proactive and creative of tools at the Council's disposal—the Special Rapporteurs, Working Groups, and Independent Experts mandated to be its 'eyes and ears'—have not escaped the scrutiny of the Chinese authorities. In the June 2018 session of the Council, the Chinese government chastised

Special Rapporteur on Freedom of Opinion and Expression David Kaye for criticising China's Cyber-Security Act (United Nations Office at Geneva 2018). He had also cited Chinese companies, such as Tencent and WeChat, as examples of businesses engaged in forms of censorship and online content management.

Last June, the report of the UN expert on extreme poverty and human rights—who had visited China in August 2016—was slammed by the Chinese delegation (UN Office at Geneva 2017 and 2017b). His efforts to call for the release of detained lawyer Jiang Tianyong met with assertions that Jiang, and others advocating for human rights, were merely criminals.

While China's aversion to scrutiny is not unique, the clear restrictions they placed on the expert during his visit, including surveillance of his staff and harassment of civil society contacts, goes well beyond acceptable cooperation and may amount to a policy of intimidation and reprisal.

Finally, China exhibits outsized influence in the part of the UN that holds the purse strings. Budgetary requests of the Office of the United Nations High Commissioner for Human Rights (OHCHR) have been held hostage in retaliation to High Commissioner Zeid meeting certain Chinese activists, or being involved in certain events (Reuters 2016). In late June, *Foreign Policy* reported that China, 'hardening' its position, was seeking targeted elimination of UN jobs tasked with monitoring human rights in conflict areas (Lynch 2018).

Uyghur rights activists Dolkun Isa. PC: Darshanwashimkar.

Among its discretionary contributions, however, China has increased funding to the Human Rights Office for at least one thing—support to the Special Rapporteur on the Right to Development.

Civil Society Access and Participation

The final area in which China has stepped up its engagement and implemented more ambitious policies is in the area of civil society access and participation.

China continues to play a ringleader role among governments seeking to shut out civil society voices in the UN Economic and Social Council (ECOSOC) NGO Committee. Their efforts have created an environment where states can, with immunity, permit political and economic interests to take precedence over a commitment to support civil society. As a result, NGOs seeking the right to access and speak at UN proceedings face intense questioning—including over their use of the terms 'the Tibetan Autonomous Region' or 'Taiwan, Province of China', regardless of the country in which the organisation is based.

Even when organisations receive accreditation, it apparently does not mean that they can participate fully. The case of Uyghur rights activists Dolkun Isa, documented by my organisation and many others, as well as in media reports, is illustrative in this regard (ISHR 2018).

In April 2017, Mr Isa sought to attend the UN Permanent Forum on Indigenous Issues at the UN headquarters in New York. Despite being fully accredited to participate at the event, at one point during the conference he was approached by UN security officers who instructed him to leave the premises. No reason was given and he was not permitted to reenter the UN grounds. There was a repeat removal of Mr Isa in April 2018.

The Chinese government has long accused Mr Isa of being a terrorist. When the red alert from Interpol was lifted in February 2018, the Chinese Ministry of Foreign Affairs repeated its ad hominem attack against Mr Isa. It is worth noting further that the UN Department, which oversees secretariat services for ECOSOC, is headed by former Chinese diplomat Liu Zhenmin.

For many UN conferences, permission to participate can be given on an ad hoc basis, without requiring an official ECOSOC accreditation. Indeed, this is the case overall for access to UN grounds and buildings. Taiwanese civil society members have reported being turned away from, or facing barriers to, entry to meetings of the UN on labour, health, and human rights—even when their advocacy is focussed on individuals detained in China, a UN member state (Focus Taiwan 2017).

The Human Rights Council in Session. PC: Hrbrief.com.

Because of the risks of retaliation against them by the government, many human rights defenders in China are reluctant to participate in the UN at all. Defender Cao Shunli, who was detained en route to Geneva to contribute to China's rights review and later died from lack of medical care while in detention, has become a potent symbol of the cost of undertaking advocacy (CHRD 2013; Kaiman 2014). In theory, they could still 'attend' meetings virtually, or review documents and provide input. But the final and perhaps most widespread barrier is the lack of information in Chinese language. Budgetary battles over the most core functions of the human rights system are perennial, so 'minor' issues of translation or additional live streaming end up far down on the list of demands, or are the first items to get reduced in a budget negotiation.

Does It Really Matter?

China's efforts to leverage political and economic pressure, meddle in or obstruct procedure, and raise the costs for NGOs to gain access to the UN are mutually reinforcing. They seem to point to a policy of remaking the UN—and particularly its human rights bodies—in China's image, one based on mutual respect, cooperation, and intergovernmental dialogue. In this version of the United Nations, legitimate scrutiny of violations is dismissed as 'interference in internal affairs' and the essential voices of civil society are constrained or even silenced.

Despite this multipronged assault on the human rights system, the UN has nonetheless shown its ability to be resilient and to reflect the concerns of individuals working on the ground—and in a handful of cases, actually impact the lives of those detained for their activism.

UN experts on torture included forced conversion therapy as a form of torture or cruel treatment throughout the review of China (UN Committee against Torture 2015 and

2016). Their recommendations to the Chinese government not only provide legal commentary to inform domestic lawsuits, but also help build international jurisprudence on the issue.

In the summer of 2016, UN experts expressed concern about the health, treatment, and detention conditions of free speech activist Guo Feixiong, after he began a hunger strike against ill-treatment and refusal of access to adequate medical care. This was the third time they had spoken up—and, apparently, this time it worked. The pressure from these experts, in addition to social media and direct actions and diplomatic requests, made a difference: Guo was able to see his sister, gain access to books, and was eventually transferred to another prison (ISHR 2017).

Finally, Chinese lawyers working to support victims of domestic violence discovered, through engaging with UN experts on violence against women, that there are international best practices in restraining orders. As this is an area lacking detail in the current Anti-domestic Violence Law, the potential for constructive legal advocacy is promising.

A Call for Engagement

The withdrawal of the United States from the Council should not be an excuse to disengage. The absence of the ability of the United States to put China under the spotlight at the Council will be strongly felt, but it is critical that we not paint all efforts to counter China's attempts to remake at the Council as anti-China, or allow responses to be bipolar and, as the Chinese delegation often reminds us, politicised. This does not help those of us who see the Council as an important space for victims' testimony and solidarity, and who believe that the risks posed by Chinese government strategies at the Council are serious.

In a joint statement delivered on 19 June (available on www.webtv.un.org), these risks were made perfectly clear. China, backed by the Likeminded Group, set out a long list of ways in which the current head of human rights and his team had proven 'dissatisfactory'. This was followed in short order by a clear set of criteria that they expected of that office in the future. This included a statement urging that 'ensuring transparency in OHCHR work is of paramount importance'. In a somewhat ironic twist, neither the statement nor its list of signatories had been made public at the time of writing this article (July 2018). Even this small example demonstrates exactly why a human rights system 'with Chinese characteristics' is entirely incompatible with the demands of the human rights movement—and why the current system, despite its flaws, is nonetheless worth fighting for. ■

Nobel Peace Prize winner Liu Xiaobo died on 13 July 2017, aged 61. PC: Handout.

Remembering Liu Xiaobo One Year On

Jean-Philippe BÉJA

On 13 July 2017, more than eight years after his arrest, Liu Xiaobo died of liver cancer in a Shenyang hospital. He was the first Nobel Peace Prize laureate to die in prison since 1936, when Carl Von Ossetski, a pacifist who had been jailed by Hitler, died in a prison hospital in Berlin. In this essay, Jean-Philippe Béja offers some glimpses into Liu's extraordinary life, highlighting the significance of his legacy for new generations of activists.

When he learned that Liu Xiaobo had won the Nobel Peace Prize, Vaclav Havel—who had not been acknowledged by the Nobel Academy—was extremely happy. Although his doctor had strictly forbidden him to drink alcohol, he opened a bottle he kept hidden for the great occasions, and drank to his success. When asked to write a foreword for the collection of Liu's works that I edited, he did it enthusiastically. In 2011, the Czech dissident who had spent many years in prison before being rewarded with the presidency of the Czechoslovak Republic, died in Prague, aged 75.

Liu Xiaobo was not so lucky: on 13 July 2017, more than eight years after his arrest, he died of liver cancer in a Shenyang hospital, surrounded by plainclothes policemen who had not allowed him one minute of intimacy with his wife Liu Xia. He was not the first Nobel Peace Prize laureate to die in prison. Before him, in 1936, Carl Von Ossetski, a pacifist who had been jailed by Hitler, died in a prison hospital in Berlin. Germany was then in the hands of the Nazis.

To add insult to injury, Liu Xiaobo was incinerated the day after he died, and his wife was forced to proceed to a 'sea burial', dispersing his ashes in the sea near Dalian so that there would be no grave where his supporters could gather to mourn him.

Liu Xia's Plight

Liu's wife, a poet and artist who had never been involved in politics, spent eight and a half years under house arrest. Her crime? To have been Liu Xiaobo's wife, and to have refused to clearly break with him (*huaqingjiexian*). During all these years, she was isolated from the world, followed by plainclothes policemen wherever she went, and only allowed to be driven 400 miles to the Jinzhou jail to see her husband for half an hour every month. Fifty-two years after Yu Luoke denounced the 'blood theory' (*xuetong lun*) that stipulated that political positions are transmitted through family association, 40 years after the famous Third Plenum of the Eleventh Central Committee launched the policy of reform and opening up, a woman was deprived of her freedom only because she was related to a man that the Party had deemed 'an enemy of the State'!

After Xiaobo died, she could not collect the letters he had written her during his imprisonment, and could not see his medical reports to understand when he was diagnosed with cancer. Everything had disappeared, the authorities said, in a convenient fire that engulfed the Jinzhou jail just two weeks before his death. In July 2018, thanks to the pressure exerted on the Chinese government by German Chancellor Angela Merkel, she was allowed to leave China and has since settled in Berlin.

I rushed to see her, but although she is now safe in Germany, she refuses to give interviews or to have her declarations published. Her freedom will not be complete as long as her younger brother Liu Hui is under parole and can be sent back to jail at the whim of the Party leaders. But she reminded me: 'I don't understand politics, anyway, and I am not interested.'

Liu Xiaobo, giving a speech at Tiananmen Square on 2 June 1989. PC: Scott Savitt.

A Born Provocateur

When they met in the early 1980s, Liu Xiaobo, like her, did not understand politics. A student at Jilin Normal University, he did not take part in the Democracy Wall Movement (*minzhu qiang*), but worked in a group of poets in his native province. A staunch individualist, a Nietzschean, he made a name for himself as a 'black horse' (*heima*) on the Chinese literary scene with an article entitled 'Crisis: The Literature of the New Epoch Faces a Crisis' (Liu 1986). In this article, he denounced liberal intellectuals' self-satisfaction, their tendency to consider themselves the only victims of Maoist terror, and to assume the posture of a counsellor to the Prince. He exhorted them to cut the umbilical chord with the Party-state and 'think for themselves'. His words deeply shocked liberal and conservative writers alike. A born provocateur, he declared in 1988 that if it took 100 years of British presence for Hong Kong to become what it now was, China should be colonised for 300 years to reach that degree of modernity (Jin 1988).

This iconoclasm makes Liu Xiaobo a direct heir to the May Fourth intellectuals who did not hesitate to vehemently denounce Chinese traditional culture. A successful intellectual, he was invited to the most famous Western universities—the dream of all Chinese intellectuals at that time—as he was widely different from his fellow writers.

But when confronted with history, Liu Xiaobo changed. He was in New York as a visiting scholar at Columbia when the 1989 pro-democracy movement shook his motherland. He immediately decided to go back and went straight to Tiananmen, where he stayed until the massacre. He did not refrain from criticising the students' behaviour, saying that they were not acting democratically. He also criticised them for asking the government to reverse the verdict it had passed on their movement by declaring it a 'counterrevolutionary turmoil': 'Why do our fellow citizens feel so grateful towards reversal of verdicts? To send a righteous person to hell is an exorbitant privilege, to reverse the verdict is so too' (Liu 1989, 277).

The students did not blame him for his attitude, and on the night of 3 June he helped convince them to leave the Square. After the massacre, he took refuge in the home of an Australian diplomat, but after a few days, he could not stand to be safe while his students and friends were being pursued by the police. He was arrested and sent to Qincheng Prison for a year. During his imprisonment, he declared in a televised interview on CCTV that nobody had died on the Square on that night. Although it was true, he later deeply regretted granting this interview to the Party's official mouthpiece.

Liu Xiaobo and his wife Liu Xia. PC: Supplied by the author.

This decided the fate of Liu Xiaobo. In his words: 'June 1989 has been the major turning point in my life which is just over one half of a century in length' (Liu 2012a, 321); 'I feel that those who perished that day are looking down on me from above … I do my best to make every word from my pen a cry from the heart for the souls of the dead' (Liu 2012b, 293). The elitist Nietszchean turned into a caring activist and philosopher. 'When the famous members of the elite refuse, at the most dangerous moment, to rise in order to defend their ethics and their conscience, when they refuse to pay the individual price, the masses do not have the duty to support them' (Liu 2002, 8).

Speaking Truth to Power

During the 1990s, Liu worked hand in hand with Ding Ziling and the Tiananmen Mothers in order to obtain the truth about the massacre. June Fourth led him to appreciate the courage of ordinary citizens who gave their lives to protect the students. The years he was free were spent launching petitions to protest the Party's repression, to denounce the oppression of marginalised citizens, writing on the children exploited in brick factories, on the fate of migrant workers (*nongmingong*), and enjoining his fellow citizens to dare speak truth to power. 'Dictatorships need lies and violence in order to maintain the coercion and fear upon which they depend … No single person, of whatever status, can fight back against regime violence alone, but the refusal to participate in lying is something that every person can accomplish. To refuse to lie in day-to-day public life is the most powerful tool for breaking down a tyranny built on mendacity' (Liu 2012b, 295).

Like Vaclav Havel, Liu Xiaobo exhorted his compatriots to live in truth. His penetrating analyses of the regime, his conviction that the peaceful growth of an independent civil society was the best way to fight the tyranny of the Party, and his deep engagement with non-violence made him one of the most remarkable

Vaclav Havel (1936–2011).
PC: Jiri Jiroutek.

Chinese intellectuals of the twenty-first century. After his release from three years in a reeducation-through-labour camp in 1999, he became one of the most respected personalities in the dissident sphere. He enjoyed the esteem both of old Party cadres disgusted by the 4 June massacre, such as Mao's former secretary Li Rui; of intellectuals active in the 1980s, such as historian Bao Zunxin with whom he developed a profound friendship; and of the younger generation, such as Liu Di and Yu Jie who became active after 1989. In such a fragmented milieu, this is a very remarkable achievement, which probably explains why Liu received such a heavy sentence in 2009.

Although the Party has consistently tried to erase his image—his essays and articles were never published in China after 1989—he still enjoys a strong support in dissident circles, and his all-out engagement with non-violence will definitely influence the future behavior of the opposition. His commitment to the cause of democracy, his emphasis on the necessity to uphold the memory of the June Fourth Massacre, his unceasing protest against human rights violations will continue to inspire the activists who dare rise against the reign of strong men. Liu's call to his fellow citizens to use truth to undermine a system built on lies makes his legacy more important than ever in an increasingly repressive China. ■

General Wang Zhen (1908–93). PC: Wikimedia Commons.

Xinjiang Today: Wang Zhen Rides Again?

Tom CLIFF

Following the intra-communal violence of early July 2009 in Urumqi, many Han invoked Wang Zhen's notorious approach to management of Xinjiang's non-Han population as the solution to what they termed the 'ethnic problem'. Today, Xi Jinping appears to have found his Wang Zhen in the figure of Chen Quanguo, Party Secretary of Xinjiang since August 2016.

Nostalgia for the boyishly brutal Wang Zhen flooded across Han Xinjiang in the days, weeks, and months following the intra-communal violence of early July 2009 in Urumqi. Many Han invoked Wang Zhen's notorious approach to management of Xinjiang's non-Han (and in particular Uyghur) population as the solution to what they termed the 'ethnic problem' (*minzu wenti*).

One legend—with a number of variations, as all good legends must have—venerates disproportionate response. According to this story, in 1950, as Wang Zhen's forces were spreading down into southern Xinjiang, a Han man had unthinkingly or insensitively prepared a meal of pork in a Uyghur village, and was killed or badly beaten for the transgression. Upon hearing about this, Wang Zhen had his troops surround the village so no one could escape. He then forced the villagers to hand over the perpetrators and publicly executed them in the village square. Next he had his troops slaughter two or three pigs and boil them up in a large cauldron; at bayonet point, the troops then forced each and every remaining resident of the village to eat a bowl of boiled pork. Given the shortage of meat to feed his own soldiers, this was surely a high-cost exercise.

Two clear points can be drawn from such stories: a) Wang Zhen held the view that Uyghurs existed in Xinjiang at the sufferance of the Han-led Chinese Communist Party (CCP), and acted on that belief; b) many Han idolise Wang Zhen for, as they see it, keeping Uyghurs under control. Reflecting on what could have been done to prevent the July 2009 violence—which is widely understood across China as the indiscriminate killing of Han, including pregnant mothers, by Uyghurs of all ages and sexes for no apparent reason—some older Han in Korla reconstituted Wang Zhen's memorable (and possibly apocryphal) contribution to the ethnic policy debate. As head of the military government in Xinjiang from 1950 to 1952, Wang Zhen had apparently sized up Uyghurs as 'a troublemaking minority', and wrote to Mao Zedong advocating that they be 'thoroughly wiped out' to avoid any future problems. Even Mao felt that this was a little extreme—or at least premature—so he redeployed Wang. Now, it seems that tragedy and farce have converged: Mao's successor-emulator, Xi Jinping, has found his Wang Zhen.

Chen Quanguo, current Communist Party Secretary of the Xinjiang Uyghur Autonomous Region. Photo: Ts.cn.

Taking Up Unfinished Business

As Party Secretary of Xinjiang, Chen Quanguo has apparently taken up Wang Zhen's unfinished business. But while Wang Zhen just wanted Uyghurs to get out of the way of his developmental plans or be wiped away completely, the current system is both destructive and inclusive. What is playing out in Xinjiang is a composite version of twentieth-century authoritarian fantasies and popular dystopias that is made possible by twenty-first-century technology (Clarke 2018; Vanderklippe 2017).

The system starts with total surveillance (Millward 2018). When Uyghurs have any communication with people outside China (including their own relatives), they get visits from the Public Security Bureau within an hour or two, and suffer repetitive questioning about who the caller was, what they are doing overseas, and what they spoke about. The police, of course, know exactly what they spoke about because they were listening. The point is to let the Uyghurs know that they are being watched and listened to very closely. Every action and every utterance goes onto an unseen scorecard, and saying or doing 'the wrong thing' could well have you taken off to one of the many political reeducation centres that Chen Quanguo dramatically expanded as soon as he took over the reins in Urumqi (Radio Free Asia 2017a). Simply having spent time overseas whilst not in the company of an authorised tour group puts you under suspicion: students studying in Islamic countries such as Egypt or Turkey have been told to return to China, then met at the airport and immediately whisked away for reeducation.

The next step is to subject select Uyghurs—and now also Kazakhs and other non-Han people—to a totalising regime of physical and psychological abuse. Horrific, and credible, reports of what goes on inside the political reeducation camps have been coming through since the beginning of 2017: inmates made to repeatedly recite lines of gratitude to the Party while being tortured with white noise, contortion, and marching exercises; sleep deprivation to break their spirit (ChinaAid 2018). The high rate of deaths in custody supports reports of vicious beatings and intrusive physical torture (RFA 2017b, 2018b). An estimated 5 to 10 percent of the Uyghur population of Xinjiang—up to 800,000 people—is now locked up in these camps, with more being taken in all the time (HRW 2017; RFA 2018a).

Graffiti on the external wall of an apartment building inhabited by Uyghur families within an oil company compound. Photo: Tom Cliff.

Overseas, in a dormitory near you, Uyghur students wake screaming in a cold sweat; they are having nightmares about their family members back in Xinjiang, or their own future without a home or a family. Their families have told them not to return under any circumstances, and now refuse to take their calls. Sub-prefectural police departments in Xinjiang send text messages to Uyghurs from their area who have been living overseas for years, demanding passport and residency information. The logic is consistent with social control practices within China: 'You are originally of our locale, you belong to us.' But these police are not primarily aiming to gather information, they are sending a warning: 'We know your telephone number, we know your name, we know where your family members live in Xinjiang. Be careful, don't be critical.' In such ways, family members residing in Xinjiang are used as leverage in attempts to control the activities of Uyghurs living overseas (Denyer 2018; U.S. Embassy 2018). All this, too, amounts to a very high-cost exercise—and on a much larger scale than Wang Zhen's pork.

Political and Financial Costs

The cost is both financial and political. The upkeep cost of this surveillance state can only be estimated, but it is undoubtedly very high (Zenz 2018). The political cost is immeasurable: over the past two decades, repressive practices aimed at Uyghurs in Xinjiang have negatively impacted interethnic relations, provoked a series of violent incidents, and caused Xinjiang residents to feel insecure, irrespective of their ethnicity. Han, Hui, Kazakh, and Uyghur people alike fear for personal or family members' safety and economic prospects; many even fear the environment in which they live, and the place to which they all feel that they belong. And although the Chinese state media claimed in March 2017 that the number of violent terrorist incidents had dropped with 'religious extremism notably curbed', my sense is that these feelings of insecurity have increased dramatically over the very same period (Cao and Cui 2017; Xinhua 2018). This is clearly no basis upon which to build a harmonious, moderately prosperous society, as is the stated aim of the Party-state in Xinjiang and across the country (An 2017).

So, why is the Party-state doing this? I raised this question in a recent discussion with a senior colleague. We should assume, I said, that we do not know the ultimate aim of the Chinese leadership in Xinjiang—and thus we do not know what motivates their policies and practices. 'That's a bit conspiratorial, isn't it?' my colleague replied. 'They say that they want to prevent violent terrorist attacks, promote economic development, and assure long-term social and political stability. Why wouldn't they want that?'

'Why not?' I now return to the question. I do not have the answer, of course, because I do not have access to any of the internal communications—far less to informal and unspoken communications—that might give me clues as to what that answer might be. But I do have a proposed starting point. I think it is important to reject once and for all the idea that Chinese leaders do not realise the effects of what they are doing. Chinese leaders do not need policy advice from foreign critics. They have access to much more and better information; they have legions of people to gather and process this information. The leaders themselves are neither stupid nor inexperienced in matters of social management. They, too, can surely see that the hyper-securitisation of Xinjiang is producing widespread feelings of insecurity and consuming vast amounts of human, material, and political resources, and thereby laying the groundwork for social and political instability for decades into the future (Rife 2018). And thus my questions 'Why are they doing it? What do they hope to achieve?' become relevant. ■

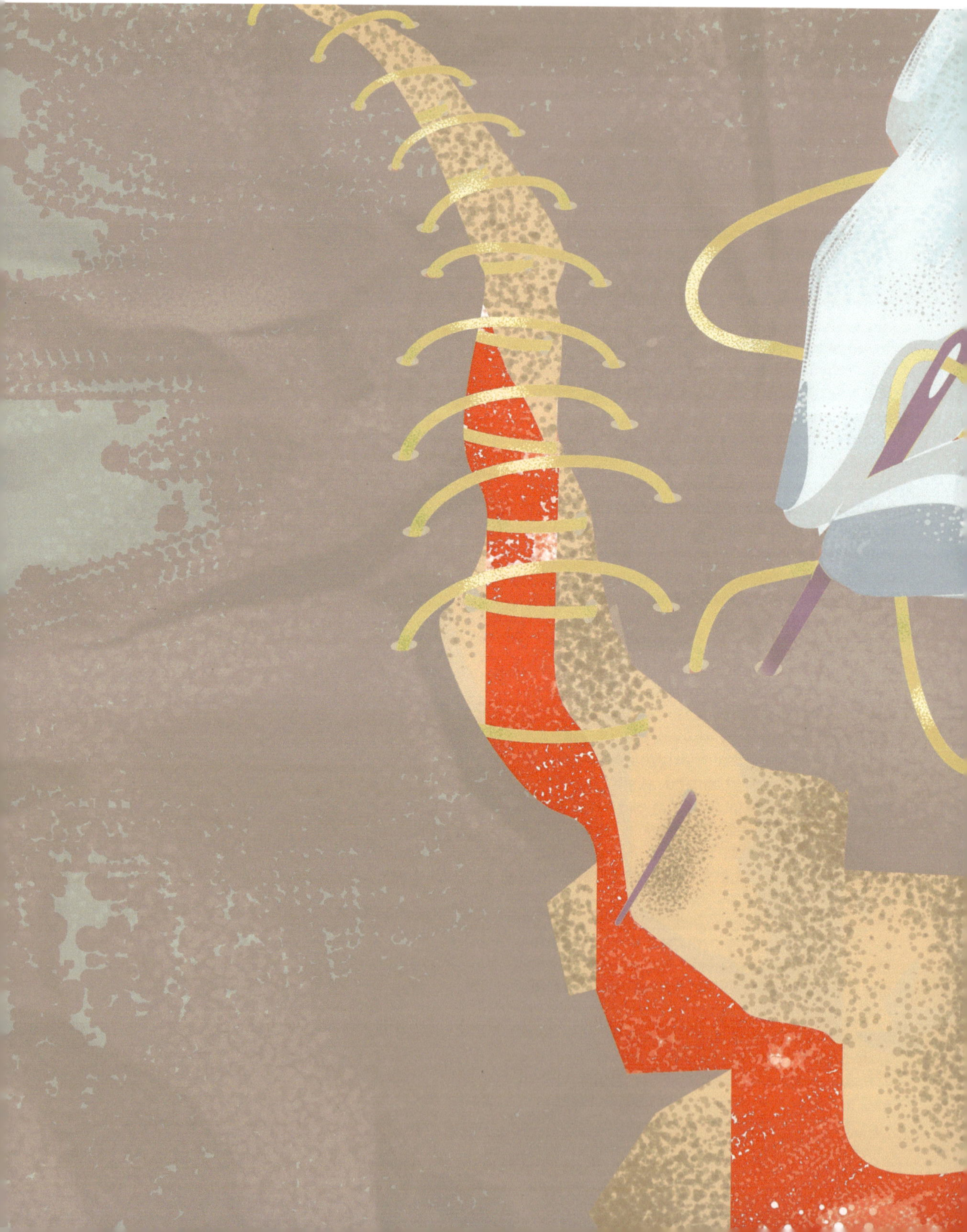

STATES OF EMERGENCY

The Sichuan Earthquake Ten Years On

'Reconstructing the homeland in the aftermath of disaster. When you drink the water, remember its source: be grateful to the Party!' Photo by the author.

Be Grateful to the Party!

How to Behave in the Aftermath of a Disaster

Christian SORACE

During the earthquake that hit Sichuan province in 2008, over 7,000 classrooms in shoddily constructed schools collapsed, killing at least 5,000 children. Grieving parents staged protests and called for an official investigation to punish the officials andcontractors found responsible for the tragedy. The Communist Party responded with more than just censorship, imprinting its own narrative on the rescue and reconstruction, so the slogans written by grieving parents are now doubly buried underneath monuments to the Party's glory and benevolence.

On 12 May 2018 at 2:28pm, when children were attending school, a 7.9 magnitude earthquake struck the Wenchuan region of Sichuan province. Over 7,000 classrooms in shoddily constructed schools collapsed. The killer buildings were dubbed 'tofu-dregs schoolhouses' (*doufuzha xiaoshe*)—toufu-dregs are soft and mushy remnants from the process of making tofu, a metaphor for slipshod construction coined by former premier Zhu Rongji during an inspection visit in 1998 to the site of a newly-built dam that had collapsed. In Sichuan's schools, at least 5,000 children died. Grieving parents staged protests and called for an official investigation into why the schools collapsed and punishment of the officials and building contractors found responsible for the tragedy.

Travelling through the wreckage at the end of May 2008, a couple of weeks after the quake, poet and self-styled barefoot ethnographer Liao Yiwu (2009, 100) documented the rage of grieving parents condensed in the following slogans:

> Demand justice for the dead students and teachers of Juyuan Middle School
> Demand that the government severely punish the murderers responsible for the collapsed school buildings of Juyuan Middle School!
>
> Recover the debt of blood for the people responsible for causing the 'toufu-dreg construction' of school buildings!

The Communist Party responded with more than censorship. It imprinted its own narrative on the rescue and reconstruction. During my 18 months of fieldwork between January 2012 and August 2013, I photographed and wrote in my notebook numerous slogans praising the Communist Party's disaster relief effort:

> An earthquake doesn't care, the Party does.
>
> In times of disaster, the Party is there
> In this life, walk with the Party.
>
> Be grateful to the mighty Communist Party for our new roads, new bridges, and new houses.
>
> Reconstructing the homeland in the aftermath of disaster. When you drink the water, remember its source: be grateful to the Party!

In the contrast between these two sets of observations lies the source of the Communist Party's authority: the ability to control the discursive parameters through which people talk about, engage, and make sense of their world. Or, as Xi Jinping insists, patriotic citizens must defend their 'discursive rights' (*huayuquan*) to 'tell China's stories well' (*jianghao Zhongguo de gushi*).

Those who tell a different story have no such rights. The slogans written by grieving parents are now part of the landscape of ruins, hieroglyphs of lost futures. They are doubly buried underneath monuments to the Party's glory and benevolence. In China, words like 'manmade disaster' (*renhuo*), 'responsibility' (*zeren*), and 'blood debt' (*xuezhai*) are added to the rubble of words that cannot be excavated. An inverted Tower of Babel that reaches down to the abyss.

Affective Sovereignty

The Communist Party's 'discursive rights' are central to its authority and power because words are not disembodied modes of communication but attach us to the world. The Communist Party unabashedly organises political life on the basis of this understanding. In the body politic, words and affects are not the private domain of the individual but the social ties that hold together public life. As a result, how people in China talk and feel falls under the jurisdiction of Party sovereignty—what I call *affective sovereignty* (Sorace 2019).

In the aftermath of the 2008 Sichuan earthquake, the Party encouraged disaster victims to 'bid farewell to sorrow and face the future' (*gaobie chuangtong, mianxiang weilai*), and to move out from under the dark clouds of 'tragedy' and into the radiance of 'heroism' (*cong beizhuang xiang haomai*). Less than a handful of months after the earthquake, all Chinese citizens were asked to 'transform the public enthusiasm' (*minzhong reqing*) for disaster relief into preparation for the Olympics, and to 'overcome disaster and welcome glory' (*chuanyue zainan, yingjie guangrong*)—the implication being that the expression of individual grief, as negative affect, would be an affront to national pride.

The Communist Party provides the acceptable guidelines for the expression and temporality of grief. One must not mourn for too long or let grief get in the way of optimism. Sadness must not metastasise into rage. Face the future rather than the past. The past is a dangerous place to live. Above all, do not dwell on the questions posed by the dead (Bandurski 2015). All of this affective corralling and cajoling is depersonalising and merciless. The imperative to surrender to the demands of the world is eloquently captured by Roland Barthes' (2010, 126) reflections on mourning his mother's death. '*I resist the world, I suffer from* what it demands of me, from its demands' (emphasis added) to rejoin the charade that life continues as if nothing changed. There is an unrelenting reality principle thrown up in response to death, and in China it is the Communist Party who defines the reality to which one must surrender in order to survive.

In the earthquake zone, those who were left cold by the warm embrace of the Party were labelled 'unruly subjects' (*diaomin*). As one internal Party document put it: for 'individual parents who are emotionally out of control (*xinli shiheng*) and engage in physical conflict' a 'public security conversation' would be needed.

The Miracle of Post-disaster Reconstruction

The Communist Party's official narrative of the post-2008 Sichuan earthquake reconstruction is that it was a 'miracle' (*qiji*). The reconstruction is celebrated as an example of how 'hard work for two to three years can leap across (*kuayue*) twenty years of monumental change'. Over five million people rendered homeless by the earthquake—more than the entire population of Los Angeles—were moved into new homes within a three-year period. Celebrating this 'miracle', on the third anniversary of the earthquake, the *People's Daily* praised the Communist Party for being capable of this kind of 'faith', 'mobilisation capability', and 'ideological dedication to the people.'

Far from disseminating empty propaganda, the Communist Party was reenacting a variation of its foundational narrative of legitimacy: without Party benevolence, disaster victims would be helpless, scattered, and exposed to the devastating power of nature. For the individual, nature is terrifying and deadly, but under the Party's collective leadership, wisdom, and protection, nature can be defeated. Another way of saying, without us, there is only chaos (*luan*). In this familiar mantra resonates the Party dictum 'without the Communist Party, no new China' (*meiyou Gongchandang, meiyou xin Zhongguo*), conveying the message *don't ask too many questions and be grateful*. Two years after the earthquake, the Communist Party organised 'gratitude education' (*gan'en jiaoyu*) activities among the earthquake survivors. The gift of the reconstruction required affective reciprocation.

For the Communist Party to be the agent of salvation, the devastation caused by the Sichuan earthquake could not be perceived or discussed as a 'manmade catastrophe' (*renhuo*) in which school buildings collapsed due to shoddy construction materials, corruption, and regulatory negligence. The Sichuan earthquake was a 'natural disaster' (*tianzai*), for which no one could be held responsible. The Communist Party's authority in the earthquake zone rested on the fragile distinction between 'natural disaster' and 'manmade catastrophe'. The discourse of 'natural disaster' had to be reinforced like a structurally damaged building on the verge of collapse. Official media outlets were banned from reporting on the 'toufu-dreg' schools, dead children, and protesting parents. Party authorities were tireless in asserting that the Sichuan earthquake was 'beyond any doubt a natural disaster' and 'an act of nature that could not be prevented'.

Activists, like Tan Zuoren, who persisted in asking uncomfortable questions were arrested on charges of 'incitement to subvert state power' (*shandong dianfu guojia zhengquan*). Most China watchers view this crime to be a meaningless, catch-all category for the state security apparatus to arrest whomever they deem threatening. I suggest, however, that it means what it says. As Mao once quoted Confucius, 'a single word may rejuvenate a country (*yi yan xing bang*), a single word may bring disaster to a country' (*yi yan sang bang*). Or as Confucius (2014, 37) also said, 'in the matter of language, a gentleman leaves nothing to chance.'

Orphans

The government never publically released the names of the schoolchildren who died during the earthquake, despite its promise to do so. To keep that promise would mean answering, or at least acknowledging, artist and activist Ai Weiwei's questions: 'Who are they? What pain did they endure while alive, what grief do they provoke, now dead?' (Sorace 2014). It would mean allowing the names of the dead to live on in the questions of the living. Ai Weiwei's memory wall only provides a temporary shelter for names orphaned from their owners.

Despite Ai Weiwei's international fame, the Chinese Communist Party has discursively defeated him at home. When it is not censored, Ai's confrontational message and style of activism does not resonate with the majority of Chinese citizens. His activism and artwork on the earthquake shook without damaging the Party's discursive hegemony. Instead of following Ai's call to reject 'the erasure of your memory' and reflect on the lives and deaths of the earthquake victims, most Chinese citizens commemorate the Communist Party's response to the Sichuan earthquake and celebrate its hosting of the 2008 Beijing Olympics. Twin dates marking China's glory and reappearance on the world historical stage. These triumphs cannot be interrogated without calling into question the symbolic foundations of the Communist Party's legitimacy.

Discursive Dictatorship

In his book on censorship, Nobel Prize winning author J.M. Coetzee (1997, 15) reflects on how the language of the state permeates the soul, and slips into the lines of even the most precise and vigilant of writers. Coetzee's point is that we cannot escape from the language under which we are pinned: 'For there is nothing outside the theater, no alternative life one can join instead. The show is, so to speak, the only show in town. All one can do is to go on playing one's part, though perhaps with a new awareness, a comic awareness.' As long as the Chinese Communist Party is writing the script, it will remain in power.

Discursive control is a more likely explanation of Xi Jinping's governance strategy than some despotic urge to become emperor. It is also entirely foreign to the English-speaking China commentariat who believes that words are the mere shadow games of power, and that Communist Party discourse is empty propaganda. Perhaps the parents of dead children whose names cannot be publically commemorated would disagree.

But the Communist Party's power depends on more than the redaction of memory—it is revitalised through the capture of emotions. After all, there are endless ways to touch the heart: the relief of still being alive; the dread of uncertainty; the submission to optimism; the exhaustion of speaking to a brick wall—all reasons to be grateful to the Communist Party. ■

Volunteers aiding in the Sichuan earthquake recovery efforts. Photo taken by the author.

The World is Yours!

Youth and Civic Engagement from Sichuan to Parkland

Bin XU

In the wake of the 2008 Wenchuan earthquake, millions of volunteers were driven by sorrow, love, and compassion to travel to Sichuan to help with the relief effort. This spontaneous and self-organised movement of idealistic youths was unprecedented in contemporary Chinese history. However, many of them failed to transcend the boundary between simple volunteering and the type of activism necessary to address the causes of suffering in the wake of the earthquake.

If I had to select only one place to tell the stories of the 2008 Sichuan earthquake, I would choose Beichuan High School.

At 2:28 pm, 12 May 2008, Beichuan High was torn apart by a 7.9-magnitude earthquake. The main building collapsed and buried most of the students. Parents rushed to the school, calling their children's names and hoping they could rescue them by digging through the rubble with their bare hands and simple tools before heavy-duty machinery arrived. Most of their efforts, however, proved to be in vain. More than 1,000 students, roughly 30 to 50 percent of the total school population, died.

Beichuan High was one of the first places that Premier Wen Jiabao visited in the wake of the quake. Against the background of ruins, he quickly established his image as a 'grandpa' by tearfully comforting the parents and promising an all-out rescue effort. Wen visited the school eight times. During a visit to the school's temporary campus, Wen wrote down a phrase on a blackboard, 'Adversities reinvigorate a nation!' (*duonan xinbang*), which became one of the official catchphrases about the earthquake.

About the same time as that visit from Wen Jiabao, Siyi, a young volunteer from Guangdong, was cleaning Beichuan High's dorm building, which fortunately remained standing. During her task, she came across a piece of paper containing a handwritten love letter. Siyi could not remember the exact words or whether it was from a boy or a girl. 'But we've gone through that age, and I wasn't so much older than them,' said Siyi, 'so I felt this love letter was very special and then took a picture.' Did the student who wrote or received the letter survive? She did not know. The message, like most adolescent love letters, probably ended up nowhere, leaving nothing but a scar on a young heart. But it was found in a place where life was even more fragile than a piece of paper and evaporated as easily as a morning dewdrop. Siyi said the love letter was one of the things that compelled her to stay in the quake zone for several months, in difficult conditions—sleeping in tents and with no running water.

Siyi was one of millions of volunteers driven by sorrow, love, and compassion to go to Sichuan to help the rescue and relief effort. They are the main characters of my book *The Politics of Compassion: The Sichuan Earthquake and Civic Engagement in China* (2017). They cried in front of computers and televisions and decided to do something. They organised themselves into groups and travelled from places as far away as Beijing and Shanghai. Numerous tearful eyes watched this huge wave of grassroots volunteering with surprise and delight, and many joined them. The volunteers, most of whom were young, wore t-shirts with enthusiastic slogans, cleaned toilets in crowded shelters, delivered food and water to hard-to-reach areas, and taught in tent schools.

This wave of volunteering was even more extraordinary and significant when it was placed in the context of the history of the People's Republic. Youth and altruism were two things prized by the Communist leaders of yore (Gold 1991). The youths, who were not contaminated by the 'old society' before 1949, were expected to build a brand new, communist world. Mao made a famous speech to praise the youth:

> The world is yours, as well as ours, but it is eventually yours. You young people, full of vigour, are blossoming, like the sun at eight or nine in the morning. Our hope is placed on you.

Note that this 'morning sun' speech was delivered to a crowd of selected elite youths, who were 'red' and smart enough to study in the Soviet Union in the 1950s. Thus, the 'you' in 'the world is yours' referred to a privileged social class represented by this particular audience. This nuance was rarely noticed, however. Communist altruism was largely embodied by Lei Feng, a young model soldier who represented not only selflessness but also loyalty to the Party. Even at the end of the Mao years, when many became disillusioned with the empty political rhetoric, a sizable army of volunteers were still mobilised by the government and their work units (*danwei*) to work in the devastated Tangshan area after the massive earthquake in 1976.

Nevertheless, the Sichuan earthquake was the first time so many volunteers spontaneously self-organised or were organised by civic associations, rather than by the state or their *danwei*. At the time, these young volunteers shattered the bias toward them—'a generation of little emperors' (*xiaohuangdi*). They seemed to instantiate China's promising future. In that moment and place, Wen's words made sense: the adversities did seem to reinvigorate a generation.

Under the Night Sky, the Stars

Siyi said that the most memorable thing about working in the quake zone was the sight of stars twinkling over the rubble, illuminating the dark Sichuan night sky. She told me: 'That's something you'll never see in cities. They're so beautiful.' This somewhat deceptive simplicity and beauty made many volunteers wish to stay in the quake zone forever. It was deceptive, because during their brief stay the volunteers could temporarily leave behind all the challenges in their day-to-day life. All human relations were reduced to the 'helper-helped' connection, and, probably more importantly, the volunteer assumed the role of a helper imbued with a somewhat condescending feeling of being needed and loved. Thus, it did not come as a surprise that the volunteers, consciously or unconsciously, attempted to be cocooned in the nice, warm comfort zone of volunteering.

Outside the comfort zone, however, the wounds of the quake were left open and raw. Many volunteers had the experience of teaching in a tent school. Not far from their tent was a pile of ruins, which the volunteers passed on a daily basis. This pile of ruins might entomb 100 or 200 students. Altogether 5,335 students died in their schools, according to official statistics. 'It was because of the earthquake!' explained the official media. But few volunteers really believed this narrative, given that many of them saw rebars in the ruins as thin as chopsticks, concrete mixed with large amounts of sand, and sometimes no rebars or concrete at all. They also heard stories of, and even saw first hand, how the students' bodies were dug out of the rubble, dead and rotten. They felt the unspeakable trauma of the parents. All these experiences would have naturally led many volunteers to a simple question: 'Why did so many schools collapse?'

Nevertheless, very few volunteers asked the question. The interviews recorded in my book show an ethical and political dilemma they faced. They wondered: 'I volunteered because I wanted to reduce the people's suffering, but should I cross the boundary to address the causes of their suffering, through serious and open public deliberations, and even activism to find out causes of the suffering?'

Those who answered yes joined the campaigns launched by Ai Weiwei and Tan Zuoren to collect and verify the names of student victims. They were harassed, pursued, threatened, expelled, and detained. Tan Zuoren was sentenced to five years in prison.

Those who answered no felt a sense of guilt that kept gnawing at their conscience. It was one thing to make angry comments online as a distant netizen; it was quite another if one as a volunteer actually went there, talked with the embittered survivors, and had to directly face this dilemma. Volunteers used all kinds of rhetorical devices to get around the difficult questions they faced on a daily basis—telling themselves: 'It's normal in this society'; or 'I can't change anything, and so I'll forget about it'; or simply 'I don't care'. Their apathy was not a result of an actual threat from the authorities, but a fear of imminent danger implied in the political context. That was what most Sichuan volunteers chose to do.

Even grimmer is the scenario of a 'spiral of silence': the more repressive the political context is, the less likely one is going to talk about or act on the issue of injustice; the less one talks about or acts on the issue, the more repressive the context becomes. In the end, with no hope to take action, one somehow loses the ability and desire to talk about the issue and silently buries it in the quiet realm of unconsciousness.

Reshaping Memory

This collective silence led to the state's unchecked representation of the past—or official forgetting of some parts of this past. Official commemorations were held, and memorials were built to celebrate the 'victory of the battle against the earthquake'. The largest memorial was built right on Beichuan High's old campus. The memorial has two main buildings and many grassy mounds. The burgundy colour of the buildings fits well with the green of the mounds. Nice and clean. But, too clean. Most ruins were wiped out, but the ruins of the main classroom building which buried more than 1,000 students were too big to be removed. Instead, they are covered by a huge grassy mound with only an inconspicuous banner to tell visitors that the students and teachers of Beichuan High died there. No details. No numbers. No names. No explanations. It is also located in a place far from the normal shuttle route, so many visitors may not bother to walk that far. This strategy is what I call the 'topography of forgetting'—the state reshapes the topography of a disaster site to reshape memory.

Driven by sorrow, compassion, and the 'can-do' spirit, the Sichuan volunteers accomplished something extraordinary. They transcended their group boundaries and particular interests to participate in one of the biggest waves of collective action in recent decades. But many of them failed to transcend the boundary between the 'nice, warm, and harmless' volunteering, and the activism that aims to address the causes of the suffering of the people they helped. The ultimate reason for this failure is the repressive political system, which is generally successful in subduing challenges to its legitimacy. But the political dynamics in China are complex. The system and the people constitute and reinforce each other; the boundary between the two is always blurred and porous. Not everyone can become Tan Zuoren. But everyone's superficial compassion, silence, and inaction perpetuate the unspeakable suffering of the victims, whom everyone claims to help.

I am not putting myself on a moral high ground in relation to the volunteers. I was one of them. I faced the same dilemma they did, but in a different way. I went to Sichuan first as a volunteer, then to collect data for my dissertation. The emotional toll of this research was certainly heavy. As a father, I often felt my heart was bleeding when listening to stories and seeing the ruins. Yet, I used their suffering as the 'data' to write my dissertation, to get my degree, and later to publish a book with a university press, hoping to use the book to convince the tenure committee to allow me to keep my job. I did little to reduce their misery, except for a brief period of volunteering and some donations. In all these years, I have repeatedly asked myself: am I exploiting their suffering? How can I—an academic who wrote some rarely cited articles and an English-language book which may only sell several hundred copies—address the causes of their suffering socially and politically? Honestly, I have no definitive answers.

The only thing I can do (and did) was to use my privilege as an academic writer to let people know what had happened and what my take on the issue was. I gave lectures in the United States and China, within and outside academia. In a public lecture in China, someone in the audience even brought up the tragedy of the Great Leap Forward famine—his relatives starved to death and women in his village were married to better-off outsiders to keep their current husbands and children alive—and this person was a village Party secretary! China never stops surprising an observer. So far, no National Security agent has bothered to invite me for a tea or chase me around. So, instigating these kinds of public conversations is the type of small action I am able to do now. Am I doing enough? Probably not. Am I doing the right thing? Perhaps yes. But how many of my fellow Sichuan volunteers are able to do even these small things, especially as they would have little to gain but a lot to lose if they do? Very few.

From Sichuan to Parkland

When I was writing this essay, a generation of American youths, who are now growing up in the shadow of Donald Trump, had to face their own tragedy and an existential challenge on a bloody Valentine's Day. On 14 February 2018, a man with a semi-automatic gun killed 17 students in Marjory Stoneman Douglas High in Parkland, Florida. My sorrow was intensified by a coincidental geographic adjacency in my past. We once lived in Miami for a few years, and my daughter's violin teacher resided in a neighbourhood close to Parkland. I quickly found the similarities between Sichuan and Parkland: children died in their schools; there were 'thoughts and prayers'; the incident provoked a storm. I even cynically expected the same subsequent trajectory: after a heated debate, nothing substantive would be done, and, like Sichuan, Parkland would be forgotten or, at best, become an empty signifier like 'Columbine'.

Nevertheless, the event took a decisive turn. The youths in Stoneman Douglas High stood up for themselves. They self-organised into groups but gave a collective middle finger to the superficial 'thoughts and prayers', or to adults' lies about the 'mental illness' of the killer, or to stories about 'good guys with guns defending children from bad guys with guns'. They eloquently told the politicians who took money from the National Rifle Association a clear 'Shame on you!' They walked out of their schools. They drove to Tallahassee to pressure the Florida state legislators on gun control laws. When the petition failed at the state level, they organised a nationwide March for Our Lives, on 24 March in Washington, D.C., and almost all major cities in the United States. Parents stood with them, drove them to protests, and helped them, but it was the students, who were of the same age as those victims in Beichuan High, who occupied the front stage.

I observed this whirlwind and joined the March with sorrow, admiration, and enthusiasm. In my head cycled *The Last Gunshot*, a song by my favourite singer Cui Jian, which, according to speculation, may be a roundabout commemoration of the Tiananmen Square movement in 1989. The lyrics fit well with my hope:

> A stray bullet hit my chest.
> All of a sudden, the past flooded my heart.
> Oh, the last gunshot!
> Oh, the last gunshot!

The students in Tiananmen Square fell and never stood up again. The students in Parkland fell, but their classmates stood up and rode the wave. It would be naïve to explain their bravery only by their individual characters. Rather, it is a bravery enabled by the current political context, which, despite its defects and hypocrisy, still contains law-regulated space for open defiance. This space is much smaller and, in some situations, unthinkable in China. The Parkland students could go to the state capitol to press legislators without being threatened or detained, while the volunteers connected to Tan Zuoren and Ai Weiwei were detained and harassed without explanation. The Parkland students could organise a nationwide march, while Sichuan volunteers did not even have the desire to talk about the issue, since it was impossible for them to change anything. The public sphere also protected this space for the Parkland students' political engagement. In a CNN 'town hall', Senator Marco Rubio was grilled by the teenagers and their parents. In Sichuan, some protesting parents were repeatedly detained and placed under surveillance, and the media were muted. Even if the efforts fail, as television host Stephen Colbert said in his programme on the Parkland shooting, the youths still have a last resort: 'This is an election year. If you want to see change, you have to go to the polls to tell the people who will not protect you that their time is up' (Russonello 2018). For the Sichuan volunteers, the last resort was no resort at all.

A Candle in the Wind

My reader, before you laugh at my naiveté, allow me to say that I am fully aware of the struggles and hardships the youth encounter in the United States and of the complexity of American politics. History is replete with American examples of slaughtered and silenced youth, such as the Kent State shooting and the killing of the Freedom Summer volunteers. I taught these events for years. But this cannot overshadow the difference between the two political systems and corresponding personal choices. Although no one would guarantee the success of the Parkland youths, they can at least do something. We adults hear their angry voices, and many of us express our own anger by joining them. In contrast, in the ten years since the Sichuan earthquake, any such attempt by the Chinese youth has been suppressed easily. All we hear is a deathly silence underpinning the state's loud self-congratulations on its successful response to the disaster.

If I sound pessimistic about Sichuan and China, let me end with a more upbeat quote from Lu Xun, who cherished hope for Chinese youths despite his deep disappointment with them.

> I hope that Chinese youths will walk out of the cold air. Simply walk upward. Don't listen to the cynics. If you can do something, do something. If you can say something, say something. If you have heat, then give out light. Even if you are a firefly, you can shine in the darkness. You don't have to wait for a torch. If there is no torch in the end, then you are the only light.
>
> Lu Xun, *Hot Wind*, No. 41 (author's translation)

Almost a century later, we still cannot say if Lu Xun's hope has any chance of becoming reality, but let us carry it like a candle in the wind. The world may be absurd enough for us to give up, but it is nevertheless our choice to continue pursuing meaning in a meaningless world. Perhaps, in the end, the Great Helmsman had a point, even anachronistically: 'The world is ours, as well as yours, but it is eventually yours!' ■

The ruins of a hospital in rural Sichuan. Photo: Dominiqueb, Flickr.com.

Sichuan, Year Zero?

KANG Yi

The aftermath of the Sichuan earthquake has witnessed the development of a variety of indigenous NGOs. While the first two years after the earthquake were a 'honeymoon' period for local governments and NGOs, after 2010 feelings became more mixed. On the one hand, a series of policies openly acknowledged the important role of social organisations in supplying public goods and social services; on the other, new laws and regulations not only restricted the activities of overseas NGOs in China, but also severely limited access to foreign funding for domestic organisations.

I still clearly remember how during my visits to the quake-struck areas one year after the Wenchuan earthquake, local officials would unanimously commend the various social organisations and volunteer groups for their enthusiastic, industrious, and effective relief efforts. Back then, I also witnessed the establishment of a number of indigenous NGOs. In recent years, however, I have found at my field sites that local government support towards social organisations has floundered. I have also heard more and more complaints from NGO representatives about the difficulty of working with local officials. As the tenth anniversary of the Wechuan earthquake approaches, the time is ripe to look back and ask whether the earthquake really was a major turning point for Chinese society, as it was presented at that time (Shieh and Deng 2011;

Teets 2009). Conversely, looking forward, is it still possible to say that a vibrant civil society is on the rise in China?

Throughout my field research in the areas affected by the Wenchuan earthquake over the past nine years, I have witnessed the development of a variety of indigenous NGOs—a term in which I also include non-profit organisations voluntarily organised by citizens, even if they do not have an official registration—which actively assisted in the post-disaster recovery and continued working in local communities after reconstruction was completed. In particular, I looked at their evolving interactions with local governments. The first two years after the earthquake were a 'honeymoon' period for local governments and NGOs. In interviews, both sides frequently highlighted each other's 'collaborative role' in post-disaster rehabilitation. However, after 2010, feelings were more mixed. On the one hand, a series of policies openly acknowledged the legitimate and important role of social organisations in supplying public goods and social services in China, facilitating their registration and encouraging them to seek funding from the government and various domestic foundations in order to provide social services. However, the 2017 Foreign NGO Management Law not only restricted the activities of overseas NGOs in China but also severely limited access to foreign funding for domestic NGOs, threatening their very survival (Franceschini and Nesossi 2017). When I returned to Sichuan in recent years, I found that the divergence in the development trajectories of different types of NGOs was becoming more apparent.

Does the Walker Choose the Path?

Many NGOs that gained official registration in the earthquake-affected areas between 2009 and 2010 were sponsored, entirely or partially, by local civil affairs bureaus through quasi-official organs such as social work associations (*shehui gongzuo xiehui*). From their inception, these NGOs eagerly established alliances with government agencies, and thus state actors had great confidence in their loyalty. Like parents rearing their children, local governments generously offered economic support and policy favours to them. For instance, despite the lack of experience of these NGOs, local government agencies continuously contracted them for various public services and even entrusted them with large-scale pilot policy programmes. In return, these NGOs carefully catered to the government's needs and satisfied the bureaucratic culture of upward reporting, enabling the relevant officials to take the credit. Unsurprisingly, such organisations easily grew and expanded over the years, and even engaged in a limited degree of policy advocacy. Such groups quickly came to dominate, or even monopolise, the local NGO 'ecosystem'. However, depending on continuous state support, sooner or later they began resembling government agencies themselves, which, in the eyes of residents and of certain sober officials, diminished their value as a third party standing between the state and citizens.

After the earthquake, a few survivors and volunteers decided to found NGOs by themselves, without any support from the local state. Such grassroots organisations had neither abundant resources nor close contact with state actors, and thus usually had a hard time fending for themselves in the years after their establishment. To survive, they actively expanded their networks to seek donations and advice. Through these networks, they made friends from different parts of the world and gained exposure to foreign civil society practices and knowledge. Given their limited resources and narrow scope, the government often paid little attention to them, and generally regarded them in a positive light. However, as these grassroots organisations steadily grew—securing funding from a wide range of non-governmental sources, building professional expertise, and gaining wider support in the local communities—local governments inevitably took notice and attempted to intervene in their development, compelling them to demonstrate loyalty. While striving to keep an optimal distance from the government, these NGOs cautiously avoided offending local officials who could have easily threatened their survival. Some eventually drew closer to the government, applying for government-funded projects and seeking opportunities to ingratiate themselves with powerful government authorities.

Overseas NGOs also played a crucial role in post-earthquake relief, rehabilitation, and reconstruction. They swiftly arrived at the quake-struck areas and joined the relief work. Throughout the rehabilitation process, they provided a variety of different kinds of support (e.g., funding, human resources, technical assistance, etc.) to earthquake survivors, local governments, and indigenous social organisations. They were generally well received by residents and local officials. After things became more stable, quite a few overseas NGOs formally established local branches or supported the founding of indigenous NGOs in order to continue participating in community building. New organisations that received generous overseas sponsorship actively launched various public services programmes, which were warmly welcomed by local governments.

Nonetheless, officials tolerated a certain degree of NGO autonomy only as long as they could harness the resources of these organisations for their own benefit and, as time went by, tensions gradually emerged. Local officials not only continuously asked these NGOs to contribute resources and ideas to fulfil governmental agendas, but also increasingly intervened in their operations to ensure that they followed the directives of local authorities. NGO staff members had to spend their time drafting and submitting proposals and reports requested by officials, even if they regarded such activities as being a waste of resources and hence handled them perfunctorily. In turn, feeling dissatisfied, officials intentionally made things difficult for these organisations. In the past few years, the diminishing ability to determine local policies and priorities, as well as the government's bureaucratic style and administrative interventions, has frustrated quite a few overseas NGOs that funded local NGO activities. One after another, they have reduced or withdrawn their financial support. In 2016 and 2017, many analysts were discussing the chilling effects of the Foreign NGO Management Law, but what I had observed in Sichuan in previous years showed that even without explicit legal intervention, local governments would discourage overseas support and funding to local NGOs by simply taking a predatory approach: all they had to do was consume the overseas resources of these organisations and marginalise their impacts in local governance.

In recent years, with the passing of the Chinese Charity Law that relaxed registration and fundraising requirements for domestic NGOs, private philanthropic foundations have been on the rise (Simon and Snape 2018; Teets 2018). Many foundations have actively supported grassroots NGO development in Sichuan, especially in the areas of post-disaster recovery and community rebuilding. At the same time, as the Chinese government has acknowledged the legitimate role of NGOs in supplying social services, NGOs in Sichuan now have various channels to seek government contracts for public service provision. When I visited the quake-struck areas in 2017, I found that almost all local NGOs, including those previously supported by overseas funding, had turned to domestic funding sources such as purchase-of-service contracting by different government agencies and flexible grant schemes from domestic foundations. The NGO representatives I talked to generally viewed foundations as an alternative—often preferable—source of funding compared to the government, in light of their more efficient, flexible, and constructive 'investment' approach and business management style. However, they also understood that foundations scarcely deviated from the agenda of the state, as they relied on the permission and support of the authorities. While the new funding game provides relatively stable financial support to NGOs, it forces them into competitions where they must actively accommodate the preferences of the funders. Some adjustments might be constructive for the purpose of organisational development, but most of these changes actually distracted NGOs from their original mission.

A New Dawn for Chinese Civil Society?

For many, 2008 was a 'Year Zero' for Chinese civil society, as the relief and reconstruction process following the Wenchuan earthquake witnessed a significant surge in spontaneous grassroots action and organisations offering help to local communities in the disaster-affected areas (Roney 2011; Shieh and Deng 2011; Teets 2009; Zhang et al. 2013). Scholars closely following post-quake developments over the long term, however, are more hesitant in their assessment. For instance, Christian Sorace (2017) has illustrated the top-down nature of the reconstruction process, effectively showing how the tragedy was taken as a perfect opportunity for the Chinese leadership to demonstrate strength and leniency, but hardly created opportunities for a substantive expansion of civic participation. Bin Xu (2017) has observed the state's cruel response to complaints and claims of parents who lost their children in the earthquake, as well as the increasing marginalisation of civil society organisations. Carolyn Hsu (2017) has noted that although NGOs and social entrepreneurship are transforming China by mobilising popular resources and support to solve various social problems, the state, meanwhile, is taming their productive powers for its own ends. Thus, the game being played is very different from that which many observers predicted at that time, and the rise of Western-style civil society in China appears to be little more than a mirage.

My research echoes these recent critical works. The post-quake development trajectories of various local NGOs show that, although after the earthquake the Chinese government embraced the third-party management model and a more open associational environment, it remains unclear whether Chinese NGOs can flourish and contribute to the rise of a civil society in the western sense of the term. In fact, most of these NGOs have limited aspirations that do not extend to promoting civil society as a political space: they simply wish to avoid trouble and complement the state in serving populations in need. Moreover, the narrowing of funding sources has caused anxiety and driven NGOs to compete for the favour and patronage of donors. Recently established NGOs are likely to become government- or business-like organisations before they can demonstrate their unique value. Indeed, over the past nine years, I have witnessed NGO development in the quake zones transform from a grassroots-driven, relatively organic, and untamed process, first into a rather fluid and dynamic situation, and then into a top-down managerial set of procedures. Still, not everything is lost. The new funding game that sees the coexistence of government and business rationales, as well as recent developments like the facilitated channels for philanthropic public fundraising and NGOs' versatile strategies for self-sufficient growth, may still open new windows of opportunity for Chinese NGOs. ■

Sichuan earthquake memorial.
Photo: Pxhere.com.

Civic Transformation in the Wake of the Wenchuan Earthquake

State, Society, and the Individual

SUN Taiyi

Relations between the Chinese state and society have undergone important transformations since the Wenchuan earthquake. While the rise of voluntarism and the rapid increase of social organisations cannot be overlooked, the state continues to pursue a deliberate strategy to cultivate relationships with those organisations that support the regime, while cracking down on those that pose a potential threat. This essay examines the evolution of state-society relations by looking at three different spheres: state, society, and individuals.

On 12 May 2008, a 7.9 magnitude earthquake hit the Wenchuan region, Sichuan province, causing widespread damage in ten provinces, autonomous regions, and municipalities in China. According to official data, about 45 million people were affected by the seism, including no less than 69,229 casualties and 17,923 missing persons. The earthquake also resulted in tremendous economic loss, which has been estimated to be more than 845 billion yuan (Deng 2009).

While the direct human and economic impacts of the earthquake were significant and tragic, there were also less direct, but long-lasting consequences for state-society relations. Over one million volunteers poured into the region and mobilised their resources to support the relief work, and as many as three to five hundred non-governmental organisations (NGOs) joined the effort (Jin and Wang 2008). For this reason, 2008 has been referred to as China's 'NGO Year Zero' (NGO *yuannian*) or the 'Year of Civil Society' (*gongmin shehui yuannian*) (Shieh and Deng 2011). In the wake of the tragedy, the number of social organisations in China grew steadily, if not rapidly, and many of those Wenchuan volunteers turned into organisers and leaders of social organisations after the quake relief effort (see Gao's essay in this volume).

The evolution of state behaviour was more complex. An unprecedented visit on site by then Prime Minister Wen Jiabao on the night of the earthquake gave clear indications about the policy priorities of the state. Whether due to the temporary incapacity of local governments or to a deliberate choice to give more space to NGOs, civic engagement was tolerated, if not welcomed, to facilitate the reconstruction and recovery of the quake-struck regions. However, since 2009, and particularly after 2012, we have seen a bifurcated policy. On the one hand, there have been frequent crackdowns against those organisations and social activists considered dangerous to regime stability; on the other hand, many social organisations have earned the trust and support of local governments that to this day rely on them for service provision and delivery of public goods (see also Kang's essay in this volume).

Still, the state matters only up to a certain point. A commonly overlooked yet extremely important factor when talking about the Chinese civil society is the individuals' attitudes towards the NGOs. Unlike in Western societies where citizens tend to trust NGOs more than governments, Chinese citizens, especially in rural areas, trust NGOs much less than the authorities (World Value Survey 2015). This individual scepticism towards social organisations poses severe challenges to the development of civil society in China.

Growth of Social Organisations in China

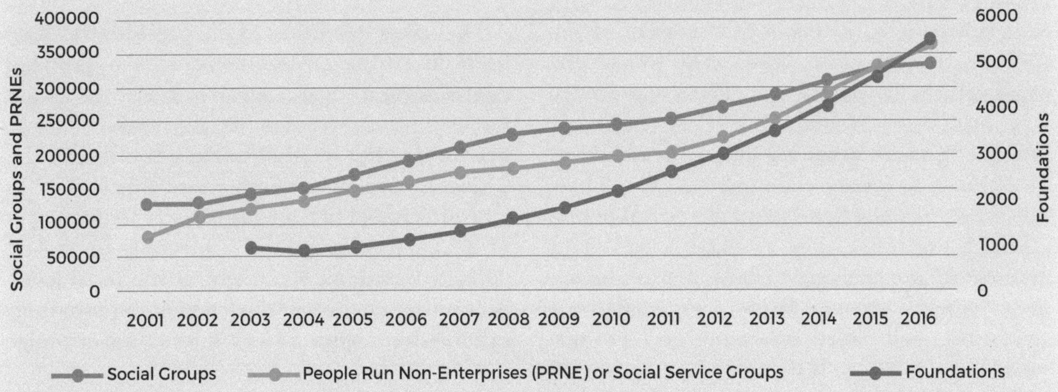

Source: Ministry of Civil Affairs Social Service Development Report (Data collected from the 2008–2016 reports)

The Awakening of Society

Since the Wenchuan earthquake, voluntary associational activities have increased steadily in China. According to reports by the Chinese Ministry of Civil Affairs, by the end of 2016, there were a total of 702,000 social organisations (*shehui zuzhi*) registered in the country, among which 336,000 social groups (*shehui tuanti*), 361,000 citizen-initiated non-enterprise units (*mingban fei qiye danwei*), and 5,559 foundations (*jijinhui*). All of the categories of organisation have increased in number steadily over the past decade.

Much of this development coincided with the boom in the number of Internet users in China. Community organisers and social activists used the Internet to organise and promote activities, which later led to the formation of official or unofficial social organisations. For example, in 2011, taking advantage of a few pictures of children beggars that went viral on Chinese social media, some activists were able to ignite a campaign to fight against child trafficking, saving at least 5,869 children from horrible fates. One year later, they established a new 'Child Safety Fund' (*ertong anquan jijin*) to continue to track and rescue victims of human trafficking.

My interviews with NGO leaders in Sichuan province reveal that many of them were first exposed to social activism in the wake of the Wenchuan earthquake, when they joined the relief efforts. Once the immediate emergency was over, they found that they had lost interest in their previous jobs and remained in Sichuan to create their own NGOs. Their initial campaigns often included a social media element, and once they reached a sufficient number of constituents to have some impact, they would create formal organisational structures and start operating as 'proper' social organisations. If successful, many would register officially.

The transformation of the social sphere can be seen not only in the increase in the sheer number of organisations, but also in the types of activities undertaken. The Wenchuan earthquake led to more intensified public scrutiny of the behaviour of officials and celebrities. Immediately after the earthquake, social activists started to report on the amounts of money donated by individual celebrities, and how the money was spent. Even though the government ended up receiving the majority of the donations, and the lack of transparency in this regard remains a controversial point to this day, the practice of society checking and monitoring the state and other powerful individuals was thus established. Officials earning modest wages but wearing luxury watches were exposed online, and in many cities individual activists started lurking outside high-end restaurants to take pictures of cars with government licence plates to expose them online. With several officials being charged with corruption and waste due to this kind of societal monitoring, it is evident that the post-Wenchuan nascent civil society was not only growing larger but also becoming more powerful.

The Bifurcation of State Policy

The recent abolition of the presidential term limit in China is testament to the growing centralisation and assertiveness of state power in recent years. At the national level, the awakening of civil society has made the Chinese state more nervous and this has led to a severe crackdown on any activity that appears to challenge the regime—especially organised collective actions. However, at the local level, in counties and townships in Sichuan province, officials have adopted a differentiated strategy.

Scholars have previously observed this strategy of distinguishing between regime-supporting and regime-challenging social organisations, arguing that the Chinese state is highly motivated to suppress and collect information from regime-challenging organisations (Kang and Han 2008). The experiences in the wake of the Wenchuan earthquake have revealed that local authorities follow another rationale in enacting this differentiation, i.e. they aim at extracting productivities from, and outsource responsibilities to, regime-supporting organisations (Sun forthcoming)—thus employing the carrot rather than the stick in most cases.

Before the Wenchuan earthquake, many local officials in Sichuan had never encountered NGOs and believed that these organisations were all anti-government. When the earthquake significantly reduced the capacity of several local governments to provide public goods and services, NGOs assisted them with the provision of goods and services. In case of problems, they even shouldered part of the blame, thus shielding certain officials from being the direct target of complaints. These experiences changed the perspectives of many local officials regarding the potential usefulness of NGOs. After the

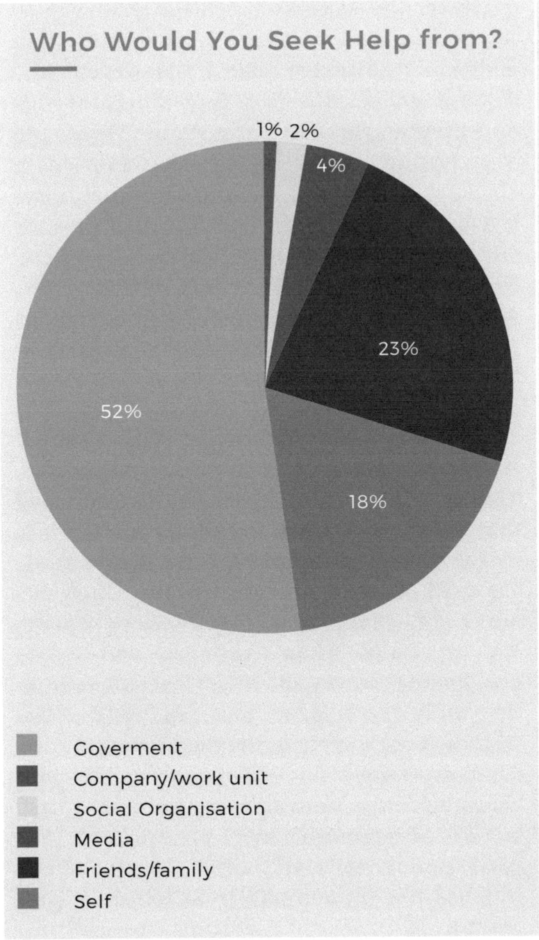

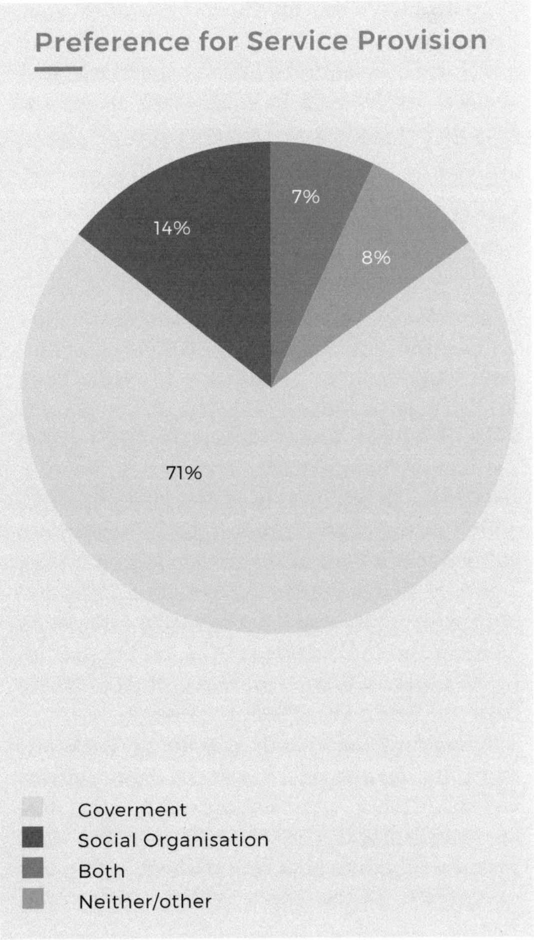

earthquake, many local governments started entrusting NGOs with service provision and other responsibilities (Sun 2017).

One example was the distribution of sticky rice dumplings (*zongzi*) during China's Dragon Boat Festival. In the past, to celebrate this traditional holiday, local governments in Sichuan province would give out free *zongzi* to villagers, but often received complaints about uneven or unfair distribution. For this reason, this became one of the tasks outsourced to NGOs and, since the transfer of responsibility complaints against the government have decreased. As one local official told me during an interview: 'If they do a good job, the government can still get the credit; but if they didn't do a good job, they will take the blame. Why wouldn't we let them help with such tasks?' With tight budgets and limited staff size, local officials in Sichuan now actively seek societal involvement in governance, as long as they do not challenge the status quo.

Sceptical Individuals

The World Value Survey and several other indexes indicate that citizens in most countries tend to have more confidence in NGOs than in their governments (World Value Survey 2015; Edelman Trust Barometer 2015; Asian Barometer Survey 2017). This is not the case for China. In addition to these survey results, which reveal that Chinese people have more confidence in their government than in NGOs, a survey that I conducted between 2014 and 2015 with 1,224 respondents in 126 villages in Sichuan also indicates that the rural population in the province is even more sceptical of NGOs than the World Value Survey average.

When rural individuals hear about NGOs—or more familiar terms such as social organisations and charitable organisations—they visualise an unorganised, less trustworthy, and less resourceful group of people without legitimacy to operate. When asked whom they would seek help from, respondents overwhelmingly chose the government (53 percent) and family/self (41 percent). Very few would seek help from other societal actors (media 4 percent, social organisation or charitable organisation 1 percent). If they had to choose between the local government and civil society for service provision, most of them (71 percent) would choose the government over social organisations (14 percent). What is surprising, is that even those who are extremely dissatisfied with the local government—those who chose one or two on a scale of one to five indicating their satisfaction with their local government—still picked the government (65 percent) over social organisations (22 percent).

The literature on civil society in China tends to depict the state as the main challenge to the non-state social actors in an authoritarian context (Gallagher 2004). However, the distrust and scepticism of individuals towards non-government associational activities and organisations might be just as important a challenge. My survey also indicates that if one is a member of any NGO, her/his trust towards NGOs will increase significantly. Therefore, NGOs in China should not only seek to deliver goods and services but should also attempt to recruit new members and empower them to be individuals that are able to carry on the mission of the organisation.

The state-society relation in China cannot simply be described as 'state versus society'. The post-Wenchuan experience has revealed that despite the tightening of the public space by the central government, local governments are quite accommodating when the conditions are right. Many new organisations sprang up, especially when they are non-regime challenging. Survey and interview results from this study also indicate that the future of the Chinese civil society in the quake zone, and in China more generally, will not only need a more accommodating state allowing for more space, but will also require a more involved citizenry participating in civil society organisations to build the population's trust towards these realities. ■

FURTHER READINGS ON THE SICHUAN EARTHQUAKE

Yi Kang, *Disaster Management in China in a Changing Era*, Springer 2014

This book shows how Chinese officials have responded to popular and international pressure, while at the same time seeking to preserve their own careers, in the context of disaster management. Using the 2008 Wenchuan earthquake as a case study, it illustrates how authoritarian regimes are creating new governance mechanisms in response to the changing global environment and what challenges they are confronted with in the process. The book examines both the immediate and long-term effects of a major disaster on China's policy, institutions, and governing practices, and seeks to explain which factors lead to hasty and poorly conceived reconstruction efforts, which in turn reproduce the very same conditions of vulnerability or expose communities to new risks.

Bin Xu, *The Politics of Compassion: The Sichuan Earthquake and Civic Engagement in China*, Stanford University Press 2017

The 2008 Sichuan earthquake killed 87,000 people and left 5 million homeless. In response to the devastation, an unprecedented wave of volunteers and civic associations streamed into Sichuan to offer help. *The Politics of Compassion* examines how civically engaged citizens acted on the ground, how they understood the meaning of their actions, and how the political climate shaped their actions and understandings. Using extensive data from interviews, observations, and textual materials, Bin Xu shows that the large-scale civic engagement was not just a natural outpouring of compassion, but also a complex social process, both enabled and constrained by the authoritarian political context.

Christian Sorace, *Shaken Authority: China's Communist Party and the 2008 Sichuan Earthquake*, Cornell University Press 2017

In *Shaken Authority*, Christian Sorace examines the political mechanisms at work in the aftermath of the 2008 Sichuan earthquake and the broader ideological energies that drove them. Sorace takes Communist Party ideas and discourse as central to how that organisation formulates policies, defines legitimacy, and exerts its power. By taking a distinctive and original interpretive approach to understanding Chinese politics, *Shaken Authority* demonstrates how Communist Party discourse and ideology influenced the official decisions and responses to the Sichuan earthquake.

Earthquake survivors line up for food at Jiuzhou stadium in Mianyang. Photo: Raul Vasquez, Flickr.com.

The Power of the Square

Post-earthquake Activism in Mianyang

GAO Huan

The year 2008 saw an explosion of civic activities in China, ignited by the devastating earthquake in Sichuan province. Even amid this widespread activism, Mianyang city stood out as a unique site of popular mobilisation, with local people becoming active, self-organised, and creating a network of new NGOs that exists to this day. This kind of activism was a rare thing in Sichuan, where most cities only created new NGOs with the help of external actors. In this essay, Gao Huan considers how Mianyang's distinctive pattern of local mobilisation was enabled by public spaces, in particular the emergency shelter at Jiuzhou Stadium.

The year 2008 saw an explosion of civic activities in China, ignited by the devastating earthquake in Sichuan province. Countless volunteers, non-governmental organisations (NGOs), informal associations, and loosely connected Internet-based groups devoted themselves to disaster relief activities (see Xu's essay in this volume). Even amid this widespread activism, Mianyang city stood out as a unique site of popular mobilisation. Though a poorer city without much civic activity before the earthquake, Mianyang locals became surprisingly active and self-organised, creating a network of new NGOs that exists to this day. This kind of activism was a rare thing in Sichuan, where most cities only created new NGOs with the help of external actors. Mianyang's distinctive local mobilisation, I argue, was enabled by public space. In particular, the emergency shelter at Jiuzhou Stadium in Mianyang was a uniquely large, visible, and accessible venue, providing not only the physical site but also a symbolic centre for grassroots mobilisation.

The Jiuzhou Stadium

Mianyang is an inconspicuous city in Sichuan, located roughly 110 kilometres northwest of the provincial capital, straddling the Longmen Mountains to the west and the Chengdu plain to the east. In 2007, it had a population of 5.38 million, with a per capita GDP of 11,354 yuan—just below the provincial average (Sichuan Bureau of Statistics 2008). The earthquake hit this city especially hard, causing 21,963 deaths, 9,174 missing people, and a total economic loss measuring 25 billion yuan (Sichuan Provincial Government 2009, 17–37 and 52).

In the evening of 12 May, only a few hours after the earthquake, nearby residents began gathering around Jiuzhou Stadium, as the area provided a suitable place to wait out aftershocks. The stadium is a sports multiplex located at the western edge of Fucheng district, the urban core of the city. It sits on a 13.6-hectare lot, with a river running along its northern and the eastern edge, and a major city road to the south. The entire area is large, open, and flat, with multiple structures and carefully manicured lawns and greenery. The structures of the stadium were mostly undamaged by the earthquake.

On the morning of 13 May, as tens of thousands of people who escaped the ruins of Beichuan finally arrived in urban Mianyang amid the pouring rain, the Party secretary of Mianyang decided to let the evacuees take shelter in the stadium. On this first day, over 18,000 people streamed into the structure in the span of a few hours (Heng 2011). Premier Wen Jiabao visited on the afternoon of 13 May, and this exposure may have encouraged other earthquake victims, as more and more homeless individuals from all around Mianyang poured in. Tents filled the lots around the stadium and spilled over to the street and the riverbank area. Though emergency shelters were continuously being set up around Mianyang, Jiuzhou Stadium remained flooded with evacuees. One week after the earthquake, at its busiest, it housed between 40 and 50,000 people, based on different estimates (Zhou 2010, 198; Beichuan County Government 2016, 301). It was the largest emergency shelter in all of Sichuan (Zheng, He, and Cao 2008). The bulk of people only dissipated towards the end of May, but the stadium did not fully empty until more than a month and a half after the earthquake, on 29 June. Even in the relatively calm last week of June, it housed over three thousand evacuees. The crowd at Jiuzhou was the single largest public gathering created by the earthquake, and it provided the site and the means for robust popular activities.

Organisational Challenges

Tens of thousands of desperate people housed in one stadium meant to hold less than 6,000 created enormous challenges for the city. From preventing communicable diseases to managing waste disposal, everything became disproportionately difficult given the population density. The situation was made even more chaotic by waves of reporters, volunteers, support personnel, and local people looking for lost family and friends who turned up at the site. The local government of Mianyang dedicated as many resources as it could to the management of the stadium. At first, on 13 May, it sent about 400 city employees (Mianyang Local Gazetteer Office 2009). In the following days, new personnel were continuously added, and at the peak of activity nearly 1,000 city employees worked around the clock at the stadium (Zhou 2010, 198). In April 2016, an activist who had been a city employee at the time told me: 'For more than a month the Mianyang prefecture government did nothing else; everything was put on hold.' Due to this Herculean effort to manage Jiuzhou Stadium, Mianyang officials did not have spare manpower left to organise volunteers; in fact, they came to depend on self-organised volunteers for crucial services.

Lang, a well-off businesswoman, was among the locals who gathered at the stadium on 13 May. She found utter chaos: newly arrived donations were piling up at every unloading bay, and local people like her who wanted to help milled about aimlessly. Lang went directly to the highest-ranking official on the spot, asking permission to organise volunteers and to help with the reception and distribution of supplies. Officials first wanted the Mianyang Communist Youth League (CYL) to organise volunteers, but when they could not locate CYL officials in the midst of the chaos, Lang obtained permission to organise as she saw fit. With official sanction, the businesswoman quickly rounded up other volunteers and together they received, catalogued, and distributed all the water, food, and other supplies they found at one particular unloading bay. Seeing how efficient these self-organised volunteers were, and relieved to have one fewer task to take care of, government officials let Lang's team manage this unloading bay throughout Jiuzhou's tenure as an emergency shelter.

In addition to managing supplies, Lang and other volunteers helped evacuees to start an evening dance group. According to Lang, a few days later, though people were being fed and clothed, they needed something uplifting to do. One evening, she and a few volunteers set up candles and speakers in a lot just across the street from the main structure of the stadium and invited people to join them in folk dances in the makeshift square. When this quickly grew into a nightly gathering with hundreds of people, local officials did not object to the initiative. Lang's activities demonstrated that, in this moment, members of the general public faced remarkably few restrictions when it came to the use of the space around them. After the stadium was cleared of evacuees, Lang's team launched several long-term projects in Mianyang and one year later managed to register a formal NGO. For years, she continued fruitful collaboration with many other local volunteers whom she had first met at the stadium.

In April 2016 I interviewed another activist surnamed Wang. He had started a volunteer team when he was in university, though it had never expanded beyond the campus. On 13 May, after mobile phone service stabilised, he called many of his university friends and together they went to Jiuzhou Stadium. Once there, they also took on the task of receiving and distributing supplies. Unlike Lang, they did not even ask for permission in the midst of the chaos. According to Wang, it was not always smooth sailing, as his team came into conflict with government officials working at the location. However, despite the conflict, they were still permitted to work, as it was impractical for officials to keep them out, given the bustling crowds. Wang's team of volunteers had been on indefinite hiatus since they had left university, but their experience at Jiuzhou Stadium gave them a new boost of energy to resume regular community services and take on new charity projects. In a short time, they became involved with earthquake reconstruction activities and also became a valuable member of Mianyang's newly created NGO scene.

An Ark of Life

A major public building used as an emergency shelter for more than a month and a half was a rare occurrence in the post-earthquake landscape. To control the chaos, most local officials across the region opted for distributed emergency shelters and for rapidly recreating pre-earthquake communities. For example, the city of Shifang began relocating evacuees to less affected areas close by and had them board with locals in private homes (Deyang Bureau of Civil Affairs 2008). Most villagers were eager to help, but their particular volunteerism was situated in private homes: there were no crowds, no unending public activities, and very little media presence. The city of Dujiangyan built prefabricated homes in record speed, and evacuees began moving into this temporary housing as early as 23 May. These temporary housing communities were administered by existing village leaders or urban residents' committees; they were closed off to outsiders, constantly patrolled by volunteers and the police force, and every visitor had to sign in and sign out (Dujiangyan Government 2008). Earthquake evacuees in Shifang and Dujiangyan quickly left public spaces and also the public eye. For this reason, it became more difficult for volunteers or NGOs to bring them donations, to offer them counselling, or to organise activities for them. Indeed, NGOs working with earthquake victims in temporary housing communities could only enter by invitation from the local authorities.

This was in stark contrast to Jiuzhou Stadium, which for several weeks remained a highly visible and accessible public space. Doors to the stadium could not be closed, as evacuees in dire need and workers offering essential goods and services were constantly coming and going. Tents spilled into surrounding lots and green space and could hardly be surrounded by a wall. Visits by high-level officials and media attention further increased the cost of forcefully restricting access to the area. Also, due to adverse natural conditions across a large swath of Mianyang, maintaining a high-capacity shelter like Jiuzhou Stadium was helpful for local authorities. As a result, Mianyang residents gained a rare public space. There, volunteers' daily interactions with earthquake victims both encouraged and enabled sustained activism, and their encounter with fellow local activists created the foundation for future collective actions and organisation building.

In the wake of the earthquake, Jiuzhou Stadium acquired a grand and elevated reputation: media reports called it nothing less than an 'ark of life' (*shengming fangzhou*), and local activists still remember it fondly by this name many years later. While this may be in part state propaganda at work, there is no denying the importance of Jiuzhou, both for disaster relief and the development of NGOs in Mianyang after 2008. Nearly all local activists began their NGO careers at Jiuzhou. While Mianyang NGOs remain constrained by restrictive regulations today and are constantly reshaped by government interference, they still represent something new and authentically grassroots. ■

Still from Red White, by Chen Zhong.

Documenting the Earthquake

Marina SVENSSON

Unlike previous disasters in China, the Sichuan earthquake was extensively documented in images and film, leaving behind an archive of national trauma unparalleled in Chinese contemporary history. This essay examines 16 documentary films produced by filmmakers in the wake of the disaster. These visual testimonies help preserve individual memories of a traumatic event that to a large extent is unaccounted for in the official media and cultural productions.

Parents and bystanders were among the first to provide footage of the Sichuan earthquake, shakily recorded on their mobile phones and camcorders. In contrast to earlier natural disasters, such as the Tangshan earthquake in 1976, the Sichuan earthquake has been extensively documented in images and on film. To date, at least ten filmmakers have produced 16 independent documentary films on the earthquake and its aftermath. Many filmmakers ended up tracing the ways in which people coped with their experiences during months and even years following the disaster.

Unsilencing Grief

In late May 2008, directives were issued to domestic media that prevented them from reporting on poor school construction and protesting parents seeking justice for the untimely deaths of their children. The images of desperate families with photos of their dead children kneeling in front of officials, marching to local government buildings, or trying to protect and secure child graves, were only seen in foreign media and, later, in many of the independent documentary films. The lack of transparency and accountability for the deaths, and the silenced voices of the mourning parents, triggered a number of individuals—including activists such as Tan Zuoren and prominent artist Ai Weiwei—to travel to the disaster zone to gather information. Several independent filmmakers, who felt a strong sense of obligation to record the national trauma, also arrived early to the scene in order to document voices and stories that had been erased in the official media.

Many parents, activists, filmmakers, and concerned citizens thus came to challenge the official narrative of national unity, responsible leadership, heroism, and gratitude that dominated the official media. The filmmakers helped parents to bear witness to their trauma and fight for justice, and in some cases also became engaged in the investigations themselves (particularly evident in the case of Ai Xiaoming and Ai Weiwei). Many filmmakers continued to follow events and individuals' stories over the years that followed, documenting not only the official reconstruction effort, but also the struggles of the affected families to overcome their losses, to heal, and rebuild their lives.

Documenting Disaster

The ten filmmakers discussed in this essay have diverse backgrounds, motivations, and approaches to documentary film (see Box 1 for the list of films and directors). Some of them have a background in film studies or had made several films before they turned their lenses on post-quake Sichuan—examples include Du Haibin, Chen Zhong, Zhao Qi, Fan Jian, and Mu Zijian. At least three filmmakers come from Sichuan, i.e. Chen Zhong, Ma Zhandong, Mu Zijian, and thus had knowledge of local dialects and customs, which also show in the deeper engagement their films have with the communities depicted.

Those who arrived early on the scene started filming without having secured any funding—for instance, Du Haibin had to borrow a camera as he rushed to the area without preparation. A few of them later managed to get funding from international funding organisations and broadcasters. For example, Fan Jian's film *The Next Life* (2011) was a coproduction with the Japanese TV station NHK, whereas Zhao Qi's film *Fallen City* (2014) received funding from a range of institutions, including the IDFA Bertha Fund, Sundance Fund, NHK, ITVS, Knowledge Network, YLE, NRK, and premiered on PBS. Unsurprisingly, those films that received support through international financing are of better technical quality in terms of editing, colouring, and sound, and they have also been more widely screened abroad. Du Haibin's film *1428* was one of the first films produced after the quake, with funding from CNEX, and it received the Best Documentary Award at the 2009 Venice International Film Festival. Other films have had more limited exposure abroad and at various unofficial film festivals in China.

Whereas some filmmakers spent a relatively short period of time in the area, many ended up making several visits over the subsequent years (for example Chen Zhong, Ma Zhandong, Fan Jian, and Zhao Qi). Their films are, therefore, able to probe more deeply into the long-term rebuilding process, and the lasting impacts on individuals, families, and communities touched by the tragedy. The films show different styles and aesthetics, ranging from observational, expository, participatory, to performative modes. Many filmmakers adopted an observational style and engaged with individuals and communities over a long period of time (Chen Zhong, Ma Zhandong, Fan Jian, Zhao Qi, and Mu Zijian). Another group of filmmakers approached the topic from a more activist and expository perspective (Ai Xiaoming and Ai Weiwei). One should, however, distinguish between Ai Xiaoming's more participatory mode of filmmaking, making ample use of the footage shot by local citizens themselves, and Ai Weiwei's more performative and confrontational mode.

There are also differences between the first films made in the aftermath of the disaster and those that documented developments over a longer period of time. The initial films often have a very raw, direct, and fragmented character. This is fitting, as it illustrates how people experience and articulate the first shock and the almost unbearable pain after a major traumatic event—examples include Pan Jianlin's *Who Killed Our Children* and Du Haibin's *1428*. Pan's film documents different voices and accounts of the disaster, providing a sense of the grief and struggles of parents to get answers regarding how and why their children had died, and giving a picture of how chaotic the immediate aftermath of the disaster was. Du's *1428* takes its title from the exact time the earthquake occurred on 8 May. The first footage was shot just a few days after the earthquake struck and provides vivid documentation of the massive scope and extent of the destruction.

Stills from *1428* documentary by Du Haibin.

The film lacks a main character and storyline, although a father and his son who live in a shack are some of the recurrent figures in the film. The use of powerful imagery of ruins and debris, the lack of voices or an explicit narrative, and the disjointed structure of the film give the viewer a sense of what living in a disaster zone can be like.

Later films, such as those by Chen Zhong, Ma Zhandong, and Fan Jian, among others, focus more on the disaster's impact on individual families and communities. They address their efforts to rebuild their lives, their emotional healing, and their coming to terms with the disaster. A recurrent topic in many of these latter films is the struggle of families to have a second child after the death of their first-born during the earthquake. In many cases, it was an only child who had died and, while they now were allowed to have a second child, many couples felt emotionally torn over this decision, and in addition had difficulties conceiving. For instance, Fan Jian's film *The Next Life* depicts the ordeals of a family who lost their eight-year-old daughter and who later, only after several IVF treatments, finally manage to get pregnant again.

The later films also provide fascinating accounts of different customary practices and the role of religion during times of mourning and trauma. For example, in *Red, White* Chen Zhong focuses on a Daoist temple in Shifang municipality and the role of different ritual and burial practices, which gives his film a strong ethnographic character and shows the important role religion played in the healing process. Some of these later films do not explicitly address the destroyed schools, protests, or calls for justice among parents, but instead show how individuals deal with their loss in more personal and intimate ways. Whereas these movies offer some hope for healing and show human resilience in the face of adversity, the more expository films made by Ai Xiaoming and Ai Weiwei discussed above offer no such comfort. They reveal unhealed (and perhaps unhealable) trauma, lack of redress and official accountability, as well as repression. The argumentative narrative,

Stills from *1428* documentary by Du Haibin.

engagement with victims, and confrontation with officials in these films underscores the ways in which filming is a form of civic engagement and social activism for filmmakers such as Ai Xiaoming and Ai Weiwei.

Archiving Trauma

Although the modes of filming as well as the topics and perspectives are highly variegated, the different films together constitute a valuable repository and archive of national trauma unparalleled in Chinese contemporary history. Whereas documentary films may not help people to get redress, and their circulation in China at the moment is very limited, these visual testimonies help preserve individual memories of a traumatic event that to a large extent is unaccounted for in the official media and cultural productions. They not only provide an important visual repository that will help individual citizens to remember one of China's most devastating events but also provide important materials for scholars who want to study the sociopolitical context of the earthquake, as well as customs and belief systems in Sichuan. ■

Documentaries and Filmmakers

At least ten different filmmakers have together made 16 films documenting the Sichuan earthquake and its aftermath.

Who Killed our Children (Pan Jianlin)
Red, White (Chen Zhong)
One Day in May (Ma Zhandong)
Tears in Ashes (Jia Yuchuan)
1428 (Du Haibin)
Our Children; Citizen Investigation; Why are the Flowers so Red; River of Oblivion; Enemy of the State (Ai Xiaoming)
Little Red Cheeks; 4851; Disturbing the Peace (Ai Weiwei)
The Next Life (Fan Jian)
Fallen City (Zhao Qi)
One Child (Mu Zijian)

WINDOW ON ASIA

PC: Benjamin Canizales.

Cambodia's Prime Minister Hun Sen. PC: Wikimedia Commons.

'Hun Sen Won't Die, Workers Will Die'

The Geopolitics of Labour in the Cambodian Crackdown

Sabina LAWRENIUK

Over the past year, the Cambodian government has engaged in a full-frontal assault on freedoms of expression, association, and assembly. The latest development has seen Cambodia effectively becoming a one-party state, after the ruling party swept all 125 seats on offer in the National Assembly at the polls held in July 2018. In this essay, Sabina Lawreniuk examines the ways in which both labour politics and China have played a role in these changes.

In September 2018, the European Parliament tabled a high-stakes debate on the aggravated human rights situation in Cambodia. Under threat was the continued inclusion of Cambodia in the European Union's Everything But Arms (EBA) trade scheme. The EBA agreement—introduced by the EU in 2010 to promote economic growth in the world's Least Developed Countries—grants Cambodia and 48 other beneficiary states tariff-free imports to the EU market, as the name suggests, on every product except arms and armaments. Yet this access comes with one, albeit significant, catch: a clause in the agreement binds beneficiaries to recognise and uphold fundamental human and labour rights conventions.

It is not hard to parse where the Cambodian government has fallen foul of this requirement over the last 12 months. Rather, it is more difficult to accurately convey the intensity of the government's full-frontal assault on freedoms of expression, association, and assembly; a nuclear response to electoral decline in the 2017 local elections and the subsequent fear of losing power in national elections in 2018. Encompassing the closure of newspapers and radio stations, dispersal of protests, and increased surveillance of civil society in public records and online, the so-called 'crackdown' peaked with the imprisonment of the main opposition party leader, Kem Sokha, before the ultimate dissolution of the opposition party itself at the behest of Cambodia's injudiciously partial Supreme Court. Without a credible opponent on ballots, the government swept to victory at the national polls held in July 2018; its 77 percent share of the vote delivering an unprecedented clean sweep of all 125 seats on offer in the National Assembly.

Nothing New under the Sky

'Descent into outright dictatorship', screamed the *Cambodia Daily*'s headline on the morning of 4 September 2017, when news broke of Sokha's arrest. The sentiment, if not strictly hyperbolic, was somewhat disingenuous. Cambodia's democratic credentials have not been recently shed. Instead, they have been long stretched by a government brought to power in a bloody 1997 coup and a leader who self-identifies as the 'strongman of strongmen'—the sixth-longest serving non-royal head of state in the world. For many years, however, Cambodia's rulers have had to take care to mask the autocratic tendencies of their tenure; the nation's economic dependency on aid and then preferential trade, like the EBA, rendering the government beholden to maintain at least a façade of liberal progress to satiate the 'good governance' strings that come attached.

There is little chance that the EU's watchdogs have, until now, simply missed the evidence of a deeper malaise. The red flags signalling a democratic deficit have always been prominent: from the long-standing harassment, detention, and assassination of peaceful human rights defenders like Chea Vichea, Chut Wutty, and Tep Vanny, to ratcheting up efforts to deter civil society organisation through dubious, hostile legislation. More likely, the trade-offs between popular power and stability have been weighed by the EU and accepted, where these have tipped in its favour—in this case, shoring up a regional ally and trading partner, as well as delivering rapid rates of economic growth that have won Cambodia middle-income status, thus serving up a ready exemplar of neoliberal development logic.

Here, the electoral cycle has been the historic rhythm to which the waxing and waning of Cambodia's democratic aspirations and aspersions have been pegged. The government's control has tended to tighten during election season, only to cede once results have been returned. In this way, the leadership has managed to tread a path between its benefactors' demands for liberal development and its own concern for the continued restitution of its command. Indeed, with the 2018 election now out of the way, there have already been signs of a return to Cambodia's own brand of normalcy. Sokha and other political prisoners like Tep Vanny have been released, if under unusual license: Vanny, having had her original conviction overturned by royal pardon, has been handed down a new suspended sentence for earlier charges; Sokha remains under house arrest, confined to the few streets around his home in the capital.

However, for many commentators these reversals signal the onset of a customary softening of the government's stance in the post-election setting. Significantly, among their number appears to be the EU, whose response has been a mirroring of this relaxation of attitude. At the time of writing (September 2018), the threat of withdrawal of the EBA looks to have been rescinded. In its final resolution, passed on 13 September, the EU Parliament watered down its assertive rebuke of the Cambodian government's actions. While reiterating calls for the immediate and full release of Kem Sokha and reinstatement of his party, strongly worded sentiment denouncing 'sham elections' and an 'illegitimate government' that appeared in an early draft motion was diluted to 'concerns over conduct' and 'credible process' in the accepted edit; the proposition of a broad response, like suspension of the EBA, became targeted sanctions aimed at individuals responsible for the most serious abuses of rights.

Plus ça change, then, has been the response in some circles, as the always uneven, sometimes uneasy, yet timeworn truce between the two sides, Cambodia and the EU, appears to have been reinstated. Nevertheless, there are indications beneath the banality of surface impressions that the balance of power has significantly shifted. For one thing, from the Cambodian side this return to normalcy has been accepted with nothing akin to the good grace of old. Instead, the Cambodian government's inclination to regard its admonition with hostility rather than humility has been markedly evident. 'Hun Sen won't die, workers will die,' the Prime Minister himself has warned icily whenever the menace of sanctions like the revocation of EBA looms. A government statement decried the September resolution as 'biased', 'reckless', and 'insensitive'.

Wooing the Workers

There is a fundamental truth to Hun Sen's words. His party's focus on garment workers throughout the recent electoral campaign is, perhaps, a sign of the government steeling itself for impact. Indeed, the garment sector, whose rapid expansion over the past two decades has been the ballast of Cambodia's booming economy, is heavily reliant on the EU market, with almost 50 percent of Cambodia's exports of clothing and footwear heading there in 2017 (ILO 2018). The loss of the EBA would represent a significant threat to the viability of a sector where for buyers, as manufacturers know, the bottom line is always the bottom line. The imposition of tariffs would cost the sector somewhere in the region of 700 million USD, risking the flight of investors and thus placing the 800,000 jobs in the industry in jeopardy.

The government's concerted overtures to garment workers since last summer—increased wages, improved social security benefits, and personal audiences with the Prime Minister—are, in part, a response to this threat: an effort to forge new alliances between the ruling party and a group which, though sizeable, it has typically ignored in its electioneering—concentrating instead on its traditional bedrock of support in rural areas. Yet this favourable attention also serves as early insurance against any potential fallout from the EU's actions. Indeed, while making these efforts to win esteem among garment workers, the Cambodian government has also pushed a preemptive narrative that links any punitive reprisals from the EU to the backstage meddling of exiled opposition leader Sam Rainsy, now based in Paris. The latest statement on the EU's September resolution, for example, acerbically references 'a notorious opposition figure' in its opening paragraph, and goes on to frame Rainsy as having an active role in the EU's process, claiming that 'this resolution was finalised with his assent' (Mission of the Kingdom of Cambodia to the European Union 2018).

The promotion of this narrative is also aimed at decoupling the traditional links between Sokha and Rainsy's party—the Cambodia National Rescue Party (CNRP)—and workers, who have been a strong base of support for the opposition. The political crisis that broke in 2013, though it had the opposition leadership as its figurehead, was fuelled by the rising discontent of workers, when a general strike called in the wake of a disputed election brought not tens, but hundreds of thousands of people on to the streets and the government almost to its knees. Alongside its softer appeals for the favour of workers, it is this kind of uprising that the government has sought to prevent through a concomitant punitive regime targeting the trade union movement. A new, draconian Trade Union Law passed in 2016 has all but paralysed many once-vibrant organisations. A mix of half-baked clauses and unachievable conditions, characteristic of Cambodia's preference for rule by, rather than of, law have made it hard if not impossible for many local branches to fulfil the criteria to formally reregister with the Ministry of Labour, as required. Instead, their operations are left in a precarious grey area of the law. Many leaders are now too frightened of the threat of carceral penalties to join their members on the picket line.

Yet the government patronises and dangerously underestimates workers if it believes that this unrest is whipped up only by the actions of trade union bosses and opposition leaders, and that by dispensing with the latter the concerns of the former will simply go away. Two decades of stagnating and declining wages are intuitively sensed by workers in their stalled livelihoods and waylaid aspirations of improved living conditions and life chances. Banning protests and curtailing unions addresses the symptoms but not the cause of Cambodia's recent wave of disquiet, which underneath this rough dressing of calm is otherwise left to fester.

Warming Up to China

It is the increasing inability of the Cambodian government to manage the rising discontent of workers within the strictures of its donor-directed liberal façade that underlies, at least in part, Cambodia's significant geopolitical manoeuvres of recent years. Worker consent, happiness, and democratic acquiescence to the current regime's rule has proved incompatible with its ruthlessly exploitative brand of neoliberal crony capitalism, where the continued impoverishment of those at the bottom is driving the massed wealth of a few at the top. The killing of five striking workers by military police during the 2013 unrest shows just how thin this veneer of liberal propriety has been stretched.

Accordingly, the Cambodian government has warmed of late to China's advances in the region, a key node in the Chinese Belt and Road Initiative. China's financing and loans come with their own strings attached, accused by some of being 'debt trap diplomacy'—the perils of which countries like Sri Lanka have become all too aware of in recent months (Abi-Habib 2018). Yet, despite the risks, China does provide a ready supply of funds with a 'don't ask, don't tell' approach to internal affairs. The allure of this interested apathy has proved hard to resist among Cambodia's leaders, looking to leverage against EU dictates. Today, 70 percent of Cambodia's 4.3 USD billion in bilateral debt is owed to China, whose share eclipses even that of multilateral lenders like the International Monetary Fund and World Bank. Since 2013, China has also been Cambodia's largest foreign direct investor, ploughing in an average of 1 billion USD annually, surpassing Cambodia itself in 2016 as the leading source of investment capital in the country.

It is the weight of this new backing, beyond previous Western dependencies, that has allowed the Cambodian government to be so bullish of late in its home and foreign policy response, without fearing the consequences of highlighting the EU's shallow and often hypocritical stance. The EU's wavering resolve in tackling the crisis in Cambodia likely stems, too, from its worries about strengthening the bond between Cambodia and China, which would weaken its own influence further. Alas, as Hun Sen astutely notes, Cambodia's new win-win is likely lose-lose for workers in any eventuality. Their livelihoods are at stake whether the EU intervenes or abandons them to global industry's race to the bottom. ■

'A Worker's Soul.'
PC: Esmee Van Heesewijk
@flickr.com.

'Mr Dong [pseudonym] is one of the external hires for our project in Papua New Guinea (PNG) ... he does onsite surveying. Natives in PNG were outraged at their vehicles getting stuck in the soft soil embankments. Convinced that these roads were dysfunctional, they hit him with sticks without any forewarning ... in fact, he had nothing to do with such road conditions.'

One of Mr Dong's supervisors

'Medical examinations show the dislocation of the first joint connecting my head with the cervical vertebrae; surgery is the only treatment for this ... I suffer from severe headaches after walking for a while, and cannot lift anything, nothing at all; if I am lifting something I have to stop walking, and must sit down once my headache hits.'

Mr Dong

My Rights Have Been Left behind in Papua New Guinea

The Predicament of Chinese Overseas Workers

ZHANG Shuchi

Increasing numbers of Chinese companies are sending employees abroad as part of China's global push. Still, Chinese workers in other countries often find themselves vulnerable. By tracking the case of one employee in a Chinese enterprise in Papua New Guinea, in this essay Zhang Shuchi reveals the plight of China's relatively powerless overseas workers, an image that stands in stark contrast to the widespread depiction of an increasingly assertive and powerful Chinese global presence.

Mr Dong, a Chinese overseas worker born in the late 1980s, is employed in PNG—over 6,200 kilometres away from his hometown in northwest China. The brutal incident that occurred in PNG in May 2014 entangled him in a legal limbo in the Chinese court system that only came to a tentative conclusion four years later, when the First Intermediate People's Court of Beijing delivered its judgement of second instance. With increasing numbers of Chinese companies sending workers abroad as part of China's global push, this case has much to tell us about the increasingly globalised Chinese legal labour regime. It also reveals the plight of China's relatively powerless overseas workers, an image that stands in stark contrast to the widespread depiction of an increasingly assertive and powerful Chinese global presence.

A Legal Odyssey

From a legal perspective, the crux of the dispute in Mr Dong's case—just as in most legal cases involving work-related injuries—lies in the determination of labour relations. Who was responsible for compensating him due to his injury? In April 2013, Mr Dong started working for China Overseas Papua New Guinea Corporation (*zhong haiwai baxin gongsi*, hereafter COPNGC)—a wholly owned subsidiary of China Overseas Engineering Group Corporation Ltd. (*zhong haiwai gongcheng zeren youxian gongsi*, hereafter COEGC Ltd.)—and was dispatched to PNG to work as a surveyor on the Mendi-Kandep Highway project. Fortunately for him, compared to the common practice of sending workers overseas under murky terms of employment that do not provide legal resource to workers, the central state-owned enterprise followed formal recruitment procedures and Mr Dong signed a written employment contract. The legal loophole, however, was that the company signed the contract in their capacity as an overseas-registered independent legal entity, thus creating a jurisdictional problem. Both signatories to the employment contract agreed that the company would purchase personal accident insurance worth 500,000 yuan for Mr Dong while he was abroad.

The Regulations on Insurance against Work-related Injuries issued in December 2010 stipulate that enterprises within China must insure all their staff members against work-related injuries, and that in the absence of such insurance, enterprises shall compensate injured employees in accordance with the coverage and standards specified in the work-related injury insurance. But it is not clear which firm was directly responsible for Mr Dong's employment: the state-owned firm or its foreign-owned subsidiary. For example, neither enterprise had contributed to his social security, which was still linked to his previous employer. Given that COPNGC was foreign-owned, Mr Dong had to prove that COEGC Ltd. was his actual employer in order to be eligible for insurance compensation in China for work-related injuries.

Mr Dong sought legal assistance from Beijing Yilian Legal Aid and Research Centre of Labour (*Beijing yilian laodongfa yuanzhu yu yanjiu zhongxin*), an NGO providing professional legal support related to labour laws [disclosure: the author of this essay is Director of Research at Beijing Yilian]. With its Deputy Director Han Shichun and Lawyer Liu Wei as his attorneys, Mr Dong applied for labour arbitration in 2015 but his request was rejected because COPNGC was the signatory to his employment contract. The Chinese Labour Law stipulates that plaintiffs can take further legal action if they object to labour arbitration decisions that serve as procedural prerequisites. So, in September 2015 Mr Dong and his legal team prepared additional evidence and supporting materials and litigated a second time, continuing to request the determination of the labour relation.

A key point of Mr Dong's case was based on an understanding of the Regulations on Management of Foreign Labour Service Cooperation issued by the State Council in 2012. According to these Regulations, foreign enterprises, institutions, or individuals are not permitted to recruit workers within China who will be sent to work overseas. Being a foreign-owned enterprise, COPNGC is not eligible to directly establish labour relations with Chinese workers within China. During the trial, his attorneys argued that Mr Dong's employment contract with the foreign-owned enterprise violated this rule and should, hence, be deemed void. This would prove the existence a factual labour relation between him and COEGC Ltd. As a second prong of argumentation, the attorneys also pointed out that the Administrative Regulations on

Contracting Foreign Projects issued in July 2008 by the State Council clearly state that firms contracting foreign projects must not subcontract their projects to other companies with no commensurate qualifications. In other words, COEGC Ltd. must be responsible for subcontracting to COPNGC and is, by extension, responsible for the project on which Mr Dong worked in PNG.

The judgements of first instance and second instance, delivered respectively in January 2018 and May 2018, both supported Mr Dong's argument, ruling that labour relations existed between COEGC Ltd. and Mr Dong. In addition, in the verdict of second instance the court emphasised that the Administrative Regulations on Contracting Foreign Projects demand that firms purchase overseas personal accident insurance for dispatched workers, and that evidence showed that Mr Dong's commercial insurance policy was paid for by COEGC Ltd., further substantiating the claim that COEGC Ltd. was indeed Mr Dong's employer.

Determining labour relations was a comparatively easy process; but lengthier and more complicated procedures awaited Mr Dong, including the identification of his work-related injuries, the assessment of his work capacity, and the request for compensation from his employer.

A Blow to the Neck

In the popular imagination, on travel websites and guidebooks, PNG is exoticised as a place of spellbinding beauty and native traditions. The reality, however, is more complicated. In a recent country guide published by the Chinese government, the country is described as a place marked by conflict, unemployment, and a lack of infrastructure (Department of Outward Investment and Economic Cooperation 2017).

Obviously, Mr Dong and his coworkers were dispatched to the real PNG and not the one of the touristic imagination. PNG imposes stringent constraints on visas for foreign workers because of high domestic unemployment rates, and designates China as a 'high-risk' country (Department of Outward Investment and Economic Cooperation 2017). By the end of 2016, there were merely 1,069 Chinese dispatched workers in PNG. The conditions for this small cohort are rather dismal. Ordinary workers dispatched to PNG are entirely segregated from local communities in their daily lives. When problems arise, they lack access to the local institutions and resources that could safeguard their rights and interests. Furthermore, the local minimum wages, average wages, social security, and other benefits they receive in the PNG are significantly inferior to those in their home country. They also face a local workforce that is largely underpaid and therefore often hostile. Monthly wages for local workers approximate 800 kina, the equivalent of 1,574 yuan based on the current exchange rate, and earnings for technicians average 1,200 kina. The National Employment Law in PNG requires employers to purchase social insurance for employees, but a local labour aid agency has yet to be established.

China's Regulation on Work-related Injury Insurance stipulates that Chinese workers dispatched overseas should first join work-related injury insurance schemes in their host countries while suspending their work-related injury insurance schemes in China. Only when local insurance schemes are unavailable are they entitled to retain their Chinese insurance. But insurance is no trivial matter, especially given the poor medical conditions in host countries and the difficulties involved in seeking compensation from overseas employers. Most workers fall under the management of cooperative enterprises contracting out labour services, and not state-owned enterprises carrying out their own projects. Comparatively speaking, Mr Dong's situation was favourable because he was actually employed by the company he worked for.

Exporting Labour and Its Discontents

While extreme, the situation facing Chinese workers in PNG is far from unique. As of 2016, 4,394 central state-owned enterprises had established businesses overseas. In 2016, China's outward foreign direct investment flows and stock accounted for 13.5 percent and 5.2 percent, respectively, of the global totals, and the volume of China's outward investment flows ranked second highest among all the countries (regions) worldwide (Ministry of Commerce, National Bureau of Statistics, and State Administration of Foreign Exchange 2016; UNCTAD 2017).

Increasing rapidly alongside outward foreign direct investment are the numbers and economic contributions of overseas workers. By 2017, the number of overseas workers from China totalled 10.1 million, ranking fourth worldwide after India, Mexico, and Russia (World Bank 2017). Annual remittances from Chinese overseas workers amounted to 64 billion USD. Globally, this was second only to the 69 billion USD remitted to India. At the national level, China's unsound domestic legal institutions and its inactive participation in international labour laws and mechanisms have resulted in weak protections for the rights and interests of its overseas workers; incidents at workplaces and attacks from local communities are frequent occurrences for Chinese workers.

Traditionally, workers from countries that export capital on a large scale because of their long-term capital accumulation take up professions and positions with added value. This added value tends to increase as these countries upgrade their industries and strengthen their education and social security systems. This is not the case with regard to China, however. Statistics published a few years ago show that over 80 percent of Chinese overseas workers were still employed in labour-intensive industries, such as construction, textiles, and fishing (Fan and Yin 2013, 340).

A Subordinate Vanguard of a New Globalisation

The story related above illustrates the dismal conditions that Chinese workers have to endure overseas, often without recourse to legal protections either at home or abroad. They fall, as it were, through the cracks, and are subjected to the full brunt of the systemic risks of globalisation. While China's perceived status as a global power continues to grow, Chinese overseas workers remain subordinate and relatively powerless, even as they play a crucial role in the global expansion of their country's power.

Realistically, the short-term approach to protecting Chinese overseas workers' rights lies in initiating changes domestically in China. This includes pressing the Chinese government to shoulder more responsibility, to amend its domestic employment legislation, to expand its participation in international legal labour systems—as well as in global and regional institutions focussing on migrant workers—and to offer a series of feasible support channels, such as consular protection, early warning mechanisms, and security institutes for overseas workers. Reinforcing the protection for the rights of Chinese overseas workers has not only added novel challenges and impetuses to China's domestic legislation on employment, but has also been linked to the success of the government's Belt and Road Initiative, as well as to the expansion of the country's clout in global governance.

What happened to Mr Dong indicates that there is much more that China must do in this new era characterised by the global Chinese worker. ■

An earlier version of this essay was translated from Chinese into English by Nan Liu.

Candlelight rally in Seoul, June 2008. PC: Michael-kay Park @flickr.com.

Online Activism and South Korea's Candlelight Movement

Hyejin KIM

The Candlelight Movement of 2016 and 2017 that successfully called for President Park Geun-hye to step down is among the largest social movements in South Korean history. This movement attracted millions of participants over a sustained period of time, while maintaining strikingly peaceful demonstrations that ultimately achieved their goal. In this essay, Hyejin Kim looks at the role of the Internet and new media in fostering a new generation of activists and laying the foundation for a successful social mobilisation.

South Korea has a storied history of mass agitation for political causes. The Candlelight Movement of 2016–17, which called for President Park Geun-hye to step down, is among the largest—if not the largest—street demonstration in that history. Set against any of several measuring sticks, it was a remarkable success. It attracted millions of participants over a sustained period of time. The events were strikingly peaceful—strangers smashed up against each other and encountered police, but participants prevented violence and there was not a single fatality. And, of course, the National Assembly eventually impeached the President, who was later dismissed, tried in criminal court, and eventually sentenced to a lengthy prison term.

Globally, examples like South Korea's are rare in the present moment. At a time when 'populist' forces appear adept at mobilising discontent, and when political interests are capable of using the Internet to distort public discussion, there may be something to learn from South Korea. In fact, while the Candlelight Movement was a response to revelations that Park had been discharging her duties irresponsibly and allowing a personal associate to share inappropriately in her public power, its success hinged on more than the egregiousness of the wrongdoing.

Cold War Legacies

Demonstrations have long been a regular feature of life in Seoul. Aggrieved groups take quickly to the streets. While demonstrations indicate a liberal environment in which people are free to organise and express themselves, most have not ignited public support in the way the Candlelight Movement did. Divisions among activists have also plagued these events. The largest movements have seen divisions emerge between the unaffiliated individuals who initiated the action via online platforms and established civil society groups.

Consider an episode from 2002, an especially significant year for mass political expression in South Korea, with a presidential election and fervent celebration of the nation around the hosting of the football World Cup. That year, individuals communicating over the Internet organised a candlelight vigil to commemorate two schoolgirls who had been killed in an incident involving American soldiers. As the peaceful movement progressed, some 130 civil society organisations joined in and raised other issues. Many of these groups chanted anti-American slogans, which expressed the frustration of many at Bush-era policies, but also alienated others who had been raised in a context where such views were taboo. Surveys show that individual participation declined when these organisations entered the fray (Kim 2008, 30).

Another set of candlelight vigils took place in 2008, this time in response to perceptions that the government was careless in relaxing restrictions on the import of American beef. These demonstrations also caused tension between online activists and established civil society groups. The movement was initiated by young people who organised themselves online (Kang 2017). The youth organisers had requested participating groups not to display banners at rallies, so that the protests would stay focussed on the particular issues at stake. However, civil society groups ignored these requests, and some even displayed a very militant attitude. In one instance, members carried steel pipes to protect themselves in the event of a police encounter, or perhaps to warn off the police. These civil society groups deliberately adopted the styles of authoritarian-era anti-government activists. Participants who came prepared for confrontation contributed, in combination with the police response, to the outbreak of scuffles.

Images of militant-looking participants and of physical confrontations made it all too easy for the media to depict the 2008 candlelight protesters as disloyal activists. The figure of the violent, treasonous protester was a trope of Cold War politics in South Korea. The victims of military violence at Gwangju in 1980 were depicted in this way. The authoritarian regime had made a habit of hiring young men to initiate violence at opposition rallies, in order to perpetuate the view of critics as unpatriotic troublemakers. In 2008, these themes emerged again. Police confrontations at the demonstrations led to a downturn in the participation of individual citizens (Kim 2008, 24). In the end, despite the fact that these demonstrations were organised by a new generation of online activists employing a completely different approach to their predecessors, conservative media portrayed participants in the 2008 candlelight vigils as communist sympathisers (Shin 2016).

The foundation of the divisions among activists lies in the Cold War legacies that continue to shape South Korea's civil society. While younger activists tend to form new, often issue-specific communities through the Internet, former activists of the 1970s and 1980s remain influential in organised civil society. The latter tend to use dramatic words like 'struggle' (*tujaeng*) to describe their activities and to use songs associated with the anti-dictatorship movement, as if they were still fighting against an authoritarian regime. Furthermore, in the early 2000s, conservatives revived McCarthyist language to discredit progressives, claiming they that are pro-Pyongyang and seek to undermine the Republic of Korea. These depictions and the approach of some civil society groups could be off-putting to many middle-class Koreans who had assimilated anti-communist sentiments through political socialisation, even if they took positions favourable to redistributive policies. These political formations have driven a wedge between online-based activists focussed on particular causes and the realm of organised civil society.

Podcasts and Spoons

In the Candlelight Movement of 2016–17, however, these two groups managed to cooperate. Demands were formulated in a way that did not appear radical, which made the cause appealing to middle-class Koreans. Two new developments behind this achievement deserve attention.

First, critical discussion of politics had moved to online platforms over the previous decade. Under the Lee Myung-bak (2008–13) and Park Geun-hye (2013–17) administrations, South Korea experienced a number of setbacks in terms of political liberties. Many journalists and reporters who tackled issues that were sensitive to these presidents had to leave their positions or were demoted. These journalists and producers chose online outlets as spaces for continuing their work. In places where the government exerts strict controls on the media, the Internet can be an important tool for people to disclose injustice, as research on China has shown (Svensson 2016). In the South Korean context, this turn to online platforms did little to diminish the standing and credibility of these new media organisations. The Internet is where most people in South Korea go to get their news. According to the Reuters Journalism Research Centre at Oxford University, 77 percent of Korean news readers access media content through an Internet portal website, compared to an average in other countries closer to 30 percent (Newman et al. 2017, 126).

As critical journalists left for online media, citizens followed. This led to a radical transformation of the media landscape, with the emergence not only of new outlets but also of new formats. For instance, political podcasts have now become a form of online media that has grown in prominence over the past several years. Online media figures are extremely successful in pulling in listeners. Political programmes gain larger audiences than other traditional formats. The main platform, *Podbbang*, hosts 10,000 audio podcasts alone. Of their top ten podcasts, seven address politics.

Second, online modes of political engagement were not only critical, but also entertaining. The most prominent podcasts are humorous and fun to tune into. Online platforms have produced entertaining ways of talking about politics. One example is a discourse around 'spoon theory' (*sujeoron*), which describes people born with or without privileges, respectively, as 'gold spoon' and 'dirt spoon' (Kim 2017). Collectively, these were the most searched terms of 2015 on South Korean online portals (Choe 2015). Actors and singers whose parents were also celebrities were among the first to be labelled 'gold spoons'—they were criticised for making their way through their

Former South Korean President Park Geun-hye. PC: Wikimedia Commons.

parents' connections rather than through talent or hard work. Netizens then continued to show their creativity and make up distinct grades of privilege, such as 'diamond spoon' or 'platinum spoon'.

The 'spoon' terminology was a way to engage with the serious issue of wealth inequality. Related memes were shared for fun but they were also a means for society to learn about inequality and express concern about the issue. Other jokey discourses operated in a similar way. By presenting serious political themes in an entertaining light, the new modes of communication drew in audiences and gave these discussions a contemporary feel. In podcasts, the approach was to be overtly irreverent but at the same time hosts brought in experts and ensured that the conversation maintained substance. The style of the discussions resonates with a global Internet culture in which nothing is sacred and anything can be lampooned. Unlike previous instances of social mobilisation, spreading jokes about 'spoons' or watching someone laugh and curse the president simply does not fit with the images expected of 'pro-North Korean' forces. This style is far removed from what could be identified by conservatives as a radical—and therefore illegitimate—movement.

Rediscovering the Internet as a Progressive Force

By autumn 2016, when the Park scandal broke, many Koreans were already adept at thinking critically about the President—especially about inherited privilege, which Park, as the daughter of former dictator Park Chung-hee, represented. Ordinary Koreans were prepared to take to the streets against the sort of injustice that the scandal exposed.

These factors helped lay the groundwork for a movement that could overcome the Cold War categories that had undermined previous social mobilisations in South Korea. Now (September 2018), more than a year after a new government was formed, public debates have moved in a progressive direction. The Justice Party, a labour party, has become the second largest party in the National Assembly and has punched above its weight in setting policy discussions. Progressive issues such as the length of the working week, work-life balance, and women's status top both the political agenda and public debate. The ruling party finds itself under pressure from the Justice Party to take a progressive policy line.

There is hope to be found in the South Korean story. Mass political engagement can come in forms other than 'populist' support for anti-immigrant or racist causes. And, the Internet can also be a force for genuine political expression rather than a medium for distortion and manipulation. These points should be welcome in today's global political landscape. ■

Mekong River, 'Life on the Water.' PC: Daniel Hoerd, Flickr.com.

China and Development Aid

The Case of Anti-trafficking and Seafood in Southeast Asia

Sverre MOLLAND

Chinese-funded aid to developing countries does not require either mitigation strategies or environmental and social impact assessments. In this essay, Sverre Molland looks at the Mekong region and assesses the impact of China's increasing influence in the area on the attempts to introduce humanitarian and human rights standards in labour migration.

Back in the early 2000s, I had an informal conversation with a social impact advisor from the Asian Developement Bank (ADB) regarding the impact of Chinese aid in Laos. The advisor told me that she was concerned about the increasing influence of China on the Lao government, as it made ADB's development strategy ineffective. As Chinese-funded infrastructure did not require either mitigation strategies or environmental and social impact assessments, it made it harder for ADB (and others) to insist on such measures. Due do China's increasing prominence, she alleged, ADB risked cancelling itself out of the competitive market of infrastructure development contracts in Laos, thus losing any ability to safeguard basic social, environmental, and human rights standards.

In this essay, I use this anecdote as a point of departure to consider China's impact on another important issue within the Mekong countries: labour migration. The predicament of this ADB advisor highlights the difficulties of imposing development-led social and environmental conditionalities within a context of increasing dominance of Chinese aid. Furthermore, although infrastructure projects constitute state-led development, they take place within a neoliberal aid environment where market mechanisms structure how development actors project human rights-based conditionalities. I suggest that current efforts to introduce humanitarian and human rights standards in labour migration—commonly through discourses of anti-trafficking and modern slavery—signal a shift away from state to market actors in development. Although it may seem to bypass state-centric responses to labour exploitation, this new strategy may face a similar dilemma to the ADB consultant mentioned above due to China's growing role in the region. This, as we will see below, can be seen in the seafood industry.

Development-migration Nexus between China and the Mekong Region

One of the central changes to development aid in the Mekong region has been the ascendance of China as a bilateral aid actor. This is particularly pertinent in countries, such as Laos, where Chinese-led infrastructure, commercial agriculture, mining, and extraterritorial casinos have received considerable scholarly attention (Baird 2011; Diana 2018; Nyíri 2012; Tan 2014). The construction of a Chinese railway connecting mainland China with its Southeast Asian neighbours is one of the latest steps within this larger trend. In a country like Laos, it is a well-known fact among aid practitioners that although Western-based development assistance may have been dominant in the recent past, it is increasingly looking like a sideshow compared to Chinese aid and investment.

Parallel to this shift, given the strong focus of ASEAN and Mekong countries on infrastructure development—especially road construction—and the liberalisation of trade and mobility, labour migration has also become a central pillar in the region's development efforts. For this reason, the aid sector has given increasing attention to the development-migration nexus in the Mekong region. Partly dovetailing with the European Union, ASEAN recently introduced an internal skilled migration mobility programme under the auspices of the ASEAN Economic Community (AEC). Still, the number of skilled migrants who can now travel freely thanks to this initiative is dwarfed by the huge amount of unskilled migrants who form the backbone of key economic sectors, such as agriculture, construction, and seafood processing. Although numbers are imprecise, in Thailand alone the unskilled labour migration population is estimated to be several millions (Auethavornpipat 2017).

To date, labour migration from China to Mekong countries has been limited and primarily concerned with the Chinese labour exodus in the context of Chinese-backed investment. In fact, the main connection between China and the Mekong countries in relation to migration has arguably been through more sinister sides of migration, in particular human trafficking. For example, the United Nations has pointed to the considerable outmigration of young women from Myanmar and Laos to China, where concerns are being raised about possible trafficking and forced marriages (UNIAP 2013). Anti-trafficking has also been a central conduit for China's multilateral cooperation with Mekong governments, such as the Memorandum of Understanding on Cooperation against Trafficking in Persons in the Greater Mekong Sub-region (COMMIT), which has served as the main vehicle for multilateral engagement on anti-trafficking among Mekong countries since its conception in 2004.

Yet to fully grasp the importance of China in relation to migration and development in the Mekong region it is important to grasp how anti-trafficking discourses and practices have changed in recent years.

From State to Market Anti-trafficking Discourses

In the Mekong region, the earliest anti-trafficking interventions by development aid actors emerged during the 1990s, with the first interventions being framed as poverty-reduction strategies. However, in the subsequent decades the sector followed a global trend to include a strong law enforcement focus, coupled with awareness-raising efforts and support for victims (Molland 2012). In other words, anti-trafficking became heavily state-centric as law enforcement and immigration authorities came to play central roles in anti-trafficking responses.

Yet, anti-trafficking has faced sustained criticisms both from academics and practitioners who point out that interventions often are counterproductive, tend to prioritise border control agendas, and—partly as a result of the latter—end up working against the very people they aim to assist (Anderson 2012; Keo et al. 2014). In Mekong countries, these criticisms are paralleled by a notable donor and programme fatigue within the anti-trafficking sector. Other nomenclatures, such as 'modern slavery', have gained momentum. In contrast to anti-trafficking interventions, modern slavery places stronger focus on consumers and the corporate sector's possible complicity in exploitative and 'slave-like' labour, and enjoys considerable financial backing from philanthro-capitalists such as Australia's mining millionaire Andrew Forrest and eBay's founder Pierre Omidyar. Rather than an explicit focus on border control and police, modern slavery broadens activities to focus on 'supply chain governance' and consumer ethics. Governments too, such as Australia, the United Kingdom, and California, have all promulgated legislation that mandates companies to report on their efforts to clean up their supply chains.

While the modern slavery discourse has also been forcefully critiqued (Gallagher 2017), it is notable how it broadens activism from the state to market. Although this discourse has only recently crept into Mekong-based NGOs and UN agencies, it is striking how in that context a previous concern with 'sex trafficking' has been largely replaced with concerns regarding slavery-like work conditions, with particular attention to the Thai seafood sector. It is also here that we see the discourse of supply chain governance opening up a space where it becomes possible to think about consumer boycotts. In Thailand, this has become a political reality, with the European Union threating a boycott of Thai seafood on environmental (overfishing) and humanitarians grounds (abusive labour). In contrast to ongoing political pressure from the United States government through its annual Trafficking in Persons Report—where Thailand has been routinely poorly ranked—a potential seafood boycott has a far larger impact: the former is primarily a question of losing political face; the latter will seriously affect the Thai economy. As such, it is precisely this kind of action that advocates of 'modern slavery' suggest can have a positive impact on the work conditions of poor, unskilled migrant workers in the Mekong region and beyond.

China and Seafood

At first glance, China appears entirely absent from these developments. Although the Chinese authorities engage with the region on human trafficking issues, they do not seem to have picked up on the emerging modern slavery

Fish Market in Suzhou, China. Today China accounts for 30 percent of global fish consumption. PC: chrisUK, Flickr.

agenda in dealing with their neighbours. Nor is China a central consumer of Thai seafood. Yet, this can all easily change, and for a very simple reason.

Today, China accounts for 35 percent of total global fish production and 30 percent of global consumption (World Bank and FAO 2013). Although China has a substantial domestic seafood production, it is already the third largest importer of seafood in the world. Its role as a seafood consumer is set to increase significantly in the next few years, as the country is the fastest growing consumer of seafood globally (World Bank and FAO 2013). Given the regional proximity of Southeast Asia, countries like Thailand may become a growing market to cater to China's seafood consumption.

To date, there is no notable human rights discourse or insistence on human rights-based conditionalities relating to Chinese consumer markets and imports. Yet, there seems to be a surprising lack of reflection amongst United Nations agencies and NGO practitioners regarding how China can influence their strategies. Soon, anti-trafficking and modern slavery abolitionists may find themselves in a similar situation to the ADB consultant mentioned at the beginning of this essay: either pursue a strategy of imposing conditionalities, thus effectively locking yourself out of the very market you attempt to impact, or simply abandon any attempt to impose ethical conditions.

Two Lessons

There are two main lessons to be drawn from all this. First, tragicomically, the end result may be similar to what has been observed in the fair trade movement more broadly: moulding markets into humane emancipatory projects which ensure fair prices is hard to achieve in practice. Yet, one thing such market-based initiatives *do* achieve is to commodify social movements. Hence, despite an official claim of aid actors to be transforming markets into ethical practices, the reverse is actually taking place: markets transform aid actors.

Second, if consumers of seafood are meant to be a central actor in the eradication of 'modern slavery' in Thailand's fishing sector through ethically based conditionalities within the seafood trade, it is difficult to see how this will be effective within the context of China's emerging role as a seafood consumer. Philanthro-capitalist initiatives, such as the modern slavery agenda, may unintentionally open another space within the aid sector where China will be able to dominate just as it already does in other spheres. In the long run, a 'modern slavery' agenda in the Mekong region may end up marginalising its own space of humanitarian consumer activism, and China's growing importance in the region is at the heart of this process. ■

PC: Shutterstock.com.

Illicit Economies of the Internet

Click Farming in Indonesia and Beyond

Johan LINDQUIST

Click farms are often considered either a form of fraudulent online marketing or as a type of exploitative digital labour based on an illegitimate business operation that produces 'click spam'. There has, however, been limited research on how these entities operate, who the actors are, and how the market is organised. In an ethnographic spirit, in this essay Johan Lindquist takes click farmers not as an aberration, but rather as a starting point for approaching the 'like economy'.

Herman lives deep in densely urban Tangerang in the western part of sprawling greater Jakarta. With more than 30 million people, Jakarta is not only one of the largest urban agglomerations in the world, but is also characterised by an increasingly intense use of social media. In 2012, it was named the world's most active Twitter city (Lipman 2012). Today the same is true for Instagram Stories (Instagram 2017), a feature that allows users to post images and videos that disappear from view after 24 hours. Indonesians are among the world leaders in time spent on the mobile Internet—Internet services accessed from handheld devices—with around four hours per day (Google Temasek

2017). For many people in Indonesia today, 'connecting to the Internet' means using social media platforms. As Merlyna Lim (2018, 163) puts it, 'Facebook, in fact, is more popular than the Internet.'

Herman, who is in his early thirties, has lived through these changes. After dropping out of college he spent years teaching himself basic programming and money-making schemes, such as the sale of gaming accounts, in the Internet cafés that were pervasive in Indonesia before the rise of smartphones. With the advent of social media, he began to sell followers, first on Twitter around 2012 and more recently on Instagram, which is increasingly becoming the dominant platform in the country. With a handful of friends and neighbours, he has developed a successful and illicit online business—using second-hand computers, a rotating proxy service, a Singapore-based server, and a software application that he rents from a programmer—in order to engage in the highly competitive and volatile market centred on manipulating 'like' buttons, views, follower counts, and popularity rankings. The main groups of buyers are online shops, influencers, and politicians. People like Herman, with an impressive digital and entrepreneurial competence, but faced with a limited labour market, are at the heart of an economy with low startup costs that connects transnational chains of actors and technologies engaged in the production, distribution, and sale of followers.

Click Farms and Follower Factories

In recent years, it has become increasingly evident that there is a major global market for purchasing followers on social media platforms such as Facebook, Twitter, and Instagram. So-called 'click farms', or 'follower factories' (Confessore 2018)—persons or companies selling likes, views, and followers via unregulated online marketplaces—are at the centre of the controversy surrounding the digital 'like economy' (Gerlitz and Helmond 2013). Previous research by scholars and journalists suggest that the majority of click farms focussing on US social media platforms are based in Asian countries such as Indonesia, the Philippines, Bangladesh, and India, while most click buyers are concentrated in North America and Europe (Clark 2015, Farooqi et al. 2015).

Click farms have been considered either a form of fraudulent online marketing or as a type of exploitative digital labour based on an illegitimate business operation that produces 'click spam' (Casilli 2016; Clark 2015; see also Brunton 2013). Click farms or factories appear to localise and control 'clickwork'. This has furthered the notion that 'click farms are the new sweatshops' (DePillis 2014)—and hence, a major problem of unregulated labour specific to the global South. Both views maintain that click farms operate out of a particular territory—'offshore' entities in geographical, legal, and sociocultural terms—and need to be regulated, either because they harm industries or workers. Click farms thus appear as an ethically dubious other, outside of legal regulation.

There has, however, been very limited research on how these entities operate, who the actors are, and how the market is organised. In an ethnographic spirit, and in collaboration with media scholar Patrick Vonderau, I have attempted to respond to this popular perception of the ethical dubiousness of these entities through a form of 'ethical inversion', in which click farmers such as Herman are taken not as an aberration, but rather as a starting point for approaching the 'like economy'.

Economies of Clicks and Likes

Beginning in Indonesia—a country where I have conducted extensive research—I have met and interviewed several dozen individuals involved in the like economy. Using search terms such as *jual follower* (sell follower) reveal a wide range of sellers who can easily be contacted, for instance through WhatsApp. Among those I have interviewed, there is a large degree of geographical concentration in the Jakarta region, but some are based in larger university cities such as Bandung, Pekanbaru, Yogyakarta, and even one in Amsterdam in Holland. The great majority are young men in their late teens and twenties who are in college or have recently dropped out. The oldest, who have generally been around since Twitter boomed in 2011 (such as Herman), are in their early thirties. Most are from relatively stable lower middle-class backgrounds with parents who are entrepreneurs, office workers, or teachers. They are all self-professed *autodidakt* (self-taught), having learned how to sell followers using YouTube tutorials, Google Translate, and Internet forums. Many started out as teenagers, selling accounts for games such as World of Warcraft.

These individuals are part of an extraordinarily complex market that takes shape across national borders. Herman is at the very centre of it. He runs a website—let's call it jualfollowers.com—in which members register and then are able to log in. He has about 800 registered resellers, of which around 400 are active. He also sells directly to customers, but at a higher price. Once logged in, members can choose products from an extensive menu, which includes different kinds of Instagram followers at varying prices—female, Indonesian, Brazilian, etc. When resellers have made their choice and paid, usually through a top-up system, they can enter their customer's Instagram user ID and the followers are gradually transferred to that account. In the process, resellers make a profit, often of at least 100 percent. Much of this reselling can be done off of cell phones. Many who engage in the market do so temporarily or on the side, particularly on the level of resellers who buy from Herman.

Manufacturing Followers

Herman accesses followers in different ways. So-called *aktif* followers are real Indonesian accounts, which can be accumulated through exchange sites or sites that offer free followers in return for access to user IDs and passwords. Herman has a stock of several thousand *aktif* Indonesian followers, which he can resell. There is a significant risk, however, that the individuals who control these accounts will change their passwords or decide to unfollow the accounts to which they have been sold. So-called *pasif* followers, in contrast, are generated and developed by bots, software applications that run automated scripts, and are thus 'fake'. *Pasif* followers are of varying quality and are priced accordingly. For instance, those that lack photos and posts—and are easily identified as fake and thus at high risk of being shut down by Instagram—are cheaper than those that have a more elaborate identity and content, making them more difficult to identify as fraudulent. Herman purchases these followers from so-called SMM (social media marketing) websites such as JustAnotherPanel.com (JAS), which are located outside of Indonesia, much in the same way that his resellers do with him, thus engaging in a comparable form of arbitrage. Websites such as JAS have a so-called open API (application programming interface). Through a simple procedure that requires no programming skills, Herman can create an interface between his website and JAS that allows for a seamless integration so that followers can be purchased and resold automatically. This seamlessness is temporarily disrupted during Instagram's security updates, as the whole international market temporarily comes to a standstill.

Indonesian sellers such as Herman have limited knowledge of these international websites, but guess that they are also resellers and that the actual production of followers takes place elsewhere—perhaps in India, Russia, or Turkey, which have stronger programming and hacker cultures than Indonesia. A common conspiracy theory is that Instagram itself is the source of the fake follower business and that the most successful players have help on the inside (I have not entirely convinced Herman that I myself am not a spy from Instagram). Many of my informants, who focus strictly on Indonesian buyers, mainly for lack of English-language skills, fantasise about scaling up and becoming part of an international market, with the promise of increased profits.

The Manual Labour of the Click Economy

Among significant sellers such as Herman—who has a fluctuating turnover of around 15,000 USD per month—there is an attempt to create forms of automation. As noted, this does not require significant programming skills, except when there are security updates. For this reason, sellers like Herman who do not have these skills need to collaborate with programmers who deal with these necessary updates, or rent their software applications. There are, however, also critical forms of manual labour. Herman has a team of eight people who work in shifts around the clock. One group engages in customer service with resellers and other buyers, primarily through WhatsApp, responding to pricing queries or dealing with problems concerning the transfer of followers. If more than 50 percent of the followers Herman has sold disappear within 30 days, he offers a free refill. A second group engages in marketing through the production of price lists and related information that is widely distributed on social media, for instance through a large number of Instagram accounts. In particular, they experiment with different ways of having top posts for hashtags such as #jualfollower. Like many of the larger actors on the Indonesian market, Herman mainly uses friends, neighbours, or family members as staff, who work on the top floor of his house. He pays them a salary and frequently offers bonuses in order to improve their work performance, which pushes their salaries over the legislated minimum wage in the Jakarta region of around 250 USD per month. Most of the staff are also resellers and it is not unusual for them to move on and start their own businesses.

Engaging with current discussions about click farms and digital sweatshops through people like Herman allows for a degree of reconceptualisation. First, the labour that underpins click farming is not so much centred on 'clicking' as it is on developing new forms of automation that decrease the reliance on manual labour. Manual labour becomes necessary primarily with regard to customer service, marketing, and occasionally data-entry when automation breaks down. Although Herman keeps the bulk of the profits, he pays his workers relatively well. Rather than considering this as a strict form of exploitation—as a 'sweatshop'—it may be more productive to understand these as evolving, but unstable forms of patron–client relationships that depend on certain forms of trust and intimacy. Second, there is a rhizomatic form to the market, with unstable chains of sellers and producers. Evidence suggests that followers are not produced in one site, but take shape in a process of assembly. Once the follower becomes a commodity in itself, it can be sold and resold along multiple levels of sellers and resellers. As such, the fake follower market is strikingly similar to other forms of transnational markets, which characterise contemporary supply-chain capitalism. ■

Artwork by Krish Raghav (krishcat.com/).

Chinese Digital Ecosystems Go Abroad

Myanmar and the Diffusion of Chinese Smartphones

Elisa OREGLIA

Myanmar's recent economic opening has prompted a dramatic upsurge in access to mobile phone and Internet technologies. Lower-cost smartphones finding their way across the border from China often have limited Burmese language support and come with WeChat and other Chinese apps preinstalled. This situation is resulting in a localised form of China's digital ecosystem with Burmese characteristics.

Shan state, in northeastern Myanmar, is an important artery of commerce, connecting the country with its most important trading partner, China. Natural resources, agricultural products, and manufactured goods are carried across the border through formal channels and through the informal economy in a variety of ways. Recently, there has been a new addition to this already complex kaleidoscope: WeChat. The Chinese instant messaging/social media app that has become the staple of smartphone use in China—with over a billion monthly active users in 2018 (Statista 2018)—is finding new, enthusiastic adopters among Shan state traders, who have figured out creative ways of adjusting functions aimed at the Chinese market for their own purposes. Take WePay for example—one of the most popular features on WeChat, this built-in payment feature that makes purchasing and transferring money in China so convenient is not available in kyat, the Myanmar currency. And yet there are Burmese traders, shopkeepers, and buyers who regularly use it to conduct business both within Myanmar and across the border with China, ending up with Chinese renminbi stored in their WeChat account that theoretically cannot be cashed out and converted into kyat. They have devised clever workarounds to do so: they can cash the renminbi out through informal agents that are based in Myanmar but have business (or family) contacts in China, for a small fee; or they can buy the equivalent value in products in China that they will then import back to Myanmar. The money never materialises: it becomes a creative encounter of digital payments, barter exchanges, and cross-border trade.

Breaking the Isolation

These are very recent developments in Myanmar, a country that has been going through decades of turmoil and international isolation. Until 2014 or 2015, retail commerce was a slow and cumbersome affair. Many small town and rural business people did not have a phone—be it a landline or a mobile—and had to rely on visits from travelling agents, or go themselves to wholesale markets, typically by bus on dangerous roads or by train on slow railway lines. Myanmar had been rather secluded from the outside world during the years of the military dictatorship (1964–2011), which had not only censored media and communications, but also neglected basic infrastructure, making it exceedingly difficult and expensive for people to get and use landlines, computers, and mobile phones, among other things. Telecommunications were a state monopoly, run by Myanmar Posts and Telecommunications. In 2010, there were only 594,000 mobile phone subscribers in the country, equal to 1.14 subscriptions per 100 inhabitants, and 493,314 landline subscribers, or 0.98 per 100 inhabitants (ITU 2017a and 2017b). The cost of SIM cards was out of reach for most people, hovering around 2,000 USD in the late 2000s, and still in the hundreds of dollars in the early 2010s. Private landlines were exceedingly rare, especially outside major cities, so people used public phones, which were also expensive and unreliable. Communication for either personal or business purposes was not easy.

The situation started to change in 2011, with the economic liberalisation programme carried out by the new government. Censorship of media was dropped and the telecommunication market was opened to foreign operators—with Norwegian company Telenor and Qatari company Ooredoo winning the licence to build and operate new mobile networks. Both companies started service in August 2014, with results that went well beyond the most optimistic expectations. The price of SIM cards dropped almost overnight to 1.5 USD, and people started to acquire both SIM cards and mobile phones at a swift pace. The number of mobile subscription went from 6,832,380 in 2013 (12.83 per 100 inhabitants) to 29,029,342 (54.05 per 100 inhabitants) in 2014 (ITU, 2017b), and reached an impressive 89.8 mobile subscriptions per 100 inhabitants in 2017 (ITU 2018), while fixed telephone subscriptions still languished at about 514,385 (ITU 2017a). The country has gone mobile, not only in terms of phones, but also in terms of Internet access, with 75.1 mobile broadband subscriptions per 100 inhabitants in 2017 (ITU 2018).

As a consequence, the number of mobile phone shops has grown as exponentially as the number of users of mobile phones. But while cities and bigger towns feature shops that would not be out of place in any urban area in wealthier countries, more rural and isolated places have to make do with small shops that offer a very limited choice. An urban shop will provide the whole gamut of phones, from the latest Samsung and Apple smartphones, costing around 1,000 USD, to entry-level feature phones at 15 USD and everything in between. These phones are all imported legally, sold with full warranty, and might offer native support for Burmese language—or at least come with a Burmese font keyboard installed—not a given in a country that has long been plagued by the existence of two incompatible ways of inputting and rendering Burmese: Zawgyi and Unicode. A rural shop, on the other hand, will sell mostly Chinese brands that occupy the mid- and low-end of the market. The prices for smartphones range from 35 USD at the lowest end, to 180 USD at the upper end. Some are budget models of well-known brands such as Huawei, its subsidiary Honor, and Oppo. Others are 'local' brands, whose phones are made in China, and whose commercial distribution, marketing, and sales are managed by Chinese entrepreneurs—for example a brand called Kenbo, which (potentially by design) shares its name with a very popular brand of motorcycles. Others still are Chinese brands like Coolpad, Gionee, Vivo, Meizu, and Zopo, typically unknown in the West, but that have been gaining significant market shares in emerging economies. While these phones are cheap, and can provide smartphone capabilities and Internet access to people who would otherwise be excluded, there are trade-offs in terms of durability and usability.

A New Internet Underclass?

The overall experience of mobile phone users who buy the cheaper kind of smartphones begins not only with a much smaller choice in terms of brands and features, but also with salespeople who might not know exactly what they are selling—some general goods stores simply add a few phones to their inventory, and do not provide any kind of support nor advice—and with phones that might have been imported through informal channels. This was—and still is—particularly true in Shan state, where porous borders mean that there continues to be a significant amount of goods being smuggled in from China, including mobile phones, in order to avoid import duty (Wai 2014).

These phones are usually purchased in Chinese shops, and are not meant for the export market; while their operating system is the now ubiquitous Android, it is often the Android adapted to the Chinese market—that is, without the default suite of Google apps that come preinstalled, which are instead substituted by Chinese apps. These phones are adapted to the Myanmar market before being sold, but they maintain traces of the Chinese Internet ecosystem: the operating system is a mix of English and Chinese, rather than Burmese, even after the default language is switched to English (at the time of my research, there was no operating system in Burmese at all). This creates a set of challenges even for people who are literate—but in their own native language rather than in English or Chinese. They range from difficulties in navigating the phone interface and understanding 'housekeeping' messages, such as notices of available updates, warnings regarding memory or performance, etc., to serious obstacles in using text-based interfaces, such as SMS or search. The journey to mobile Internet use, thus, often starts in an environment that is unfamiliar, as most people did not have any experience with digital devices before getting their smartphone, and in a language (or two) not well known, or completely unknown. Even as these challenges are negotiated and work-arounds are developed, there are still barriers related to access, since connectivity is still patchy outside urban areas, the network can be very slow at peak usage times, and data cost can be significant, especially for people with limited budgets.

While affordable smartphones and the fast build-up of infrastructure have allowed millions of people to go online, mobile-only Internet access is not the panacea that it was expected to be in the early days of the debate on the so-called digital divide. More people have access to the Internet, but their Internet looks quite different from the one that users in wealthy, urban areas across the world take for granted. The 'Emerging Mobile Internet Underclass,' as Napoli and Obar (2014) called it, is using an Internet with lower levels of functionality, less content, more closed platforms, and more difficulties in creating content and looking for information than people using computers. While not all these issues were equally relevant in Myanmar, the point remains that smartphone use, and Internet use through smartphones, present serious challenges to new users, and the combination of default settings and intermediaries make a significant difference in how people are able to leverage their devices. What is preinstalled on the phone is key, as many people that face the budget and technical challenges I mentioned above will not install new apps, or if they do they will do so through intermediaries, e.g. the many shops that offer 'download and maintenance' support, for a fee.

A WeChat for All Seasons

Smartphones coming from China often have WeChat preinstalled, and Shan state already has a significant WeChat user base due to the commercial ties with China, meaning that the app is quite widespread for both business and personal use. Its features are also a particularly good match for mobile Internet users with low levels of literacy and on bad networks: much can be done by using a combination of photos, voice messages, videos, emoticons, and even the built-in Chinese to English translation capability. A market vendor I interviewed said that she took photos of the goods she needed to reorder, and sent them to her existing suppliers, who then shipped the packages via bus. The added bonus for her was that she could compose her 'order' regardless of the state of the network, which at the time was so overloaded as to be often unusable during the day, knowing everything would be sent later on, typically at night. She received a call from the bus station when her goods arrived, and went to collect them without having to wait for the agent to come and visit, or having to travel to the suppliers herself. In her case, the payment was done through the bus operator, that worked as a sort of payment clearing house for local businesses (Oreglia and Srinivasan 2016). Other bigger traders were doing international business using the same tactics. Relationships were established with suppliers (or buyers, in the case of agricultural products and natural resources) in person, which served to create the initial trust, but subsequently carried out via WeChat, including WePay payments.

Thus, WeChat, the quintessential symbol of the Chinese Internet, is being adopted and adapted in other countries. In general, the connection with China remains, as most of the use that I have witnessed has included some kind of trade link with the country. What is remarkable, however, is that this is happening outside the localisation strategy of Tencent—which launched WeChat in Burmese in 2015—and is mostly parallel to, rather than fully integrated with, the formal economy. The WeChat usage I have observed is either in Chinese or in English, but for the users it did not matter much: they rarely explored options outside the main instant messaging area, and their way of using the app bypassed written language almost entirely. The goods bought and sold on the app were sometimes bought legally, but often illicitly smuggled in or out of Myanmar, and currencies travelled equally fluidly across borders. As both the app and Chinese smartphones find a large user base in the Global South, it will be interesting to see whether the Chinese Internet becomes a sort of 'second Internet', as former Google CEO Eric Schmidt put it (Kolodny 2018), quite independent from the one led by the United States, or whether a new hybrid will emerge, that will mix Chinese and US technology with local business and social practices. ■

Coal Steam, Baganuur, Mongolia. Photo by the author.

Ulaanbaatar, City of the Future

Christian SORACE

Ulaanbaatar has come to be associated with dystopian levels of air pollution, especially in the wintertime, when the temperature drops to minus 40 degrees. In almost every account, the culprit for the devastating pollution of the capital city of Mongolia is the ger districts, areas not connected to municipal infrastructure, where people mainly rely on burning low-grade coal to keep warm. As Ulaanbaatar's future is shrouded in smoke, many older residents wistfully recall a different city from the past. And yet, to this day there is no discursive space to ask: were Ulaanbaatar and Mongolia better off under socialism?

Ulaanbaatar means 'red hero' in Mongolian, but the grandiose roots of this name today are lost, as the city has come to be associated with dystopian levels of air pollution—especially in the wintertime, when the temperature drops to minus 40 degrees (Celsius and Fahrenheit converge when it is this cold). In almost every account, the culprit for Ulaanbaatar's devastating pollution is the *ger* districts—areas not connected to municipal infrastructure, where people mainly rely on burning low-grade coal to keep warm during the harsh winter. With the surrounding mountains and river trapping the smoke coming from the fires of its poorest inhabitants, a city once considered a 'showcase of socialist progress' is now depicted as in 'crisis' with no foreseeable solution. This state of affairs has been epitomised in the popular social media hashtag #Prayforulaanbaatar.

The dominant register when discussing Ulaanbaatar is crisis. At a press conference on 11 January 2017, Mongolia's then president, T.S. Elbegdorj sounded a controversial warning: 'The pollution has reached a level where it has caused stillbirths. If this is not disastrous then what is? It has become dangerous to live in Ulaanbaatar. Ulaanbaatar has become a futile city with no future' (Boldsukh 2017). Many local residents echo this sentiment of uncertainty, a sentiment exacerbated by increasing distrust in the promises of politicians, which in turn is starting to erode faith in Mongolia's democratic institutions. Protesting the air pollution, Mongolians have marched on Suhkbaatar Square in the heart of Ulaanbaatar chanting the slogan 'we are suffocating' (*booj ukhlee*), which as Chisato Fukuda points out also means 'we are extremely frustrated' (Fukuda 2017). When I was in Ulaanbaatar in January 2017, protesters placed facemasks on several of the city's statues, including those of the socialist leader Tsedenbal (1954–84) and Mongolia's hallowed democracy activist Sanjaasurengiin Zorig, who was stabbed to death in 1998. Perhaps only the statue of Lenin, which was moved in 2012 from downtown Ulaanbaatar to the courtyard of a four-star hotel in Terelj National Park, can still breath fresh air.

S. Zorig also known as the 'Golden Swallow of Democracy'—Statue with Facemask. Photo by the author.

As Ulaanbaatar's future is shrouded in smoke, many older residents wistfully recall a different city. In the words of a friend who grew up there during the final decade of socialism: 'My Ulaanbaatar where I grew up and played no longer exists.' She is not alone in this sense of loss. Several Facebook pages are devoted to posting old photographs of socialist-era Ulaanbaatar with its clean streets, modern buildings, parks, and open spaces. The problem with such urban aesthetic reverie is that it is disconnected from the political and economic conditions of urbanisation. Socialist Ulaanbaatar was constructed out of an ideological vision grounded in different conceptions about public space and community. But people's nostalgia for Ulaanbaatar as a space seldom translates into openly expressed longing for socialism.

There is no discursive space to ask: were Ulaanbaatar and Mongolia better off under socialism? Foreign media depicts Ulaanbaatar's air pollution as a catastrophe disconnected from political and historical context, while domestic discourse focuses on finding practical and technological solutions to the air pollution crisis. The collapse of socialist political infrastructure resulted in the dissolution of herding collectives, migration flows from the grasslands to the capital, and privatisation of land driving the expansion of *ger* districts. However, the context of democratisation and land privatisation are ignored in favour of a narrative that isolates and blames the *ger* districts as the cause of Ulaanbaatar's lack of

(1) Local residents gathering coal, Nalaikh January 2017. (2) Marmot memorial statue, Nalaikh. (3) Coal scavenging, local residents. (4) Coal distribution on the side of the road. All photos by the author.

a future. From this perspective, the possibility that positive aspects of socialism were lost in the transition to democracy cannot be considered.

Mongolia's status as an 'oasis of democracy' is guarded against critical scrutiny in a way that forecloses the imagination of new political possibilities. The discourse of democracy poses an obstacle to a future whose contours may not be visible, but whose necessity can be felt in the unbearable contradictions of the present. Is it possible to act on the recognition that there may not be much that is democratic about democratic institutions under capitalism? As Slavoj Žižek (2009) has argued, free elections may counterintuitively render a government 'more impervious to criticism by [social] movements' in that leaders can respond to protestors: 'Who are you to criticise us? We are an elected government, we can do what we want!' This is not to argue for the abolition of elections but for the democratisation of political and economic life.

The temporalities of utopia and dystopia converge in the satellite city of Nalaikh, about 35 kilometres outside of Ulaanbaatar. The Nalaikh state mine opened in 1922 and ran for almost the entirety of the socialist era until 1990, when it closed down because of a fatal methane gas explosion and the disappearance of Soviet subsidies. When I visited Nalaikh in January 2017, local residents were scavenging coal from slag heaps on the outskirts of the city (see Figure 3), their survival depending on the use and sale of the remaining coal deposits. The coal from Nalaikh ends up in Ulaanbaatar's ger districts, where its combustion provides winter heat at the cost of the future.

In the midst of Nalaikh's abandoned socialist past and precarious present is a small monument commemorating the disappearance of a local species of marmot (see Figure 2). They stand alert in anticipation of their extinction. By contrast, the bodies on the slag heaps appear entirely consumed in the strenuous labour of survival. Both images pose questions. Is there a future beyond immediate survival? For what purpose is labour expended? They are uncomfortable questions because we lack convincing answers to them. But just because our political vocabularies are damaged and less able to inspire confidence does not mean that Ulaanbaatar's future should be abandoned to the impasse of the present. ■

WORK OF ARTS

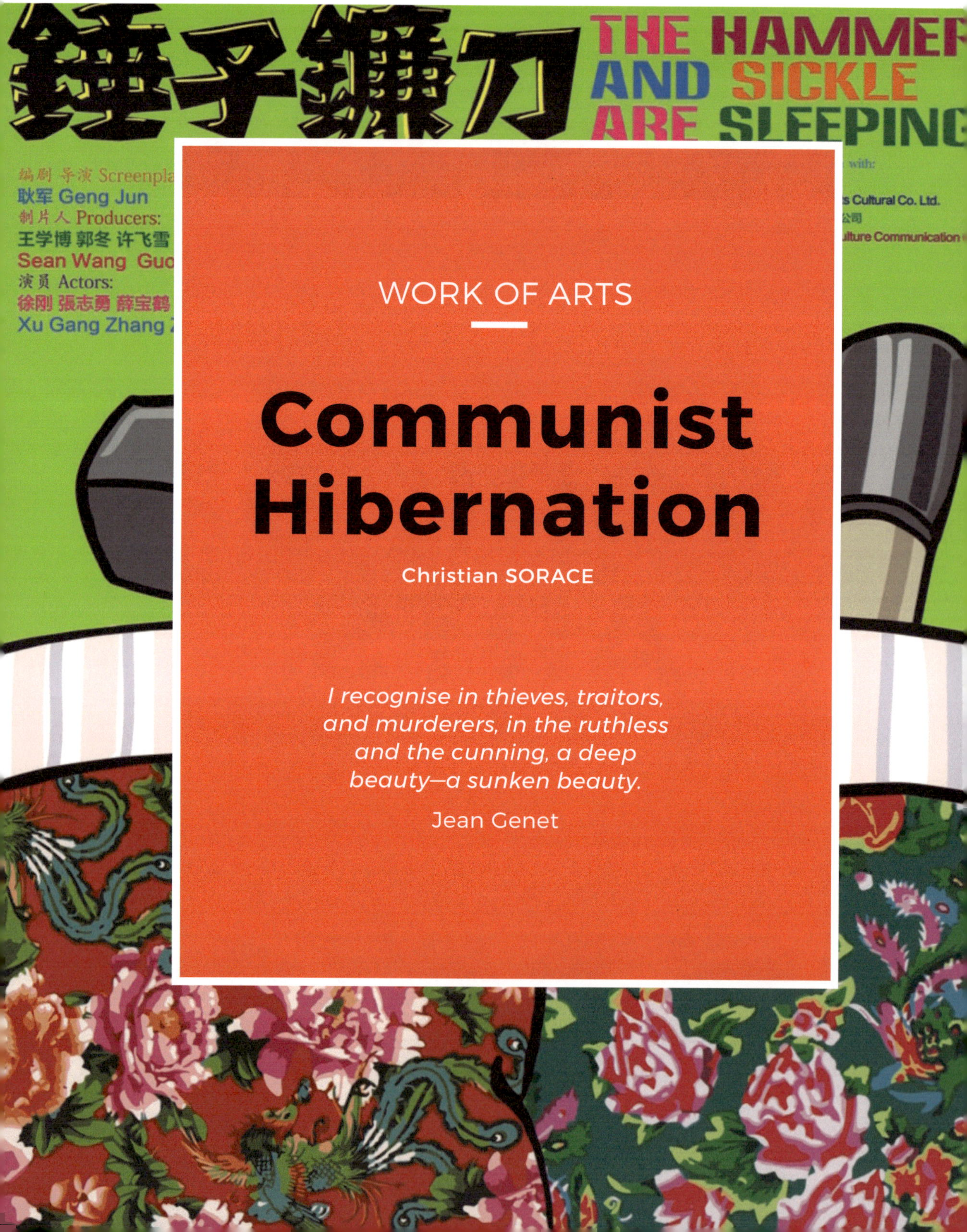

WORK OF ARTS

Communist Hibernation

Christian SORACE

I recognise in thieves, traitors, and murderers, in the ruthless and the cunning, a deep beauty—a sunken beauty.

Jean Genet

Still from *The Hammer and Sickle Are Sleeping* (2013).

Geng Jun's films are set in northeastern China where he grew up. As Geng Jun put it in an interview I conducted with him at a friend's studio in Songzhuang in August 2018:

> When people watch my films, maybe they will see different actors and actresses and characters, but the main character in my films is the setting (*changjing*). I write my stories for the setting, which is the foundation of my expression.

The landscape of China's Northeast—also known as its rustbelt region—is inseparable from its political economy. During the Mao era, the Northeast was the heartland of heavy industry (in particular, steel and machinery), natural resource extraction (oil and coal), and collective agriculture (corn, sorghum, and wheat). Its workers and farmers stood proudly at China's symbolic vanguard. However, these same political economic factors that made it attractive under the socialist planned economy rendered it vulnerable to privatisation and liberalisation during the reform era. For state-owned enterprises (SOEs) located in the Northeast, layoffs began as early as the 1980s, but dramatically intensified after the Fifteenth Party Congress in 1997 during which 'it was decided that SOEs were to evolve into profitable firms and that a chief means to achieve this goal would be the laying off of workers to cut costs' (Hurst 2009, 49). It is estimated that between 1997 and 2004 over 35 million workers were laid off throughout China (Hurst 2009, 35). This wave of layoffs had catastrophic effects on labour relations and the lives of workers in the Northeast. As Ching Kwan Lee wrote at the time: 'Many aggrieved workers find themselves going back and forth between passivity, depression, and even self-destruction, on the one hand, and outbursts of rage, desperation, and heroic acts of collective defiance, on the other' (2007, 69–70).

In the early years of reform, natural resource extraction was profitable but at the steep cost of environmental destruction, which undermined its economic sustainability. Geng Jun recalls the early 1980s as a 'golden age of state planning' in which everyone wanted to go into mining because of the relatively high salaries and perks, such as 'salted duck eggs, cured meat, and bread'. But by the 1990s, 'some mines and oil fields became increasingly desperate as they began to exhaust their deposits of mineral resources, even as prices and markets for the commodities they produced were booming' (Hurst 2009, 44–45). In our conversation, Geng Jun describes the privatisation of natural resources as a process of theft and redistribution of wealth into the hands of people with political connections. In his words: 'After people destroyed the resources of the Northeast, and made their money, they left the area and took the money with them, most likely buying real estate in places like Beijing and Hainan.' Then he quickly adds that this is a familiar story and pattern throughout China.

In terms of agricultural production, the Northeast was once regarded as the 'bread basket' of the People's Republic because of bountiful harvests of staple crops produced at economies of scale (it was for this reason that it was also coveted by the defeated Japanese imperialists). The region also boasted among the earliest and most successful models of collectivisation in the late 1950s. Even in the 1980s, the Northeast was one of the only regions in China in which there was *resistance* to decollectivisation. As the 'urban form' began to envelope agricultural land (Sorace and Hurst 2016), the region's farmers also slowly lost their lands and livelihoods. The empty field is also a metaphorical condition of life—in Geng Jun's film *Free and Easy* (*Qingsong yukuai*, 2017), the characters frequently refer to their lives as *huangfei*, meaning fields that are no longer cultivated.

Geng Jun's movies take place in Heilongjiang province after two decades of continuous layoffs, disinvestment, and disrepair. With long panoramic and tracking shots of dilapidated buildings and abandoned fields, Geng Jun's camera reveals a landscape in which time has stopped—frozen between the *no longer* and the *not yet*. In his discussion of Béla Tarr's films—another director from a socialist background—Jacques Rancière describes a similar phenomenon of 'the loss of revolutionary temporality and its future-orientation in which the present is a duration of abeyance and anticipation of the life-to-come' (2013). Recent attempts to revitalise the Northeast do not include—and perhaps do not even recognise—these people who Geng Jun describes as 'being abandoned by the age' (*bei shidai shuai diao*) and left with 'nothing to do' (*wushi kezuo*).

But Geng Jun does not offer sociological portraits of China's downtrodden. Instead, he films dark comedies that resemble what a Samuel Beckett play would be if it were staged in China's Northeast. Almost all of Geng Jun's characters are con artists and criminals with the twist that they are hilariously inept at crime. The cast of characters from his two recent films *The Hammer and Sickle Are Sleeping* (*Chuizi liandao dou xiuxi*, 2013) and *Free and Easy* include: a travelling soap salesman whose soap incapacitates anyone who smells it; a holy fool with a speech impediment and stuffy nose; a fake monk beggar; a pair of delinquent cops; a cripple; a man dressed as an elderly woman who sings revolutionary songs for money; a hapless forestry official; and laid-off workers who occasionally wander into the scene as targets of the various ongoing hustles. They are anything but the stereotype of cold-blooded criminals; in fact, there is something lovable about their mannerisms, and the sheer futility of their schemes. Besides, as Geng Jun put it, they have nothing else to do.

Falling Asleep

The title of Geng Jun's recent short film *The Hammer and Sickle Are Sleeping* conjures an image of a future that has gone away and is not coming back—at least not in any recognisable way. The once exalted emblems of proletarian unity—the hammer and sickle—are no longer put to work in constructing the future, but have become mute objects strewn amid empty factories and barren fields. Geng Jun explains his thinking behind the title in these terms: 'After farmers lose their land and workers lose their jobs, their tools become idle (*gongju jiu xianzhi le*). The hammer and sickle are sleeping. But at the same time, they can become weapons of self-protection (*fangshen wuqi*) or murder weapons (*xiongqi*).' Tools are no longer used for harvesting grain and forging metal, but are brandished as instruments of survival. A new twist to the Marxist stages of historical

A travelling salesman asks strangers to smell the soap that he is selling—one deep breath and they fall unconscious. Still from *Free and Easy* (2017).

development: after farmer and worker comes the con artist and criminal. The title of the film, however, also refers to a sabbatical from violence. As Lunar New Year approaches, one of the main characters decides to take a holiday from crime, and writes in his diary on the wall of his apartment, 'the hammer and sickle are sleeping'. It is perhaps in the decision *not to act* that promises a utopia of pure potentiality.

But we are also disarmed and vulnerable when we are asleep. In *Free and Easy*, a travelling salesman asks strangers to smell the soap that he is selling—one deep breath and they fall unconscious.

The soap does not merely incapacitate but also induces pleasurable reveries. When the police show up to question three victims, one of the workers (played by Geng Jun himself) describes feeling '... like I was having a dream. It was hot, and I was thirsty. All the women on the street were wearing beautiful dresses. I was somewhere warm.' Impatient to solve the case, the police officer cuts short the worker's narration of his dream. Later in the film, the same officer tries a bar of confiscated soap on himself and passes out. When his partner asks: 'What was it like?', the half-conscious, beatific police officer responds: 'Free and easy.'

The magical soap is more than a mere plot device; it is also an ambiguous commentary on social life. From a tradition of critical theory, it is possible to interpret the soap as people's willingness to be duped and distracted from their own exploitation—the trope of going through life asleep. After all, *the people are being robbed*. But it also possible to understand the soap as providing a momentary respite from a world with nothing to offer.

Fragile Solidarity

In a land of cutthroat capitalist competition and survival, Geng Jun's characters are surprisingly tender and empathetic to the needs of others, even the people that they are robbing.

A moment of tenderness between thieves. Still from *Free and Easy* (2017).

When the thief in *The Hammer and Sickle Are Sleeping* holds up a man on his way home carrying fireworks, oranges, and a toy gun as a Lunar New Year gift for his son, he asks the worker about his present economic state. The man responds that his boss at the mine has not paid him for months. The robber hands back the toy gun to the man to give to his son, but keeps the oranges and fireworks. Later in the film, the robber breaks into a house and as he is leaving discovers a crippled man feigning to be asleep under the blankets (who also happens to be another swindler). As he is about to depart with the stolen money, the crippled man's nephew, who is a devout Christian, comes home and invites the robber to stay for dinner. When the nephew sings a hymn to God during dinner, *the robber attempts to return the money to the person he stole it from, who refuses the offer*. In this gesture of double-refusal, a friendship and future partnership is born. The same robber later encounters (unbeknown to him) the partner in crime of the crippled man who is standing on the side of the road dressed as an elderly woman. She tells him a predictable sob story: 'I am from out of town, I came to find my relatives, but they're gone. I've been here for days now, and I don't have any money left. Can you just give me a little cash to get home?' All he can offer her are two of the oranges he stole from the worker earlier in the film. As he walks home, she performs for him by singing 'Little Bamboo Raft' (*xiaoxiao zhupai jiang zhongyou*)—a song written in 1974 during the Cultural Revolution:

> The red star shining
> Guiding me into battle
> The Revolution rising like a wave
> We will always follow the Party
> Breaking down the old world
> The new world stretches before us.

The red star is dim and no longer illuminates a path forward. The optimism for the future in the song lyrics is conspicuously out of place in the desolate landscapes of Geng Jun's movies. It also produces a rather comical effect. According to Geng Jun, this scene in particular has attracted the disapproval of the authorities:

> They thought that it wasn't appropriate for someone to beg for money by singing a revolutionary song. When I screen the movie, sometimes representatives from the local Chinese People's Political Consultative Conference (CPPCC) or Party members come and express their dissatisfaction.

On the surface, there is a comic juxtaposition of a beggar singing a revolutionary song—but at a deeper level, it raises the question: who are the heirs of the revolution? As the Communist Party stays in power through the twin mechanisms of stability maintenance and capitalist exploitation, perhaps the genuine spirit of communism is incarnated in the homosocial tenderness among thieves and liars who have 'nothing to do' and no one to rely on but each other.

Complicit Criminals

For Geng Jun, referring to his characters as 'criminals' is misleading because everyone is a criminal in Chinese society:

> All of us are criminals and participants [in the system]. It is because we are too weak and did not stand in the way that our situation has become like this. My stories are only a surface layer, but in my heart, an even deeper layer is that I am also, in fact, a criminal.

In this quote, the definition of criminal is expanded from its traditional usage in the court/penal system to indict all of society. Like his characters, Chinese people are victims of their own criminal complicity in the system which oppresses them. The ability to get by depends on a willingness to give in. Each decision not to act is a counterfactual history of the absence of freedom:

> Why is everything messed up? Why is there collusion among officials and business people? Why do we suffer hardship? It is because we never resisted or fought. Instead, we believe that we are weak. I have never thought that I film society's lowest rung and weak groups. On the contrary, I think that I film the great majority of people … . I don't know what people mean by the term 'disadvantaged social groups' (*ruoshi qunti*) [author's note: *ruoshi qunti* is a sociological term in China referring to the economically and politically dispossessed].

It is a radical statement to say that there are no disadvantaged groups in China because everyone is complicit in the maintenance of the system. You are always someone's criminal and another person's victim. But Geng Jun's comment also draws on a familiar legacy that locates sovereign power in the hands of the people. This idea is conveyed in Mencius' famous statement: 'The time is not as important as the terrain and the terrain is not as important as having unity with the people … an unjust cause finds little support' and well-known Chinese phrases, such as 'water can carry the boat or overturn it' (*shui neng zai zhou, yi neng fu zhou*). In Mao's account, as soon as the state separates from the masses, it becomes a 'paper tiger' (*zhilaohu*) that has become disconnected from the source of its power. Power is always ultimately in the hands of the people, even if they are unable to recognise it, let alone act on it.

Geng Jun finishes the interview on a pessimistic note: 'Individuals can accomplish very little on their own; communities can accomplish a lot more. But when individuals are powerless and communities are also powerless, all that remains is desperation.' But this may not be as bleak a prognosis as it seems. It is important to remember that *desperation* in Geng Jun's films *does not take itself seriously*. His characters seem to have adapted to their absurd circumstances, and are seldom discouraged by their constant failures. The insouciance of the criminal is also an emancipation from the solemn rituals of the state. Perhaps they have stumbled upon a powerful antidote to a Party-state that is incapable of laughter, and regards itself with a *deadly seriousness*. ■

Still from Zhao Liang's documentary *Crime and Punishment*, (DGenerate Films, 2007).

Crime and Punishment on a Chinese Border

Suzanne SCOGGINS

Zhao Liang's 2007 documentary Crime and Punishment *details the emergence of a local police state in a small Chinese town on the border with North Korea. The film follows national border officers who have been called in to take over the town's policing duties, and the ways in which they interact with local people. As the film unfolds, one incident after another, viewers are drawn into a world of policing which is slow, tiresome, petty, and punctuated with violence.*

Zhao Liang's documentary *Crime and Punishment* (*Zui yu fa*) provides a rare, candid window into the tedium of law enforcement in China. Filmed in a poor district of Dandong, a city along the Yalu River on China's border with North Korea, it follows a group of border officers charged with taking over law enforcement duties at the local police station. As the camera lingers long past the point of comfort on details such as the military-style folding of bed sheets or a scrap collector's pained face, the viewer is drawn into a world of policing where law enforcement is slow, tiresome, petty, and punctuated with violence.

Crime and Punishment, (DGenerate Films, 2007).

Power and Powerlessness

In the film, the border police are initially praised for their service at a station in the impoverished Zhen'an district of Dandong, having set up regular patrols and assumed a variety of duties that typically fall on the shoulders of the local people's police. These officers are attached to the army, not the Ministry of Public Security, and their presence in a largely rural area such as this is relatively rare. Unfortunately, the film does not capture the more serious security concerns that we can only guess led to this arrangement. We are instead treated to a parade of petty criminal cases that showcase the desperation and powerlessness of the residents who come into contact with the border police.

From berating a mentally ill man for making a false call about a dead body that was actually a pile of blankets, to the busting up of a mahjong game, the motley crew of officers lumbers from one small case to the next. Viewers will likely feel sympathy for the plight of the three men who get caught trying to make money off illegally harvested trees in advance of the Chinese New Year or the deaf man detained for pickpocketing a cell phone. In both cases, the police exercise casual violence on camera—smacking the suspects around in order to elicit information and a much-prized confession. In China, a case is not solved until the perpetrator has confessed—a fact acknowledged by one of the officers on camera after his colleague hauls away a suspect to an undisclosed area where a confession will presumably be coerced. In rare cases, however, the need for a signed confession can work in a suspect's favour. The deaf cellphone thief is ultimately released for lack of evidence because the officers are unable to take his statement.

Violence and Petty Harassment

Zhao weaves the theme of violence through many of the film's interactions, and rightly so, given the coercive duties that frontline agents like these are charged with performing on behalf of the state. Unsurprisingly, the more violent acts of interrogation are committed off camera. Since stations have long been required to film interrogations, removing suspects from the interrogation room, away from the cameras, in order to grease the wheels is a widespread practice, and in interviews, officers have acknowledged that they know just where to go and just where to hit in order to avoid proof that they used excessive force (Scoggins 2018). Naturally, most if not all officers are in on this game, and in one 'good cop, bad cop' scene we see the good cop grin to the camera as he tells the bad cop—who is taking the suspect away—to go easy on him.

Two cops beating a suspect's bruised face. Still from Zhao Liang's documentary *Crime and Punishment*. (DGenerate Films, 2007).

The oddly swollen faces and general lethargy of the suspects shown on camera immediately following such incidents are the physical signs of officer brutality. Yet we also see evidence that the power of the border police is not wholly unchecked. When one lumber thief is hauled back to his house to show where he illegally felled the trees, his wife sees his puffy face and begins shouting at the border officers. She follows them down the road, telling them they can enforce the law and levy fines but cannot go around beating people, especially right before the New Year. Shortly thereafter, we learn that the men were able to keep the lumber and pay a significantly reduced fine because the supervisors of the border officers feared repercussions.

Pettiness is also a theme that runs through the film. In no place is this more evident than the flashes of anger displayed by the border officers after they overhear the scrap collector's son curse the police in a phone conversation. Of all the town residents shown throughout the film, the scrap collector is most memorable. Hauling the elderly man in with his donkey and cart in order to berate him for lack of a permit seems like petty harassment enough, but the frustration and vitriol that erupt in the wake of the overheard phone conversation—replete with threats to keep his cart and kill his donkey—are difficult to watch. Rather than policing serious crimes, we see the border police and their bruised egos on full display as they harangue poor and vulnerable residents for very little in return. The scrap collector is finally let go with a warning, and he hastily drives his cart around the corner and out of sight, presumably to resume his work.

The Banality of Everyday Life

Those who make it past the first hour of an undeniably slow film will be rewarded with the promise of a murder case. As officers post notices around town, clean guns, and set up checkpoints, viewers may understandably hope that the real action is about to begin. Instead, we are treated to shots of a few normal traffic stops, a driver whose defiant refusal to stop may remind China watchers of other well-known incidents (Williams 2017), and the interception of the film's hapless lumber thieves. Because the latter two are shown back to back, the viewer is led to believe that the officers—exasperated with their inability to make progress on the case and angry at the man who refused to stop—take their frustrations out on the lumber thieves. This may indeed have been the case, but in telling their story, we miss out on a chance to see how they resolve the murder. This is a shame since the handling of murder cases in China has sparked suspicion that the government's claim of having one of the lowest murder rates in the world is fabricated (Li 2017; The Economist 2013).

Those looking for a window into the everyday life of law enforcement officers in China will not be disappointed. An early scene captures a conversation about hair dye and hair loss. One officer confides that his hair problems began after a particularly bad summer with the coast guard. He blames it on late nights, insomnia, and stress—issues that have been well documented by scholars (Scoggins and O'Brien 2016; Wang 2015; Wang et al. 2015)—and we are told that Apollo shampoo will help. As the border officers tramp through snow while patrolling isolated areas or sleep with their faces crushed into office chairs, viewers should take heart that the film's slow pace mirrors the realities of ground-level work. While this does not necessarily make for riveting viewing, its authenticity makes it a fair trade.

Blurred Boundaries

The film—released in 2007—feels especially relevant today in light of the ramping up of police presence in Xinjiang (see Cliff's essay in this volume). Reports of re-education camps and increases in government spending leave us with many questions and few glimpses into what interactions between security agents and residents actually look like on the ground (Zenz 2018a and 2018b). Although set in a very different context, the world captured by Zhao gives us remarkable insight into how law enforcement practices can blur boundaries between right and wrong, violence and mercy. Zhao peppers his scenes with shots of the officers cursorily taking care of two dogs, leaving us to wonder if the dogs represent the public or the officers themselves. The final scenes present an answer. As one officer and one dog are summarily dismissed by way of pink slip and knife to the stomach, respectively, we see how some agents of the state get caught in the gears of a force much stronger than they are. ■

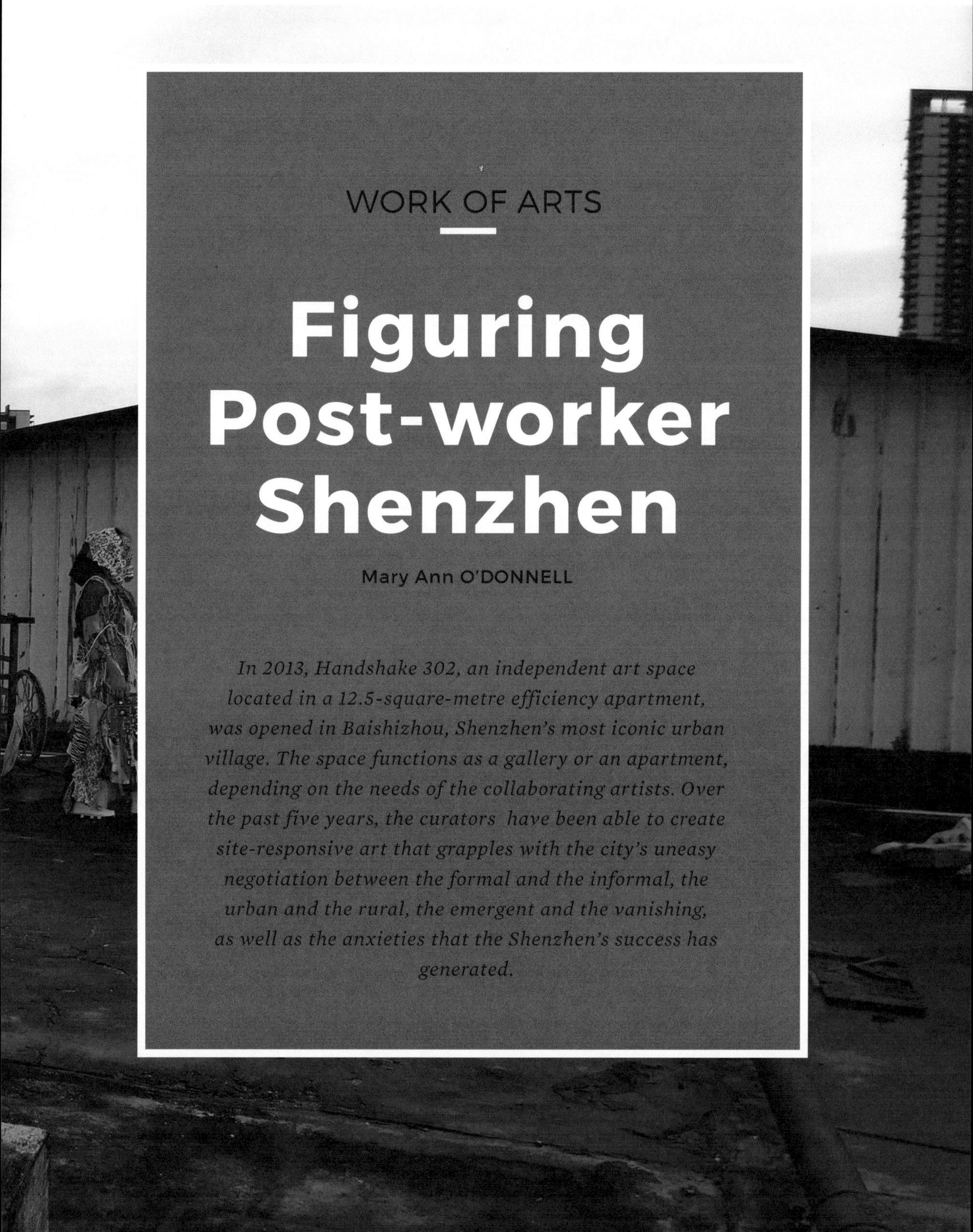

WORK OF ARTS

Figuring Post-worker Shenzhen

Mary Ann O'DONNELL

In 2013, Handshake 302, an independent art space located in a 12.5-square-metre efficiency apartment, was opened in Baishizhou, Shenzhen's most iconic urban village. The space functions as a gallery or an apartment, depending on the needs of the collaborating artists. Over the past five years, the curators have been able to create site-responsive art that grapples with the city's uneasy negotiation between the formal and the informal, the urban and the rural, the emergent and the vanishing, as well as the anxieties that the Shenzhen's success has generated.

In 2013, Zhang Kaiqin, Wu Dan, Liu He, Lei Sheng, and I opened Handshake 302, an independent art space located in a 12.5-square-metre efficiency apartment in Baishizhou—Shenzhen's most iconic urban village. The space functions as a gallery or an apartment, depending on the needs of the collaborating artists. Over the past five years, we have created and curated site-responsive art that grapples with the city's uneasy negotiation between the formal and the informal, the urban and the rural, the emergent and the vanishing, as well as the anxieties that the city's success has generated. Our decision to open an art space in Baishizhou was made in the context of the ongoing demolition of Shenzhen's urban villages and the forced relocation of their residents. In this essay, I introduce several artworks that present Baishizhou, its post worker demographics, and the emergence of Shenzhen as a 'creative' city.

Trainers (2017), photography by Zheng Kuai, Handshake 302 artist-in-residence, October 2017.

Washing Feet and Coming on Land

Handshake buildings and the narrow alleys in between comprise the defining architectural features of an 'urban village' (*chengzhongcun*)—Shenzhen's informal but not disorganised working class neighbourhoods. Built by village collectives in the 1990s, Shenzhen's urban villages continue to evoke the city's rural origins, its status as 'China's first city without villages' notwithstanding. These brutal tenements are called 'handshakes' (*woshoulou*) because it is possible to reach from one's window across a narrow alleyway and shake hands with a neighbour. Not that anyone actually reaches into the alleys, except to hang laundry on the innumerable electrical wires connecting Baishizhou's 2,340 buildings and estimated 35,000 rental units.

The official Baishizhou footprint occupies roughly 0.73 square kilometres. Overseas Chinese Town (OCT) abuts its northern, southern, and eastern borders, and the Shahe Golf Club lies next to its western edge. Internally, vernacular Baishizhou comprises

six sections that point to the neighbourhood's history—the Shahe Industrial Park and the five villages—Baishizhou, Shangbaishi, Xiabaishi, Xintang, and Tangtou. Their administrative integration is an artefact of collectivisation. In 1959, the villages were designated Shahe Farm, a provincial-level outpost of the Guangming Overseas Chinese Dairy in northern Shenzhen. Four of the villages are located north of Shennan road, and the fifth—the actual Baishizhou village—is hidden away behind the Window of the World theme park, south of Shennan road. Since at least 2012, the corporation that represents the five villages has been in negotiation with LVGEM, the appointed real estate company, over compensation for demolishing village-held properties.

Roughly a decade ago, Shenzhen began to squeeze manufacturing out of its borders—first from the Special Economic Zone (SEZ) and then from its outer districts. They squeezed out textiles, electronics, and toy factories like 'toothpaste from a tube', as a friend once described it to me. When Shahe's eastern factories were demolished in 2016, they were already being used for storage and as transfer stations in the online economy. The surviving factories in the eastern section of the industrial park were gentrified into restaurants, cheap studio space, and even microbreweries. Today, as Baishizhou hovers at the edge of annihilation, it has an estimated population of 140,000 people, although like many other Shenzhen statistics, this number disintegrates upon inspection. Does it include the roughly 1,800 members of the historic villages? The former workers and staff of Shahe Industrial Park? Residents of the housing developments that are only accessible from Baishizhou, but technically not built on the Baishizhou footprint? Or does it represent the registered population in the four community stations (*shequ gongzuozhan*) through which 'Baishizhou' is administered? Like much in Baishizhou, demographic figures operate as placeholders for information we believe should be on record, but somehow hovers just beyond confirmation.

During her residency at Handshake 302, second generation Shenzhen migrant Zheng Kuai photographed a pair of athletic trainers that had been hung out to dry. The trainers dangle above accumulated grime and dank gutters and, like Van Gogh's *Shoes* (1886), point to the contemporary organisation of labour and its shifting topographies. In homage to Heidegger's now famous interpretation of Van Gogh's painting (Heidegger 2008), we might describe the toilsome tread of a rural migrant, who left his natal village wearing a t-shirt and blue jeans, cheap socks and synthetic shoes, carrying a middle-school diploma to pursue dreams of a better life. The shoes, we imagine, became soiled and sweat stained in the walk from the tenement to his job. Did he wash the shoes himself or did the woman who cares for him do it? We wonder because the effort to clean the shoes points to care, to a gentle self-respect and the ambition to rise beyond one's current status. But it is just as likely that he earns his wages in a job where cleanliness is mandatory.

Several decades ago, when Shenzhen actually was the 'factory of the world', the migration that brought millions of rural workers to the SEZ was described as 'washing feet and coming on land' (*xijiao shang'an*)—a reference to the rice paddies where farmers worked barefoot. The expression is explicitly southern and coastal. Villagers from Shenzhen, for example, also used the expression to describe no longer having to work in the oyster industry, which had been central to the area's pre-reform economy. Indeed, rural urbanisation in Shenzhen is easily imagined as post-mud. During the heyday of industrial manufacturing, when oyster fields, rice paddies, and lychee orchards were being transformed into a paved network of industrial parks, commercial centres, and housing estates, the city oozed and belched as construction sites pumped out thick cords of sludge. Today, however, teams of sanitation workers keep the sidewalks clean. The men wear trainers and formal shoes, the

Baishizhou Superhero (2014), installation by Liu Wei.

women wear high heals and shiny sandals, and all expect—and are expected—to keep their feet clean and dry.

A National Bildungsroman

Shenzhen's official history has figured the city as the male subject of a national bildungsroman. Located in the plaza of the Shenzhen history museum, for example, the public sculpture *Path Breaking* (1993) reinterprets the character *chuang*—which depicts a horse charging through a gate—as the creative spirit of China at the threshold of a new world. *Chuang* is a northern expression, evoking generations of workers leaving the country's central plains to work in the northeast of China and Mongolia. Eyes fixed on the road before him, legs powerfully braced, arms flexed in anticipation, and fingers gripping the iron frame of the door that for too long isolated China from the world, the central figure of the statue embodies national will to power. Similarly, the statue of Deng Xiaoping on Lianhua Mountain represents the city through heroic masculinity, a leader confidently striding forward into the world (via Hong Kong). In contrast, projects completed at Handshake 302 have attempted to figure Baishizhou, its residents, and, more ambitiously, their urban agency and contributions.

Consider, for example, *Baishizhou Superhero*, one of the first installations at Handshake 302. In this oeuvre, Liu Wei's playful cartoon characters transformed Handshake 302 into a magic telephone booth. Visitors stepped into the space and through the power of a photo stand-in became one of seven possible urban village superheroes—Methane Man, Wonder Granny, Stir Fry Fly, the Amazing Beer Babe, Village Guardian, Super Dog, or Cat-a-go-go. Friends could then take pictures of each other as they impersonated some of the most visible forms of labour in Baishizhou. At first glance, the installation seems a tacky party game until we remember that these jobs—deliveryman, child care provider, food hawker, beer waitress, and village fireman—constitute entry level access to Shenzhen's post-manufacturing economy. After all, these superheroes provide the services and social network that Shenzhen's informal residents need to make themselves at home in a city which denies them the social welfare benefits concomitant with local household registration (*hukou*).

In fact, the city's demographics have shifted as quickly as its ever-changing mission statement precisely because it has structured its *hukou* to retain desired migrants and exclude people who are considered 'temporary'. During the 1980s, for example, only transfers from an urban work unit (*danwei*) were granted the right to permanence through a Shenzhen *hukou*. Migrants with an official registration worked to build the city's administrative apparatus as well as its infrastructure, while informal migrants worked in township and village industrial parks, engaged in quasi-legal commercial activities, or laboured on construction teams. In the 1990s, during the city's boom, the majority of migrants came to work in the city's informal economy. Professional migrants came to work as architects, designers, accountants, and lawyers, securing a Shenzhen *hukou* via state-owned enterprises, while the majority of migrants continued to labour without formal inclusion in the municipal apparatus. In this important sense, Shenzhen was always already post-worker, because workers were defined by their exclusion from the city. Workers lived in dormitories and urban villages, which were by definition transitional. When, in 2005, the city began restructuring from manufacturing to creative production, Shenzhen began attracting young creatives, even as factory workers were forced to leave the city or to change jobs, finding work in service or as small capital entrepreneurs. In 2016, then Municipal Party Secretary Ma Xingrui announced that the city's administrative population had breached 20 million, but its *hukou* population remained less than 3.5 million.

Thus, at a second glance, the insidious charm of *Baishizhou Superhero* becomes even more apparent. The Shenzhen Dream hinges on the fact that migrants come to the city in order to improve their material lives. Within the maelstrom of globalisation, however, the latent potential of human beings to transform themselves has been limited by the imperatives of commodification. The superpower of an unpaid grandmother, for example, is to create value by providing unpaid childcare so that both fathers and mothers can join the gendered labour force, as deliverymen or waitresses. The superpower of all Baishizhou migrants is, in fact, the power to sell their labour on an unregulated market for as long as their bodies hold out. A popular expression maintains that migrant workers 'sell their youth' (*chumai qingchun*). As individuals, there are limits to the scale of transformation. When a deliveryman's legs can no longer pump a bicycle or when a waitress' breasts succumb to gravity, these workers are replaced by younger, more energetic migrants. And there is the fantastic allure of the superhero myth—unlimited strength to endure and transcend physically exhausting and emotionally alienating jobs in order to realise oneself as a proper Shenzhener with a local *hukou*, propriety, and salaried job. After all, those who do not leave Baishizhou continue to exist in the liminal space between hometown and Shenzhen, their figure not yet determined.

A Model of Post-industrial Restructuring

The rise of Shenzhen as a creative city has been a result of national-level planning decisions and municipal-level interpretations. By 2000, a mere 20 years into the reform era, the Chinese government had already recognised that many cities had 'over-zoned'. Especially in the Pearl River Delta, competition within and between cities meant that industrial zones were no longer effective catalysts for modernisation. This was also true in Shenzhen, where low-end manufacturing of textiles and shoes—and artificial Christmas trees, plastics, and soap dishes—had already moved to neighbouring Dongguan. The new national strategy required that cities restructure their economies from assembly manufacturing to higher-value markets, including graphic design and high-quality printing, fashion and trade fairs, technology, research and design, biotech, and financial services. Today, creatives have joined the city's transient population, living in urban villages to save money and time on their daily commute.

In the fall of 2014, when 23-year-old Fu Honghong accepted a graphic design job at a firm in OCT, she did not know that Baishizhou existed. University had allowed Fu to transfer her rural *hukou* to a provincial city and her new job was the first step toward achieving a Shenzhen *hukou*, which would give her children access to the city's public schools and medical system. Before she started her job, Fu learnt that the firm did not provide housing and the salary was less than the monthly rent in an OCT housing estate. Rather than share an apartment with five roommates or lease an apartment that was a one-hour commute away from her office, Fu decided to rent a one-bedroom apartment in neighbouring Baishizhou. This would allow her to reduce commuting time, save money toward a down-payment on a condominium, and to forward remittances to her parents. 'I have,' she admitted with a shy laugh, 'bland goals. I want a family and a house in a convenient part of the city.'

The relationship between Baishizhou and the OCT illustrates the city's ongoing transformation. In late 2005, for example, Shenzhen launched its restructuring with the Shenzhen Hong Kong Bi-City Biennale of Urbanism\Architecture (UABB) in the eastern industrial zone of OCT. Within several years of its establishment, the UABB had achieved international recognition and was generally acknowledged as Shenzhen's most important cultural event, heralding the city's ambitions to elevate its standing from a glorified industrial park to creative city. Shenzhen succeeded. Previously considered by many to be an over-ranked manufacturing town, it is now domestically acknowledged as China's fourth city after Beijing, Shanghai, and Guangzhou. Outside China, Shenzhen has been represented as one of the country's most important creative hubs. The goal of the UABB has since expanded to exploring urban possibility within the larger context of the Pearl River Delta mega cities and, more recently, China's expansion into the South China Sea via the Belt and Road Initiative.

The OCT has not only symbolised Shenzhen's rise as a creative city, but has also been deployed as a national model for post-industrial restructuring. In addition to the UABB, which the OCT hosted in 2005, 2007, and 2011, the area has attracted many of Shenzhen's most important architecture firms, design studios, and cultural institutions to take up residence in its factory buildings, including

Floating Desires (2015), installation by Fu Honghong.

the city's leading independent modern art and design museums. While its theme parks seem dated, the OCT housing estates and starred hotels provide fantasy experiences, where staff dress as gondoliers, greeting guests with practiced smiles and offers of help. Nevertheless, the OCT model of creativity is not easily reproduced, primarily because its success has depended upon two factors: free land via the work unit system of development that prevailed in Shenzhen during the early 1980s; and shunting the cost of workers' living expenses onto Baishizhou and other urban villages, a business practice which became prevalent in Shenzhen after Deng Xiaoping's Southern Tour in 1992.

On the one hand, the OCT was developed by a national ministry that did not have to pay for land. This came about as a result of the 1980 Sino-Vietnamese War. In 1980, the national government relocated roughly one hundred Sino-Vietnamese refugees to Shahe and Guangming, while other refugees were sent to cities and farms in Guangdong and Fujian Provinces. The daughter of one refugee mentioned that her parents had been jealous of relatives who had been settled outside Huizhou, which was 'a real city' and not 'a rural backwater' like Shenzhen. Based on the presence of these refugees, when Shenzhen intensified its modernisation efforts in 1985, the Ministry of Overseas Chinese Affairs was given 4.8 square kilometres of Shahe land to develop. The Ministry appointed Singaporean urban planner Meng Daqiang to consult on OCT's overall plan, which emphasised a garden layout and the separation of manufacturing and residential areas. This plan proved beneficial. By 1990, it was clear that neither Shahe nor OCT industrial parks could compete with industrial parks in Luohu and Shekou, which were located next to the Port of Hong Kong and the Port of Shekou, respectively. Instead, OCT decided to use its location as a suburb to both Luohu and Shekou to develop theme parks and leisure areas for the city's growing population and Hong Kong businessmen.

On the other hand, in the early 1990s, Shenzhen pioneered the restructuring of socialist work units. In the Maoist system, urban *danwei* provided factory workers with housing, medical insurance, and education opportunities for their children. In contrast, in the 1980s, Shenzhen enterprises began hiring workers who did not have a local *hukou*, enabling factories to provide housing, medical insurance, and education opportunities only to a small percentage of workers. Most of these workers moved into handshake rentals, which, given the distribution of villages throughout the city, were located within proximity of any official development. The majority of young creatives who work in OCT, for example, live in Baishizhou until they can afford upscale rents or make the down-payment on a condominium.

Fu Honghong's installation at Handshake 302, *Floating Desires* represented her experience of walking between her job as a graphic designer in OCT and her shared rental in Baishizhou. Dreams and ambition like plastic wrap and styrofoam lunch boxes glut the alleys and accumulate in the overfull garbage cans. The debris and steam, crowds and shouting, disconcert recent arrivals and long-term residents alike. Although immaterial, these bland desires—to find a job, to meet a life partner, to buy a house, and move from an urban village into Shenzhen proper—have informed the shape of Baishizhou. Fu created this map out of double-sided tape, plastic wrap, and acrylic paints. The materials themselves are easily found in Baishizhou, where garbage pickers collect the rubbish littered around overfull garbage cans. Just up the street from the art space, a 40-something (50-something?) auntie sits in front of a stairwell leading up to a hotel with rooms to rent by the hour or the night; no one stays longer than a week unless things do not work out. She hunches over her cellphone, ensconced on a cheap wooden chair that can be purchased from one of the second-hand furniture stores in a nearby alley. Fu says: 'It took a month to see past the odours and grime. Now I see that there's no time to rest, but if it weren't for Baishizhou, there wouldn't even be a place to start. We just keep working, compelled by desire and Shenzhen dreams.'

Ghostly Matters

The ghosts of China's violent inclusion in the modern world system haunt Shenzhen. One trips over colonial ghosts along Chong-Ying street in eastern Shenzhen and rubs up against the ghosts of overseas Hakka throughout Longgang district. Ghosts have settled beneath the Yantian reservoir when Tangtou village was submerged so that the East River Waterworks could be constructed circa 1958, and they flit along the banks of the Shenzhen and Pearl Rivers, memories of those who drowned trying to swim from 'Red China' to the 'Free World' during the Cold War. Maoist workers haunt the renovated factories of the Shekou Industrial Zone, and the ghosts of rural migrants manifest in the city's demolished urban villages. Indeed, the uncanny presence of disappeared history has not only accompanied the city's emergence as China's fourth city, but also, and more importantly, defined it. These immanent hauntings also appear as 'stages of development' in normative accounts of the city's post-Mao rise from a 'fishing village' to modern metropolis.

In January 2018, no other place in Shenzhen materialised encapsulated the city's ghastly topography as completely as Baishizhou, where it was still possible to find architectural traces of every era of the city's modern history. In the northern section of Baishizhou, which does not consist of the actual Baishizhou village, but rather an amalgam of the Shahe Industrial Park Shangbaishi, Xiabaishi, Xintang, Tangtou, and gated communities, one could find freshwater wells that had been dug during the late Qing, an old munitions warehouse that was used during the war against Japan, and rural Hakka dormitories that were built in 1959 for Tangtou families displaced by the East River Waterworks project. There were two-story factories first built in the early 1980s, two-and-a-half family villas that were built in the

Specter (2017) construction and performance by Sabrina Muzi. Handshake 302 artist-in-residence, June 2017.

late 1980s, and handshake buildings from the 1990s, as well as thousands of restaurants, mom and pop shops, and neon signage that have flourished as hundreds of thousands of people have used Baishizhou as their gateway to the Shenzhen dream. The ghosts that haunt Baishizhou also anticipate a seemingly inevitable future when the neighbourhood has been demolished and replaced with high-end housing estates, office complexes, and state-of-the-art cultural spaces.

Handshake artist-in-residence, Sabrina Muzi constructed a shamanic cape and handheld props from objects that had been found or donated in Baishizhou, her artistic practice itself a reflection of the highly organised work of garbage collection, sorting, and resale that defines life in Baishizhou. She hired three people to perform as the spectre, their identities distinguished by the objects in their hands—one carried a discarded control board, one carried a glowing staff, and one carried a small flashlight. The performers posed at and walked through several of Baishizhou's representative spaces, including a market street, a restaurant, and the Baishizhou subway station. In each space, the juxtaposition of the spectre to the residents of Baishizhou highlighted the tenacious informality of the area. In one ecstatic image, the 'control board spectre' walks in front of a temporary storage facility, which was constructed illegally on the rooftop of a condemned factory. In the foreground are discarded tyres and boxes, which have been organised for future reuse. In the background, just beyond the pastel tiles of Xintang are the high-end high-rise apartment buildings in neighbouring OCT.

Muzi's colourful cape and formal poses arrested a gaze, but the wires and flickering lights of the props suggest the conditions of haunting Baishizhou. Like Zheng Kuai's focus on Baishizhou's wires, *Spectre* takes reckoning with Baishizhou not only as a liminal space, but more precisely as a transient space. To live in Baishizhou is not necessarily to be from a rural area, but rather to be ruralised with respect to the city proper. The current residents do not simply live in the shadow of demolition and relocation, but rather the spectre of demolition transvalues the work and lives of Baishizhou residents. They materialise suddenly and just as abruptly vanish into viscous uncertainty—apparitions like electricity, flickering across and between the neighbourhood's dense network of wires. ■

WORK OF ARTS

Rural Migrant Workers in Independent Films

Representations of Everyday Agency

Eric FLORENCE

The recent wave of evictions of tens of thousands of rural migrants in Beijing has served as a harsh reminder of the subaltern condition of many of these people in today's China. This essay examines how rural migrant workers have been represented in Chinese independent documentary films. It points to the importance of conceptually linking the political economy, sociology, and cultural politics of labour in order to apprehend the subject-making processes of migrant workers in today's China.

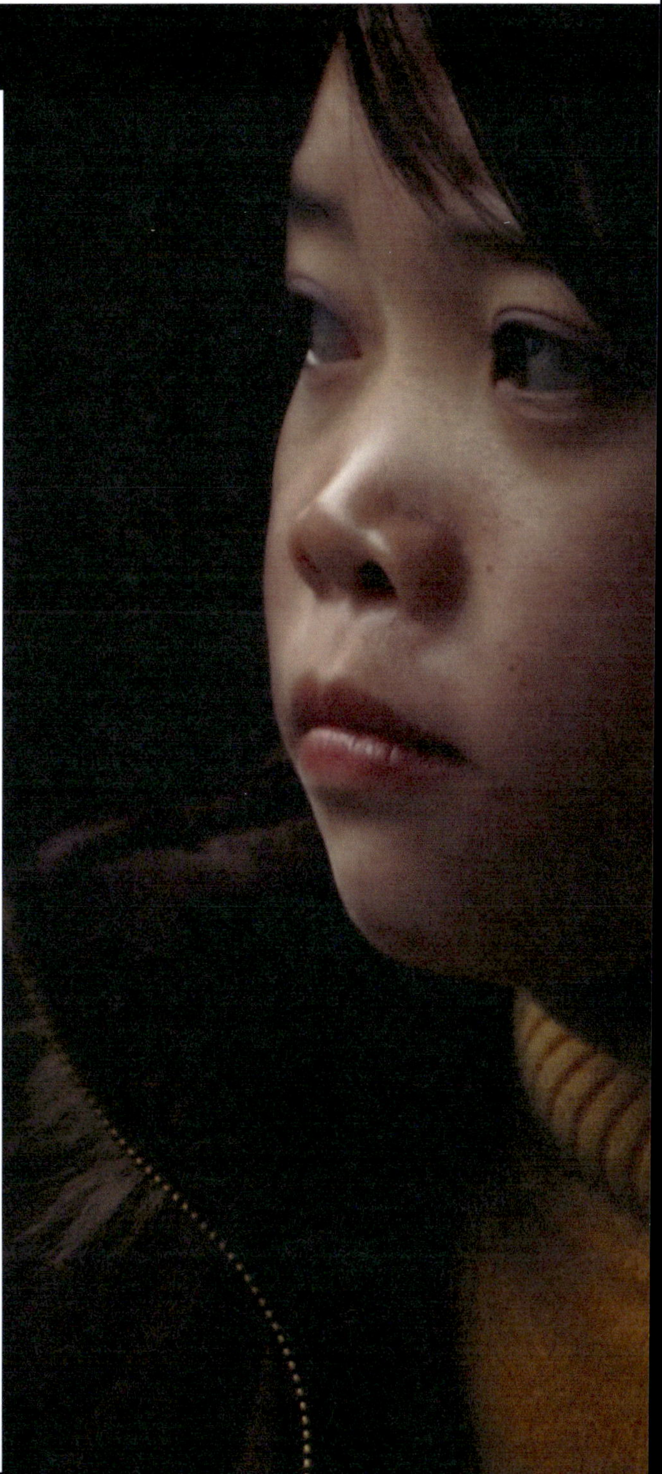

> It's like guerrilla warfare. What matters is to get water. Everything is demolished around here, there is no water... Once the migrants school is demolished, you'll have nowhere to go to. How do you think that makes me feel? I can only blame myself for not giving you a better life.
>
> *When the Bough Breaks*, Ji Dan (2010)

The recent demolition of entire areas in the suburbs of Beijing and the ensuing wave of evictions of tens of thousands of rural migrants have served as harsh reminders of the subaltern condition of many of these people in China today. Several contributions in this volume focus on the ongoing debate on precariousness in contemporary China, shedding light on the complex changes affecting labour regimes and the increasingly diverse and fragmented labour landscapes across the country. In this essay, I will delve into a different but related issue: how rural migrant workers have been represented through a specific form of intervention—Chinese independent documentary films. The importance of looking at the ways various categories of rural migrants are represented, and how migrants themselves take part in their own self-representation—the so-called cultural politics of labour—hinges upon the assumption that both the study of the political economy and sociology of labour on the one hand, and the study of the cultural politics of labour on the other, are needed to apprehend the subject-making processes of migrant workers in today's China (Sun 2014).

Although the relationship between rural migrants and filmmakers is an unbalanced one, an exploration of independent documentary

>>

films provides a glimpse into how migrants' desires, aspirations, hopes for a better life, and their quest for social mobility, engage with—and are strongly shaped by—historically produced institutional and structural forces. Rural-to-urban migration processes in post-Mao China are deeply rooted in large-scale structural inequality of power and access to wealth. They have also been shaped by politico-institutional configurations, and by the relationship between Party-state, market forces, and capital. Hence, we can consider rural migrants in post-socialist China as standing within historically, culturally, and institutionally constituted 'matrixes' of power (Ortner 2006), i.e. the rural-urban chasm, the reformed institutions and mechanisms of demographic control and appropriation of labour, and a whole network of multi-layered hegemonic discourses.

In the late 1980s and first half of the 1990s, many of the mainstream media accounts shared an overall homogenising depiction of rural workers. Starting from the second half of the 1990s, in parallel with similar processes taking place in the fields of Chinese social sciences, media, and popular literature, some documentaries began to deconstruct the image of voiceless hordes of unsightly people 'pouring blindly' into Chinese cities (Florence 2006). Since the late 1990s, the channels of mediation of migrant workers' lives and toil in the cities have become increasingly diversified, including through popular literature, radio, TV shows, photography, and films. With digital advancements over the past decade or so, online forms of representation by both workers themselves—what Jack Qiu has defined as 'worker-generated content' (Qiu 2009)—and by urban elites, such as journalists or NGO activists, have become increasingly widespread. The categories of migrants covered by this specific form of cultural politics have also become more varied, with the inclusion of not only young factory workers, but also miners, domestic workers, vagrants, etc.

A Bottom-up View

Independent documentary films such as such as Li Hong's *Return to Phoenix Bridge* (1997), Wu Wengugang's *Life on the 'Jianghu'* (1999), Du Haibin's *Along the Railway* (2001), Ying Ning's *Railroad of Hope* (2002), Ai Xiaoming's *The Train to My Hometown* (2008), Fan Lixin's *Last Train Home* (2010), Ji Dan's *When the Bough Breaks* (2010), Guo Zongfu's *Coal Miner* (2012), Huang Weikai's *Drifting* (2005), Zhao Dayong's *Nanjing Lu* (2010), and Xu Tong's *Wheat Harvest* (2012) depart from the more mainstream—often paternalistic and at times voyeuristic—cinematic representations of rural migrants (Sun 2014). With their uninterrupted long sequence-shots, they provide the subjects with enough time to narrate their experiences in full. While each of these films possesses its own specificity in terms of form and cinematic arrangements, they share a bottom-up perspective, often focussing on ordinary people from all walks of life who narrate their experiences and reflect on their lives, as well as on society as a whole. For such filmmakers, building a relationship of confidence with the subjects requires a quasi-ethnographic approach that implies living with them for extended periods of time (in some cases for one year or more). Berry and Rofel highlight that it is out of this relationship that the 'social and political commentary of the film' is able to develop (Berry and Rofel 2010, 11). Duan Jinchuan, one of the pioneering figures of new style Chinese documentaries, similarly stressed the importance of building a relationship with the filmed subjects (Lü 2003, 96; see also Robinson 2010).

In light of this, *Return to Phoenix Bridge*, widely referred to as one of the earliest independent documentaries focussing on the everyday life of female migrant workers, managed to de-dramatise the depiction of these women. This was accomplished through the use of long sequences simply concentrating on these women's daily chores and living conditions. In *Along the Railroad*, a 2001 film focussing on the lives of vagrants living beside the railway tracks in Baoji, Shaanxi province, Du Haibin provided a platform for people who can hardly find space to voice their views on their own lives, or on society more broadly. Hence, to some extent, the film opened up a space for making visible the subjectivities of people located at the lowest rungs of society, the so-called 'blind migrants' (*mangliu*). By leaving ample time for the subjects' narration, making their everyday life visible along with the space they live in and their emotions and aspirations, the rather homogenising category of 'blind migrant' is somehow fissured. The long sequence shots exposed quite crudely the very harshness of their everyday living conditions, as well as their own reflections on the precariousness of their existence. As one of the characters in the film said: 'Nowhere to stay when it was cold, nothing to eat when hungry, no doctors to see when sick. It made me feel sad about my life.'

To some extent, such exposure stood at logger's head with the quite mainstream—but far from undisputed—idea that personal efforts inevitably lead to improvement in one's condition, a value which has become a major mode of legitimation of access to wealth and status in post-Mao China.

An Embodied Characterisation of the Rural Condition

Through the subjects they portray, through their narratives, and through the bodies of their characters, the documentary films explored in this essay hint at powerful markers of the politico-historically produced rural-urban chasm and the traps of the political economy underpinning rapid economic growth in post-Mao China. The way these films mediate the rural conditions experienced by migrants is again, on the whole, quite different from that of the mainstream media narrative of the 1980s and 1990s, which linked material poverty to

Wheat Harvest, Xu Tong (2012).

Still from *Railroad of Hope*. Ying Ning (2002).

subjective or cultural poverty characterised by the 'low quality' (*di suzhi*) of the rural populace (Yan 2008; Sun 2013). They do so in an embodied manner, by enabling the expression of the rural condition as lived experience that often causes hardship and suffering.

In filmic representations, one sees a recurring background of poverty, disease, and material constraints, such as debts, unaffordable health or education costs, family normative pressures, and violence. In her latest book, Pun Ngai describes how in the 1980s and 1990s, policies related to agriculture, education, and health in the countryside combined with political economies in urban areas to produce labour markets that favoured massive and rapid capital accumulation. She also describes how these policies have enabled 'a production regime within which a separation exists between the production sphere in industrial regions and social reproduction in rural areas' (Pun 2016, 33–34). In a specific passage of *Railroad of Hope*, one of the first documentary films shot with a DV camera by filmmaker Ying Ning, this embodied hardship of the rural condition takes on a highly tragic and intense form in the tale of a woman who—in front of her child—explains that almost 20 years before she had been forced to marry a man she did not know, and that since then she had to live with this extraordinarily heavy load so as not to sadden her parents and to preserve her son's future:

> The woman: 'Since 1982 I have lost any joy in life.'
>
> The filming assistant: 'If you were to live again, what kind of life would you wish to have?'
>
> The woman: 'I have no wishes any more.'

These Chinese documentary films also enable the viewers to get a glimpse of the multiplicity, complexity, and ambivalence of the motives that rural migrants put forward in order to explain their decisions to leave their hometowns: compelling rural poverty (debts, cost of health and education), the wish to become more independent from their family, the hope to discover the world out there, etc. Along with the vast scholarship on rural-to-urban migration in China, they show that human experiences can never be reduced to a simple monocausal narrative. Chinese independent documentary films also allow us to approach the simultaneously empowering and highly constrained dimension of migrants' agency, showing how it develops both against the background of historically and institutionally produced economic forces (Brettel and Hollifield 2007, 21).

Remote Mountain, a film shot in 1995 in an illegal mine shaft in the Qinlian mountains, Qinghai province, more than 3,000 metres above sea level, features a compelling explanation of why three young people filmed in the mine had decided to migrate to work in such a dangerous environment. Hu Jie filmed the bodies of these minors very closely, and because of the narrowness of the shaft, one hears their breath as they dig and excavate full baskets of coal. In one specific passage, one of the men carrying a heavy yoke, replies to the filmmaker's question as to why he is still working in the shaft despite being critically ill with pneumoconiosis:

> What I think of this? This is in order to live. We are here in order to earn a living, to get married, rebuild the house, send our kids to school. This is in order to live.

Railroad of Hope (2002) offers another perspective on the agency of rural migrants. The film revolves around the question of why these migrants decided to leave their mountainous hometown in Sichuan province to work in cotton fields in remote Xinjiang. Much of the film tends to lend credence to the idea that, while they were not literally compelled to leave, a set of powerful forces at home and in the destination area have somehow pushed them to get out of their hometown. The film also mediates the agency and the capacity of rural migrants to reflect on their lives, as well as on the factors limiting their endeavours. Two segments of this movie demonstrate how powerful material forces shape people's decisions. In the first, a terribly disfigured young woman, injured while toiling in a factory, exemplifies not only the constraints of the countryside, but also the structural violence of labour regimes in post-Mao China. The strength of this scene lies in the invisible but compelling forces that make this young lady, whose face has been irremediably damaged and who received minimal financial compensation for the injury, once again leaves her hometown to labour in the cotton fields in Xinjiang.

In the second segment, two women in their forties reply to the question: 'Do you feel happy?'

> Woman 1: 'Well I don't know, really. I am not sure what this means. Happy people don't need to go far away to get a job.'
>
> Woman 2: 'It's all for our children and our parents.'
>
> Woman 1: 'This is not a happy life. Happiness is to stay at home. When two kids have to go to school, one may not afford it, we have to get out.'

One should note that younger people in the same film tend to put forward reasons more related to positive and 'emancipatory values', such as the will to change one's condition compared to their older counterparts. What this shows is that the decisions these people make are interwoven and shaped by a number of forces, such as normative family and gender expectations, expectations regarding social mobility, material constraints related to health and education costs, as well as a politics of desire constructed within the migration

Still from *When the Bough Breaks*, Ji Dan (2010).

process. These elements all combine to shape migrant workers' subjectivities and agency in complex ways.

When the Bough Breaks

The movie which, I argue, manages to show most powerfully the complex ways in which rural migrants' aspirations and will engage with material forces—both at home and in the workplace—is *When the Bough Breaks*, a 2010 documentary by pioneer filmmaker Ji Dan (Litzinger 2016). The filmmaker spent a year with a family of scrap collectors she had met in 2004 while working on a film project on a Beijing school. Five years later, she heard that the eldest female sibling in the family had vanished—it is never quite clear in the movie whether she died, but she was supposedly forced into prostitution at some point. The film focusses on the relationship between the parents—in particular, the crippled father who lost one leg—and the two remaining daughters. Xia, the eldest daughter, holds on to one single project with extraordinary determination: to enable her younger brother to attend a good high school and later university. Xia's perseverance and determination to succeed in her goal is contrasted by the father. He and his wife are originally at best ambivalent about their daughter's plan. He first agrees to it, recognising that 'education enables you to get anything', but later strongly opposes it, aware of what this dream would cost him and his family. At some point, Xia's mother, exhausted, tells her daughter: 'You know, it is already so tough right now, with this project of yours, the bough might break.' The father's entire body is so full of scars, exhaustion, hardship, and suffering. His body bespeaks precariousness, liminal subsistence, which leans towards physically and psychological collapse, alcoholism, and violence.

Through these characters of the father and daughter, in a single documentary Ji Dan manages to shed light on the complexity of what shapes the agency of rural migrants in today's China: a mix of powerful aspirations to improve one's condition and equally powerful forces that tend to maintain them in a subaltern position. Throughout the film, the daughter is ready to make any sacrifice—such as dropping out of school herself to earn money—so that her younger brother can enter a good high school. At one point, Xia says: 'I'll sell my blood to send him to school if I have to.' A series of implicit questions run through the film: what kind of political economy pushes people to endure such hardships and make such sacrifices? Would it not be wiser to listen to Xia's brother, who, perhaps tired of shouldering such normative pressure, at one point suggests that it might be better to simply let him attend an ordinary school? But by doing so, would this not prevent him from having any chance of accessing university? And would this not essentially be making a concession to some kind of social determinism according to which rural people ought to only perform the jobs for which they are suited? These are complex issues relating to the institutionally unfair nature of the education system, the structural obstacles to social mobility, and the enduring subaltern condition of rural migrants. Ji Dan manages to mediate this tension and complexity in an incredibly powerful way.

In conclusion, these Chinese documentaries allow us to approach core dimensions of the subaltern condition of migrant workers—of their determination, agency, and modes of engagements with the world. To a certain extent, these films provide subtle insights into the societal and socioeconomic transformations linked to unprecedented growth and massive capital accumulation that took place in China over the last three decades. They not only shed new light on the experiences of migrant workers by making their hopes, desires, and embodied hardships visible, but also illustrate how all this suffering constitutes an important, if not fundamental, part of such transformations. ■

WORK OF ARTS

Plastic China
Beyond Waste Imports

Yvan SCHULZ

Still from *Plastic China* by Wang Jiuliang.

China Wasting Away

In the last two years, the issue of waste exports to China has attracted considerable media and public attention. As a result, awareness of the social and environmental impact of the global trade in recyclables has increased substantially, both within and outside of China. Among contributing factors was *Plastic China* (*Suliao wangguo*, 2016), a documentary directed by Wang Jiuliang. Since its release, the film has become indissociable from the issue of waste exports, and it gained even more prominence after July 2017, when the Chinese government announced a wide-ranging ban on 'foreign waste' (*yang laji*) (Liebman 2018). However, the film's relevance extends far beyond the issue of waste management. In this essay, I argue that *Plastic China* should be considered as a rich social commentary and critique, and interpreted in the light of China's tradition of independent documentary-making in the reform era.

Wang is a recognised authority on the topic of waste in China. He rose to prominence a few years ago thanks to his first film, *Beijing Besieged by Waste* (*Laji weicheng*, 2012), which revealed the existence of a great number of unauthorised and unmonitored dumpsites around Beijing. The film also alerted people in China to the dangers of haphazard waste management, and drew attention to the sheer mass of waste generated by a city the size of Beijing.

Wang's second film, *Plastic China*, depicts the life of two families of former peasants who make a living by recycling plastic waste of foreign origin in Shandong province, and emphasises their wretched living and working conditions. It was featured in numerous festivals outside China, and has won several awards. In China, the film went viral in

January 2017 before quickly disappearing from the Internet—thereby following a pattern that affects most of Wang's work (Zhao 2017).

Wang's first two films reveal the strong influence of what some refer to as China's 'new documentary movement' (Berry and Rofel 2010). This is obvious in, among others, his choice of topic (China's economic growth and opening to the world as experienced by the country's underclass), his relationships with subjects (long-term involvement, much like that of an anthropologist), and his cinematographic style (observational realism involving on-the-spot and spontaneous shooting, a director who stands behind the camera, and the absence of voiceover). *Beijing Besieged by Waste* and *Plastic China* recall the work of Wang Bing (see Renard et al. 2014 and Persico 2010) and Zhao Liang (see Sorace 2017), among other leading Chinese independent filmmakers.

With *Plastic China,* Wang aimed to raise awareness of his homeland's role in the global waste trade, and expose its negative repercussions on the Chinese population and environment. In 2014, Wang released an early, less narrative but more explanatory version of his documentary addressed at the media, in which he clearly framed the issue as environmental dumping. That same year, he expressed his intention to undertake a follow-up project on waste imports beyond plastics, which he tentatively titled *Dumping Ground of the World* (*Shijie de laji chang*) (Liu 2014). It is therefore not surprising that *Plastic China* is generally invoked, both within and outside of China, in connection with the global capitalist system that, for many years at least, allowed relatively rich countries to pass the burden of pollution on to China.

As mentioned above, the film has been particularly closely associated with the issue of waste imports since July 2017, when the Chinese central government hit headlines domestically and internationally by announcing a ban on imports of 24 categories of waste, including many types of plastics (Voice of America 2018). Several experts I engaged with in recent months put forward the idea that the film prompted officials in Beijing to take this kind of action, or at least influenced them significantly (see also Lü 2018). What is certain is that the film can serve as a justification for the outright ban on waste imports—irrespective of whether Wang ever regarded a ban as the proper solution to the problems he documented. In this sense, *Plastic China* has arguably played a key role in the recent evolution of the trade in recyclable waste.

However, the film is all too often reduced to its function as a tool for denouncing environmental dumping. This is regrettable, for two main reasons. First, this narrow focus fails to do justice to the richness and complexity of Wang's second, cinema version of *Plastic China,* which—unlike the first version targeting the press—constitutes a broad social commentary and critique. Second, this prevents us from understanding why the film was censored in China, when the denunciation of waste imports actually fits with the Chinese state's increasingly restrictive policies on this issue since the 2010s. To compensate for this narrow focus, we need to look beyond the predominant reading.

Plastic China as Commentary and Critique

One first reason why *Plastic China* should be considered as a comprehensive reflection on the contemporary condition in China is that this is consistent with the director's intention. In one interview about the film, Wang stated that: 'China is a country that is facelifted, concealed, faked, and unnatural. In other words, though it looks good exteriorly, it has a lot of interior problems' (Kanthor 2017). In another one, he explained, in reference to the film's title that:

> The [word] 'plastic' here has two meanings: first it refers to the plastic waste, but at a deeper level it refers to the weakness beneath our surface prosperity; the way plastic surgery only improves appearance, not the reality. Years of rapid growth have made China appear prosperous, but pollution is having a huge impact on health … while China's growth appears incredible, it is actually cheap and fragile. (Liu 2014)

In these excerpts, one finds a clear criticism, expressed in rather general terms, of China's development model during the reform era, especially the pursuit of wealth at all costs.

Another factor that justifies adopting a broad interpretation of *Plastic China* is the wide range of social issues addressed by Wang.[1] First of all his film tackles the problem of labour exploitation. The prosperity of China's coastal regions relies on a massive inflow of migrant workers from the interior, who rarely have much bargaining power regarding their working conditions. In the film, Peng Wenyuan—who comes from Sichuan province, belongs to the Yi ethnic group, and is almost illiterate—complains repeatedly about his salary. He asks Wang Kun, his boss and the owner of the recycling workshop the Pengs work in, for a raise. But Kun—who is Han, from Shandong province, and can read and write—refuses, telling Wenyuan that he can always leave if he is not satisfied. In the cinema version of *Plastic China*, the concept of labour exploitation applies more clearly within China and even among former peasants than it does between China and the highly industrialised countries from which waste is imported. Thus, in a way, Wang departs from the perspective of environmental dumping. His focus on the daily life of two families in a shared domestic space, where exploitation unfolds in an intimate setting, allows him to give an otherwise commonplace phenomenon a particularly raw and emotional dimension.

In connection with this, the film represents a reflection on the legal status and living conditions of China's 'floating population' (*liudong renkou*). In China, rural migrants are generally registered in their place of origin but spend most of their time living far away from their hometowns. During the reform era, this has prevented them from enjoying key rights and public services in their place of residence. Since 2014, China's household registration system (*hukou*) is being eased with a view to, among other things, give migrants better access to healthcare and education. However, implementation of this reform only begun several years into the shooting of Plastic China (which lasted from 2011 to 2016), and remains patchy to this day. The Pengs' precarious existence and the fact that they are basically left to fend for themselves is striking for both Chinese and foreign viewers. Among the film's many harrowing scenes is that of Peng's wife giving birth to her fourth child in the Wangs' garden, with what looks like a total absence of medical assistance. The film does not tell its audience how this situation came about, but it is easy to associate it with rural migrants' generally limited access to healthcare.

The documentary is also a meditation on issues of gender inequality. The picture of China's gender regime that emerges from *Plastic China* is one of entrenched patriarchy, at least in the countryside, where boys are still valued more than girls (*zhongnan qingnü*). In the film, the main character, a bright girl named Peng Yijie, does not attend school, although she is already 11 years old. Viewers learn that this has to do with her status as a migrant, her family's meagre earnings, and her father's alcoholism. However, it is also strongly implied that Yijie's gender played a role in her parents' decision to neglect her education. At some point, Wang Kun pushes for Yijie to attend a local kindergarten, even offering to cover the costs, yet Yijie's father, Peng Wenyuan, refuses, preferring that she continue to sort plastics, do household chores, and take care of her younger siblings. This contrasts with the situation of Wang Qiqi, Kun's son, who is sent to the kindergarten so that he can pick up literacy skills early on in the hope that he will get access to a high-earning job later in life, ideally in an office in Beijing—it should be noted, however, that Qiqi is not only a boy, but also an only child.

A further issue highlighted in the film is that of conspicuous consumption. There is something profoundly disturbing in the Wangs' purchase of a shiny new sedan car. The family obviously lives on very little, and Wang Kun, the breadwinner, has a possibly serious affliction that affects his capacity to work, and remains undiagnosed and untreated, partly because he fears that seeking medical attention could result in high expenses. Yet, towards the end of the film, the Wangs spend their entire savings—and even borrow money—to purchase a vehicle for which they seem to have little practical need. Acquiring this potent status symbol allows them to have the feeling—and give others the impression—that they have achieved wealth, and moved up the social ladder. The question remains, however, whether this was worth the enormous sacrifice in financial security, and viewers are left wondering what will happen to the family if Wang Kun is diagnosed with a serious illness.

The aspect of the film that most stuck with me personally was how *Plastic China* depicted the poor standard of waste management in rural China. Some scenes in the film take place in a dumpsite, where waste is burned in the open, or next to a river, where it accumulates. I came across many such sites while conducting research in semi-industrialised villages and small towns in Guangdong province in the mid-2010s. Some of them were located in rural recycling hubs, but many were not. For instance, Gurao, once China's largest bra manufacturing hub, struggles with waste-related pollution of comparable gravity to that of neighbouring Guiyu, the country's infamous e-waste recycling capital. Work done by environmentalists Chen Liwen and Mao Da from China Zero Waste Alliance (*Ling feiqi lianmeng*) suggests that waste management is either lacking or highly inefficient in the Chinese countryside as a whole, and that much remains to be done in this field (Chitwood 2018).

The film also resonated with the study of China's so-called 'informal' recycling world that I conducted in the mid-2010s (Schulz 2018). Through my interviews with self-made entrepreneurs who live in the countryside or have rural origins, I came to the conclusion that, as a rule, these people did not enjoy any support from state authorities for changing their methods or upgrading their facilities in order to cause less pollution, and better protect workers. There were virtually no incentives to comply with environmental and safety regulation, and local authorities made little effort to improve the sector—in large part because officials at the village or town level had a stake in rapid, unbridled economic growth. In recent years, crackdowns have become commonplace in rural recycling hubs, largely due to pressure from authorities at the county level and above, and they often cause recycling bosses to lose everything (Schulz 2019). Such a context makes it very risky for the latter to adopt a long-term perspective and invest in new equipment or techniques. This also explains why Wang Kun's plastic recycling workshop, like many others, relies on manual labour and a couple of unsophisticated and antiquated machines.

Plastic China and the Chinese Condition

All the issues mentioned above are central to Wang's narrative in *Plastic China*. It is important to stress that, while these features of China's contemporary condition can be observed in rural recycling hubs, they are not unique to these places. Indeed, they cut across borders and sectors of economic activity. An important implication is that improving the lives of the people who live in rural recycling hubs and engage in waste sorting and processing requires more than putting an end to waste imports—especially if imports are substituted with domestic waste, of which there is no shortage in China.

This brings us to the topic of censorship. If *Plastic China*'s message really boiled down to nothing more than a plea against waste imports and the pollution they cause, then the film would not be an obvious target for the Chinese censors. After all, this type of message is consistent with recent official discourse and practice, which lay great emphasis on environmental protection, leadership in global trade, and national sovereignty. If anything, there is considerable overlap between Wang's film and the 'foreign waste' rhetoric that accompanies state authorities' action in the field of transboundary movements of waste since the early 2010s, and predates the ban announced in July 2017. Moreover, *Plastic China* contains virtually no direct criticism of any government, state-owned enterprise, or other powerful entity—a key difference with *Under the Dome* (*Qiong ding zhi xia*, 2015), another documentary on China's environmental predicament that also went viral and disappeared from the Internet in a matter of days.

Yet, something in *Plastic China* must have bothered Chinese censors, and prompted them to intervene. In the absence of any recognisably subversive content, I would argue that it was the image of China conveyed by Wang's bleak and shocking depiction of the country's recycling sector that struck a nerve. Since taking office as president, Xi Jinping has striven to distinguish his government from the previous one. He has vowed to break with the past, and usher in a 'new normal' (*xin changtai*)—later morphing into a 'new era' (*xin shidai*)—in which the country's true wealth would reside in 'clear waters and green mountains' (*lüshui qingshan*), and its prosperity would rely on moderate and sustainable growth. It is against this backdrop that *Plastic China* came out in 2016. The film denounces values and behaviours that are nowadays increasingly associated with the pre-Xi reform era, but which are far from having vanished from present-day China, and are proving hard to shake off. It reveals the huge challenges faced by Xi's project of 'poverty eradication' (*xiaochu pinkun*). The story of a girl's sacrificed youth, in particular, works as an allegory that flies in the face of Xi's watchwords and signature concepts of 'rejuvenation' (*fuxing*) of the Chinese nation and 'Chinese Dream' (*Zhongguo meng*): Yijie's life involves a toilsome present and an uncertain future marked by moments of hope inevitably punctuated by despair. Her dreams are daydreams, a way for her to escape the harsh reality she experiences on a daily basis. They take her elsewhere, to a place where she can picture a better life, and—most damning of all—it looks like this could be abroad.

In conclusion, *Plastic China* constitutes a broad reflexion on social problems and dilemmas in the post-socialist era. The film clearly belongs to China's 'new documentary movement', which has created an important space for social commentary and critique since the early 1990s (Berry and Rofel 2010). There are clear signs that this space is shrinking nowadays, yet this does not stop many independent filmmakers from pursuing their mission (Berry 2017). Despite censorship, Wang Jiuliang has managed to reach a wide audience with *Plastic China*, and have considerable impact. Immediately afterwards, he embarked on a new project. Interestingly, it does not look further into waste imports, as Wang had originally planned, but instead addresses construction and real estate's impact on the surface of the earth, in particular through mineral extraction and the desolate landscapes it produces in China (Wang 2016). Once again, though, Wang has a holistic way of tackling the issue, and his real concern is China's changing relationship to the land under capitalism—a broad project if there ever was one. ■

(1) I gratefully acknowledge the contribution of Marina Svensson and other participants in the 2018 Made in China Summer School, who pointed to several of these social issues and helped me become more aware of them.

WORK OF ARTS

The Last Days of Shi Yang

Ivan FRANCESCHINI

What follows is a fictionalised account of the last days of Shi Yang (1889–1923) based on the prison diaries included in the commemorative volume Shi Yang jinian wenji *(Museum of the 7 February Massacre, Wuhan 1988). Shi Yang was a* weiquan *lawyer ante litteram, and to this day he remains an inspiration to many labour activists in China. The Chinese Communist Party (CCP) celebrates him as a martyr of the revolution, the irony of which will not escape those who are aware of the plight of human rights lawyers and labour activists in the country today. That in April 2018 the Chinese government passed a new law to protect the reputation and honour of 'its' heroes and martyrs can be seen as further adding to the irony.*

When they knocked at his door on the afternoon of 7 February 1923, Shi Yang had just come home after a day in court. Guns in hand, a dozen uniformed policemen rushed into the room, led by a detective in plain clothes. The officer was the first to break the silence: 'The boss of our department wants to meet you for a chat. Hurry up!' An experienced lawyer, Shi Yang was not easily intimidated: 'Who is your boss?' 'The head of Hankou police, don't you understand? Stop talking and follow me!' 'Since the director of such an important department has ordered you to come in person to fetch me, I will obviously come. Just please don't be so aggressive. There is no need.' Compliant, he followed them outside, despite the protests of his wife who insisted on accompanying him. 'And why would you do that? Go back inside. I didn't violate any law: wherever they take me, there is nothing to worry about,' he reassured her.

Shi Yang (1889–1923), lawyer by trade and a member of the Chinese Communist Party. He was one of the early leaders of the Chinese labour movement.

Actually, Shi Yang was well aware that the situation was not that simple. Tension had been mounting in the city for days, since the previous week, when the police in Zhengzhou had blocked the founding congress of a trade union that would have represented all railway workers along the Beijing-Hankou line. Rumour had it that the order had come directly from Wu Peifu, the warlord pulling the strings of the government in Beijing, a shady character who fancied himself a poet. This decision had come completely by surprise, considering that until the previous day Wu had posed as a staunch supporter of worker rights. Embittered, the railway workers had decided to hold their congress anyway, which had led to a wave of arrests. Further enraged, union leaders had decided to launch a general strike along the whole railway line, putting forward a series of demands that included the firing of the general director of the railway, the reimbursement of all expenses incurred by the workers to organise the congress, the clearing of all union spaces by the police, and—why not?—one day of paid leave a week and a week of holiday for the Spring Festival. The strike had started at noon on 4 February.

The worker leaders who had organised the mobilisation had no experience in handling a strike of that size. Shi Yang was one of them. Now 34, the son of a poor family from the countryside of Hubei province, he had studied law and became a lawyer, eventually managing to open his own law firm. A member of the newly established Chinese Communist Party since 1922, he had never joined the secret work of the organisation, preferring to carry out his activities in the light of day. He worked ceaselessly to defend the poor and marginalised, representing workers and trade unionists without any concern for the threats coming from the rich and powerful. As a legal consultant for the Beijing-Hankou Railway Worker Association, Shi Yang had played a fundamental role in the organisation of the congress of 1 February, as well as in the ensuing events. When the skirmishes had started, he had joined a secret meeting in which trade union leaders had decided what to do. Together with Lin Xiangqian, he had been put in charge of the coordination of the strike in the Hankou area. That very night he had taken a train back to Wuhan.

The general strike had lasted only three days, before being drowned in blood. 35 workers were killed, including Lin Xiangqian, who had been decapitated in front of his colleagues on a platform of the railway station in Hankou after refusing to give the order to go back to work. Three more worker leaders had shared the same fate, their horribly disfigured heads left hanging from telegraph poles as a warning. Shi Yang was certainly aware of all this—the whole city was abuzz with sordid rumours about the violence of those days—but he still decided to lie to his wife, to spare her a few more hours of relative peace before what he suspected would come.

Along the way the policemen started to drag him as if he were a common criminal. 'Whatever law I violated, I am available to follow you to the local court to go through judgment according to the law. I will not come to the police station just to have my rights violated,' he kept saying. The response was always the same: 'We have our orders. It is not up to us.' Once at the police station, they entered from a side door. Inside, a couple dozen fully armed officers surrounded him. Another official in plain clothes took him to a small room, where they both sat down.

Shi Yang then asked the man: 'What law did I violate for you to drag me here?' 'We summoned you because of the strike. We want to discuss things with you in order to find a solution.' 'The government is really giving me too much importance! Who am I to solve a wave of strikes that is propagating worldwide? Still, there is always one reason why the wind blows. If you want to solve the problem, you have to consider its fundamental roots. These protests have four causes: the horrible working conditions in the factories, the lack of freedom of association for the workers, low wages, and long working hours. Do you want to solve the problem? Then improve the conditions in the factories, allow the workers to join trade unions, raise the salaries, and shorten work hours. Is it that hard? What need is there to ask for my advice?'

The lawyer spoke for more than one hour and a half, until dinnertime. Since he had also skipped lunch, he was hungry. An official went to fetch him some food, but suddenly other policemen arrived to take him to a military court on the other side of the Yangtze river. 'Wait until he eats something,' somebody remarked. But Shi Yang got impatient: 'Let's cross the river immediately. What's the point of eating if the time of death is close?' Once outside, he found himself in a corridor formed by over two hundred armed policemen standing in two rows. Thirty more officers surrounded him, while two detectives held him by his arms and shoulders.

A huge crowd had gathered along the road to the pier. They were people with tense and severe looks, boiling with rage at the thought of the recent betrayal. The men who were escorting him knew that it would take only the smallest spark to trigger a riot. They loaded Shi Yang on the small steamboat that would take him on the other side of the river. On the short trip across the water, the lawyer began to harangue his captors: 'Many poor people live in misery, the workers deserve our pity, all Chinese—whether poor, rich, noble, or humble—are under the yoke of international imperialism. All Chinese people should unite to fight against this threat. We should stop killing each other and put an end to exploitation by the foreigners!' Many a guard lowered his eyes, and when he finished talking one of them was crying: 'If only we did as this man says, China would prosper and be at peace in less than three years!'

At the military tribunal, Shi Yang was searched and forced to strip. Among the officials, he saw a familiar face, but there was no hint of recognition in the other person's eyes. After a while, he was taken to the military jail, where his hands and feet were cuffed and

A photo that Shi Yang (third from the left) and his colleagues took in Wuhan in 1922 to celebrate the establishment of an association of workers and traders.

he was thrown into a cell along with other common criminals, one of whom had already spent five years in that place. Now that the irons impaired his movements, it was this other prisoner who helped him to get on his bed. By that time, it was already 11pm, but he could hardly sleep. He did not worry for himself, but for his family: without him his wife, his daughter, and his younger brother would have no source of livelihood.

The following morning, on 8 February, after a basic breakfast that he found hard to digest, he was taken to the military court. There he told the judge all about his experiences in the patriotic movements that had erupted in China in 1919. Questioned about his ties with the trade unions, he said that as a lawyer he had indeed assisted workers and unionists, but always within the boundaries of the existing laws, as professional ethics demanded. The judge then asked: 'It is true that it is legal for lawyers to represent workers and unionists, but in Wuhan there are so many lawyers. Why do these people always come to you?' Shi Yang then replied: 'Actually, there are many other people out there who are doing the same job as I do.' 'Then explain why official bodies pay attention only to you!' 'The reason is simply that I have taken part in every patriotic movement since 1919. I have done so openly, putting my face on it, and presenting countless complaints and petitions to the authorities. Now officials and bureaucrats in many departments deeply hate me and want my demise.'

The judge showed some sympathy: 'I don't really get many of the things you say, but you can give your testimony and then we will investigate. In any case, even if this case has been opened on the initiative of several government departments in Wuhan, you are famous and therefore society will pay a lot of attention to your trial. Moreover, I myself have studied law, so you can rest assured that I will judge you with equanimity and fairness. But you also have to consider that this is a military court, so unlike an ordinary tribunal it just follows orders. When you provide your testimony, don't voice any complaint: if someone wants to accomplish great things in this world, he must be ready to suffer, there is no choice. Accept a few days of mistreatment, wait quietly, and everything will sort itself out.' But Shi Yang was too stubborn, and as soon as the judge had finished talking he went on a tirade against the Chinese tradition of keeping prisoners in irons inside their cells, which he deemed a barbarian custom that civilised countries had abandoned a long time before.

The session lasted the whole morning and most of the afternoon. At about 5pm, the lawyer was led back to his cell. He had just been cuffed, when a young official came down and gave the order to release him from his restraints: 'Mister Shi Yang is a man of culture, take off the irons and take care of him. From now on, he will not be subjected to these methods.' He also ordered the transfer of his two roommates to another cell and a change of blankets, not only for him, but for all prisoners. That evening, Shi Yang wrote a couple of letters, one to his family, another to a friend in Shanghai who had been arrested for an unspecified reason. After that he went to sleep.

He spent the following day in his cell, drafting his own testimony. The day was over soon and, before he could even realise it, it was already 10 February. On that day, Shi Yang drafted a petition on behalf of all inmates to demand better living conditions in the prison. At 1pm, he received a package with some food sent by his family and at 4pm they came to deliver clean clothes and to change bed sheets. In the evening, he wrote some letters and then he went to sleep.

We do not know how Shi Yang spent the following two days, which turned out to be his last on earth. His final thoughts are contained in the last page of his prison diary, dated 13 February. On that grey winter day, Shi Yang woke up at 7am, had breakfast, and then went back to lie down. Having nothing better to do, he picked up the pen and started writing the first few verses of a poem entitled 'The Joy of Prison':

> Everybody says that prison is suffering
> On the contrary, I am sitting here happy
> I have free food to fill my belly
> I have free food to cover myself.

We will never know whether Shi Yang planned to complete the poem. Two days later at dawn he was taken to the prison yard, where an officer put a bullet in his head. Although the trial was still under way, a telegram from Beijing had demanded his immediate execution. And orders from Beijing could not be questioned. ■

CONTRIBUTOR BIOS

AU Loong Yu

Au Loong Yu is a writer based in Hong Kong. His book *China Rise: Strength and Fragility* was published by Merlin Press in 2012.

David BANDURSKI

David Bandurski is Co-director of the China Media Project, an independent research and fellowship programme founded in 2004 at the University of Hong Kong's Journalism & Media Studies Centre. His research focuses on media policy and propaganda, the political discourse of the Chinese Communist Party, and trends in journalistic professionalism such as investigative reporting. David is the author of *Dragons in Diamond Village* (Penguin 2016), a book of reportage about urbanisation and social activism in China, and co-editor of *Investigative Journalism in China* (Hong Kong University Press 2010). He is currently a Richard von Weizsäcker Fellow at the Robert Bosch Academy in Berlin.

Jean-Philippe BÉJA

Jean-Philippe Béja is Emeritus Senior Research Fellow at the National Center for Scientific Research and the Center for International Studies and Research at Sciences-Po, Paris. He has worked for decades on relations between society and the Party in China, and has written extensively on intellectuals and on the pro-democracy movement in the People's Republic of China. He also works on Hong Kong politics. He edited *The Impact of China's 1989 Tiananmen Massacre* (Routledge, 2011), *Liu Xiaobo, La philosophie du porc et autres essais* (Gallimard, 2011), and *Liu Xiaobo, Charter 08 and the Challenges of Political Reform in China* (Hong Kong University Press, 2012, co-edited with Fu Hualing and Eva Pils).

Stefan BREHM

Stefan Brehm is a Researcher at the Centre for East and South-East Asian Studies, Lund University, and co-founder of Globalworks Lund AB, a start-up specialising in big data analytics for social and environmental governance (ESG). Stefan is an economist by training and has studied modern Chinese in Germany and Taiwan.

Sarah M. BROOKS

Sarah M. Brooks leads the programmatic and advocacy work of the International Service for Human Rights (ISHR) to support defenders in the Asian region (with particular focus on China) as well as defenders of migrant and refugee rights. Sarah also supports ISHR's work in corporate accountability and leads organisational change in digital security. She comments on her work, transnational feminism, and geopolitics on Twitter @sarahmcneer.

Chris King-Chi CHAN

Chris King-Chi Chan is an Associate Professor of Sociology at the Department of Social and Behavioural Sciences, City University of Hong Kong. He researches Chinese labour and civil society, and he is the author of *The Challenge of Labour in China: Strikes and the Changing Labour Regime in Global Factories* (Routledge 2010).

Julie Yujie CHEN

Julie Yujie Chen is a Lecturer in the School of Media, Communication, and Sociology at the University of Leicester. Chen studies digital labour and examines how technologies, cultural contexts, and existing socioeconomic structures impact on the experience of digital work from the workers' perspective. Her latest publication is *Super-sticky WeChat and Chinese Society* (Emerald Publishing Limited 2018).

Nellie CHU

Nellie Chu is Assistant Professor of Cultural Anthropology at Duke Kunshan University in Kunshan, China.

Tom CLIFF

Tom Cliff is an ARC Postdoctoral Fellow in the School of Culture, History, and Language at the Australian National University. Tom is currently investigating the role of the informal institutions of family and enterprise in responding to economic uncertainty and the ageing population in China. He has conducted long-term fieldwork in Xinjiang, and his book *Oil and Water: Being Han in Xinjiang* has been published by Chicago University Press in June 2016.

Geoffrey CROTHALL

Geoffrey Crothall is Communications Director at China Labour Bulletin (CLB). He has worked at CLB since 2007 and was the Beijing correspondent for the *South China Morning Post* from 1991 to 1996.

Daniele DAINELLI

Daniele Dainelli is a photographer from the Contrasto photo agency. He first gained international recognition with the work *Metropolis,* a series of color photographs depicting global metropolises. In 2001, he moved to New York, where he documented the changes in the wake of the 11 September tragedy. At the same time, he started a project about artists' communities, which went on to win the 2002 Canon Prize for best photographic project. In 2003, he joined 13 other Contrasto photographers in the *Eurogeneration* project, an initiative that documented youth lifestyles in 25 countries of the European Community, culminating in an exhibition at Palazzo Reale in Milan and a book. Since 2004, he has been based in Tokyo, where he has been pursuing long-term photographic projects between Japan and China.

Magnus FISKESJÖ

Magnus Fiskesjö was formerly on the staff of the Swedish Embassy in Tokyo and Beijing, and served as Director of Sweden's Museum of Far Eastern Antiquities. He currently teaches anthropology and Asian studies at Cornell University.

Eric FLORENCE

Eric Florence is Director of the French Centre for Research on Contemporary China (CEFC), Hong Kong, and Senior Researcher at the Centre for Ethnic and Migrations Studies, University of Liege.

Ivan FRANCESCHINI

Ivan Franceschini is a Postdoctoral Fellow at the Coral Bell School of Asia Pacific Affairs, The Australian National University. His research focuses on labour and civil society in China and Cambodia, but he is also interested in Chinese modern history and literature, as well as literary translation. He has published several books related to China, on topics ranging from human trafficking to digital activism, from labour struggles to civil society. With Tommaso Facchin, he is the co-director of the documentaries *Dreamwork China* (2011) and *Boramey* (forthcoming in 2019). Currently, he is researching the social impact of China's presence in Cambodia.

GAO Huan

Gao Huan is a PhD Candidate in the Department of Government, Harvard University. Her research focuses on emergency management, local governance, and civil society development in contemporary China.

Jane HAYWARD

Jane Hayward is a Research Fellow at the Department of Government, London School of Economics and Political Science, and former postdoctoral researcher at the Institute for Contemporary China Studies in the School of Public Policy and Management, Tsinghua University. Her work examines the social and political processes by which the Chinese state is becoming integrated into the global capitalist economy, focussing on China's peasant question, and related questions of urbanisation.

HUANG Yu

Huang Yu is a Postdoctoral Fellow in the Division of Social Science, Hong Kong University of Science and Technology. Her research interests include industrial automation and robotisation, science and technology studies, labour studies, agrarian change, and rural development in China.

Tamara JACKA

Tamara Jacka is Professor in the Department of Political and Social Change, in the College of Asia and the Pacific, the Australian National University. She is a feminist scholar with research interests in gender and rural-urban inequalities, rural-urban migration, and social change in China. She is the author of *Rural Women in Urban China: Gender, Migration, and Social Change* (ME Sharpe 2006), *Women, Gender and Rural Development in China* (co-authored with Sally Sargeson, Edward Elgar 2011) and *Contemporary China: Society and Social Change* (co-authored with Andrew Kipnis and Sally Sargeson, Cambridge University Press 2013). She is currently writing an historical ethnography, examining transformations in everyday practices in a village in the central Chinese province of Henan.

Thomas Sætre JAKOBSEN

Thomas Saetre Jakobsen works at the Department of Geography, Norwegian University of Science and Technology. He recently defended his PhD in Human Geography, where he focussed on the rural-urban mobility of work and aspirations among migrant labour in Southwestern China. In his research Thomas focuses on the uneven geographies of accumulation, agrarian transformations, social reproduction, and solidarity in China and beyond.

Hyejin KIM

Hyejin Kim teaches Political Science and Global Studies at the National University of Singapore. She is the author of the books *International Ethnic Networks and Intra-ethnic Conflict: Koreans in China* (Palgrave Macmillan 2010) and *Jia: A Novel of North Korea* (Cleis Press 2007). Her new book, about transnational education corporations and education policy in Asia, will come out in 2019.

Sabina LAWRENIUK

Sabina Lawreniuk is a Leverhulme Early Career Fellow at Royal Holloway, University of London. Her current research uses a feminist geopolitical approach to study the intersections of work, inequality, and activism, with a focus on the Cambodian garment sector.

LI Qiaochu

Li Qiaochu is a project coordinator at the Department of Sociology, Tsinghua University. Her research focuses on labour issues and civil society in contemporary China. She has been involved in the volunteer organisation and processing of assistance-related information following the Beijing evictions.

Kevin LIN

Kevin Lin is China Programme Officer at the International Labor Rights Forum. His research interests focus on labour and employment relations in China's state sector, and China's labour movement and civil society.

Johan LINDQUIST

Johan Lindquist is Professor of Social Anthropology and Director of the Forum for Asian Studies at Stockholm University in Sweden. He is the co-editor of *Figures of Southeast Asian Modernity* (University of Hawai'i Press 2013), the author of *The Anxieties of Mobility: Development and Migration in the Indonesian Borderlands* (University of Hawai'i Press 2009), and the director of B.A.T.A.M. (DER 2005).

KANG Yi

Kang Yi is an Assistant Professor of Government and International Studies at Hong Kong Baptist University. She received her PhD in Political Science from Yale University. Her research relates to the politics of non-democratic systems, civil society, and post-disaster management. She is author of *Disaster Management in China in a Changing Era* (Springer, 2015).

Nicholas LOUBERE

Nicholas Loubere is Associate Senior Lecturer at the Centre for East and South-East Asian Studies, Lund University. His research examines microcredit and digital finance in rural China, and Chinese migration to Africa for resource extraction.

Sverre MOLLAND

Sverre Molland is a Senior Lecturer in Anthropology at the Australian National University. His research examines the intersections between migration, development, and security in a comparative perspective, with specific focus on governance regimes and intervention modalities in mainland Southeast Asia. He has published extensively on human trafficking and labour migration in Southeast Asia and is the author of *The Perfect Business? Anti-Trafficking and the Sex Trade along the Mekong* (University of Hawaii Press 2012).

Elisa NESOSSI

Elisa Nesossi is an ARC Research Fellow at the Australian Centre on China in the World, the Australian National University. Her research focuses on the administration of criminal justice in places of detention in China and alleged abuses of power in the Chinese criminal justice system.

Mary Ann O'DONNELL

Mary Ann O'Donnell is an independent artist-ethnographer and co-founder of the Handshake 302 Art Space in Shenzhen. Since 2005, she has been blogging at Shenzhen Noted (shenzhennoted.com). With Winnie Wong and Jonathan Bach, she co-edited the volume *Learning from Shenzhen* (University of Chicago Press 2017).

Lynette H. ONG

Lynette H. Ong is an Associate Professor of Political Science at the Munk School of Global Affairs & Public Policy, University of Toronto. She is the author of *Prosper or Perish: Credit and Fiscal Systems in Rural China*, (Cornell University Press 2012). Her current research addresses state power and state control in China, in the area of urbanisation. Follow her on twitter: @onglynette.

Elisa OREGLIA

Elisa Oreglia is a lecturer in Global Digital Cultures at King's College London. She studies the circulation, adoption, and use of digital technologies in Asia, with a specific focus on China and Southeast Asia.

Andrea Enrico PIA

Andrea Enrico Pia is an Associate Professor in the Department of Anthropology, London School of Economics and Political Science. His work investigates the entanglements of political, legal, technical, and ethical issues with the appropriation, distribution, and circulation of common water sources in contemporary China. His interest lies in exploring questions of scarcity, human cooperation, and environmental justice. He also writes on sustainability, rural politics, and the Chinese State in comparative perspective.

Sarah ROGERS

Sarah Rogers is a Research Fellow at the University of Melbourne's Centre for Contemporary Chinese Studies. She is a geographer who studies hydropolitics, agrarian change, and poverty alleviation in central China.

Yvan SCHULZ

Yvan Schulz obtained his PhD from the Anthropology Institute, University of Neuchâtel in February 2018. He currently works as a postdoctoral researcher at the China Centre, University of Oxford. His research explores China's state project of ecological modernisation from the angle of e-waste reuse and recycling.

Suzanne SCOGGINS

Suzanne Scoggins is an Assistant Professor of Political Science at Clark University. Her research interests include policing, protest management, bureaucratic politics, rights consciousness, and authoritarian control in reform era China. Her book manuscript, *Policing in the Shadow of Protest*, looks at the police bureaucracy in China, and explores how different patterns of bureaucratic control over local police affect law enforcement personnel and local state security.

SONG Jiani

Song Jiani is a researcher at Beijing Yilian Legal Aid and Research Center of Labor, a local NGO committed to advancing labour rights and to improving labour law in China. Her research interests include internal migration, labour issues, and civil society in contemporary China.

Christian SORACE

Christian Sorace is an Assistant Professor of Political Science at Colorado College. He is the author of *Shaken Authority: China's Communist Party and the 2008 Sichuan Earthquake* (Cornell University Press 2017). He is currently conducting research on the urbanisation of the grasslands in Inner Mongolia, China, and *ger* districts in Ulaanbaatar, Mongolia.

SUN Taiyi

Sun Taiyi is an Assistant Professor of political science at Christopher Newport University. His interests focus on disaster politics, civil society, and the dynamics of state-society relations. His current research deals primarily with the development of the public sphere and the accumulation of social capital after disasters.

Wanning SUN

Wanning Sun is Professor of Media Studies at the University of Technology Sydney. She has conducted ethnographic research about the lives of China's rural migrants over the past 15 years. Her latest book on this topic is *Subaltern China: Rural Migrants, Media, and Cultural Practices* (Rowman & Littlefield 2014). She is currently completing a monograph on how inequality impacts on rural migrants' experience with love and intimacy.

Marina SVENSSON

Marina Svensson is Director of the Centre for East and South-East Asian Studies at Lund University. Her main fields of research include: human rights debates; legal developments and struggles; cultural heritage issues; investigative journalism, journalism cultures, and China's media ecology; documentary film and visual cultures; and China's digital society.

Bin XU

Bin Xu is an Assistant Professor in the Department of Sociology at Emory University. His research focuses on how an authoritarian state interacts with a burgeoning civil society and on collective memory. His latest book is *The Politics of Compassion: the Sichuan Earthquake and Civic Engagement in China* (Stanford University Press 2017).

YU Chunsen

Yu Chunsen is an early career researcher, studying rural migrants' employment and social security within the Chinese hi-tech processing and assembly manufacturing industry in Chongqing and Shenzhen. He was awarded a PhD in Chinese Studies Research and an MA both from King's College London in the United Kingdom.

ZHANG Lu

Zhang Lu is an Associate Professor of Sociology and Global Studies at Temple University. Her research concentrates on labour and labour movements, globalisation, development, and the political economy of China. She is the author of the award-winning book, *Inside China's Automobile Factories: The Politics of Labor and Worker Resistance* (Cambridge University Press 2015).

ZHANG Shuchi

Zhang Shuchi is a researcher and practitioner at Beijing Yilian Legal Aid and Research Center of Labor, a labour NGO in the Chinese capital. He is currently reading a masters in International Human Rights Law at the University of Essex.

ZHANG Yueran

Zhang Yueran is a doctoral student in sociology at the University of California-Berkeley. His research focuses on political economy, (de mobilisations, and the interaction between states and class forces in the Global South. He has also been involved in labour and left organising both in China and the United States.

John Aloysius ZINDA

John Aloysius Zinda is Assistant Professor of Development Sociology at Cornell University. He studies how people respond to environmental and developmental interventions, and the consequences for social and ecological change, with a focus on land management in China.

Mimi ZOU

Mimi Zou is the inaugural Fangda Career Development Fellow in Chinese Commercial Law at the University of Oxford. She obtained her law doctorate and master's degrees with distinction from Oxford. Her extensive publications in the area of employment law have received international recognition, including being awarded the International Association of Labour Law Journals Marco Biagi Prize in 2016.

BIBLIOGRAPHY

ANYBODY OUT THERE? THE CHINESE LABOUR MOVEMENT UNDER XI

Changes and Continuity: Four Decades of Industrial Relations in China (CHRIS KING-CHI CHAN)

Caixin. 2017. 'Guangdong zuidi gongzi biaozhun gaiwei "sannian yitiao" [The Minimum Wage in Guangdong Transformed to Adjustment in Every Three Years].' *Caixin,* 4 March. china.caixin.com/2017- 03- 04/101062231.html.

Chan, Anita. 2018. 'The Relationship between Labour NGOs and Chinese Workers in an Authoritarian Regime.' *Global Labour Journal* 9, no. 1: 1–18.

Chan, Chris King-Chi. 2012. 'Class or Citizenship? Debating Workplace Conflict in China.' *Journal of Contemporary Asia* 42, no. 2: 308–27.

Chan, Chris King-Chi. 2010. *The Challenge of Labour in China: Strikes and the Changing Labour Regime in Global Factories.* London: Routledge.

Chan, Chris King-Chi, and Elaine Sio-Ieng Hui. 2017. 'Bringing Class Struggles Back: A Marxian Analysis of the State and Class Relations in China.' *Globalizations* 14, no. 2: 232–44.

Chan, Chris King-Chi, and Elaine Sio-Ieng Hui. 2014. 'The Development of Collective Bargaining in China: From "Collective Bargaining by Riot" to "Party State-led Wage Bargaining".' *The China Quarterly* 217: 221–42.

Chen, Jay Chih-Jou. 2015. 'Zhongguo weiquan zhengtixia de jiti kangyi: taizichang dabagong de anli fenxi [Popular Protest in an Authoritarian Regime: A Wildcat Strike in Southern China].' *Taiwanese Sociology* 30: 1–53.

China Labour Bulletin. 2016. 'As China's Economy Shifts to Services in Q3, So Too Does Labour Unrest.' *China Labour Bulletin,* 21 October. www.clb.org.hk/content/china's-economy-shifts-services-q3-so-too-does-labour-unrest.

Chuang. 2018. '"The Mastermind": A Third Young Leftist Speaks Out on the November 15th Incident.' *Chuang,* 20 January. chuangcn.org/2018/01/the-mastermind.

Dou, Xuewei. 2017. 'Local Trade Union Reform in Shenzhen: Practice and Experience.' Paper presented at the international workshop 'Labour in Rising Powers: China in Comparison with India and Brazil,' held at the City University of Hong Kong on 15 and 16 September.

Duan, Yi. 2015. 'Gongyunxing laogong NGO de qianjing yu tiaozhan [Prospects and challenges for labour NGOs of the labour movement type].' *Gongmin*, 20 May. xgmyd.com/archives/17927.

Froissart, Chloé. 2018. 'Negotiating Authoritarianism and Its Limits: Worker-led Collective Bargaining in Guangdong Province.' *China Information* 32, no. 1: 23–45.

Lee, Ching Kwan. 2007. *Against the Law: Labor Protests in China's Rustbelt and Sunbelt*. Berkeley: University of California Press.

Lee, Ching Kwan. 1998. *Gender and the South China Miracle: Two Worlds of Factory Women*. Berkeley: University of California Press.

Mitchell, Tom. 2015. 'End of China's Migrant Miracle: Toil and Trouble.' *Financial Times*, 7 June. www.ft.com/content/dc3db3e4-fef9-11e4-94c8-00144feabdc0.

National Bureau of Statistics of China. 2017. *Zhongguo tongji nianjian 2016* [China Statistical Yearbook 2016]. Beijing: Zhongguo Tongji Chubanshe.

National Bureau of Statistics of China. 2013. *Zhongguo tongji nianjian 2012* [China Statistical Yearbook 2012]. Beijing: Zhongguo Tongji Chubanshe.

National Bureau of Statistics of China. 2011. *Zhongguo tongji nianjian 2010* [China Statistical Yearbook 2010]. Beijing: Zhongguo Tongji Chubanshe.

Pun, Ngai. 2005. *Made in China: Women Factory Workers in a Global Workplace*. Durham, NC, and Hong Kong: Duke University Press and Hong Kong University Press.

Siu, Kaxton. 2018. 'From Dormitory System to Conciliatory Despotism: Changing Labour Regimes in Chinese Factories.' In *Made in China Yearbook 2017: Gilded Age*, edited by Ivan Franceschini and Nicholas Loubere, 48–51. Canberra: ANU Press.

Yin, Han. 2018. 'Chinese Crane Operators Protest for Better Pay, Working Conditions.' *Global Times*, 1 May. www.globaltimes.cn/content/1100323.shtml.

China's Labour Movement in Transition (GEOFFREY CROTHALL)

China Labour Bulletin. 2017a. 'China's Walmart Workers: Creating an Opportunity for Genuine Trade Unionism.' *China Labour Bulletin*. www.clb.org.hk/sites/default/files/Walmart%20report%20Final.pdf.

China Labour Bulletin. 2017b. 'Why Has There Been a Drastic Reduction in Worker Protests in Dongguan?' *China Labour Bulletin*, 28 September. www.clb.org.hk/content/why-has-there-been-drastic-reduction-worker-protests-dongguan.

China Labour Bulletin. 2016a. 'Labour Activist Meng Han Sentenced to 21 Months.' *China Labour Bulletin*, 4 November. www.clb.org.hk/content/labour-activist-meng-han-sentenced-21-months.

China Labour Bulletin. 2016b. 'What Happens When the Boss Actually Abides by the Law during a Factory Closure in China?' *China Labour Bulletin*, 1 February. www.clb.org.hk/en/content/what-happens-when-boss-actually-abides-law-during-factory-closure-china.

China Labour Bulletin. 2015. 'The Lide Shoe Factory Workers' Campaign for Relocation Compensation.' *China Labour Bulletin*, 22 June. www.clb.org.hk/en/content/trying-hit-moving-target-lide-shoe-factory-workers-campaign-relocation-compensation.

China Labour Bulletin. 2014a. 'Unity Is Strength: The Story of the Guangzhou University Town Sanitation Workers' Strike.' *China Labour Bulletin*, 16 October. www.clb.org.hk/en/content/unity-strength-story-guangzhou-university-town-sanitation-workers-strike.

China Labour Bulletin. 2014b. 'Taking a Stand: Trade Union Chairman Fights Back against Walmart.' *China Labour Bulletin*, 24 June. www.clb.org.hk/en/content/taking-stand-trade-union-chairman-fights-back-against-walmart.

Feng, Emily. 2017. 'China's Laid-off Workers Pose Daunting Welfare Challenge.' *Financial Times*, 16 November. www.ft.com/content/de33f222-af09-11e7-aab9-abaa44b1e130.

Tu, Chonghang. 2015. 'Dongguan 'qiye daobichao' beihou de zhuanxing zhentong [The Transformation Pain behind Dongguan's Wave of Factory Closures].' *Beijing News*, 25 November. www.xinhuanet.com/info/2015-11/25/c_134852198.htm.

Zhao, Yinan. 2015. 'Premier Meets with Group of Innovators over Coffee.' *China Daily*, 8 May. www.chinadaily.com.cn/china/2015-05/08/content_20654522.htm.

Gongyou: The New Dangerous Class in China? (YU CHUNSEN)

China Labour Bulletin. 2010. 'Bentian gongren bagong yaoqiu tigao jiben gongzi [Honda Workers Go on Strike and Request to Increase Basic Salary].' *China Labour Bulletin*, 19 November. www.clb.org.hk/content/本田工人罢工要求提高基本工资.

China News Weekly. 2010. 'Nanhai bentian fugong gongren qude jubuxing shengli [Workers of Nanhai Honda Return to Work: Workers Have Achieved Part of Success].' *China News Weekly*, 3 June. style.sina.com.cn/news/2010-06-03/094562469.shtml.

Friedman, Eli. 2012. 'China in Revolt.' *Jacobin*, 8 January. www.jacobinmag.com/2012/08/china-in-revolt.

Hurst, William. 2017. 'The Chinese Working Class: Made, Unmade, In Itself, For Itself, or None of the Above?' In *Made in China Yearbook 2016: Disturbances in Heaven*, edited by Ivan Franceschini, Kevin Lin, and Nicholas Loubere, 16–19. Canberra: ANU Press.

Lau, Mimi, and Will Clem. 2010. 'Hundreds Clash as Labour Strife Widens.' *South China Morning Post*, 9 June. www.scmp.com/article/716586/hundreds-clash-labour-strife-widens.

Lee, Ching Kwan. 2007. *Against the Law: Labour Protests in China's Rustbelt and Sunbelt*. Berkeley: University of California Press.

Lu, Xun. 1927. *Zai Zhonglou Shang* [On the Clock Tower]. www.marxists.org/chinese/reference-books/luxun/12/033.htm.

Lü, Tu. 2013. *Zhongguo xingongren: mishi yu jueqi* [Chinese New Workers: Lost and Rise]. Beijing: Legal Publishing House.

Lü, Tu. 2015. *Zhongguo xingongren: wenhua yu mingyun* [Chinese New Workers: Culture and Destiny]. Beijing: Legal Publishing House.

New Taipei City Government. 2014. 'Xinbei shizhengfu gongyou gongzuo guize [New Taipei City Government on Workers' Working Regulations].' New Taipei City Government Secretariat, 26 May. 新北市政府工友工作規則 (103/05/26修訂))(PDF格式).

Owens, Timothy J., Dawn T. Robinson, and Lynn Smith-Lovin. 2010. 'Three Faces of Identity.' *Annual Review of Sociology* 36: 477–99.

Pun, Ngai, and Chris King-Chi Chan. 2008. 'The Subsumption of Class Discourse in China.' *Boundary 2* 35, no. 2: 75–91.

Pun, Ngai, and Huilin Lu. 2010. 'Unfinished Proletarianisation: Self, Anger, and Class Action among the Second Generation of Peasant-workers in Present-day China.' *Modern China* 36, no. 5: 493–519.

SFTU (Shandong Federation of Trade Unions). 2006. 'Shandongsheng zonggonghui guanyu gongyou chuangye xingdong de shishi yijian [Shandong Federation of Trade Unions about the Opinions of Implementation of Workers' Actions of Entrepreneurship].' Jining Trade Union Federation, 29 May. www.jngh.org/a/bangfubaozhang/ghjy/2013/0529/1422.html.

Smith, Chris, and Ngai Pun. 2017. 'Class and Precarity in China: A Contested Relationship.' In *Made in China Yearbook 2017: Gilded Age,* edited by Ivan Franceschini and Nicholas Loubere, 44–47. Canberra: ANU Press.

Standing, Guy. 2016. 'The Precariat, Class and Progressive Politics: A Response.' *Global Labour Journal* 7, no. 2: 189–200.

Swider, Sarah. 2015. *Building China: Informal Work and the New Precariat*. New York: Cornell University Press.

The Economic Observer. 2010. '"Bagong" you name kepa, kezeng ma? [Is the Strike so Horrible and Hateful?].' *The Economic Observer*, 1 July. www.eeo.com.cn/observer/shijiao/2010/07/01/174266.shtml.

Wang, Tongxin, and Hongli Wang. 2013. 'Shenzhen xinshengdai nongmingong de zongti zhuangkuang [Shenzhen New-generation Rural Migrant Workers' General Situations].' In *Shenzhen xinshengdai nongmingong diaocha baogao*, edited by Tongxin Wang and Yujuan Zhai, 34–68. Beijing: China Legal Publishing House.

Woronov, Terry. 2015. *Class Work: Vocational Schools and China's Urban Youth*. Stanford, CA: Stanford University Press.

Xie, Jianshe. 2005. *Xinchanye gongren jieceng: shehui zhuanxingzhong de nongmingong* [New Industrial Workers: Rural Migrant Workers within Social Transformation]. Beijing: Social Sciences Academic Press.

Yang, Chunhua. 2010. 'On the Issue of the New Generation of Migrant Workers.' *Issues in Agricultural Economy* 4: 80–84.

Yang, Shuo. 1950. *Yalujiang nanbei* [North and South of the Yalu River]. www.people.com.cn/GB/channel1/10/20001010/265308.html.

Ye, Shengtao. 1925. *Zai minjian* [Among the People]. www.zgwxmz.com/m/xiandaiwenxue/051010052016/1017.html.

The Struggles of Temporary Agency Workers in Xi's China (ZHANG LU)

All-China Federation of Trade Unions. 2012. 'Laowu paiqian diaoyan baogao: Dangqian woguo laowu paiqian yonggong xiankuang diaocha [Report on Labor Dispatch: Surveys on the Current Use of Labour Dispatch in China].' ACFTU Internal Report, Beijing.

China Labour Bulletin. 2017a. 'Hundreds of Volkswagen workers in northeast China demand equal pay.' *China Labour Bulletin*, 27 February. www.clb.org.hk/content/hundreds-volkswagen-workers-northeast-china-demand-equal-pay.

China Labour Bulletin. 2017b. 'Volkswagen worker representatives arrested at Changchun plant.' *China Labour Bulletin*, 6 June. www.clb.org.hk/content/volkswagen-worker-representatives-arrested-changchun-plant.

China Labour Bulletin. 2017c. 'Chinese Volkswagen workers call on German parent company to assume responsibility for violations.' *China Labour Bulletin*, 13 July. www.clb.org.hk/content/chinese-volkswagen-workers-call-german-parent-company-assume-responsibility-violation.

Gonos, George 1997. 'The Contest Over 'Employer' Status in the Postwar United States: The Case of Temporary Help Firms.' *Law & Society Review* 31, no. 1: 81–110.

Peng, Wenzhuo. 2016. 'Meiti xi lanyong laowu paiqian nan genzhi [Why Is It Difficult to Cure the Abusive Use of Labour Dispatching?].' *Worker's Daily*, 5 January 2016, 5.

Pringle, Tim. 2016. 'A Class against Capital: Class and Collective Bargaining in Guangdong.' *Globalizations* 14, no. 2: 245–58.

Ruckus, Ralf. 2018. 'VW workers in China and elsewhere in struggle while the company starts historic transformation.' Preface to the German translation of Lu Zhang, *Inside China's Automobile Factories: The Politics of Labor and Worker Resistance* (Cambridge 2015), Mandelbaum.

Vosko, Leah F. 2010. *Managing the Margins: Gender, Citizenship and the International Regulation of Precarious Employment*. New York: Oxford University Press.

Wong, Chun Han. 2016. 'China's Slowing Growth Forces Rethink on Worker Protections.' *Wall Street Journal*, 29 November. www.wsj.com/articles/china-looks-to-loosen-job-security-law-in-face-of-slowing-economic-growth-1480415405.

Xia, Nü. 2018. 'Has the Workers' Protest at FAW-VW Ended?' *Gongchao*, 15 January. www.gongchao.org/2018/01/15/has-the-workers-protest-at-faw-vw-ended.

Zhang, Lu. 2015. *Inside China's Automobile Factories: The Politics of Labor and Worker Resistance*. New York: Cambridge University Press.

Robot Threat or Robot Dividend? A Struggle between Two Lines (HUANG YU)

Acemoglu, Daron, and Pascual Restrepo. 2017. 'Robots and Jobs: Evidence from US Labour Markets.' *NBER Working Paper No. 23285*. www.nber.org/papers/w23285.pdf.

Braverman, Harry. 1988. *Labour and Monopoly Capital: The Degradation of Work in the Twentieth Century*. New York: Monthly Review Press.

Butollo, Florian, and Boy Lüthje. 2017. '"Made in China 2025": Intelligent Manufacturing and Work.' In *The New Digital Workplace: How New Technologies Revolutionise Work*, edited by Kendra Briken, Shiona Chillas, and Martin Krzywdzinski, 42–61. London: Palgrave.

Chen, Li-Kai, Mona Mourshed, and Andrew Grant. 2013. 'The $250 Billion Question: Can China Close the Skills Gap?' *Mckinsey and Company*. www.mckinsey.com/~/media/mckinsey/industries/social%20sector/our%20insights/the%20250%20billion%20question%20can%20china%20close%20the%20skills%20gap/the%20dollar%20250%20billion%20question%20can%20china%20close%20the%20skills%20gap.ashx.

Guo, Rui. 2016. 'Jiqi shengji shi Dongguan gongren daliang shiye 90 hou nongmingong cheng qiantu juewang [Machine Upgrading Results in Massive Unemployment in Dongguan, Post-90s Migrant Workers Say They Are Hopeless].' *Phoenix Net*, 29 February. news.ifeng.com/a/20160229/47626474_0.shtml.

Huang, Yinchuan, and Peng Fu. 2017. '"Jiqi dairen" de chengben jingsuan [The Cost Breakdown of "Machines Replacing Humans"].' *Nanfang Daily*, 24 July. epaper.southcn.com/nfdaily/html/2017-07/24/content_7655509.htm.

Huang, Yu, and Naubahar Sharif. 2017. 'From "Labor Dividend" to "Robot Dividend": Technological Change and Workers' Power in South China.' *Agrarian South: Journal of Political Economy* 6, no. 1: 53–78.

IFR (International Federation of Robotics). 2018. 'Robot Density Rises Globally.' *International Federation of Robotics*, 7 February. ifr.org/ifr-press-releases/news/robot-density-rises-globally.

IFR (International Federation of Robotics). 2017. 'Robots: China Breaks Historic Records in Automation.' *International Federation of Robotics*, 16 August. ifr.org/ifr-press-releases/news/robots-china-breaks-historic-records-in-automation.

Jianxiaojiao. 2017. 'Nanian huakai fangzhi gongren yin shiye za jiqi, jiqi huanren li women haiyou duoyuan? [In 'Nothing Gold Can Stay' Textile Workers Smash Machines, How Far is Robotization Away from Us?].' *Jianjiao Buluo*, 9 October. www.jianjiaobuluo.com/content/10789.

Jin, Lu. 2017. 'Zidonghua qudaile 80 wan ming gongren que chuangzaochu 350 wan ge xingongzuo [Automation Replaces 800,000 Workers But Creates 3.5 Million New Jobs].' *Tencent Technology*, 8 September. tech.qq.com/a/20170908/019354.htm.

Klorer, Elena, and Matthias Stepan. 2015. 'Off Target: China's Vocational Education and Training System Threatens the Country's Rise to Industrial Superpower Status.' Mercator Institute for China Studies, 2 October. www.merics.org/fileadmin/templates/download/china-monitor/China_Monitor_No_24_EN.pdf.

Kwong, Robin. 2012. 'Terry Gou: Managing "1m Animals".' *Financial Times*, 20 January. next.ft.com/content/be3d2550-f9e6-34c0-91fb-afd639d3e750.

Liu, Chenchen. 2014. 'Reporting from Beijing: China Announces Modern Vocational Education Development Strategy 2014–2020'. Embassy of Switzerland in China, 29 July. www.sinoptic.ch/textes/education/2014/20140729_Ambassade.de.Suisse_Apprentissage.en.Chine-en.pdf.

Ministry of Agriculture. 2018. '2016 nian nongcun jiating chengbao gengdi liuzhuan ji jiufen tiaochu qingkuang [Information on the Transfer of Family Contract Land and Dispute Mitigation].' Ministry of Agriculture and Rural Affairs, 5 January. jiuban.moa.gov.cn/zwllm/tzgg/tz/201710/t20171017_5842411.htm.

Ministry of Industry and Information Technology. 2017. 'Sanbuwei guanyu yinfa "zhizaoye rencai fazhan guihua zhinan" de tongzhi [Announcement on the Three Ministries Issuing The Development Planning Guidelines for Manufacturing Talents].' Ministry of Industry and Information Technology, 24 February. www.miit.gov.cn/n1146295/n1652858/n1652930/n3757016/c5500114/content.html.

Morris-Suzuki, Tessa. 1988. *Beyond Computopia: Information, Automation and Democracy in Japan*. New York: Routledge.

Noble, David Franklin. 1979. 'Social Choice in Machine Design: The Case of Automatically Controlled Machine Tools, and a Challenge for Labour.' *Politics and Society* 8, no. 3–4: 313–47.

Pun, Ngai, and Jenny Chan. 2012. 'Global Capital, the State, and Chinese Workers: The Foxconn Experience.' *Modern China* 38, no. 4: 383–410.

Sharif, Naubahar, and Yu Huang. 2019. 'Industrial Automation in China's "Workshop of the World".' *The China Journal* 81, 1–22.

Tian, Aili, and Hui Cai. 2018. 'Yige jiqiren chuangzao 3.6 ge gangwei, AI chanyehua chuangzao wuda jiuye xinfangxiang [One Robot Creates 3.6 Jobs, The AI Industry Forges Five New Directions of Employment].' *Southern Metropolis Daily*, 25 January. epaper.oeeee.com/epaper/D/html/2018-01/25/content_5844.htm.

Trobe, Frank. 2016. 'Collaborative Robots Are Broadening Their Marketplaces.' *The Robot Report*, 4 March. www.therobotreport.com/collaborative-robots-are-broadening-their-marketplaces.

Worker Empowerment. 2017. 'Diaocha baogao: fuwuye gongren laodong zhuangkuang diaocha baogaoji [Research Report on the Labor Condition of Service Industry Workers].' *Worker Empowerment*, 17 August. www.workerempowerment.org/zh/%E8%AA%BF%E6%9F%A5%E5%A0%B1%E5%91%8A/384.

Writing Group for 'Socialist Political Economy'. 1976. *Socialist Political Economy* (Unpublished). Shanghai.

Wuhua. 2017. 'Rengong zhineng keneng hui rang ni shiye, danshi buhui rang renlei shiye [Artificial Intelligence Might Make You Unemployed, But Won't Let Human Beings Unemployed].' *Welle Studio*, 5 May. www.douban.com/note/618928476.

Xia, Licheng. 2018. '2020 nian, rengong zhineng jiang chuangzao gengduo de jiuye jihui, ye hui you gengduo de ren shiqu gongzuo [By 2020, AI Will Create More Job Opportunities, But Will Also Cause More Unemployment].' *Sohu*, 14 May. www.sohu.com/a/231500788_100101980.

Xing, Lijian. 2016. "Bei jiqi huanxialai de yuangong jixu tongchou anzhi [It Is Necessary to Coordinate the Arrangement of Workers Displaced by Machines]." *Beijing Youth Daily*, 27 May. www.xinhuanet.com/2016-05/27/c_1118940767.htm.

Xinhua. 2005. '"Jiqi huanren" de xi yu you: Guangdong Gongguan shoujia "wuren gongchang" dundian diaocha [The Joy and Concerns Regarding the "Replacing Humans with Machines": Investigation on the First "Workerless Factory" in Dongguan, Guangdong].' *Xinhua*, 31 July. news.xinhuanet.com/fortune/2015-07/13/c_1115909116.htm.

Yoshino, Jiro. 2017. 'China Emerging as a Service Robot Powerhouse.' *Nikkei*, 5 September. asia.nikkei.com/Tech-Science/Tech/China-emerging-as-a-service-robot-powerhouse.

Zheng, Bin. 2017. 'Jiuye "shashou" haishi "zhushou" [Job "Killer" or "Helper"].' *Economy Daily*, 15 August. paper.ce.cn/jjrb/html/2017-08/15/content_341586.htm.

Zhou, Jianping, and Chenyue Jiang. 2016. '"Jiqi huanren" dachao xia de gongren: youren shengji, youren cheng kan budao xiwang [Workers in the Wave of "Machines Replacing Human Labor": Some Get Upgrading, Some Claim Hopeless].' *The Paper*, 24 September. www.thepaper.cn/newsDetail_forward_1533577.

Zuo, Mandy. 2016. 'Rise of the Robots: 60,000 Workers Culled from Just One Factory as China's Struggling Electronics Hub Turns to Artificial Intelligence.' *South China Morning Post*, 21 May. www.scmp.com/news/china/economy/article/1949918/rise-robots-60000-workers-culled-just-one-factory-chinas.

A 'Pessoptimistic' View of Labour NGOs (IVAN FRANCESCHINI AND KEVIN LIN)

Chan, Anita. 2018. 'The Relationship between Labour NGOs and Chinese Workers in an Authoritarian Regime.' *Global Labour Journal* 9, no. 1: 1–18.

Chan, Chris King-Chi. 2018. 'The Future of Labour NGOs: A Response to Two Mindsets.' *Hong Kong Confederation of Trade Unions*. en.hkctu.org.hk/mainland-china/position-and-analysis/the-future-of-labour-ngos-a-response-to-two-mindsets.

Chan, Chris King-Chi. 2013. 'Community-based Organizations for Migrant Workers' Rights: The Emergence of Labour NGOs in China.' *Community Development Journal* 48, no. 1: 6–22.

Chen, Feng, and Xuehui Yang. 2017. 'Movement-oriented Labour NGOs in South China: Exit with Voice and Displaced Unionism.' *China Information* 31, no. 1: 155–75.

Chen, Jay Chih-Jou. 2015. 'Zhongguo weiquan zhengtixia de jiti kangyi: taizichang dabagong de anli fenxi [Popular Protest in an Authoritarian Regime: A Wildcat Strike in Southern China].' *Taiwanese Sociology* 30: 1–53.

Duan, Yi. 2015. 'Gongyunxing laogong NGO de qianjing yu tiaozhan [Prospects and challenges for labour NGOs of the labour movement type].' *Gongmin*, 20 May. xgmyd.com/archives/17927.

Franceschini, Ivan. 2014. 'Labour NGOs in China: A Real Force for Political Change?' *The China Quarterly* 218: 474–92.

Franceschini, Ivan and Elisa Nesossi. 2018. 'State Repression of Chinese Labor NGOs: A Chilling Effect?' *The China Journal* 80: 111–29.

Franceschini, Ivan and Elisa Nesossi. 2017. 'The Foreign NGOs Management Law: A Compendium.' In *Made in China Yearbook 2016: Disturbances in Heaven*, edited by Ivan Franceschini, Kevin Lin, and Nicholas Loubere, 60–67. Canberra: ANU Press.

Friedman, Eli. 2018. 'Collective Bargaining in China is Dead: The Situation is Excellent.' In *Made in China Yearbook 2017: Gilded Age*, edited by Ivan Franceschini and Nicholas Loubere, 56–59. Canberra: ANU Press.

Froissart, Chloé. 2018. 'Negotiating Authoritarianism and Its Limits: Worker-led Collective Bargaining in Guangdong Province.' *China Information* 32, no. 1: 23–45.

Froissart, Chloé. 2005. 'The Rise of Social Movements among Migrant Workers: Uncertain Strivings for Autonomy.' *China Perspectives* 61. journals.openedition.org/chinaperspectives/526.

Fu, Diana. 2017a. 'Fragmented Control: Governing Contentious Labor Organizations in China.' *Governance: An International Journal of Policy, Administration and Institutions* 30, no. 3: 445–62.

Fu, Diana. 2017b. 'Disguised Collective Action in China.' *Comparative Political Studies* 50, no. 4: 499–527.

Gramsci, Antonio. 1963. *Lettere dal carcere*. Torino: Einaudi.

Howell, Jude. 2008. 'Civil Society and Migrants in China.' In *Migrant Labour and Social Development in Contemporary China*, edited by Rachel Murphy, 171–94. London: Routledge.

Lee, Ching Kwan. 2016. 'Precarization or Empowerment? Reflections on Recent Labour Unrest in China.' *Journal of Asian Studies* 75, no. 2: 317–33.

Lee, Ching Kwan, and Yuan Shen. 2011. 'The Anti-Solidarity Machine? Labor Nongovernmental Organizations in China.' In *From Iron Rice Bowl to Informalization*, edited by Sarosh Kuruvilla, Ching Kwan Lee, and Mary E. Gallagher, 173–87. Ithaca and London: Cornell University Press.

Pun, Ngai, and Wai Ling Chan. 2004. 'Community Based Labour Organizing.' *International Union Rights* 11, no. 4: 10–11.

Xu, Yi. 2013. 'Labor Non-governmental Organizations in China: Mobilizing Rural Migrant Workers.' *Journal of Industrial Relations* 55, no. 2: 243–59.

The Jasic Mobilisation: A High Tide for the Chinese Labour Movement? (AU LOONG YU)

HRIC (Human Rights in China). 2018. 'HRIC Urges International Attention on 32 Jasic Workers and Supporters Detained, Disappeared.' *Human Rights in China*, 7 December. www.hrichina.org/en/press-work/hric-bulletin/hric-urges-international-attention-32-jasic-workers-and-supporters-detained.

Li, Mingqi. 2016. *China and the 21st Century Crisis*. London: Pluto Press.

Luo, Chong. 2018. 'Jinggangshan jin he zai? [Where Has Jinggangshan Gone?].' *RedChinaCn.net*, 4 August. redchinacn.net/portal.php?mod=view&aid=36329.

Pun, Ngai. 2018. 'Guandian: Shenzhen jia shi gongren weiquan de liang da yiyi [Opinion: The Two Significant Aspects of Jiashi Workers' Rights Protection].' *BBC*, 17 September. www.bbc.com/zhongwen/simp/45217517.

Wu, Jingtang. 2018. 'Benfu shenzhen pingshan! Weile gongrenjieji de juexing, weile Mao zhuxi! [Rush to Shenzhen Pingshan! For the Sake of Working Class Awakening, for the Sake of Chairman Mao!].' *Shidai Xianfeng*, date not found. www.shidaixianfeng.tk/archives/12887.

TO THE SOIL: THE LABOUR OF RURAL TRANSFORMATION IN CHINA

China's Land Reforms and the Logic of Capital Accumulation (JANE HAYWARD)

Bray, David. 2013. 'Urban Planning Goes Rural: Conceptualising the "New Village".' *China Perspectives*, no. 3: 53–62.

Chen, Meiqiu, and Wenna Ma. 2012. 'Chengxiang jianshe yongdi zengjian guagou zhong nongmin liyi baozhang duice yanjiu— jiyu Jiangxi sheng "zengjianguagou" shidian nongmin liyi baozhan zhuanti yanjiu [System for Linking Increases in Urban Construction Land-use to Decreases in Rural Construction Land-use—A Specialist Study of Peasant Interest Guarantees in the "Increase-decrease Linking System" Pilot Programme of Jiangxi Province].' *Zhongguo tudi kexue* 26, no. 10: 9–14.

Cui, Hongzhi, and Cuifen Sun. 2014. 'Xinxing nongcun shequ jianshe: fangshi, xiaoguo, wenti ji zhengce tiaozheng—yi Henan wei li [New Rural Community Construction: Methods, Effects, Problems, and Policy Adjustments—Taking Henan as an Example].' *Rural Economy*, no. 3: 9–13.

Cui, Zhiyuan. 2011. 'Partial Intimations of the Coming Whole: The Chongqing Experiment in Light of the Theories of Henry George, James Meade, and Antonio Gramsci.' *Modern China* 37, no. 6: 646–60.

Gong, Weigang, and Qian Forrest Zhang. 2017. 'Betting on the Big: State-brokered Land Transfers, Large-scale Agricultural Producers, and Rural Policy Implementation.' *The China Journal*, no. 77: 1–26.

Hayward, Jane. 2017. 'Beyond the Ownership Question: Who Will Till the Land? The New Debate on China's Agricultural Production.' *Critical Asian Studies* 49, no. 4: 523–45.

Rosenberg, Lior. 2013. 'Urbanising the Rural: Local Strategies for Creating "New Style" Rural Communities in China.' *China Perspectives*, no. 3: 63–71.

Zhan, Shaohua. 2017. '*Hukou* Reform and Land Politics in China: The Rise of a Tripartite Alliance.' *The China Journal*, no. 78: 25–49.

Manufactured Modernity: Dwelling, Labour, and Enclosure in China's Poverty Resettlements (SARAH ROGERS)

Chuang, Julia. 2015. 'Urbanization Through Dispossession: Survival and Stratification in China's New Townships.' *Journal of Peasant Studies* 42, no. 2: 275–94.

Ingold, Tim. 2011. *The Perception of the Environment: Essays on Livelihood, Dwelling and Skill*. London: Routledge.

National Development and Reform Commission. 2016. 'Quanguo "shisanwu" yi di fupin banqian guihua [National "13th Five" Year Plan Poverty Resettlement Plan].' www.ndrc.gov.cn/zcfb/zcfbtz/201610/t20161031_824886.html.

Managing the Anthropocene: The Labour of Environmental Regeneration (JOHN ALOYSIUS ZINDA)

Cao, Jianjun, Emily T. Yeh, Nicholas M. Holden, Yanyan Qin, and Zhengwei Ren. 2013. 'The Roles of Overgrazing, Climate Change and Policy as Drivers of Degradation in China's Grasslands.' *Nomadic Peoples* 17, no. 2: 82–101.

Geall, Sam. 2015. 'Interpreting Ecological Civilisation.' *China Dialogue*, 7 June. www.chinadialogue.net/article/show/single/en/8018-Ecological-civilisation-vision-for-a-greener-China-part-one-.

Hilton, Isabel. 2013. 'The Environment in China and the Return of Civil Society.' *The China Story*, 14 April. www.thechinastory.org/2013/04/the-environment-in-china-and-the-return-of-civil-society/.

Standaert, Michael. 2017. 'As It Looks to Go Green, China Keeps a Tight Lid on Dissent.' *Yale Environment 360*, 2 November. e360.yale.edu/features/as-it-looks-to-go-green-china-keeps-a-tight-lid-on-dissent.

Urgenson, Lauren, Amanda H. Schmidt, Julie Combs, Stevan Harrell, Thomas Hinckley, Qingxia Yang, Ziyu Ma, Li Yongxian, Lü Hongliang, and Andrew MacIver. 2014. 'Traditional Livelihoods, Conservation and Meadow Ecology in Jiuzhaigou National Park, Sichuan, China.' *Human Ecology* 42, no. 3: 481–91.

Yeh, Emily T. 2005. 'Green Governmentality and Pastoralism in Western China: "Converting Pastures to Grasslands".' *Nomadic Peoples* 9, no. 1–2: 9–30.

Zinda, John Aloysius, Christine J. Trac, Deli Zhai, and Stevan Harrell. 2017. 'Dual-Function Forests in the Returning Farmland to Forest Program and the Flexibility of Environmental Policy in China.' *Geoforum*, no. 78: 119–32.

Zinda, John Aloysius, Jianmei Yang, Ximing Xue, and Hai Cheng. 2014. 'Varying Impacts of Tourism Participation on Natural Resource Use in Communities in Southwest China.' *Human Ecology* 42, no. 5: 739–51.

Beyond Proletarianisation: The Everyday Politics of Chinese Migrant Labour (THOMAS SÆTRE JAKOBSEN)

Breman, Jan. 2013. 'A Bogus Concept?' *New Left Review*, no. 84: 130–38.

Chan, Kam Wing. 2010. 'The Global Financial Crisis and Migrant Workers in China: "There Is No Future as a Labourer; Returning to the Village Has No Meaning".' *International Journal of Urban and Regional Research* 34, no. 3: 659–77.

Chang, Leslie T. 2009. *Factory Girls: From Village to City in a Changing China*. New York: Spiegel & Grau.

Chatterjee, Partha. 2006. *The Politics of the Governed: Reflections on Popular Politics in Most of the World*. New York: Columbia University Press.

Das, Veena, and Shalini Randeria. 2015. 'Politics of the Urban Poor: Aesthetics, Ethics, Volatility, Precarity: An Introduction to Supplement 11.' *Current Anthropology* 56, no. 11: 3–14.

Day, Alexander F., and Mindi Schneider. 2017. 'The End of Alternatives? Capitalist Transformation, Rural Activism and the Politics of Possibility in China.' *The Journal of Peasant Studies* 45, no. 7: 1221–46.

Ferguson, James. 1999. *Expectations of Modernity: Myths and Meanings of Urban Life on the Zambian Copperbelt*. Berkeley: University of California Press.

Frenkel, Stephen J., and Chongxin Yu. 2015. 'Chinese Migrants' Work Experience and City Identification: Challenging the Underclass Thesis.' *Human Relations* 68, no. 2: 261–85.

Huang, Philip C. C. 2011. 'China's New-Age Small Farms and Their Vertical Integration: Agribusiness or Co-Ops?' *Modern China* 37, no. 2: 107–34.

Jakobsen, Thomas Sætre. 2018. 'From the Workplace to the Household: Migrant Labor and Accumulation Without Dispossession.' *Critical Asian Studies* 50, no. 2: 176–95.

Lee, Ching Kwan. 2016. 'Precarization or Empowerment? Reflections on Recent Labor Unrest in China.' *The Journal of Asian Studies* 75, no. 2: 317–33.

Loyalka, Michelle Dammon. 2012. 'Chinese Labor, Cheap No More.' *The New York Times*, 17 February. www.nytimes.com/2012/02/18/opinion/chinese-labor-cheap-no-more.html.

McMichael, Philip. 2008. 'Peasants Make Their Own History, But Not Just as They Please . . .' *Journal of Agrarian Change* 8, no. 2–3: 205–28.

Pun, Ngai. 2005. *Made in China: Women Factory Workers in a Global Workplace*. Durham: Duke University Press.

Pun, Ngai, and Huilin Lu. 2010. 'Unfinished Proletarianization: Self, Anger, and Class Action Among the Second Generation of Peasant-Workers in Present-Day China.' *Modern China* 36, no. 5: 493–519.

Rigg, Jonathan. 2012. *Living with Transition in Laos: Market Integration in Southeast Asia*. London: Routledge.

Smith, Chris, and Ngai Pun. 2018. 'Class and Precarity in China: A Contested Relationship.' In *Made in China Yearbook 2017: Gilded Age*, edited by Ivan Franceschini and Nicholas Loubere, 44–47. Canberra: ANU Press.

Solinger, Dorothy J. 2012. 'The New Urban Underclass and Its Consciousness: Is It a Class?' *Journal of Contemporary China* 21, no. 78: 1011–28.

Walker, Kathy Le Mons. 2009. 'From Covert to Overt: Everyday Peasant Politics in China and Its Implications for Transnational Agrarian Movements.' In *Transnational Agrarian Movements Confronting Globalization*, edited by Saturino M. Borras Jr., Marc Edelman, and Cristóbal Kay. Hoboken: Wiley-Blackwell.

Inside Work: The Hidden Exploitation of Rural Women in Modern China (TAMARA JACKA)

Bray, Francesca. 2013. *Technology, Gender and History in Imperial China: Great Transformations Reconsidered*. London: Routledge.

Eyferth, Jacob. 2012. 'Women's Work and the Politics of Homespun in Socialist China, 1949–1980.' *International Review of Social History*, no. 57: 365–91.

Gates, Hill. 1989. 'The Commoditization of Chinese Women.' *Signs* 14, no. 4: 799–832.

Greenhalgh, Susan, and Edwin A. Winckler. 2005. *Governing China's Population: From Leninist to Neoliberal Biopolitics*. Stanford: Stanford University Press.

Hershatter, Gail. 2011. *The Gender of Memory: Rural Women and China's Collective Past*. Berkeley: University of California Press.

Jacka, Tamara. 2017. 'Translocal Family Reproduction and Agrarian Change in China: A New Analytical Framework.' *Journal of Peasant Studies* 45, no. 7: 1341–59.

Jacka, Tamara. 1997. *Women's Work in Rural China: Change and Continuity in an Era of Reform*. Cambridge: Cambridge University Press.

Murphy, Rachel. 2014. 'Study and School in the Lives of Children in Migrant Families: A View from Rural Jiangxi, China.' *Development and Change* 45, no. 1: 29–51.

Tang, Jia, Jinlian Liang, and Liping Mu. 2017. 'A Gender Perspective on the Impact of Rural Women Accompanying Children to School: A Case Study in B Town, Sichuan Province.' *Journal of Chinese Women's University*, no. 5: 52–58.

Wang, Jing. 'Children of Migrant Parents Left Alone to Die.' *Caixin Online*. 24 June. english.caixin.com/2015-06-24/100821862.html.

Wu, Huifang. 2016. 'The other side of development in rural China: The marginalization of women as carers and low-paid labourers.' Unpublished paper presented at the Asian Studies Association of Australia conference. Canberra, Australia.

Ye, Jingzhong. 2015. 'Land Transfer and the Pursuit of Agricultural Modernization in China.' *Journal of Agrarian Change* 15, no. 3: 314–37.

Zwolinski, Matt, and Alan Wertheimer. 2017. 'Exploitation.' In *The Stanford Encyclopedia of Philosophy*, edited by Edward N. Zalta. plato.stanford.edu/archives/sum2017/entries/exploitation.

ON A CHINESE SCREEN: MEDIA, POWER, AND VOICE IN CHINA

Changing Representations of China's Workers (WANNING SUN)

Clark, Paul. 2008. *The Chinese Cultural Revolution*. Cambridge: Cambridge University Press.

Guo, Yingjie. 2008. 'Class, Stratum and Group: The Politics of Description and Prescription.' In *The New Rich in China: Future Rulers, Present Lives*, edited by David S. G. Goodman, 38–52. London: Routledge.

Perry, Elizabeth. 2012. *Anyuan: Mining China's Revolutionary Tradition*. Berkeley: University of California Press.

Renmin wang [People's Daily Online]. 2003. 'Guandian Pengzhuang: Mingong "tiao lou xiu" ying shouyancheng? [Clash of Views: Should Migrant Workers' "Show Jumping" be punished severely?].' 15 January. www.peopledaily.com.cn/GB/guandian/27/20030115/907962.html.

Sun, Wanning. 2015. 'Workers and Peasants as Historical Subjects: The Formation of Working Class Media Cultures in China.' In *Routledge Handbook of Chinese Media*, edited by Gary Rawnsley and Ming-Yeh Rawnsley, 239–49. London: Routledge.

Sun, Wanning. 2014. *Subaltern China: Rural Migrants, Media, and Cultural Practices*. Lanham, MA: Rowman & Littlefield.

Sun, Wanning. 2012. 'Desperately Seeking My Wages: Justice, Media Logic, and the Politics of Voice in Urban China', *Media Culture & Society* 34, no. 7: 864–79.

Sun, Wanning 2009. *Maid in China: Media, Morality, and the Cultural Politics of Boundaries*. London: Routledge.

Wallis, Cara. 2013. *Technomobility in China: Young Migrant Women and Mobile Phones*. New York: New York University Press.

Yan, Hairong. 2008. *New Masters, New Servants: Migration, Development, and Women Workers in China*. Durham, NC: Duke University Press.

Zhao, Yuezhi. 2010. 'Chinese Modernity, Media, and Democracy: An Interview with Lü Xinyu.' *Global Media and Communication* 6, no. 1: 5–32.

Platform Economies: The Boss's Old and New Clothes (JULIE YUJIE CHEN)

Beijing Transportation Committee. 2016. 'Beijing Interim Administrative Measures for the Business of Online Taxi Booking Services.' *Beijing.gov.cn*. 21 December. zhengce.beijing.gov.cn/library/192/33/50/438650/107721/index.html.

Chen, Julie Yujie. 2018. 'Thrown under the Bus and Outrunning It! The Logic of Didi and Taxi Drivers' Labour and Activism in the on-Demand Economy." *New Media & Society* 20, no. 8: 2691–2711.

CLB (China Labour Bulletin). 2018. 'The Workers' Movement in China 2015–2017: A New Report from CLB.' *China Labour Bulletin*. 13 August. www.clb.org.hk/sites/default/files/%E5%B7%A5%E4%BA%BA%E8%BF%90%E5%8A%A8%E4%B8%89%E5%B9%B4%E6%8A%A5%E5%91%8A%202015-17%20final.pdf.

CLB (China Labour Bulletin). 2017. 'New Normal? Strike Map Shows Steady Trends in Worker Actions in First Half of 2017.' *China Labour Bulletin*. 15 August. www.clb.org.hk/content/new-normal-strike-map-shows-steady-trends-worker-actions-first-half-2017.

CLB (China Labour Bulletin). 2016. 'New Economy, Same Old Problems for China's Workers.' *China Labour Bulletin*. 27 April. www.clb.org.hk/content/new-economy-same-old-problems-china%E2%80%99s-workers.

China's National Information Center, and Internet Society of China Sharing Economy Committee. 2018. 'Report on the Development of the Sharing Economy in China, 2018.' Beijing, China. www.sic.gov.cn/News/79/8860.htm.

China's National Information Center, and Internet Society of China Sharing Economy Committee. 2017. 'Report on the Development of the Sharing Economy in China, 2017.' Beijing. www.sic.gov.cn/archiver/SIC/UpFile/Files/Htmleditor/201703/20170302125144221.pdf.

China's National Information Center, and Internet Society of China Sharing Economy Committee. 2016. 'Report on the Development of the Sharing Economy in China, 2016.' Beijing. www.sic.gov.cn/archiver/SIC/UpFile/Files/Htmleditor/201602/20160229121154612.pdf.

Dyer-Witheford, Nick. 2015. *Cyber-Proletariat: Global Labour in the Digital Vortex*. Toronto, Ontario, London: Pluto Press.

Foster, John Bellamy, and Robert W. McChesney. 2014. 'Surveillance Capitalism.' *Monthly Review* (blog), 1 July. monthlyreview.org/2014/07/01/surveillance-capitalism/.

Gillespie, Tarleton. 2018. *Custodians of the Internet: Platforms, Content Moderation, and the Hidden Decisions That Shape Social Media*. New Haven: Yale University Press.

Innoinsights. 2018. 'New Rules for Online-booking Taxis in Beijing From July 1', 31 May. inno.caijing.com.cn/20180531/4462975.shtml.

Lee, Ching Kwan. 2007. *Against the Law: Labour Protests in China's Rustbelt and Sunbelt*.Berkeley: University of California Press.

Liang, Fan, Vishnupriya Das, Nadiya Kostyuk, and Muzammil M. Hussain. 2018. 'Constructing a Data-Driven Society: China's Social Credit System as a State Surveillance Infrastructure.' *Policy & Internet* 10, no. 4: 415–53. doi.org/10.1002/poi3.183.

Meituan-Dianping. 2018. 'Application Proof of Meituan-Dianping.' Hong Kong: Meituan-Dianping. www.hkexnews.hk/APP/SEHK/2018/2018062202/Documents/SEHK201806250005.pdf.

National Bureau of Statistics of China. 2017. *Zhongguo Tongji Nianjian 2017* [*China Statistical Yearbook 2017*] www.stats.gov.cn/tjsj/ndsj/2017/indexeh.htm.

Rosenblat, Alex, and Luke Stark. 2016. 'Algorithmic Labor and Information Asymmetries: A Case Study of Uber's Drivers.' *International Journal of Communication* 10: 3758–84.

Shenzhen Transportation Committee. 2018. 'Several Changes to Shenzhen Administrative Measures for the Business of Online Taxi Booking Services.' 15 June. www.sz.gov.cn/jw/zwgk/jtzx/gzdt/qt/201806/t20180615_12196650.htm.

Shenzhen Transportation Committee. 2016. 'Shenzhen Interim Administrative Measures for the Business of Online Taxi Booking Services.' 28 December. www.sz.gov.cn/cn/xxgk/zfxxgj/tzgg/201612/t20161228_5797203.htm.

Srnicek, Nick. 2016. *Platform Capitalism*. Cambridge, UK: Polity Press.

Yangtze Evening Paper. 2017. 'Xianshang xianxia cheliang bu fu [Online and Offline the Cars Do Not Conform].' *Xinhua,* 15 November. www.xinhuanet.com/2017-11/15/c_1121957526.htm.

Yue, Shaoxue. 2018. 'Rank of Business Licences for Close to a Hundred Ride-haling Platforms and Their Nationwide Distribution'. 2 July. m.evpartner.com/news/detail-37434.html.

Zuboff, Shoshana. 2015. 'Big Other: Surveillance Capitalism and the Prospects of an Information Civilization.' *Journal of Information Technology* 30, no. 1: 75–89.

Rethinking Online Privacy in the Chinese Workplace: Employee Dismissals over Social Media Posts (MIMI ZOU)

Beijing Bonatongcheng Technology Co., Ltd. v. Li Chennan, Beijing Dongcheng District People's Court, Dongmin Chuzi No. 11291 (2014).

Beijing Bonatongcheng Technology Co., Ltd. v. Li Chennan, Beijing No. 2 Intermediate People's Court, Er Zhong Min Zhong Zi No. 01062 (2015).

Chen v. Di Nuo Wei Ya International Freight Forwarders (Shanghai) Co., Ltd., Hu Er Zhong Zhong, San (Min) No. 556 Labour Contract Dispute Appeal Case (2013).

NPC (National People's Congress). 2017. 'General Provisions of the Civil Law of the People's Republic of China.' 15 March.

NPC (National People's Congress). 2016. 'Cybersecurity Law of the People's Republic of China.' 7 November.

NPC (National People's Congress). 2009. 'Tort Liability Law of the People's Republic of China.' 29 December.

NPC (National People's Congress). 1986. 'General Principles of the Civil Law of the People's Republic of China.' 12 April.

Park, Susan. 2014. 'Employee Internet Privacy: A Proposed Act that Balances Legitimate Employer Rights and Employee Privacy.' *American Business Law Journal* 51, no. 4: 779–841.

Pei Shihai v. Shunfeng Express Group (Shanghai) Express Co., Ltd., Shanghai Second Intermediate People's Court, Hu 2 Min Zhong No. 3368 Labour Contract Dispute: Second Instance Civil Judgment (2016).

Pei Shihai v. Shunfeng Express Group (Shanghai) Express Co., Ltd., Shanghai Qingpu District People's Court, Qingmin Si (Min) Chu Zi No. 2538 Labour Contract Dispute: First Instance Civil Judgment (2015).

Penguin Intelligence. 2017. '2017 weixin yonghu & shengtai yanjiu baogao [WeChat User Behaviour Report].' *Tengxun Keji*, 24 April. tech.qq.com/a/20170424/004233.htm#p=1.

SAC (Standardisation Administration of China). 2017. 'Information Security Technology—Personal information security specification, GB / T 35273-2017', 29 December.

SPC (Supreme People's Court). 1988. 'Opinions on Several Issues concerning the Implementation of the General Principles of the Civil Law of the People's Republic of China (For Trial Implementation).' 26 January.

Sun Liang v. Shunfeng Express Group (Shanghai) Express Co., Ltd., Shanghai Second Intermediate People's Court, Hu 2 Min Zhong No. 1128 Labour Contract Dispute: Second Instance Civil Judgment (2016).

Sun Liang v. Shunfeng Express Group (Shanghai) Express Co., Ltd., Shanghai Qingpu District People's Court, Qingmin Si (Min) Chu Zi No. 2089 Labour Contract Dispute: First Instance Civil Judgment (2015).

Xi'an Mou Gong Ye Xuexiao v. Tang, Shaanxi Province Zhouyi County People's Court, Shaan 0124 Minchu No. 1400 (2016).

Visualising Labour and Labourscapes in China: From Propaganda to Socially Engaged Photography (MARINA SVENSSON)

Bogre, Michelle. 2012. *Photography as Activism: Images for Social Change*. Waltham, MA: Focal Press.

Chen, Shuxia. 2018. 'Ren Hang: Bodies Without Redemption.' In *Made in China Yearbook 2017: Gilded Age*, edited by Ivan Franceschini and Nicholas Loubere, 200–05. Canberra: ANU Press.

Estrin, James. 2015. 'A Chinese Miner With a Heart of Gold.' *The New York Times*, 23 June. lens.blogs.nytimes.com/2015/06/23/a-chinese-miner-with-a-heart-of-gold.

Franklin, Stuart. 2016. *The Documentary Impulse*. London: Phaidon.

Levi Strauss, David. 2003. *Between the Eyes: Essays on Photography and Politics*. New York: Aperture.

Roberts, Claire. 2013. *Photography and China*. London: Reaktion Books.

Salgado, Sebastiao. 1994. 'Interview by Ken Lassiter.' *Photographer's Forum*, September: 26.

Sontag, Susan. 2003. *Regarding the Pain of Others*. London: Penguin Press.

Svensson, Marina. 2016. '"Connectivity, Engagement and Witnessing on China's Weibo.' In *The Internet, Social Media, and a Changing China*, edited by Jacques deLisle, Avery Goldstein, and Guobin Yang, 49–70. Philadephia: University of Pennsylvania Press.

Wu, Hung. 2016. *Zooming In: Histories of Photography in China*. Chicago: The University of Chicago Press.

Documenting China's Influence (DAVID BANDURSKI)

An, Baijie. 2018. 'Xi: Spreading China's Story Key Mission.' *China Daily*, 23 August. www.chinadaily.com.cn/a/201808/23/WS5b7de976a310add14f387392.html.

Beijing International Film Festival (BIFF). 2018. 'Beijing guoji dianyingjie jilüpian danyuan kaiqi [Beijing International Film Festival Documentary Section Opens].' *DocuChina, China.org.can*, 16 April. jilu.china.com.cn/2018-04/16/content_40292808.htm.

Bruneau, Marie-Agnès. 2018. 'Sunny Side '18: China Comes Back as Copro Partner.' *Realscreen*, 29 June. realscreen.com/2018/06/29/sunny-side-18-china-comes-back-as-copro-partner.

China Daily. 2017. 'Documentary by Discovery Channel Highlights Xi Jinping's Key Role in China's Growth.' *Straits Times*, 16 October. www.straitstimes.com/asia/east-asia/documentary-by-discovery-channel-highlights-xi-jinpings-key-role-in-chinas-growth.

China.org.cn. 2015. '"China From Above" premieres on National Geographic.' *China.org.cn*, 24 September. china.org.cn/video/2015-09/24/content_36667953.htm.

Discovery Channel. 2017. 'Discovery Channel Delves into Time of Xi.' *PR Newswire*. markets.businessinsider.com/news/stocks/discovery-channel-delves-into-time-of-xi-1004110233.

DocuChina. 2017. 'Quan fang wei chuanbo tuiguang, "zhonghu zhi mei" hai wai chuanbo jihua 10 yue qidong [The Comprehensive Broadcast and Promotion: The "Beautiful China" Overseas Broadcast Plan Gets Underway in October].' *DocuChina*, 28 September. www.docuchina.cn/2017/09/28/ARTIN5G6kSHdn4cR88Izx83k170928.shtml.

Gitter, David. 2017. 'The CCP Plants the China Dream Abroad.' *The Diplomat*, 9 September. thediplomat.com/2017/12/the-ccp-plants-the-china-dream-abroad.

Li, Congjun. 2013. 'Laolao zhangwo yulun gongzuo zhudongquan [Firmly Grasping the Initiative in Public Opinion Work].' *People's Daily*. 24 September. opinion.people.com.cn/n/2013/0904/c1003-22797334.html.

Liu, Wei. 2007. 'Partnership Will Turn World's Eyes to China.' *China Daily*, 12 December. www.chinadaily.com.cn/cndy/2007-12/12/content_6314506.htm.

Meridian Line Films Ltd. 2015. 'Annual Return.' Companies House, filed 10 August. beta.companieshouse.gov.uk/company/07450293/filing-history.

State Administration for Industry and Commerce. 'Wu Zhou Chuanbo Youxian Gongsi' [China Intercontinental Communication Co. Ltd.] (91110108721478549P). National Enterprise Credit Information Publicity System, retrieved 2018. www.gsxt.gov.cn/index.html.

State Administration for Industry and Commerce. 'Wu Zhou Chuanbo Chubanshe' [China Intercontinental Press] (911100001020877768). National Enterprise Credit Information Publicity System, retrieved 2018. www.gsxt.gov.cn/index.html.

State Administration of Radio Film and Television. 2012. 'Guanyu jiakuai jilü pian chanye fazhan de ruogan yijian [Opinion on the Acceleration of Development in the Documentary Film Industry].' *CNTV*, 28 September. jishi.cntv.cn/program/jlppyzy/20120928/100206.shtml.

Tan, Huileng. 2017. 'China's Xi Preaches "Opennes" and "Cooperation" after Trump Comes Out Swinging.' *CNBC*, 10 November. www.cnbc.com/2017/11/10/chinas-xi-delivers-speech-at-apec-summit-in-vietnam.html.

VideoChinaTV. 2017. 'CICC Recognized as a Winner of 2017 Silk Road International Documentary Academic Awards.' *LinkedIn*, 15 December. www.linkedin.com/pulse/cicc-recognized-winner-2017-silk-road-international-documentary-影像中国.

Yu, Ming. 2017. 'International Co-production of Chinese Documentary Development.' *Asia Dialogue*, 5 July. theasiadialogue.com/2017/07/05/international-co-production-of-chinese-documentary-development.

Zhang, Niansheng and Zexi Hu. 2017. '"China Was on the Brink of Entering a New Chapter": VP of Discovery Networks Asia-Pacific.' *People's Daily*, 19 October. en.people.cn/n3/2017/1019/c90000-9282097.html.

The Global Age of the Algorithm: Social Credit and the Financialisation of Governance in China (NICHOLAS LOUBERE AND STEFAN BREHM)

Barmé, Geremie R., Linda Jaivin, and Jeremy Goldkorn, eds. 2015. *Shared Destiny: China Story Yearbook 2014*. Canberra: ANU Press.

Bislev, Ane. 2017. 'Contextualizing China's Online Credit Rating System.' *China Policy Institute: Analysis*, 4 December. cpianalysis.org/2017/12/04/contextualizing-chinas-online-credit-rating-system.

Bodkin, Henry. 2017. 'AI Robots Are Sexist and Racist, Experts Warn.' *The Telegraph*, 24 August. www.telegraph.co.uk/news/2017/08/24/ai-robots-sexist-racist-experts-warn.

Daum, Jeremy. 2017. 'Giving Credit.' *China Law Translate*, 4 January. www.chinalawtranslate.com/giving-credit/?lang=en.

Daum, Jeremy. 2018a. '"Who Did China Ban from Flying.' *China Law Translate*, 21 March. www.chinalawtranslate.com/who-did-china-ban-from-flying/?lang=en.

Daum, Jeremy. 2018b. 'Giving Credit 3: Inputs and Outputs.' *China Law Translate*, 15 January. www.chinalawtranslate.com/giving-credit-3-inputs-and-outputs.

Epstein, Gerald A. 2005. 'Introduction: Financialization and the World Economy.' In *Financialization and the World Economy*, edited by Gerald A. Epstein, 3–16. Cheltenham: Edward Elgar.

Fang, Lee. 2018. 'ICE Used Private Facebook Data to Find and Track Criminal Suspect, Internal Emails Show.' *The Intercept*, 26 March. theintercept.com/2018/03/26/facebook-data-ice-immigration.

Foreign Policy. 2018. 'A Summer Vacation in China's Muslim Gulag.' *Foreign Policy*, 28 February. foreignpolicy.com/2018/02/28/a-summer-vacation-in-chinas-muslim-gulag.

Heilmann, Sebastian. 2008. 'From Local Experiments to National Policy: The Origins of China's Distinctive Policy Process.' *The China Journal* 59: 1–30.

Hornby, Lucy, Sherry Fei Ju, and Louise Lucas. 2018. 'China Cracks down on Tech Credit Scoring.' *Financial Times*, 4 February. www.ft.com/content/f23e0cb2-07ec-11e8-9650-9c0ad2d7c5b5.

Human Rights Watch. 2018. 'China: Big Data Fuels Crackdown in Minority Region.' *Human Rights Watch*, 26 February. www.hrw.org/news/2018/02/26/china-big-data-fuels-crackdown-minority-region.

Hvistendahl, Mara. 2017. 'Inside China's Vast New Experiment in Social Ranking.' *Wired*, 14 December. www.wired.com/story/age-of-social-credit.

Keeley, Brian. 2007. *Human Capital: How What You Know Shapes Your Life*. Paris: OECD Publishing.

Loubere, Nicholas. 2017a. 'China's Internet Finance Boom and Tyrannies of Inclusion.' *China Perspectives* 2017/4: 9–18.

Loubere, Nicholas. 2017b. 'Cyber Loan Sharks, Social Credit, and New Frontiers of Digital Control.' In *China Story Yearbook 2016: Control*, edited by Jane Golley, Linda Jaivin, and Luigi Tomba, 213–23. Canberra: ANU Press.

Mertha, Andrew. 2009. '"Fragmented Authoritarianism 2.0": Political Pluralization in the Chinese Policy Process.' *The China Quarterly* 200: 995–1012.

Millward, James A. 2018. 'What It's Like to Live in a Surveillance State.' *The New York Times*, 3 February. www.nytimes.com/2018/02/03/opinion/sunday/china-surveillance-state-uighurs.html.

O'Neil, Cathy. 2016. *Weapons of Math Destruction: How Big Data Increases Inequality and Threatens Democracy*. New York: Crown.

Rosenzweig, Joshua, Ewan Smith, and Susan Treveskes. 2017. 'Forum: Interpreting the Rule of Law in Xi Jinping's China.' In *Made in China Yearbook 2016: Disturbances in Heaven*, edited by Ivan Franceschini, Kevin Lin, and Nicholas Loubere, 98–105. Canberra: ANU Press.

State Council. 2016. 'Guowuyuan bangongting guanyu jiaqiang geren chengxin tixi jianshe de zhidao yijian [The General Office of the State Council's Guiding Opinion on the Strengthening of the Establishment of the Personal Creditworthiness System].' www.gov.cn/zhengce/content/2016-12/30/content_5154830.htm.

State Council. 2014. 'Guunyu yinfa shehui xinyong tixi jianshe guihua gangyao (2014—2020 nian) de tongzhi [Planning Outline for the Construction of a Social Credit System (2014-2020)].' chinacopyrightandmedia.wordpress.com/2014/06/14/planning-outline-for-the-construction-of-a-social-credit-system-2014-20.

Strumpf, Dan, and Wenxin Fan. 2017. 'Who Wants to Supply China's Surveillance State? The West.' *Wall Street Journal*, 1 November. www.wsj.com/articles/who-wants-to-supply-chinas-surveillance-state-the-west-1509540111.

The Economist. 2016a. 'Test of Character.' *The Economist*, 29 September. www.economist.com/news/finance-and-economics/21707978-how-personality-testing-could-help-financial-inclusion-tests-character.

The Economist. 2016b. 'China Invents the Digital Totalitarian State.' *The Economist*, 17 December. www.economist.com/news/briefing/21711902-worrying-implications-its-social-credit-project-china-invents-digital-totalitarian.

The Economist. 2016c. 'China's Digital Dictatorship.' *The Economist*, 17 December. www.economist.com/news/leaders/21711904-worrying-experiments-new-form-social-control-chinas-digital-dictatorship.

Wade, Samuel. 2018. 'China's Surveillance State: Henan, Xinjiang, and Beyond.' *China Digital Times*, 6 February. chinadigitaltimes.net/2018/02/chinas-surveillance-state-henan-xinjiang-beyond.

Winston, Ali. 2018. 'Palantir Has Secretly Been Using New Orleans to Test Its Predictive Policing Technology.' *The Verge*, 27 February. www.theverge.com/2018/2/27/17054740/palantir-predictive-policing-tool-new-orleans-nopd.

Yu, Lean, Xinxie Li, Ling Tang, Zongyi Zhang, and Gang Kou. 2015. 'Social Credit: A Comprehensive Literature Review.' *Financial Innovation* 1, no. 6: 1–18.

HUMAN RIGHTS MADE IN CHINA

Beijing Evictions, a Winter's Tale (LI QIAOCHU, SONG JIANI, AND ZHANG SHUCHI)

AFP (Agence France-Press). 2018. 'Chinese Artist Hua Yong Detained after Documenting Mass Migrant Evictions in Beijin.' *Hong Kong Free Press*, 18 December. www.hongkongfp.com/2017/12/18/chinese-artist-hua-yong-detained-documenting-mass-migrant-evictions-beijing.

Franceschini, Ivan, and Elisa Nesossi. 2018. 'State Repression of Chinese Labor NGOs: A Chilling Effect?' *The China Journal*. www.journals.uchicago.edu/doi/abs/10.1086/696986.

Gao, Charlotte. 2017. '8 Top Chinese Intellectuals Demand Constitutional Review of Beijing's Mass Eviction.' *The Diplomat*, 27 December. thediplomat.com/2017/12/8-top-chinese-intellectuals-demand-constitutional-review-of-beijings-mass-eviction.

Haas, Benjamin. 2017. 'China: "Ruthless" Campaign to Evict Beijing's Migrant Workers Condemned.' *The Guardian*, 27 November. www.theguardian.com/world/2017/nov/27/china-ruthless-campaign-evict-beijings-migrant-workers-condemned.

Hao, Jingfang (translated by Ken Liu). 2015. 'Folding Beijing.' *Uncanny Magazine*, January/February. uncannymagazine.com/article/folding-beijing-2.

Holton, Kate, and Jamillah Knowles. 2017. 'London Tower Blocks Evacuated as 34 Buildings Fail Fire Tests.' *Reuters*, 24 June. www.reuters.com/article/us-britain-fire/london-tower-blocks-evacuated-as-34-buildings-fail-fire-tests-idUSKBN19F071.

Lo, Kinling. 2017. 'Chinese Intellectuals Urge Beijing Authorities to Stop "Forcing" Tens of Thousands of Migrant Workers Out of City in Wake of Deadly Fire.' *South China Morning Post*, 28 November. m.scmp.com/news/china/policies-politics/article/2121633/chinese-intellectuals-urge-beijing-authorities-stop.

Meng, Zhu, and Xin Gao. 2017. 'Beijing jiang jizhong 40 tian kaizhan anquan yinhuan dapaicha daqingli dazhengzhi zhuanxiang xingdong [Beijing Government Has Kicked Off 40 Days of Citywide Safety Inspections].' *People.cn*, 23 November. bj.people.com.cn/n2/2017/1123/c82840-30957026.html.

Qi, Ah. 2018. '40 tian handong qingli: Minjian zijiu shilü [The 40-day Eviction in Winter: Voices from Chinese Civil Society].' *NGOCN*, 15 January. shimo.im/docs/6t94NJ4xMpsdamPz?from=timeline&isappinstalled=0.

Rawlinson, Kevin. 2017. 'The Victims of the Grenfell Tower Fire.' *The Guardian*, 23 November. www.theguardian.com/uk-news/2017/jul/13/grenfell-tower-fire-victims-dead-missing-identified-named-so-far.

Tu, Ming, and Xiang Kong. 2017. 'Beijing daxing ximen zhen xinjian cun fasheng huozai, yizhi 19 ren siwang [Fire Breaks Out in a Building in Beijing's Ximen Township, Daxing District, Killing 19 People].' *Xinhua*, 19 November. news.sina.com.cn/c/2017-11-19/doc-ifynwnty4966179.shtml.

Wang, Jiangsong. 2017. 'Laogongjie renshi jiu Beijing da guimo qugan "wailai renkou" zhi zhonggong zhongyang, quanguo renda, guowuyuan, quanguo zhengxie de gongkaixin [Open Letter About the Mass Evictions of Migrants from Beijing to the Central Committee of the Chinese Communist Party, the National People's Congress, the State Council, and the Consultative Conference by Personalities in the Labour Field].' (@JiangsongWang, 25 November). mobile.twitter.com/JiangsongWang/status/934448437520506880.

Weiquanwang. 2017. 'Jiang Ping, He Weifang deng xuezhe lüshi dui Beijingshi zhengfu qugan wailai jumin de xingdong qi yiju de xingzheng wenjian xiang quanguo rendahui changweihui tiqing hexianxing shenzha de quanwen [Full Text of the Letter to the Standing Committee of the National People's Congress by Top Chinese Scholars and Lawyers Requesting a Constitutionality Check of the Evictions in Beijing].' *Weiquanwang*, 24 December. wqw2010.blogspot.com/2017/12/blog-post_27.html.

Zhou, Viola, and Pinghui Zhuang. 2017. 'Migrant Workers Take to Streets of Beijing to Protest against Forced Evictions.' *South China Morning Post*, 11 December. www.google.com.hk/amp/m.scmp.com/news/china/policies-politics/article/2123714/migrant-workers-take-streets-beijing-protest-against%3famp=1.

Evictions and the Right to the City (KEVIN LIN)

Wang, Jiangsong. 2017. 'Laogongjie renshi jiu Beijing da guimo qugan "wailai renkou" zhi zhonggong zhongyang, quanguo renda, guowuyuan, quanguo zhengxie de gongkaixin [Open Letter About the Mass Evictions of Migrants from Beijing to the Central Committee of the Chinese Communist Party, the National People's Congress, the State Council, and the Consultative Conference by Personalities in the Labour Field].' (@JiangsongWang, 25 November). mobile.twitter.com/JiangsongWang/status/934448437520506880.

Weiquanwang. 2017. 'Jiang Ping, He Weifang deng xuezhe lüshi dui Beijingshi zhengfu qugan wailai jumin de xingdong qi yiju de xingzheng wenjian xiang quanguo rendahui changweihui tiqing hexianxing shenzha de quanwen [Full Text of the Letter to the Standing Committee of the National People's Congress by Top Chinese Scholars and Lawyers Requesting a Constitutionality Check of the Evictions in Beijing].' *Weiquanwang*, 24 December. wqw2010.blogspot.com/2017/12/blog-post_27.html.

Outsourcing Coercion and Social Control (LYNETTE H. ONG)

Batal al-Shishani, Murad, and Dalia Elsheikh. 2012. 'How "Thugs" Became Part of the Arab Spring Lexicon.' *BBC News*, 5 September. www.bbc.com/news/world-middle-east-19467017.

Branigan, Tania. 2012. 'Chen Guangcheng: How China Tried to Lock Down a Blind Man.' *The Guardian*, 27 April. www.theguardian.com/world/2012/apr/27/chen-guangcheng-china-lockdown.

Lim, Louisa. 2014. 'The Thugs of Mainland China.' *The New Yorker*, 8 October. www.newyorker.com/news/news-desk/thugs-mainland-china-hong-kong-protests.

Ong, Lynette H. 2019 (forthcoming). 'Engaging a Huangniu: Commodification of State-Society Bargaining in China.' *Journal of Contemporary China.*

Ong, Lynette H. 2018. 'Thugs and Outsourcing of State Repression in China.' *The China Journal* 80: 94–110.

Shi, Jiangtao. 2018. 'Xi Jinping Puts China's Mafia in Cross Hairs, but Fears of Judicial Abuse Remain.' *South China Morning Post*, 26 January. www.scmp.com/news/china/policies-politics/article/2130629/xi-puts-chinas-mafia-cross-hairs-fears-judicial-abuse.

Wen, Philip. 2017. 'Rare Disclosure Sheds Light on Plight of China's Aggrieved Petitioners.' *Reuters*, 3 March. www.reuters.com/article/us-china-parliament-petitioners/rare-disclosure-sheds-light-on-plight-of-chinas-aggrieved-petitioners-idUSKBN16931T.

Justice Restored under Xi Jinping: A Political Project (ELISA NESOSSI)

Biddulph, Sarah, Elisa Nesossi, and Susan Trevaskes. 2017. 'Criminal Justice Reform in the Xi Jinping Era.' *China Law and Society Review* 2, no. 1: 63–128.

Forsythe, Michael. 2016. 'China Exonerates Man It Executed for Murder in 1995.' *The New York Times*, 2 December. www.nytimes.com/2016/12/02/world/asia/china-court-exonerates-innocent-executed.html.

Lu, Meihui. 2013. 'Henan jianfang: Li Hualiang an jue bu shi "yuan'an", "cuo'an" [Henan Procuratorate: Li Hualiang's Case Is by No Means a Wrongful Conviction].' *Yifeng Wang*, 9 May. news.ifeng.com/society/1/detail_2013_05/09/25084078_0.shtml.

Jia, Peng. 2014. 'Anhui "sha qi yuan'an" Yu Yingsheng: 17 nian yuanyu xichu de qingbai [Anhui "Kill Wife Case" Yu Yingsheng: Declared Innocent After 17 Years of Wrong Imprisonment].' *Xinjingbao*, 29 May. www.bjnews.com.cn/inside/2014/05/29/318690.html.

Ma, Shipeng. 2014. 'Yanqi si ci zhihou, Fujian Nian Bin tou du'an keneng 6 yue 25 ri zai kaiting [After Four Delays, Fujian Nian Bin's Poisoning Case May Be Reopened on June 25].' *Pengpai*, 12 June. www.thepaper.cn/newsDetail_forward_1250441.

Trevaskes, Susan, and Elisa Nesossi. 2015. 'The Sword of Discipline and the Dagger of Justice.' In *China Story Yearbook 2014. Shared Destiny*, edited by Geremie R. Barmé, Linda Jaivin, and Jeremy Goldkorn, 261–83. Canberra: ANU Press.

Wang, Yongji. 2014. 'Xi Jinping: jue bu yunxu zhifa fanfa zaocheng yuanjia cuo'an [Xi Jinping: Never Allow Law Enforcement Offences to Become Miscarriages of Justice].' *Zhongguo Xinwen Wang*, 8 January. www.chinanews.com/gn/2014/01-08/5713997.shtml.

Zhou, Xifeng. 2013. 'Jingfang kua sheng diao yu babi you kougong zao yuan'an zhen xiong louwang zai sharen [Police Cross-Provincial Transfer of Prisoners Used Coercive Methods and Cause Miscarriages of Justice, the Real Murderer Escapes the Net and Kills Again].' *Nanjing Baoye Wang*, 27 March. news.sina.com.cn/c/2013-03-27/035026651331.shtml.

Zhu, Changjun. 2017. '"Yi zui cong qing" dao "yi zui cong wu" xuyao jiannan yi yue [It Is Hard to Jump from "Suspecting Guilt from Lightness" to "Suspecting Guilt from Nothing"].' *Zhongguo Qingnian Bao*, 13 September. www.chinanews.com/sh/2017/09-13/8329460.shtml.

Confessions Made in China (MAGNUS FISKESJÖ)

Bandurski, David. 2016. 'Can Old News Shed Light on the Gui Minhai Case?' *China Media Project*, 18 January. medium.com/china-media-project/can-old-news-shed-light-on-the-gui-minhai-case-a969ea091759.

Berlatsky, Noah. 2014. 'When Chicago Tortured.' *The Atlantic*, 17 December. www.theatlantic.com/national/archive/2014/12/chicago-police-torture-jon-burge/383839.

China Change. 2017. 'Q & A with Peter Dahlin, the Swedish NGO Worker Who 'Endangered the National Security' of China.' *China Change*, 3 January. chinachange.org/2017/01/03/q-a-with-peter-dahlin-the-swedish-ngo-worker-who-endangered-the-national-security-of-china.

Fiskesjö, Magnus. 2017. 'The Return of the Show Trial: China's Televised "Confessions".' *The Asia-Pacific Journal: Japan Focus* 15 (13): 1–34. apjjf.org/2017/13/Fiskesjo.html.

France 24. 2018. 'The Victims of China's Forced Disappearances.' *France 24*, 9 February. www.france24.com/en/20180209-video-reporters-victims-china-forced-disappearances.

HKFP (Hong Kong Free Press). 2016. 'Full, Complete Transcript of Returned Bookseller Lam Wing-Kee's Press Conference and Q&A.' *Hong Kong Free Press*, 20 June. www.hongkongfp.com/2016/06/20/full-complete-transcript-of-returned-bookseller-lam-wing-kees-press-conference-and-qa.

Huang, Joyce. 2017. 'Hong Kong Publisher Gui Minhai Released, but Still Missing.' *Voice of America*, 26 October. www.voanews.com/a/hong-kong-publisher-released-but-still-missing/4086945.html.

NHK World. 2018. 'Hong Kong Bookseller Criticizes Sweden.' *NHK World*, 10 February.

Phillips, Tom. 2016. 'Mysterious Confession Fuels Fears of Beijing's Influence on Hong Kong's Top Newspaper.' *The Guardian*, 25 July. www.theguardian.com/world/2016/jul/25/south-china-morning-post-china-influence-hong-kong-newspaper-confession.

Phillips, Tom. 2018. '"A Very Scary Movie": How China Snatched Gui Minhai on the 11.10 Train to Beijing.' *The Guardian*, 22 February. www.theguardian.com/world/2018/feb/22/how-china-snatched-gui-minhai-train-beijing-bookseller-hong-kong.

Rejali, Darius. 2009. *Torture and Democracy*. Princeton: Princeton University Press.

Rønneberg, Kristoffer. 2018. 'Arrestert Forlegger Anklager Sverige for å Bruke Ham Som «Sjakkbrikke» for å Sverte Kina.' *Aftenposten*, 10 February. www.aftenposten.no/article/ap-a27GPM.html.

Xinhua. 2012. 'China Bans Forced Confessions in Investigations.' *China.Org.Cn*, 26 December. www.china.org.cn/china/2012-12/26/content_27526041.htm.

Will the Future of Human Rights Be 'Made in China'? (SARAH M. BROOKS)

CHRD (Chinese Human Rights Defenders). 2013. 'China Must Stop Excluding Civil Society from UN Human Rights Review.' *Chinese Human Rights Defenders,* 7 October. www.nchrd.org/2013/10/china-must-stop-excluding-civil-society-from-un-human-rights-review.

Emmott, Robin, and Angeliki Koutantou. 2017. 'Greece Blocks EU Statement on China Human Rights at U.N.' *Reuters,* 18 June. www.reuters.com/article/us-eu-un-rights/greece-blocks-eu-statement-on-china-human-rights-at-u-n-idUSKBN1990FP.

Eve, Frances. 2018. 'The US Withdrawal from the UNHRC Is Perfect for Xi Jinping and China.' *The Guardian,* 22 June. www.theguardian.com/world/commentisfree/2018/jun/22/the-us-withdrawal-from-the-unhrc-is-perfect-for-xi-jinping-and-china.

Focus Taiwan. 2017. 'Taiwan: Taipei Urges UN to Promote Country's Integration in Multilateral Organisations.' *Unrepresented Nations and Peoples Organisation,* 13 September. unpo.org/article/20320.

ISHR (International Service for Human Rights). 2018. 'The Backlash against Civil Society Access and Participation at the United Nations.' *International Service for Human Rights,* 30 May. www.ishr.ch/sites/default/files/documents/mappingreport_web.pdf.

ISHR (International Service for Human Rights). 2017. 'Human Rights Council Side Event: Defenders in Detention – Safeguarding the Legacy of Liu Xiaobo.' *International Service for Human Rights,* 12 September. www.ishr.ch/human-rights-council-side-event-defenders-detention-safeguarding-legacy-liu-xiaobo.

Kaiman, Jonathan. 2014. 'Chinese Activist Cao Shunli Dies after Being Denied Medical Help, Says Website.' *The Guardian,* 15 March. www.theguardian.com/world/2014/mar/14/china-activist-cao-shunli-dies-human-rights.

Lynch, Colum. 2018. 'Russia and China See in Trump Era a Chance to Roll Back Human Rights Promotion at U.N.' *Foreign Policy,* 26 June. foreignpolicy.com/2018/06/26/russia-and-china-see-in-trump-era-a-chance-to-roll-back-human-rights-promotion-at-u-n.

Reuters. 2016. 'China Angered as U.N. Rights Chief Attends Ceremony for Jailed Academic.' *Reuters,* 12 October. www.reuters.com/article/us-china-rights-un-idUSKCN12C0X2.

UN Committee against Torture. 2016. 'Concluding Observations on the Fifth Periodic Report of China' United Nations Committee against Torture, 3 February. docstore.ohchr.org/SelfServices/FilesHandler.ashx?enc=6QkG1d%2FPPRiCAqhKb7yhslEE2YuVt8GA5WKG3GEX%2BZEXqjnsVnWP%2BkQ6f9cmzWcEPJYdFWEXvIFmDTE3WtKbIKZXAKr5OVTwnh86Q4GNZXSmrqMf55xyaMPMcFusW3o2.

UN Committee against Torture. 2015. 'List of Issues in Relation to the Fifth Periodic Report of China' United Nations Committee against Torture, 15 June. www.refworld.org/docid/564ed6854.html.

UN Office at Geneva. 2018. 'Human Rights Council Holds Interactive Dialogue with Special Rapporteurs on Extrajudicial Executions and on Freedom of Expression.' The United Nations Office at Geneva, 20 June. www.unog.ch/unog/website/news_media.nsf/(httpNewsByYear_en)/89894A16234574F5C12582B2004476FF?OpenDocument.

UN Office at Geneva. 2017a. 'Council Begins Interactive Dialogue on Human Rights of Internally Displaced Persons, and on Human Rights and Extreme Poverty.' The United Nations Office at Geneva, 7 June. www.unog.ch/unog/website/news_media.nsf/(httpNewsByYear_en)/42F8EF03A6A88996C1258138005BC998?OpenDocument.

UN Office at Geneva. 2017b. 'Human Rights Council Concludes Interactive Dialogue on Internally Displaced Persons, and on Human Rights and Extreme Poverty.' The United Nations Office at Geneva, 8 June. www.unog.ch/unog/website/news_media.nsf/(httpNewsByYear_en)/B0F95625A13F165AC125813900458CE7?OpenDocument.

Wade, Samuel. 2018. 'U.S. Rights Council Exit: A Victory for China?' *China Digital Times*, 22 June. chinadigitaltimes.net/2018/06/american-exit-from-u-n-rights-council-a-crushing-victory-for-china.

Remembering Liu Xiaobo One Year On (JEAN-PHILIPPE BÉJA)

Jin, Zhong. 1988. 'Zhuanfang Liu Xiaobo [An Interview with Liu Xiaobo].' *Jiefang Yuebao* [*Liberation Monthly*], December.

Liu, Xiaobo. 2012a. 'I Have No Enemies: My Final Statement.' In *Liu Xiaobo: No Enemies, No Hatred*, edited by Perry Link, Tienchi Liao, and Liu Xia, 321–26. Cambridge, MA: Harvard University Press.

Liu, Xiaobo. 2012b. 'Using Truth to Undermine a System Built on Lies.' In *Liu Xiaobo: No Enemies, No Hatred*, edited by Perry Link, Tienchi Liao, and Liu Xia, 292–99. Cambridge, MA: Harvard University Press.

Liu, Xiaobo, 2002. 'Minjian fanduipai de pinkun [The Unofficial Opposition's Poverty].' *Minzhu Zhongguo* [*Democratic China*] 6, 8.

Liu, Xiaobo. 1989. 'Pingfan: Xiandai zhongguo zui da de beiju [Rehabilitation: Modern China's Greatest Tragedy].' In *Tiananmen 1989*, Taibei, Lianjing Press.

Liu, Xiaobo. 1986. 'Weiji, xin shiqi wenzue mianlin weiji [Crisis: The Literature of the New Epoch Faces a Crisis].' *Shenzhen Qingnianbao* [*Shenzhen Youth Daily*], 3 October.

Xinjiang Today: Wang Zhen Rides Again? (TOM CLIFF)

An, Baijie. 2017. 'Xi Pledges "New Era" in Building Moderately Prosperous Society.' China Daily, 19 October. www.chinadaily.com.cn/china/2017-10/19/content_33428169.htm.

Cao, Yin, and Jia Cui. 2017. 'Terror Attacks Down, but Attempts Remain High, Study Finds.' China Daily, 21 March. www.chinadaily.com.cn/china/2017-03/21/content_28621171.htm.

ChinaAid. 2018. '20 Prisoners Mentally Break Down in Chinese Detention Camp.' ChinaAid, 5 April. www.chinaaid.org/2018/04/20-prisoners-mentally-break-down-in.html.

Clarke, Michael. 2018. 'In Xinjiang, China's "Neo-Totalitarian" Turn Is Already a Reality.' The Diplomat, 10 March. thediplomat.com/2018/03/in-xinjiang-chinas-neo-totalitarian-turn-is-already-a-reality.

Denyer, Simon. 2018. 'China Detains Relatives of U.S. Reporters in Apparent Punishment for Xinjiang Coverage.' Washington Post, 28 February. www.washingtonpost.com/world/china-detains-relatives-of-us-reporters-in-apparent-punishment-for-xinjiang-coverage/2018/02/27/4e8d84ae-1b8c-11e8-8a2c-1a6665f59e95_story.html.

HRW (Human Rights Watch). 2017. 'China: Free Xinjiang "Political Education" Detainees.' Human Rights Watch, 10 September. www.hrw.org/news/2017/09/10/china-free-xinjiang-political-education-detainees.

Millward, James A. 2018. 'What It's Like to Live in a Surveillance State.' The New York Times, 3 February. www.nytimes.com/2018/02/03/opinion/sunday/china-surveillance-state-uighurs.html.

RFA (Radio Free Asia). 2017a. 'New Guidelines on Uyghur "Signs of Extremism" Issued to Xinjiang Authorities.' Radio Free Asia, 11 November. www.rfa.org/english/news/uyghur/guidelines-11072017153331.html.

RFA (Radio Free Asia). 2017b. 'Uyghur Woman Dies of Condition Left Untreated in Chinese Police Detention.' Radio Free Asia. 12 December. www.rfa.org/english/news/uyghur/death-12122017164350.html.

RFA (Radio Free Asia). 2018a. 'Uyghur Inmates in Xinjiang's Korla City Endure Overcrowded Re-Education Camps.' Radio Free Asia, 3 January. www.rfa.org/english/news/uyghur/camps-01032018155622.html.

RFA (Radio Free Asia). 2018b. 'Uyghur Father of Two Dies After Falling Ill in Xinjiang Re-Education Camp.' Radio Free Asia, 12 April. www.rfa.org/english/news/uyghur/father-04122018153525.html.

Rife, Roseann. 2018. 'A Police State in Xinjiang in Which Moderate Voices Are Silenced Is Not What China Needs to Achieve Stability.' South China Morning Post, 17 January. www.scmp.com/comment/insight-opinion/article/2128581/police-state-xinjiang-which-moderate-voices-are-silenced-not.

U.S. Embassy. 2018. 'Spokesperson Heather Nauert's Statement on Xinjiang.' U.S. Embassy & Consulates in China. 20 April. china.usembassy-china.org.cn/spokesperson-heather-nauerts-statement-on-xinjiang.

Vanderklippe, Nathan. 2017. 'China Probes Deeper into the Lives of Uyghur Minority in Xinjiang.' The Globe and Mail, 29 December. www.theglobeandmail.com/news/world/scholars-shocked-by-changes-in-chinas-xinjiang-comparing-it-to-north-korea-and-apartheid-era-southafrica/article 37455333.

Xinhua. 2018. 'Religious Extremism Notably Curbed in Xinjiang: Senior Chinese Official.' Xinhua Net, 14 April. www.xinhuanet.com/english/2018-04/14/c_137111356.htm.

Zenz, Adrian. 2018. 'China's Domestic Security Spending: An Analysis of Available Data.' The Jamestown Foundation - China Brief, 21 March. jamestown.org/program/chinas-domestic-security-spending-analysis-available-data.

STATES OF EMERGENCY: THE SICHUAN EARTHQUAKE TEN YEARS ON

Be Grateful to the Party! How to Behave in the Aftermath of a Disaster (CHRISTIAN SORACE)

Bandurski, David. 2015. 'The Politics of Senseless Tragedy.' *China Media Project*, 17 August. medium.com/@cmphku/the-politics-of-senseless-tragedy-12cc9230fa4.

Barthes, Roland (translated by Richard Howard). 2010. *Mourning Diary*. New York: Hill and Wang.

Coetzee, J. M. 1997. *Giving Offense: Essays on Censorship*. Chicago: University of Chicago Press.

Confucius (edited by Michael Nylan, translated by Simon Leys). 2014. *The Analects*. New York: W.W. Norton & Company.

Liao, Yiwu. 2009. *Dizhen fengrenyuan* [Earthquake Insane Asylum]. Taipei: Yunchen Wenhua Shiye Fengu Youxian Gongsi.

Sorace, Christian. 2014. 'China's Last Communist: Ai Weiwei.' *Critical Inquiry* 40, no. 2: 396–419.

Sorace, Christian. 2017. *Shaken Authority: China's Communist Party and the 2008 Sichuan Earthquake*. Ithaca: Cornell University Press.

Sorace, Christian. 2019. 'Extracting Affect: Televised Cadre Confessions in China.' *Public Culture*.

The World is Yours!: Youth and Civic Engagement from Sichuan to Parkland (BIN XU)

Gold, Thomas B. 1991. 'Youth and the State.' *China Quarterly* 127: 594–612.

Russonello, Giovanni. 2018. 'Stephen Colbert Stands With Florida Students Fighting for Gun Control.' *The New York Times*, 21 February. www.nytimes.com/2018/02/21/arts/television/stephen-colbert-florida-shooting-students.html.

Xu, Bin. 2017. *The Politics of Compassion: The Sichuan Earthquake and Civic Engagement in China*. Stanford, CA: Stanford University Press.

Sichuan, Year Zero? (KANG YI)

Franceschini, Ivan, and Elisa Nesossi. 2017. 'The Foreign NGOs Management Law: A Compendium.' In *Made in China Yearbook 2016: Disturbances in Heaven*, edited by Ivan Franceschini, Kevin Lin, and Nicholas Loubere, 60–67. Canberra: ANU Press.

Hsu, Carolyn. 2017. 'Social Entrepreneurship and Citizenship in China: The Rise of NGOs in the PRC.' *The Asia-Pacific Journal* 15 no. 3: 1–10.

Kang, Yi. 2017. 'The Development of Grassroots Chinese NGOs Following the Wenchuan Earthquake of 2008: Three Case Studies, Four Modi Vivendi.' *Voluntas* 28, no. 4: 1648–72.

Roney, Britton. 2011. 'Earthquakes and Civil Society: A Comparative Study of the Response of China's Nongovernment Organizations to the Wenchuan Earthquake.' *China Information* 25, no. 1: 83–104.

Shieh, Shawn, and Guosheng Deng. 2011. 'An Emerging Civil Society: The Impact of the 2008 Sichuan Earthquake on Grass-roots Associations in China.' *The China Journal* 65: 181–94.

Simon, Karla, and Holly Snape. 2018. 'China's Social Organisations after the Charity Law.' In *Made in China Yearbook 2017: Gilded Age*, edited by Ivan Franceschini and Nicholas Loubere, 118–21. Canberra: ANU Press.

Sorace, Christian. 2017. *Shaken Authority: China's Communist Party and the 2008 Sichuan Earthquake*. Ithaca and London: Cornell University Press.

Teets, Jessica. 2009. 'Post-earthquake Relief and Reconstruction Efforts: The Emergence of Civil Society in China?' *The China Quarterly* 198: 330–47.

Teets, Jessica. 2018. 'The Rise of Foundations: Hope for Civil Society in China?' In *Made in China Yearbook 2017: Gilded Age*, edited by Ivan Franceschini and Nicholas Loubere, 122–25. Canberra: ANU Press.

Xu, Bin. 2017. *The Politics of Compassion: The Sichuan Earthquake and Civic Engagement in China*. Stanford: Stanford University Press.

Zhang, Xi, Lixin Yi, and Dong Zhao. 2013. 'Community-based Disaster Management: A Review of Progress in China.' *Natural Hazards* 65: 2215–39.

Civic Transformation in the Wake of the Wenchuan Earthquake: State, Society, and the Individual (SUN TAIYI)

Asian Barometer Survey. 2017. www.asianbarometer.org.

Deng, Guosheng. 2009. *Responding to Wenchuan: An Analysis of Relief Mechanism in China*. Beijing: Peking University Press.

Edelman Trust Barometer. 2015. www.edelman.com/insights/intellectual-property/2015-edelman-trust-barometer.

Jin, Weixing, and Chunyu Wang. 2008. 'Yi you jin 130 wan renci zhiyuan zhe canjia wenchuan dizhen jiuzai [Close to 1.3 million volunteers have participated in Wenchuan earthquake relief].' *Xinhua News Agency* 25 February. www.yn.xinhuanet.com/topic/2008-06/21/content_13605664.htm.

Kang, Xiaoguang, and Heng Han. 2008. 'Graduated Controls: The State-society Relationship in Contemporary China.' *Modern China* 34, no. 1: 36–55.

Shieh, Shawn and Guosheng Deng. 2011. 'An Emerging Civil Society: The Impact of the 2008 Sichuan Earthquake on Grassroots Associations in China.' *The China Journal* 65: 181–94.

Sun, Taiyi. 2017. 'Earthquakes and the Typologies of State-society Relations in China.' *China Information* 31, no. 3: 304–26.

Sun, Taiyi. Forthcoming. 'Deliberate Differentiation by the Chinese State: Outsourcing Responsibility for Governance.' *The China Quarterly*.

World Value Survey. 2015. www.worldvaluessurvey.org/WVSContents.jsp.

The Power of the Square: Post-earthquake Activism in Mianyang (GAO HUAN)

Beichuan County Government. 2016. *Wenchuan teda dizhen Beichuan kangzhen jiuzai zhi* [Records of Rescue and Relief after the Wenchuan Earthquake in Beichuan]. Beijing: Fangzhi Chubanshe.

Deyang Bureau of Civil Affairs. 2008. 'Deyang shi minzhengju guanyu kangzhenjiuzai gongzuo de xubao [Follow-up Report from Deyang Bureau of Civil Affairs on Disaster Relief Work].' 26 May.

Dujiangyan Government. 2008. 'Guanyu zai jizhong anzhi dian kaizhan guanli gongzuo xingji pingding de tongzhi [Announcement on Starting Management Rating in Transitional Housing Communities].' *Duweiban* [2008]201. 29 December.

Heng, Jie. 2011. 'Kexue juece: zhihui yu qianzhan de zhuxian [Scientific Decision Making: Themes of Wisdom and Foresight].' *Lianzheng Liaowang* 5: 19–22.

Mianyang Local Gazetteer Office. 2009. *Mianyang nianjian 2009* [Mianyang Yearbook 2009]. Beijing: Fangzhi Chubanshe.

Sichuan Bureau of Statistics. 2008. *Sichuan tongji nianjian 2007* [Sichuan Statistical Yearbook 2007]. Beijing: Zhongguo Tongji Chubanshe.

Sichuan Provincial Government. 2009. *5.12 Wenchuan teda dizhen Sichuan sheng zaihai sunshi tongji pinggu ziliao huibian* [Collection of Materials on Disaster Damage Statistics in Sichuan after the Wenchuan Earthquake]. Internal Document.

Zheng, Degang, Guanghua He, and Hongtao Cao. 2008. "456 wan zhenqu qunzhong tuoshan anzhi [4.56 Million Residents from the Earthquake Region Appropriately Settled]." *People's Daily*, 19 May.

Zhou, Jianyu. 2010. 'Mianyang Jiuzhou tiyuguan yingji anzhi zhenzai qunzhong de chenggong jingyan [Successful Experience in Using Jiuzhou Stadium in Mianyang as an Emergency Shelter].' In *Yingji guanli guoji yantaohui*, edited by Liqun Wei and Hong Yi, 197–202. Beijing: Guojia Xingzheng Xueyuan Chubanshe.

WINDOW ON ASIA

'Hun Sen Won't Die, Workers Will Die' The Geopolitics of Labour in the Cambodian Crackdown (SABINA LAWRENIUK)

Abi-Habib, Maria. 2018. 'How China Got Sri Lanka to Cough Up a Port.' *The New York Times*, 25 June. www.nytimes.com/2018/06/25/world/asia/china-sri-lanka-port.html.

ILO (International Labour Organisation). 2018. *Cambodian Garment and Footwear Sector Bulletin*, Issue 7. Phnom Penh: ILO.

Mission of the Kingdom of Cambodia to the European Union. 2018. *Communique of the Mission of the Kingdom of Cambodia to the European Union*. 13 September. en.freshnewsasia.com/index.php/en/11131-2018-09-14-15-53-02.html.

My Rights Have Been Left behind in Papua New Guinea: The Predicament of Chinese Overseas Workers (ZHANG SHUCHI)

Department of Outward Investment and Economic Cooperation. 2017. *Duiwai touzi hezuo guo bie zhinan babuya xin jineiya 2017 nianban* [*Guide for Countries and Regions on Overseas Investment and Cooperation 2017 – Papua New Guinea*]. fec.mofcom.gov.cn/article/gbdqzn/upload/babuyaxinjineiya.pdf.

Fan, Jiaoyan and Rensheng Yin. 2013. *2016 niandu zhong guo duiwai zhijie touzi tongji gongbao [Study on Legal Systems for Protecting the Rights and Interests of Chinese Overseas Workers]*. Beijing: China Economic Publishing House.

Ministry of Commerce, National Bureau of Statistics, and State Administration of Foreign Exchange. 2016. *2016 niandu zhongguo duiwai zhijie touzi tongji gongbao [Statistical Bulletin of China's Outward Foreign Direct Investment in 2016]*. fec.mofcom.gov.cn/article/tjsj/tjgb/201709/20170902653690.shtml.

UNCTAD. 2017. *World Investment Report 2017: Investment and the Digital Economy*. Geneva: United Nations Publication. unctad.org/en/PublicationsLibrary/wir2017_en.pdf.

World Bank. 2017. Migration and Remittances: Recent Developments and Outlook. *Migration and Development Brief 27*. pubdocs.worldbank.org/en/992371492706371662/MigrationandDevelopment Brief27.pdf.

Online Activism and South Korea's Candlelight Movement (HYEJIN KIM)

Choe, Yeon-jin. 2015. '"Geumsujeo" namjaga ...["Gold spoon" man...]'. *Chosun Ilbo*, 30 December. news.chosun.com/site/data/html_dir/2015/12/30/2015123000311.html.

Kang, Jiyeon. 2017. 'Internet Activism Transforming Street Politics: South Korea's 2008 "Mad Cow" Protests and New Democratic Sensibilities.' *Media, Culture & Society* 39, no. 5: 750–61.

Kim, Hyejin. 2017. '"Spoon Theory" and the Fall of a Populist Princess in Seoul,' *Journal of Asian Studies* 76, no. 4: 839–49.

Kim, Seon-hyuk. 2009. 'Minjuhwa ihuui Hangugui jiphoe siwi minjujuui [(Protests and democracy in South Korea after democratisation].' In *2008 jiphoesiwireul tonghae bon siminsahoe peurojekteu, II [Project on Civil Society as Seen through the 2008 Protests, II]*, edited by EAI and Jungang Ilbo. Seoul: East Asia Institute, 2009.

Newman, Nic et al. 2017. *Reuters Institute Digital News Report 2017*. University of Oxford and Reuters Institute.

Shin, Wooyeol. 2016. 'Conservative Journalists' Myth Making in South Korea: Use of the Past in News Coverage of the 2008 Korean Candlelight Vigil.' *Asian Studies Review* 40, no. 1: 120–36.

Svensson, Marina. 2016. 'Connectivity, Engagement and Witnessing on China's Weibo.' In *The Internet, Social Media, and a Changing China*, edited by Jacques deLisle, Avery Goldstein, and Guobin Yang, 49–70. Philadelphia: University of Pennsylvania Press.

China and Development Aid: The Case of Anti-trafficking and Seafood in Southeast Asia (SVERRE MOLLAND)

Anderson, Bridget. 2012. 'Where's the Harm in That? Immigration Enforcement, Trafficking, and the Protection of Migrants' Rights.' *American Behavioral Scientist* 56, no. 9: 1241–57.

Auethavornpipat, Ruji. 2017. 'Assessing Regional Cooperation: ASEAN States, Migrant Worker Rights and Norm Socialization in Southeast Asia.' *Global Change, Peace & Security* 29, no. 2: 129–43.

Baird, Ian G. 2011. 'Turning Land into Capital, Turning People into Labor: Primitive Accumulation and the Arrival of Large-scale Economic Land Concessions in the Lao People's Democratic Republic.' *New Proposals: Journal of Marxism and Interdisciplinary Inquiry* 5, no. 1: 10–26.

Diana, Antonella. 2018. 'Liquid Labourscape: Ad Hoc Experimentation in a Chinese Special Economic Zone in Laos.' In *Made in China Yearbook 2017: Gilded Age*, edited by Ivan Franceschini and Nicholas Loubere, 80–83. Canberra: ANU Press.

Gallagher, Anne T. 2017. 'What's Wrong with the Global Slavery Index.' *Anti-Trafficking Review* no. 8.

Keo, Chenda, Thierry Bouhours, Roderic Broadhurst, and Brigitte Bouhours. 2014. 'Human Trafficking and Moral Panic in Cambodia.' *The ANNALS of the American Academy of Political and Social Science* 653, no. 1: 202–24.

Molland, Sverre. 2012. *The Perfect Business? Anti-Trafficking and the Sex Trade Along the Mekong*. Honolulu: University of Hawaii Press.

Nyíri, Pál. 2012. 'Enclaves of Improvement: Sovereignty and Developmentalism in the Special Zones of the China-Lao Borderlands.' *Comparative Studies in Society and History* 54, no. 3: 533–62.

Tan, Danielle. 2014. 'Chinese Networks, Economic and Territorial Redefinitions in Northern Lao PDR.' In *Transnational Dynamics in Southeast Asia*, edited by Sirivanh Khntaphane, Christian Taillard, and Nathalie Fau, 422–52. Singapore: Institute of Southeast Asian Studies.

UNIAP. 2013. *Report on an Exploratory Research about Migration and Human Trafficking to China in Luang Namtha and Phongsaly, Lao PDR*. Vientiane: UNIAP.

World Bank and FAO. 2013. *Fish to 2030: Prospects for Fisheries and Aquaculture*. Washington: World Bank Report Number 83177-Glb.

Illicit Economies of the Internet: Click Farming in Indonesia and Beyond (JOHAN LINDQUIST)

Brunton, Finn. 2013. *Spam: A Shadow History of the Internet*. Cambridge: MIT Press.

Casilli, Antonio. 2016. 'Never Mind the Algorithms: The Role of Click Farms and Exploited Labor in Trump's Election.' 30 November. www.casilli.fr/2016/11/20/never-mind-the-algorithms-the-role-of-exploited-digital-labor-and-global-click-farms-in-trumps-election.

Clark, Doug. 2015. 'The Bot Bubble: How Click Farms Have Inflated Social Media Currency.' *New Republic*, 21 April. newrepublic.com/article/121551/bot-bubble-click-farms-have-inflated-social-media-currency.

Confessore, Nicholas, Gabriel J.X. Dance, Richard Harris, and Mark Hansen. 2018. 'The Follower Factory.' *The New York Times*, 27 January. www.nytimes.com/interactive/2018/01/27/technology/social-media-bots.html.

DePillis, Lydia. 2014. 'Click Farms are the New Sweatshops.' *The Washington Post*, 6 January. www.washingtonpost.com/news/wonk/wp/2014/01/06/click-farms-are-the-new-sweatshops.

Farooqi, Shehroze, Muhammad Ikram, Gohar Irfan, Emiliano De Cristofaro, Arik Friedman, Guillaume Jourjon, Mohamed Ali Kâafar, Muhammad Zubair Shafiq, and Fareed Zaffar. 2015. 'Characterizing Seller-Driven Black-Hat Marketplaces: The Curious Case of SEOClerks and MyCheapJobs.' *Semantic Scholar*. www.semanticscholar.org/paper/Characterizing-Seller-Driven-Black-Hat-Marketplaces-Farooqi-Ikram/eb21af3109cd70be0ab81bbf4384c55c641595f1.

Gerlitz, Carolin, and Anna Helmond. 2013. 'The Like Economy: Social Buttons and the Data-Intensive Web.' *New Media & Society* 15, no. 8: 1348–65.

Google Temasek. 2017. 'e-Conomy SEA Spotlight 2017: Unprecedented Growth for Southeast Asia's $50B Internet Economy.' www.thinkwithgoogle.com/intl/en-apac/tools-research/research-studies/e-conomy-sea-spotlight-2017-unprecedented-growth-southeast-asia-50-billion-internet-economy.

Instagram. 2017. 'Celebrating One Year of Instagram Stories.' instagram-press.com/blog/2017/08/02/celebrating-one-year-of-instagram-stories.

Lim, Merlyna. 2018. 'Dis/Connection: The Co-evolution of Sociocultural and Material Infrastructure of the Internet in Indonesia.' *Indonesia*, no. 105: 155–72.

Lipman, Victor. 2012. 'The World's Most Active Twitter City? You Won't Guess It.' *Forbes*, 30 December. www.forbes.com/sites/victorlipman/2012/12/30/the-worlds-most-active-twitter-city-you-wont-guess-it/#2f9e8a1855c6.

Chinese Digital Ecosystems Go Abroad: Myanmar and the Diffusion of Chinese Smartphones (ELISA OREGLIA)

ITU (International Telecommunication Union). 2017a. Fixed Telephone Subscriptions 2000–2016. www.itu.int/en/ITU-D/Statistics/Documents/statistics/.../Fixed_tel_2000-2016.xls.

ITU (International Telecommunication Union). 2017b. Mobile Cellular Telephone Subscriptions 2000–2016. www.itu.int/en/ITU-D/Statistics/Documents/.../Mobile_cellular_2000-2016.xls.

ITU (International Telecommunication Union). 2018. Myanmar Profile. www.itu.int/net4/itu-d/icteye/CountryProfileReport.aspx?countryID=42.

Kolodny, Lora. 2018 'Former Google CEO Predicts the Internet Will Split in Two — And One Part Will be Led by China.' *CNBC*, 20 September. www.cnbc.com/2018/09/20/eric-schmidt-ex-google-ceo-predicts-internet-split-china.html.

Napoli, Philip. M., and Jonathan A. Obar. 2014. 'The Emerging Mobile Internet Underclass: A Critique of Mobile Internet Access.' *Information Society* 30, no. 5: 323–34.

Oreglia, Elisa, and Janaki Srinivasan. 2016. 'Intermediaries, Cash Economies, and Technological Change in Myanmar and India.' Institute for Money, Technology, & Financial Inclusion. blog.imtfi.uci.edu/2017/10/intermediaries-cash-economies-and.html.

Statista. 2018. Number of monthly active WeChat users from 2nd quarter 2011 to 2nd quarter 2018.

Wai, Khin Hsu. 2014. 'Struggling with Smugglers on the Border.' *Myanmar Times*, 10 November. www.mmtimes.com/business/12217-struggling-with-smugglers-on-the-border.html.

Ulaanbaatar, City of the Future (CHRISTIAN SORACE)

Boldsukh, Chintushig. 2017. 'Vice Speaker calls for the impeachment of the President.' *The UB Post*, 13 January. theubpost.mn/2017/01/13/vice-speaker-calls-for-the-impeachment-of-the-president.

Fukuda, Chisato. 2017. 'A Fight to Breathe.' *Medical Anthropology Quarterly*, 29 March. medanthroquarterly.org/2017/03/29/a-fight-to-breathe.

Žižek, Slavoj. 2009. *In Defense of Lost Causes*. London: Verso.

WORK OF ARTS

Communist Hibernation (CHRISTIAN SORACE)

Hurst,William. 2009. *The Chinese Worker after Socialism*. Cambridge: Cambridge University Press.

Lee, Ching Kwan. 2007. *Against the Law: Labor Protests in China's Rustbelt and Sunbelt*. Berkeley: University of California Press.

Rancière, Jacques. 2013. *Béla Tarr, The Time After* (translated by Erik Beranek). Minneapolis: Univocal Publishing.

Sorace, Christian, and William Hurst. 2016. 'China's Phantom Urbanisation and the Pathology of Ghost Cities.' *Journal of Contemporary Asia* 46, no. 2: 304–22.

Crime and Punishment on a Chinese Border (SUZANNE SCOGGINS)

Li, Yan. 2017. 'China Has One of the Lowest Murder Rates in the World.' *People's Daily Online*, 21 September. en.people.cn/n3/2017/0921/c90000-9272100.html.

Scoggins, Suzanne E. 2019 (forthcoming). *Policing in the Shadow of Protest*. Unpublished Book Manuscript.

Scoggins, Suzanne E., and Kevin J. O'Brien. 2016. 'China's Unhappy Police.' *Asian Survey* 56, no. 2: 225–42.

The Economist. 2013. 'Murder Mysteries.' *The Economist*, 6 April. www.economist.com/china/2013/04/06/murder-mysteries.

Wang, Xiaohai. 2015. 'Empowering the Frontline Police Officers to Cope with Police Social Service Role Strain in China.' *International Journal of Criminology and Sociology* 3: 20–45.

Wang, Yanan, Lu Zheng, Tianhong Hu, and Quanquan Zheng. 2014. 'Stress, Burnout, and Job Satisfaction: Case of Police Force in China.' *Public Personnel Management* 43, no. 3: 325–39.

Williams, Sophie. 2017. 'Traffic Policeman Desperately Clings to Car's Bonnet after Driver Refuses to Stop for an Inspection and Accelerates Straight into the Officer.' *Daily Mail*, 24 February. www.dailymail.co.uk/news/peoplesdaily/article-4256202/Policeman-clings-car-bonnet-driver-fails-stop.html.

Zenz, Adrian. 2018a. 'New Evidence for China's Political Re-Education Campaign in Xinjiang.' *China Brief* 18, no. 10. jamestown.org/program/evidence-for-chinas-political-re-education-campaign-in-xinjiang.

Zenz, Adrian. 2018b. 'China's Domestic Security Spending: An Analysis of Available Data.' *China Brief* 18, no. 4. jamestown.org/program/chinas-domestic-security-spending-analysis-available-data.

Figuring Post-worker Shenzhen (MARY ANN O'DONNELL)

Heidegger, Martin (edited by David Farrell Krell). 2008. *Basic Writings*. New York: HarperCollins.

Rural Migrant Workers in Independent Films: Representations of Everyday Agency (ERIC FLORENCE)

Berry, Chris, and Rofel, Lisa. 2010. 'Alternative Archive: China's Independent Documentary Culture.' In *The New Chinese Documentary Film Movement: For the Public Record*, edited by Chris Berry, Lu Xinyu, and Lisa Rofel, 117–34. Hong Kong: Hong Kong University Press.

Brettell, Caroline B., and James F. Hollifield, eds. 2007. *Migration Theory: Talking Across Disciplines*, Second Edition. New York and London: Routledge.

Florence, Eric. 2006. 'Debates and Classification Struggles Regarding the Representation of Migrant Workers.' *China Perspectives* 65: 15–27.

Hansen, Mette Halskov. 2013. 'Recent Trends in Chinese Rural Education: The Disturbing Rural-Urban Disparities and the Measures to Meet Them.' In *Economy, Society and Politics in Twenty-First Century China: Striving for a New Development Paradigm*, edited by Eric Florence and Pierre Defraigne, 165–78. New York and London: Routledge.

Litzinger, Ralph. 2016. 'Regimes of Exclusion and Inclusion: Migrant Labor, Education and Contested Futurities.' In *Ghost Protocol : Development and Displacement in Global China*, edited by Ralph Litzinger and Carlos Rojas, 191–204. Durham and London: Duke University Press.

Lü, Xinyu. 2003. *Jilu zhongguo: Dangdai zhongguo xin jilupian yundong* [Documenting China: Contemporary China's New Documentary Movement]. Beijing: Sanlian shudian.

Ortner, Sherry. 2006. *Anthropology and Social Theory: Culture, Power, and the Acting Subject*. Durham and London: Duke University Press.

Pun, Ngai. 2016. *Migrant Labor in China: A Post-Socialist Transformation*. Cambridge and Malden: Polity Press.

Qiu, Jack Linchuan. 2009. *Working-Class Network Society: Communication Technology and the Information Have-less in Urban China*. Cambridge and London: MIT Press.

Sun, Wanning. 2014. *Subaltern China: Rural Migrants, Media and Cultural Practices*. Lanham: Rowman & Littlefield.

Plastic China: Beyond Waste Imports (YVAN SCHULZ)

Berry, Chris, and Lisa Rofel. 2010. 'The New Chinese Documentary Film Movement: For the Public Record (Introduction).' In *The New Chinese Documentary Film Movement: For the Public Record*, edited by Chris Berry, Lü Xinyu, and Lisa Rofel, 3–14. Hong Kong: Hong Kong University Press.

Berry, Chris. 2017. 'The Death of Chinese Independent Cinema?' *Asia Dialogue*, 3 July. theasiadialogue.com/2017/07/03/the-death-of-chinese-independent-cinema.

Chitwood, Matthew. 2018. 'Trash Management in Rural China.' *Institute of Current World Affairs*, 9 June. www.icwa.org/trash-management-in-rural-china/.

Kanthor, Rebecca. 2017. '"Plastic China" Documentary Looks at Underbelly of Recycling in China.' *Plastic News*, 7 March. www.plasticsnews.com/article/20170307/NEWS/170309925/plastic-china-documentary-looks-at-underbelly-of-recycling-in-china.

Liebman, Adam. 2018. 'No More of Your Junk.' *The New Internationalist*, 5 December. newint.org/features/2018/11/01/chinese-waste-ban.

Liu, Qin. 2014. 'Film: How China Became the World's Rubbish Dump.' *Chinadialogue*, 1 May. www.chinadialogue.net/culture/6947-Film-How-China-became-the-world-s-rubbish-dump/en.

Lü, Kuo-chen. 2018. 'Chung kuo chin yang la chi tu yin wei t'a [China's Ban on Foreign Waste is All Because of Him].' *T'ien Hsia Tsa Chih*, 2 October. www.cw.com.tw/article/article.action?id=5092329.

Persico, Daniela. 2010. *Wang Bing. Il Cinema Nella Cina Che Cambia*. Milano: Agenzia X.

Renard, Caroline, Isabelle Anselme, and François Amy de La Bretèque, eds. 2014. *Wang Bing. Un Cinéaste en Chine Aujourd'hui*. Aix-en-Provence: Publications de l'Université de Provence.

Schulz, Yvan. 2018. *Modern Waste: The Political Ecology of E-scrap Recycling in China*. PhD dissertation: University of Neuchâtel.

Schulz, Yvan. 2019 (forthcoming). 'Scrapping "Irregulars": China's Recycling Policies, Development Ethos and Peasants Turned Entrepreneurs.' *Journal Für Entwicklungspolitik*.

Sorace, Christian. 2017. 'Paradise under Construction.' In *Made in China Yearbook 2016 Disturbances in Heaven*, edited by Ivan Franceschini, Kevin Lin, and Nicholas Loubere, 128–31. Canberra: ANU Press.

Voice of America. 2018. '"Suliao wangguo" zai yin re yi: Zhongguo xianzhi jinkou ke huishou wu yiweizhe shenme? ["Plastic China" Triggers A Hot Debate Once Again: What Do China's Limits on Recyclable Goods Imply?].' 21 March. www.voachinese.com/a/china-recycler-20180320/4307521.html.

Wang, Jiuliang. 2016. 'Guanyu zhongguo dadi de 20 zhang zhaopian [About 20 Pictures of the Earth in China].' *Yixi Talk*, 22 December. wemedia.ifeng.com/6721032/wemedia.shtml.

Zhao, Kiki. 2017. 'China's Environmental Woes, in Films That Go Viral, Then Vanish.' *The New York Times*, 28 April. www.nytimes.com/2017/04/28/world/asia/chinas-environmental-woes-in-films-that-go-viral-then-vanish.html?_r=0.

MADE IN CHINA
JOURNAL

中華全球研究中心
AUSTRALIAN CENTRE ON
CHINA IN THE WORLD

Australian
National
University
PRESS

LUND
UNIVERSITY

Made in the USA
Las Vegas, NV
03 November 2026

57421905R00200